Online Promotions
Winning Strategies and Tactics

Bill Carmody

Wiley Computer Publishing

John Wiley & Sons, Inc.
NEW YORK · CHICHESTER · WEINHEIM · BRISBANE · SINGAPORE · TORONTO

Publisher: Robert Ipsen
Editor: Cary Sullivan
Assistant Editor: Christina Berry
Managing Editor: Gerry Fahey
New Media Editor: Brian Snapp
Text Design & Composition: Lachina Publishing Services

Published by John Wiley & Sons, Inc.
Published simultaneously in Canada.

This publication is designed to provide accurate and authoritative information in regard to the subject matter covered. It is sold with the understanding that the publisher is not engaged in rendering professional services. If professional advice or other expert assistance is required, the services of a competent professional person should be sought.

Printed in the United States of America.

10 9 8 7 6 5 4 3 2 1

To my wife Elena, my partner in this world and in the next. For my mother who taught me to love. For my father who taught me to be the best person I can be. For my brother who continues to teach by example. And for my best friend Jaymes, thank you for always being there for me.

Contents

Foreword   xiii

Introduction   xvii

Acknowledgments   xxiii

Chapter 1   **Promotional Marketing Basics**   1

What Is a Sweepstakes?   1
    Random Draw Sweepstakes   4
    Automatic Entry   6
    Qualified Entry Sweepstakes   7
    Instant Win Sweepstakes   8
    Preselected Sweepstakes   10
    Second-Chance Sweepstakes Drawing   11

What Is a Contest?   12
    So Why Run a Contest?   14
    Essay Contests   15
    Photography and Art Contests   18
    Games as Contests   18
    Programming Contests   19
    Other Contests   19

Other Types of Promotions   20
    Product Sampling   20
    Electronic Coupons and Smart Rebates   21
    Loyalty Programs   24

How Do You Know When to Use What?   27
    Launching a New Web Site, Product, or Service   28
    Build Awareness/Reinforce Attributes   30

Drive Sales   32

Drive Traffic   33

Build Brand Loyalty/Product Preference   35

Reinforce Brand Identity   36

Generate Ideas for an Effective Ad Campaign   37

Collect Demographic Information and Get
    Permission for Future Marketing   38

Increase Memberships   41

Initiate Trial/Create Interest   43

Conclusion   45

Chapter 2   **Why Online Promotions Work**   **47**

Overview of Online Advantages   48

Speed   50

Research   51

Technology   51

Immediacy   52

Viral   52

Environmental   53

Control   54

Permission   54

Data and Information   55

Fun   55

Costs   56

Success   56

Participation   57

Email   57

Integration   58

New   58

Evolution   58

Mobility   59

Ongoing   59

Ideal   59

Instant Win Games: Becoming More Interactive   60

Why Instant Is Better   60

Taking Full Advantage of the Medium   61

Interactive without Instant Win   66

Email Components: Why They Work   68

Permission to Send Email   69

Adding Personalization   70

Pointers: Adding Links to the Email   71

Punch: Adding Creative Design   72

If It's Good, It Will Be Forwarded   73

Mobile Devices   73

Immediate Feedback and Response   74

Real-Time Reporting   75
Analyzing Results   75
Responding in Real Time   76

Conclusion   77

Chapter 3   Planning an Online Promotion   79

Starting with a Clear Objective   80
Avoid Multiple Conflicting Objectives   82

Taking Time to Plan   84
Avoiding Less Important Short-Term Gains   84
From Chaos to Smart Marketing   85
The Right Customer at the Right Price   85
Long-Term Benefits of Planning   86

When Online, Do as Your Users Do   86
How to Be a Good Consumer   87
Finding Online Promotions   88
How Do You Know What's Good?   89

Data Collection: Building Your Own Database   90
Begin with a Plan   91
Designing the Database   91
Collect Only the Data You Plan to Use   92
Effectively Use the Database   92
Managing the Data   93

Conclusion   94

Chapter 4   Protecting Yourself and Your Company Online   95

Privacy and Security Issues   96
Privacy: What's Your Customer's Information Worth?   96
FTC: Self-Regulation and Privacy Online   98
Children's Online Privacy Protection Act (COPPA)   99
European Union Data Protection Directive   106
Tell-a-Friend Emails   107
Security: Creating a Safe Environment   109

Overview of the Legal Aspects of Online Promotions   115
Illegal Lotteries   116
Sweepstakes Registration   119
Contest Registration   120
1099 Filings   121
Official Winners List   122
Ending the Promotion   123

Preparing the Official Rules   124
Why Are Official Rules Important?   124
Can Changes Be Made to Official Rules?   125
Checklist for Chance Promotions   125

Disclaimers and Abbreviated Rules   133
Getting Professional Help   135

Cautions for Legal Compliance   135
Avoid Deception   135
Use of the Word *Free*   136
Equitable Means of Entry   136
Investigation of Official Winners   137
Enforcement   137

International Promotions and Foreign Laws   137
Country-Specific Guidelines   142
Translating Your Promotions into Multiple Languages   142
Avoiding Cultural Blunders   143

Conclusions   143

Chapter 5   Outsourcing versus In-House Resources   145

When to Call a Promotional Marketing Agency   147
Strategy   147
Legal   150
Technical   154
Creative   157
Media   159
Partnerships   162
Customer Support   165
Administration   169
Fulfillment   173
Research/Analysis   176
Summary of Recommendations   180

Finding Vendors, Consultants, and Other Resources   180
Online Promotions Agencies   180
Strategy Consultants   182
Legal   182
Technical   183
Creative   183
Media   184
Partnerships   184
Customer Support   184
Administration   185
Fulfillment   185
Research/Analysis   185

Asking the Right Questions to Determine a Good Fit   186
Strategy   186
Legal   188
Technical   189
Creative   191

Media   192
Partnerships   194
Customer Support   195
Administration   196
Fulfillment   198
Research/Analysis   199

When and How to Fire Your Promotions Agency   201
When to Fire Your Promotions Agency   201
How to Fire Your Promotions Agency   202

How to Start an In-House Promotions Group   202
Starting with the Right In-House Resources   203
Evaluating Your Ongoing Needs   204

Conclusion   204

Chapter 6   How to Create a Multibrand Promotion   207

Starting with a Clear Objective   208
Avoid Multiple Objectives   208

Identifying Ideal Partners   209
The Gets: Satisfying Your Biggest Needs   210
The Gives: What You're Willing to Offer   211
Complementary Partners List   211

Put Yourself in Your Partner's Shoes   212
Contacting Potential Partners   212
Keeping Track of Responses   213
Selecting the Right Partner   213

Who Is in the Driver's Seat?   215
What to Do with a Weak Quarterback   216
The Production Schedule   216
Key Milestones   217
Flowcharts and Other Documentation   217
Contingency Plans   219

Create Partnership Agreements   219
Avoid Contract Templates   220
Amendments to Partnership Agreements   220
Terminating the Agreements   220

Manage the Ongoing Relationship   221
Prelaunch   221
At Launch   222
During the Promotion   222
Concluding the Promotion   223

What Could Have Been Done Better?   223
Creating Your Own Benchmark   224
Log Files   226

	Custom On-Demand Reports	227
	Database Analysis	228
	Protect Your Customer's Privacy	228
	Compare Your Results with Research Reports	229
	Conclusion	229
Chapter 7	**Promoting the Promotion**	**231**
	Where and How to Advertise Your Online Promotion	232
	Online Resources	232
	Offline Resources	239
	Targeted Offline Media	246
	Why Targeted Offline Media Works	247
	Why Offline Media Can Be More Effective	247
	Problems with Banners	248
	The "Catch 22" of Email Marketing	249
	The Long-Term Perspective	249
	Integrating Communities and Portal Sites Effectively	250
	What Defines an Internet Community?	250
	Portal Sites	252
	Nontraditional and Experimental Advertising	254
	Online Media Vehicles	255
	Offline Media Vehicles	261
	Conclusion	264
Chapter 8	**What to Do after the Promotion**	**265**
	Measuring the Results of Your Promotion	266
	On-Demand Reports	267
	En Masse Reports	271
	Spotting Trends	274
	Managing and Integrating Your Promotional Database	275
	Managing the Promotional Database	276
	Integrating the Promotional Database	278
	Following Up with Special Discounts and Offers	280
	Differential Marketing	281
	When Promotions Are Not Enough	284
	Loyalty Programs	284
	Planning Your Next Promotion	286
	1. Begin with the Objective	286
	2. Integrate Your Online Promotions	287
	3. Keep Up with Technology	287
	4. Listen and Learn	288
	5. Promote the Promotion	289
	6. Identify Reporting Needs *before* Launch	289

7. Opt-In: Ask for Permission   290
8. Begin a Relationship   291
9. Build Your Database Marketing Efforts   291
10. Ensure Legal Compliance   292

Conclusion   292

Chapter 9   The Future of Online Promotions   293

Integrating Your Online and Offline Marketing Efforts   294
When Online Promotions "Grow Up"   294
Offline Promotions for Online Brands   297

Mobile Devices   298
Promotions on PDAs and WAPs   298
Global Positioning Satellite Technology   299
Built-In Scanner Technology   300
V-Commerce   300
When "V" Is for Voice   301
When "V" Is for Vehicle   305

High-End Interactive Promotions   307
Macromedia's Flash   308
3D Environments   309
Multiuser Gaming   310
Digital Video Disks   311
Beyond Television   313

Conclusion   315

Thank You   315

Index   317

Foreword

Sweepstakes, games, and contests have been effective marketing tools for decades in large part because—no matter how often they hear or see the words "no purchase necessary"—many consumers think they need to buy something to enter. Or, they at least feel that buying the product is easier than going through the hassle (and often the expense) of using the "alternative means" of entry.

But consumers are getting smarter, and their perception of promotion is changing, due in large part to the Internet's rapid rise as a vital channel of communications. The Internet is also making it easier for anyone to enter any promotion at just about any time.

In the mid-1990s, there was tremendous debate about the potential for marketing on the Web. Until that point, the medium had been primarily employed as a communications channel for government workers, academics, and technical professionals. All information was delivered free of charge, and there were no marketing messages to muck up the process. The Internet would never serve as an advertising vehicle because those users would never accept it.

What many prognosticators failed to realize is that, for better or worse, marketing messages are as much a part of our entertainment-focused culture as movies, TV programs, or sports. People like to buy things (they aren't called consumers for nothing), and they will tolerate a certain amount of marketing to help them make their purchase decisions. So as the Internet audience has become more mainstream, the antipathy toward marketing has disappeared.

Consumer attitudes about those marketing messages and the ways in which consumers responded to those messages changed also. As a medium, the Web has given consumers more power than ever before over the messages they receive. Yes, the proliferation of cable television networks and, more importantly, the invention of the remote allowed viewers to click away from commercials. But a truly accurate measure of how many people did so was never attainable.

On the Internet, marketers know exactly how many people are ignoring their ads because they know exactly how many people have viewed them. What's more, the Internet gives consumers the power not only to ignore the messages they don't want to see but also to *find ones they do.*

In a survey conducted for *PROMO Magazine* during the summer of 2000, 1,000 consumers who classified themselves as "Internet-savvy" were asked why they logged on. More than half said they wanted to look for special offers on products and services. Nearly half said they spent time actively looking for sweepstakes and contests to enter.

The results suggest that the Internet is fostering a new consumer who is more aware of promotional offers: a consumer who not only appreciates purchase incentives but may even demand them. (More than 80 percent, for instance, said they "expected" food products to offer some kind of purchase incentive.)

This increased power and awareness have made traditional advertising more difficult because proper media placement is no longer enough. Consumers are not passively letting marketing messages pass by them, but actively choosing which messages they receive. That puts the burden on marketers to find ways to make sure messages are captivating. In many cases, the best way to reel in consumers is with promotional offers.

Once the Web proliferates through devices other than computers—wireless phones, pagers, and PDAs on one side, interactive TV on the other—the need for marketers to incentivize purchase will become even more profound.

The Internet is a wonderful tool for disseminating messages and collecting data, but it cannot be treated as a separate piece of the marketing plan. In the aforementioned *PROMO* survey, nearly as many respondents said they learn about promotions from newspaper and magazine ads (57 percent) as identified the Internet (60 percent). And only 16 percent said they participated in promotions exclusively online. Compared with other communication mediums, the Internet is faster, easier to use, and more engaging for consumers. But it's not the only medium marketers must leverage.

Here's a perfect example: In 1999, Buick executed a golf vacation sweepstakes communicated through TV spots, print ads, and Internet advertising. Consumers were invited to enter on a special Web site or through a toll-free telephone number. Almost 91 percent of the ultimate 155,000 entries arrived via the Web—but Buick probably wouldn't have received as many responses had it advertised solely on the Internet.

Consumer promotion has always been stigmatized as the "ugly stepchild" of the marketing world, the tactics smart marketers utilized only when they needed to score quick sales lifts. All of the glory (and most of the budget allocations) went to advertising, considered the best way to turn little-known products into internationally recognized brands. But there are good reasons why Procter & Gamble decided in 2000 to use the Internet as the primary channel through which to launch new products: It's cheaper than other channels, lets marketers alter strategies almost immediately, and provides the best means for establishing true two-way communication between brand and consumer.

In fact, the Internet could be the mechanism through which professionals will stop treating "advertising" and "promotion" as disparate disciplines with different objectives, and instead will focus more simply on "marketing communications" that effectively put a brand in touch with its target audience.

There are, to be sure, dangers involved here. Place too much emphasis on the promotion and your brand gets lost in the mad dash for rewards. When that happens, customers disappear as soon as a competing brand comes up with a better offer. And on the Web, your competitor is just a click away—as many failed dot coms that put the marketing cart before the product-and-service horse have learned the hard way.

PROMO Magazine tapped Bill Carmody as its "Internet" columnist because he not only understands this new medium better than most but he also recognizes its place in the overall marketing plan. He's not a "techie" who views the Internet as the be-all-end-all of marketing; he's not an industry dinosaur refusing to acknowledge the marketplace changes brought about by the Internet. He fully understands the medium's vast potential, but he knows its potential pitfalls just as well.

Likewise, this book is designed to help both the dot-com entrepreneur who needs a lesson in promotion and the marketing executive who needs a course on effective Internet strategies. Either way, it should prove an insightful and informative read.

Peter Breen
Editor, *PROMO Magazine*

Introduction

From 1996 to 2001, it is safe to say that I have become an online promotional marketing expert. Having started my Internet marketing career in 1994, I began with my first online promotion in February 1995 for CBS.com's NCAA tournament while working with Marden-Kane at Modem Media. In this promotion, CBS had advertised the URL of its Web site on national television during its pretournament coverage of the NCAA tournament and told viewers that they could go to the Web site and enter to win tickets to the next year's NCAA tournament.

CBS's NCAA tournament was a landmark promotion for many reasons. This was the first online promotion where a URL had been broadcast on national television and drove traffic from one medium to another. This was the first major promotion to take advantage of the Web for data collection (although there had previously been several promotions for the big three online services—America Online, CompuServe, and Prodigy). With the NCAA supplying the tournament tickets, this promotion was also one of the first multibrand promotions on the Web.

And, when the Web servers couldn't handle the increased volume of traffic produced by a URL being broadcast on national television, CBS's NCAA tournament promotion was the first online promotion to experience technical problems—although certainly not the last.

After my extremely valuable education with the CBS NCAA tournament promotion, I became more and more interested in promotions. At the time of the CBS promotion, I couldn't tell you what the difference was between a sweepstakes or a contest. What I *could* tell you was that online promotions seemed to work for some reason. At the time I couldn't explain why, but I found it fascinating that suddenly several hundred consumers who wouldn't have even thought to type in www.cbs.com were fighting to submit their entries.

With that promotion, CBS had built its first database of online consumers—a list of individuals (including their email addresses) who had accessed the Internet *while watching the pretournament coverage of the NCAA tournament*. This was one small step for CBS, but a giant leap for the online promotional marketing industry.

The more I thought about promotions, the more I wanted to learn more about them. I was fascinated by a promotion's ability to get people to do things. From visiting a Web site to driving sales, it was clear that promotions had an uncanny ability to accomplish a marketer's objective. What marketer could disagree with the bottom line success—*measurable* success—that promotions brought to the table?

I joined Marden-Kane full time in January 1997. Marden-Kane is a 45-year-old promotional marketing firm (one of the oldest in the business) that is accredited with developing the very first scratch-off ticket. When I joined Marden-Kane, I had a lot to learn about sweepstakes, contests, and games, but, at the same time, I had brought a wealth of online knowledge and expertise that was needed to create successful online promotions. Now, as Chief Marketing Officer of Seismicom, I am responsible for the integration of online and offline marketing efforts for some of the top brands in the world and online promotions continues to be a significant part of my responsibility.

Overview of the Book

With several years of online promotions experience, I am writing this book to share what I have learned. My objective is that, by the end of this book, you will have a clear understanding of what it takes to create successful online promotions. From promotional marketing basics to the future of online promotions, this book takes a step-by-step approach to the planning, production, execution, and conclusion components that represent the complete circle of online promotions.

Online promotions are a proven technique that helps marketers satisfy their objectives. Until now, however, marketers have had to rely solely on the experience of their promotional marketing agency or attend online promotional marketing seminars in order to learn about how to build, manage, and execute successful online promotions. I was compelled to write this book because of the lack of information that existed on this incredibly important and effective aspect of marketing online.

While I believe this book to be the first comprehensive source for information about online promotions, I do not expect that it will be the last. As technology continues to evolve at a rapid rate, so too will the applications of online promotions. This book will identify some of these future trends in online promotions and provide a look forward at what technologies are likely to impact the promotions industry. Because this book focuses on the fundamentals of online promotions, I am confident that future technologies will only enhance the various applications that will become available to marketers in the future.

How This Book Is Organized

This book is organized into nine chapters. The first chapter is a primer for anyone not already familiar with the basics of promotional marketing. From the basics, the book provides an overview of why online promotions are successful and then covers each aspect of an online promotion, including the legal aspects, outsourcing versus in-house resources, multiple brands, advertising the promotion, results and analysis, as well as future technologies that will impact online promotions.

In Chapter 1, "Promotional Marketing Basics," the focus is on the basic fundamentals of promotional marketing (online or traditional). This chapter explains the difference between a sweepstakes and a contest and all the various kinds of sweepstakes and contests that exist. This chapter also covers other kinds of promotional marketing techniques such as coupons, rebates, and loyalty programs. Most importantly, this chapter reviews when each tactic works best.

From the basics, Chapter 2, "Why Online Promotions Work," covers the advantages of online promotions. This is an in-depth look at why online promotions have become such an important aspect of successful marketing utilizing the Internet. This chapter takes a look at why instant win games are so appealing to an online audience and why email marketing continues to be a successful component to online promotions.

With Chapter 3, "Planning an Online Promotion," the focus turns from the ethereal aspects to the step-by-step approach of creating successful online promotions. Starting with a clear objective is the first (and arguably the most important) step in this process. The importance of taking time to plan is stressed as well as the significance of doing what your consumers are most interested in doing online. This chapter also describes why data collection is such a critical aspect to successful online promotions and how the resulting database should be built.

For many, Chapter 4, "Protecting Yourself and Your Company Online," will be referred to often as a guide for legal compliance when constructing an online promotion. While specific laws may change or be interpreted differently over time, the basic principles of promotional law, privacy, and security will remain unchanged. Thoroughly understanding the legal implications of online promotions is the first step in minimizing potential risk and protecting your company online. If an online promotion is illegal, it doesn't matter how compelling it might be—the risk is not worth the reward.

Chapter 5, "Outsourcing versus In-House Resources," addresses the challenge most marketers face between running promotions internally or outsourcing them. This chapter helps you take a good hard look at your internal resources and identify what (if anything) should be outsourced. For the components that clearly should not be kept internally, this chapter shows where to find vendors, consultants, and other resources. It also provides a laundry list of questions to ask as well as a guide for the responses you should be looking for to determine a good fit.

Chapter 6, "How to Create a Multibrand Promotion," deals with partnership promotions—be they online or traditional. This chapter will help you identify ideal partners for your promotion and take you through the process of contacting these partners and creating a partnership agreement. Once the partnership is formed, this chapter will provide the necessary steps to manage the ongoing relationship throughout the promotion and evaluate what could be improved for future multibrand promotions.

Without the proper amount of advertising support, your online promotions may be a waste of time and money. Chapter 7, "Promoting the Promotion," covers where and how to advertise your online promotion so that you can get the biggest bang for your buck. This chapter explores the use of both online and offline media and explains which can be more effective. It also covers more nontraditional and experimental advertising vehicles that should be considered.

Chapter 8, "What to Do after the Promotion," helps you measure the results of your online promotion. By reading this chapter *before* your next online promotion, you are likely to get the kinds of information you need to make intelligent decisions and truly evaluate the success or failure of your online promotions. This chapter also describes best practices for managing and integrating your promotional database as well as when and how to follow up with special discounts and offers to keep the momentum going. This chapter concludes the circle of online promotions and ends with planning your next online promotion.

Chapter 9, "The Future of Online Promotions," takes a look at the importance of integrating your online and offline marketing efforts. This chapter explores recent trends and technology developments that are likely to impact the promotions industry, including mobile devices and v-commerce (which can stand for both "voice" and "vehicle").

Who Should Read this Book

When I first began my career in the promotional marketing field, I had extensive online marketing experience, but precious little promotional marketing experience. As my promotional marketing experience grew, I realized that there were two groups of marketing professionals in the online promotions business: traditional promotions experts who were slowly learning about the Internet and Internet experts who were slowly learning about promotions. This book caters to both groups by providing sufficient information about both sides of the equation. Because this book begins with the basics of promotional marketing and then segues into online promotions, it will provide a solid foundation for people who may be new to *both* the online and traditional promotional marketing.

For experienced veterans in the promotional marketing industry, this book will reveal that successful online promotions are not too far off from successful traditional promotions once you have a clear understanding of the Internet. After all, it stands to reason that what works in an offline environment should also work in an online environment. For the most part this is true. If you are one of those experienced veterans, then I recommend that you skim Chapters 1 and 6 as each deals with traditional promotional marketing topics with which you will already be familiar.

If you are *not* an experienced promotional market veteran, fear not. Chapter 1 will bring you up to speed on the fundamental concepts you need to understand about traditional promotions in order to create successful online promotions. If you are a direct marketing specialist, you will feel right at home with the database aspects associated with online promotions and may find that online promotions are the magic bullet you've been looking for to create highly segmented databases.

If you are in the advertising industry, you will discover that online promotions are a wonderful marketing tactic that will help generate response. While advertising agencies tend to specialize in building brands, online promotions help drive sales and get consumers to take action. For this reason, this book will likely appeal to brand managers and marketing specialists of many diverse fields of business.

Overall, this book will provide ideas on how to satisfy current online marketing objectives. As Thomas Edison put it, "Your idea needs to be original only in its adaptation to the problem you are currently working on." My goal is that this book will provide you with the necessary tools and techniques to guide you through the process of building and managing online promotions. If you find that any particular section drills down farther than you are interested, you can always skim over that section and move on to the next one. Because this is the first comprehensive source on the topic of online promotions, I have done my best to leave no stone unturned.

What's on the Web Site

It is important to note that there is a companion Web site that accompanies this book. The Web site provides hands-on examples of different kinds of promotions, provides a template for a sample online sweepstakes, and provides links to various resources that will support you in your efforts to create successful online promotions.

The URL for the companion web site is `http://www.wiley.com/onlinepromotions/`

This companion Web site will be updated from time to time as new online promotions examples and new vendor resources become available. I urge you to take advantage of the companion Web site and get a feel for the resources available to you either now or once you have completed this book. In addition to this companion Web site, I have provided URL links throughout each chapter for additional information and helpful examples. While you need not be near a computer while you are reading this book, I urge you to check out some of these links and support information.

Summary

Successful online promotions can help you achieve your marketing objectives—often at a fraction of the cost of traditional promotions. This book will provide you with the information you need to plan, produce, execute, and measure your online promotions. It will show you what kinds of online promotions to use given specific marketing objectives and provide examples from previous successful online promotions. This book will provide you with the foundation you need to create, manage, and execute successful online promotions. After reading this book, you will have a clear understanding of each aspect that goes into building online promotions.

At the very least, this book will show you how to keep out of legal trouble when creating your online promotions and provide you with the resources you need for flawless execution. At best, this book will become a comprehensive resource that you can turn to time and time again as you experiment with new technologies and adaptations of previously successful promotional campaigns.

I wish you all the best with your future online promotions and am confident that, with the right tools and information, you can achieve the positive results that so many companies are currently enjoying.

Bill Carmody

Acknowledgments

This book would not be possible without the loving support of my friends and family. While they all thought I was insane for writing a book the same year I married, moved to the west coast, and started a new company, they provided the support I needed just the same.

Special thanks to Melton Cartes for all your help with the illustrations and cover art—you are a Photoshop master and Illustrator genius.

It has been great working with John Wiley Publishing, especially with Cary Sullivan and Christina Berry who patiently guided me through the process of publishing a book. Special thanks to Nedra Nash Kowalik, who spent countless hours making more copy edits to the book than I care to think about.

Thank you, Peter Breen, for writing the foreword to this book, and Dan Hanover, for continuing to keep me updated on trends and developments in the promotions industry. To Ken Florin, I thank you for your legal insights and continued support. To Marden-Kane, the oldest promotions agency in the business, thank you for providing a magnificent learning environment where I received my initiation into the promotions industry.

I would like to thank each of my colleagues at Seismicom—David Flaherty, Kathy Mitchell, Doug Litwin, Greg Gotts, Melton Cartes, Garrett Culhane, Lisa Valentine O'Beirne, Shannon Boysen, Jeffrey Miller, Cathy Crampton, and Julie Ebner—who have each provided insights and helpful information along with their support of this book. I am proud to be part of a company that is dedicated the success of our clients.

And last, but not least, I'd like to thank the many individuals within corporate America who have made a deep impact on my career, especially Howard DeBow (Visa); Chris Geisert, Dave Dekema, Kristin Murphy, Stefanie Rothschild, and Diane Hurley (America Online); Joel Ehrlich (Warner Brothers); Jaymes Graeber (Intel); Amy McDougall (Cisco Systems); Chris Russo (NFL); Henry Bar-Levav (Oven Digital); Di-Ann Eisnor (Eisnor); Gregg Alwine (B-12); Quaid Saifee (WIT); and Samantha Saturn (Saturn Networks). Thank you all for your support and valued coaching in the business world.

Promotional Marketing Basics

Think of this first chapter as the equivalent to a college course entitled, "Promotional Marketing 101: An Introduction to Promotional Marketing." If you consider yourself a promotions expert, then you can breeze through this chapter to confirm what you already know. For most marketers, however, this will serve as a solid foundation from which all our online promotions tools and techniques will be formed. This chapter covers the legal definitions of a *sweepstakes* and a *contest*, and provides an in-depth look at several variations of each. From there we move to other types of promotions, including coupons, rebates, and loyalty programs. Once each major promotions tactic is discussed, the chapter closes with an important section on knowing when to use each of them.

What Is a Sweepstakes?

If you know the answer to this question, then you may not need to spend much time in this section, but knowing how legislators define a sweepstakes versus a contest is important when determining the best promotional tactic to meet your marketing objectives.

Simply put, a *sweepstakes* is a game of chance.

All promotions are subject to state and federal lottery laws, which define a lottery as having three elements: prize, chance, and consideration. If a promotion has all three elements, then the promotion is not a sweepstakes or a contest, but a lottery that is in violation of state and federal lottery laws.

Prize + Chance + Consideration = Lottery (Illegal Promotion)

Think about a state lottery. In order to get the $30 million jackpot, you have to buy a lottery ticket. You have the *prize* of $30 million. You have one *chance* at winning that lottery jackpot for each lottery ticket you buy. And you have *consideration* when you paid to purchase the lottery ticket. So what's the problem?

Lotteries are a form of gambling. Gambling is illegal in most of the United States, and is tightly controlled by the government. If everyone could have all three elements of prize, chance, and consideration, what would stop businesses from opening up casinos on every street corner or opening up their own lotteries to compete with the states?

Gambling is addictive. Part of the American dream is to strike it rich and everyone wants to believe that they can get something for nothing. The fact that someone actually wins sends a powerful message to all the people who didn't. "Sure you didn't win this time, but someone's got to win and it might as well be you." The highly effective tag line for the New York State lottery reinforced the key message, "Hey, you never know."

That is precisely the psychology behind a lottery. You don't know. There is a chance, albeit a small one, that you could win millions of dollars. While the probability is most often compared to the odds of someone being struck by lightning (more than once), consumers still have faith that their day will come. This is such powerful psychology, no wonder so many businesses want to tap into its essence. The solution is to tap into the power of a lottery while at the same time avoiding the legal problems associated with it.

To avoid having a state or federal legislator knock at your door, you must remove one of the three elements of prize, chance, or consideration so that you have either a sweepstakes or a contest instead of an illegal lottery. When looking at the equation, it's obvious you can't remove the element of prize or else your promotion wouldn't be very appealing.

Snapple did a funny takeoff on this idea with their "Win Nothing" sweepstakes. They made it seem to the consumer (at least at first glance) that they had removed the element of the prize from the lottery equation. Television and radio ads featured consumers opening the caps to their Snapple bottles and screaming with joy that they had won *nothing*. The prizes, of course, were actually there, but in the form of the negative. An example of a "Win Nothing" prize from Snapple was "No car payments for a year," where the consumer could win a cash prize equivalent to 12 months of car payments.

This was a brilliant campaign that got even deeper into the consumers' psyche. Snapple played on the fact that most consumers *don't* win. Snapple used a brilliant slice of creative and turned the common message "Sorry, You Didn't Win. Please Try Again" into a positive one.

Had Snapple actually run a promotion without prizes, it would have been a first for the promotional marketing industry, but almost certainly would have been a failure. After all, the prizes are what drive the promotion in the first place. From a million dollars to a new car to a fabulous vacation package, prizes provide the incentive for consumers to perform the action you are requesting. Take away the incentive and you kill the promotion.

So how do you turn an illegal lottery into a sweepstakes? Simple: You take away the element of consideration. That's the "No Purchase Necessary" disclaimer you hear at the end of every radio or television sweepstakes commercial. By removing the element of consideration, you have transformed your illegal lottery into a sweepstakes.

$$\text{Prize} + \text{Chance} + \cancel{\text{Consideration}} = \text{Sweepstakes}$$

Consideration is not just a purchase. Nor is consideration as black or white as most of us would like. The word *consideration* originally comes from the legal profession when discussing contracts. Specifically, *consideration* means something of value to the people who are making the contract.[1] A sweepstakes, in essence, is a contract from your company to your consumers. The official rules for the sweepstakes outline the contract set forth by your company to its participants (your consumers), who agree to follow the contract in order to participate in your sweepstakes.

Consideration is a much-debated issue, with way too much gray area. If you got several promotional lawyers in a room together, you'd probably end up with different counsel as to what constitutes consideration. For example, consideration can come into play when consumers are asked to complete a lengthy survey. That is, some lawyers would argue that if you forced someone to take an hour out of his or her busy schedule to answer your questions, then that 1 hour of time would be enough to satisfy the requirement of consideration.

Until recently, some lawyers believed that forcing a consumer to go online to participate in a promotion could be construed as consideration. The theory went like this: (1) Consumers have to pay for Internet access. (2) In order to participate in the online promotion, you must have Internet access. (3) Therefore, consumers pay to participate. Online sweepstakes without "free" methods of entry have all three elements of prize, chance, and consideration. Lawyers who agreed with this theory told their clients that they must include an alternate "free" method of entry, such as opening up a Post Office box for consumers to send in entries via regular mail.

Recently, however, the state of Florida ruled that online access in and of itself does not constitute consideration. The state of Florida realized that there are ways to get free Internet access with services such as NetZero.com, FreeInternet.com, and Bluelight.com (just to name a few). When combined with free Internet access that most consumers can get via their public library, the state of Florida decided that having to go online to enter into sweepstakes did not constitute consideration.

Regardless of Florida's ruling, many conservative companies who want to avoid the consideration issue altogether still provide an alternate "free" method of entry. The word "free" is in quotes because even sending a postcard to a P.O. box costs the consumer postage. But this "free" method of entry is by far the least disputed

---

[1] Term taken from nolo.com (a self-help legal Web site).

and has the most legal precedents. In the promotional marketing industry, legal precedents are the key. I will dive further into this and other legal issues in Chapter 4, "Protecting Yourself and Your Company Online."

Please do not be put off by this brief legal overview of the term *sweepstakes*. The fact is that many companies posting online sweepstakes right now do not know the legal definitions. This is a problem because, while Internet-based sweepstakes can be truly effective, they can also cause significant problems for your company if they don't follow the legal guidelines set forth by federal and state governments.

This section only scratches the surface of the consideration issue to show you what's going on behind the scenes. The purpose of this section is to get you familiar with the true definition of a sweepstakes so you won't make the common mistake of interchanging the word *sweepstakes* with *contest*. I'll talk about the specifics of what makes a contest later on, but right now, just remember that *a legal sweepstakes has both elements of prize and chance*—and no consideration.

Random Draw Sweepstakes

While the underlying foundation of a sweepstakes is always the same (that is, *no consideration*), there are different kinds of sweepstakes. The most common kind is a *random draw* sweepstakes. The prizes in a random draw sweepstakes are awarded at the end of the promotion from the total number of entries received.

You can easily determine a random draw sweepstakes from the "Odds of Winning" section in the official rules. In a random draw sweepstakes, the odds of winning are always defined as being determined based on the total number of entries received. True odds of winning cannot be accurately established in a random draw sweepstakes until the conclusion of the promotion. A company has no idea how many consumers will enter the sweepstakes.

In a heavily promoted sweepstakes, a company might receive tens (even hundreds) of thousands or perhaps several million entries. Because a sweepstakes has the element of chance, judging these entries is not a problem. The official judge simply combines all methods of entry (online, write-in, in-store, phone, or other entry methods) and randomly selects the winners based on the number of prizes that have been set aside for the sweepstakes. Thus, if 152,384 people enter to win a single prize of a car, the odds of winning that car would be 1 in 152,384—but this would not be known until the last official entry was received.

From 1994 to 2000, random draw sweepstakes have been the most common type of online promotion. There are many reasons for this. First, random draw sweepstakes are usually the easiest form of sweepstakes to administer. While the official rules for one sweepstakes should never be reused for another sweepstakes, the official rules for a random draw sweepstakes tend to be the simplest to write and have fewer legal complexities. I'll go into greater detail about why you shouldn't use the same official rules for different sweepstakes in Chapter 4, "Protecting Yourself and Your Company Online." The short answer is: While your sweepstakes may not change, the legislation surrounding your sweepstakes is constantly evolving. Even though your sweepstakes may be identical, the state and federal laws governing your sweepstakes may change and therefore will require changes in your official rules.

There tend to be fewer chances for breakdowns once a random draw sweepstakes is launched, and the winner selection is by far the least complicated of sweepstakes promotions. With a random draw sweepstakes, there are no requirements for "seeding" instant winners—online or in the real world. This means that there is virtually no risk of accidentally telling someone he or she is a winner, when, in fact, he or she is not. In most cases, winners are selected after all the sweepstakes entries are received. This gives you (and/or your promotions agency) the chance to look at all the eligible entries and ensure that the sweepstakes was conducted fairly—before winners are selected and notified.

From a technology perspective, a company need only set up an online entry form to collect the required information. There is not a lot of heavy back-end work required to collect data from an online entry form, at least in comparison to other forms of promotions. Figure 1.1 is an example of how a simple random draw sweepstakes looks online.

As you can see in Figure 1.1, there are typically five HTML pages associated with a random draw sweepstakes:

1. Entry Form Page

2. Official Rules Page

3. Thank You Page

4. Missing Required Information Page

5. Duplicate Entry Page

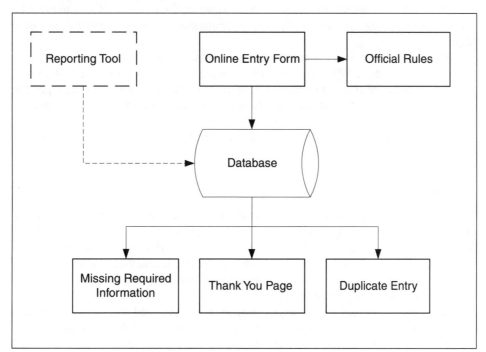

Figure 1.1 Diagram of a random draw sweepstakes.

While the contents of these five HTML pages will change for each random draw sweepstakes, the format will not vary. In essence, a consumer is asked to complete an online entry form and submit his or her entry. The entry is checked to ensure that all required information was entered. If the submitted entry is incomplete, it will be sent back to the consumer to complete for successful entry submission. If the entry is successfully submitted, the consumer will receive the thank you page. If the consumer tries to enter more times than the sweepstakes allows (as specified by the official rules), then he or she will receive the duplicate entry message.

Because the format of the sweepstakes doesn't change, companies can use random draw sweepstakes to learn about their customers. By simply changing the prizes offered and the creative approach to the sweepstakes, companies can measure the effectiveness of their offers and determine what drives their customers. By asking a few optional demographic questions, companies can further learn more about the profiles of their consumers (age, income, education, and other important marketing information).

Random draw sweepstakes have been—and continue to be—used to define the target audience of a Web site. With the use of this sweepstakes tactic, companies are able to go beyond simple statistical data on their Web sites (hits, page views, etc.). Now, marketers can accurately describe who their target audience is and what motivates them.

One of the key reasons why random draw sweepstakes are the most common source of online sweepstakes is that one of the sweepstakes entry form questions will often be, "Would you like to receive special email offers and information from XYZ Company?" This simple question gave birth to the massive "opt-in" email industry (opt-in is discussed in more detail later in the chapter). Consumers who respond with a "Yes" to this question give permission to the company to market to them.

Seth Godin has written a comprehensive book entitled *Permission Marketing* (Simon & Schuster, 1999) that does a fantastic job of explaining just how important it is to get consumers' permission to market to them. Specifically, how getting consumers' permission to market to them and not abusing that privilege enables companies to "turn strangers into friends and friends into customers."

I will discuss how to effectively use random draw sweepstakes later in this chapter.

Automatic Entry

How many times have you heard the statement "When you purchase [XYZ product], you're automatically entered to win [ABC prize]"? How is this legal? While there are many debates over the definition of consideration, purchase is not one of the debated topics. In every sense, a purchase is consideration, and yet somehow there are companies touting that you're automatically entered into a sweepstakes when you purchase their product.

This is both true and legal—legal, that is, when you add the proper legal disclaimers such as "No purchase necessary. Void where prohibited. Must be 18 years of age or older to participate. For official rules, please send a self-addressed stamped envelope to [address]." The reason is that when you read the official rules, you will see that there is a "free" method of entry. This is usually in the form of a

P.O. box that was set up for the promotion, but can also be an 800 number or a Web site.

The automatic entry (with purchase) into the sweepstakes is only *one* of the methods of entry. By also having an alternate "free" method of entry, the company is not in violation of state and federal lottery laws that prohibit having all three elements of prize, chance, and consideration. As long as the company discloses the other methods of entries in the official rules and makes those official rules publicly available, then the company can offer the automatic method of entry into the random draw sweepstakes. At the end of the promotion, all automatic entries received with a purchase are combined with the free method(s) of entry and a winner is (or winners are) selected.

Automatic entry with purchase is an extremely powerful way to urge consumers to purchase your product. By highlighting the prizes offered in the sweepstakes, companies can provide one more reason why their target audience should purchase now rather than at some later date.

Clearly, most consumers will not purchase a bad product just to be entered into a sweepstakes, but an automatic entry with purchase promotion can help encourage your target audience to purchase your product over a similar product offered by your competition.

Qualified Entry Sweepstakes

A *qualified entry* sweepstakes looks and smells a lot like a random draw sweepstakes. The one difference is that a consumer must do something in order for his or her sweepstakes entry to be eligible. The most common example of a qualified entry sweepstakes is a quiz or trivia-based sweepstakes where the consumer receives one entry for each correctly answered question.

To avoid potential consideration problems, the official rules will usually provide consumers with a way to get all the correct answers by sending a self-addressed stamped envelope requesting the answers. Companies using qualified entry sweepstakes online can use relevant links to provide clues or to send consumers to specific Web pages where they can find the answers and submit their responses.

Qualified entry sweepstakes are especially effective if the objective of your promotion is to educate your target audience. If you have a new product, for example, and you wish to educate consumers as to why your product is superior to a competitor's, you could use a qualified entry sweepstakes to get consumers to learn about the features or benefits of your product.

If you want to promote a new television show, you could provide a key word or phrase during the new program that your target audience must submit in order to be entered into the sweepstakes. An in-store display could provide the answers to a quiz, so consumers are driven into a physical store to find the answers that they can submit online. As more physical store locations come online, this will be one of many tools that these companies will use to drive traffic to and from their retail stores and their Web sites.

Treasure hunts also fall into the category of qualified entry sweepstakes. This is an extremely effective way to generate awareness of a Web site's guts. As the log files will attest, one of the most common problems that a Web site experiences is that consumers only go to the home page and maybe two or three pages more before they wander off to something else. Companies have found that using treasure hunts to encourage consumers to dive deeper and deeper into their content can be an effective tool. The premise is that if consumers are exposed to more areas of the site, they are more likely to come back for additional content. A consumer receives additional entries into the sweepstakes for each sweepstakes treasure icon discovered. The more treasure icons found, the more chances to win the prizes offered.

Instant Win Sweepstakes

Instant win games are the darlings of the promotions industry and continue to be so online. With instant win comes instant gratification. Unlike random draw sweepstakes, consumers don't have to wait 6 to 8 weeks to find out if they're a winner—they know immediately. With the immediacy of the Internet, instant win games have become a clear choice for successful online promotions.

Online scratch-off games became popular in 1995 even before the right technologies existed. Some of the first online scratch-off games used animated graph-

---

CASE STUDY: BLUE SHIELD OF CALIFORNIA'S WEB SITE (MYLIFEPATH.COM)

In 1998, Blue Shield of California launched a new service for its customers—a Web site known as *mylifepath.com.* This site was full of useful information for customers, all relating to their health and well-being. In a postlaunch promotional effort, Blue Shield wanted to not only reinforce the concept of *mylifepath.com,* and drive incremental site traffic, but also get registered users to then drill down into all the useful information that this site provided.

In order to get registered members to dive deeper into the content, one of the promotional tactics that Blue Shield of California used was a treasure hunt. The premise was that each week, treasure icons would be "buried" within the contents of the site. When registered members came across one of these treasure icons, all they had to do was click on it to receive an entry into the sweepstakes. Each time a consumer found a specific treasure icon, he or she would receive another entry into the sweepstakes.

Each week, the treasure icons were moved to different areas of the site. This encouraged consumers to investigate the deeper content areas of the Web site and thus expose them to all that the site had to offer.

Blue Shield of California was happy with the increased number of page views associated with this promotion, but found that most consumers did not find all of the treasure icons each week. While the sweepstakes did, in fact, encourage consumers to get deeper into the site, the treasure hunt feature of the sweepstakes alone could not sustain consumer's interest in content that was not relevant to them. That is, if you were a male, it was not likely that you would spend much time searching for a treasure icon within the female breast cancer content area (unless you knew someone who could use this information).

The "treasure hunt" feature of the promotion overall did, however, encourage members to dig deeper into the site, thereby exposing viewers to more of the total content of the mylifepath.com.

ics to simulate a user scratching off the game ticket. That is, you would click on an online scratch-off ticket, and the static image would refresh the page with an animated image scratching itself off.

Later, when Java was introduced, online scratch-off games received the technology boost they deserved and allowed consumers to use their mouse to scratch off online game cards to reveal their winning status. Not only did Java technology allow consumers to use their mouse to control which areas were scratched off, but Java allowed for sound as well. Now consumers could get both a controlled audio and video experience with real-time feedback. This technology not only allowed for instant gratification of the prize winner status but provided a unique experience that did not require any additional software to be downloaded. However, Java is not foolproof. Some corporate firewalls do not allow Java into their networks. The best Java-based instant win games include a text link so that consumers without Java can see their instant winning status (via a graphic image and/or text message, for example).

Some versions of online scratch-off tickets use Macromedia Shockwave or Flash technologies. While these games tend to be more graphically robust, they require that users of older Web browsers download software plug-ins to participate. This download, while usually fast, creates another barrier to participation in the promotion that some marketers are unwilling to entertain.

It is important to note that instant win games and scratch-off games are *not* synonymous. What distinguishes an instant win sweepstakes from another kind of sweepstakes is the immediacy of the results. With the technology that exists today, promotional marketing firms are going beyond the traditional scratch-off games to create unique games that can only be played on the Internet.

For example, a credit card company might use the visual effect of sliding an electronic credit card through an ATM machine to start the wheels of a virtual slot machine spinning. A shipping company might use the virtual popping of bubble wrap to be the action that reveals the sweepstakes message. There is simply no end to the creative possibilities that exist with online instant win games. Using Java, ActiveX, Flash, or a host of other technologies, the online promotional marketing industry is constantly being revolutionized.

Another distinguishing characteristic of an instant win game is the fact that there is a preset number of game plays, which, in turn, allows the odds of winning a particular prize to be disclosed in the official rules. The issue of having a preset number of game plays on instant win games began with the printing of physical game cards, as promotional marketers were forced to determine the total universe of game plays *prior* to the launch of the promotion.

Contrary to popular belief, this aspect of instant win games does not change for online instant win games. This is an important issue because the Internet allows you to easily modify your database. If you project that there will be 1 million game plays, and it turns out that in the first week only 10,000 people play the game, you *cannot* change the odds of winning by reducing the universe of game plays. The reason is that if you modify the game, the first 10,000 people will have different odds of winning than the next 10,000.

This goes entirely against the grain of the Internet where making changes along the way is simply a part of doing business. Because things *can* be modified or changed online in a matter of seconds doesn't mean that they should—especially from a legal point of view. The problem is that most companies holding online promotions expect these kinds of modifications during the online promotion. Instead, the only fair way to administer instant win games is to let them run their course.

If you overestimate the total number of game plays, it is likely you will have prizes left over. Unclaimed prizes can be placed in a second-chance drawing (as discussed later in this chapter). If you underestimate the number of game plays, the only damage is that the promotion will end prior to its projected end date. It's a tradeoff that both companies and agencies struggle with, but changing the odds during the promotion is not the answer. The best results come with making projections and then analyzing results—plain and simple. The more online instant win games you do, the more accurate your projections are likely to be.

Preselected Sweepstakes

A *preselected* sweepstakes is similar to an instant win game from the consumers' point of view. A preselected sweepstakes means that all the prizes in the promotion were randomly drawn *prior* to the launch of the sweepstakes. Preselected sweepstakes usually occur in traditional direct mail where the universe of recipients is known prior to the mailings. The phrase "You may have already won" was born from this type of sweepstakes, as the winning consumers were already selected before the direct mail was sent out. Preselected sweepstakes allowed television broadcast stations to produce their "Watch & Win" games. Consumers would pick up a free game piece at a local supermarket, or in their *TV Guide*, or by writing in. When the show aired, a message would be broadcast to consumers. All consumers who had that same message in their game card would be winners and could redeem the card for the appropriate prize.

Preselected sweepstakes are now being used effectively for email programs. Consumers who participate receive a unique code via email that they must match up with a specific Web site. The consumer visits the site to see if the codes match— if so, they send an email confirmation or complete a prize claim form.

One question you might ask with a preselected sweepstakes is how the consideration issue is dealt with. In a traditional sweepstakes, consumers who find out about the promotion can simply enter the promotion through completing the appropriate entry form (online or through the mail). But with a preselected sweepstakes, the universe of eligible consumers is already defined. It must be, or one winner cannot be predetermined. But how is this possible? How do you limit your universe of consumers who are eligible to participate?

The simplest answer is that you do just that: You limit your universe to "current members" or a "current list" that is described in the official rules of the sweepstakes. As long as there is no inducement to become part of the list for the purpose of obtaining sweepstakes entries, you're in the clear.

Say, for example, you have an existing database of members to your site. You can use this membership database to send out your preselected sweepstakes. The promotion is only open to existing members of your Web site. In this way, your list is not discriminatory and not created as an inducement to become part of the list. It is simply a closed sweepstakes. The key is to remove any inducement to become part of the list and to ensure that the list selected would not be deemed discriminatory by a regulator.

But what if the purpose of the preselected sweepstakes *is* to include people who are not on an existing list? One alternative is to *not* limit your universe to a predefined list and to set aside more game plays. As long as consumers are not forced to join a list to participate in the promotion, additional game plays can be set aside and distributed to consumers not on the list. There will be a limited number of additional game plays available, but as long as your estimates are based on reasonable projections, you can still have a complete universe from which you can preselect winners.

This holds true for email programs just as it does for direct mail and other forms of traditional preselected sweepstakes. You can limit the email recipients to existing lists (either created by you or purchased from a list broker). In this case, you would identify this requirement in your official rules—that you must be a named recipient of the mailing in order to participate. Otherwise, you can send an email for an official entry *while supplies last*.

On the back end, the promotional agency simply preselects winning email addresses from the list of eligible consumers and keeps this list for winner verification. The winning emails are sent out from the same email address, but the randomly generated nonwinning codes are replaced with winning codes.

Preselected email sweepstakes are an extremely effective tool for driving traffic from your opt-in email list of consumers back to your Web site. By the very definition of "opt-in," consumers have asked for more information about your company's products and services. By overlaying a preselected email campaign, you effectively augment the distribution of information with an enticing reason to come back to your Web site.

Second-Chance Sweepstakes Drawing

A second-chance sweepstakes occurs in addition to another form of sweepstakes. Second-chance sweepstakes are most common as a follow-up to online instant win games, where not all prizes were awarded instantly. Because the grand prize is usually awarded at the end of the promotion, the second-chance drawings usually coincide with the grand prize drawing. As long as the consumers' contact information was received, everyone who entered into the first sweepstakes online is automatically eligible for the second-chance drawing.

This is a nice tie-in to the disappointing, "Sorry You're Not An Instant Winner . . ." as you can now add, "But You Have Been Entered Into Our Second-Chance Drawing." The latter part of the message leaves the consumer with a sense of hope that it's still possible to win even though he or she didn't win instantly.

Traditional instant win games don't always capture information about the consumer, so in order for a consumer to be eligible for the second-chance drawing, he or she must submit contact information to a designated P.O. box. However, with online sweepstakes, contact information is usually captured ahead of time for winner verification and validation purposes. Thus, the second-chance drawings can happen automatically.

Consumers who write in (using the designated "free" method of entry) will be added into the second-chance drawing as well. Once all second-chance prizes have been awarded, all the winners are posted and the sweepstakes is complete.

What Is a Contest?

A contest is not a sweepstakes. Some people use the terms *contest* and *sweepstakes* interchangeably, but a contest has a very different legal definition than a sweepstakes. Whereas a sweepstakes removes the element of consideration from the lottery equation, a contest removes the element of chance.

Simply put, a contest is a game of skill.

Prize + ~~Chance~~ + Consideration = Contest

What's interesting about removing chance from the contest equation is that companies can legally require participants to pay for their entries into the promotion. Some companies will go as far as to pass on all or part of the promotional cost to the entrants. You might recall some contests on the backs of cereal boxes saying, "Send $4.95 and your 50-word essay to . . ."

Industry awards are often set up as contests. By requiring that you pay $500 to $1,000 for your entry into the "[Insert Industry Here] Awards," the sponsor has created an industry-specific contest that, depending on the number of entries received, may actually *make* money for the sponsor. Imagine, creating a promotion that not only helps generate awareness of your brand but also can provide supplemental income.

But before you quit your day job to set up profit-making contests online, let's review some of the reasons why most companies *don't* charge their consumers to enter into their contests. While there are exceptions to every rule, the following are generally true about contests.

1.   Contests elicit a much lower response than sweepstakes.

2.   Contests are much more time-consuming.

3.   Contests are much less effective "action motivators"—they require thought and skill, which do not have the "act now" push of a sweepstakes.

4.   Contests are more expensive than sweepstakes.

By removing the element of chance from the contest equation, the promotion is no longer a sweepstakes. What you have done is create a promotion where every submitted entry must be judged.

Think about that for a second. In a sweepstakes, a company might receive thousands (and in some cases millions) of entries. Yet, winner selection is not a problem because winners are randomly selected. But what if you had to read and score a 100-word essay attached to each of those entries?

The components of the promotion to be judged (essay, photo, art, or game, for example) consist of preset criteria that are defined in the contest's official rules. A contest is any game of skill whereby entries are judged on creativity, uniqueness, beauty, or other criteria outlined in the official rules. In this chapter I will review the differences between various types of contests. But before we jump into that, I would like to clarify another long-debated issue: What is the definition of *skill*?

Unfortunately, as was the case with the definition of *consideration,* the definition of skill according to state and federal legislators is not clearly defined. While there is legal precedent at both the federal and state levels for what constitutes a skill promotion, there is no one easy legal definition of what constitutes skill. Rather than make up a definition, let's examine the true difference between chance and skill.

If there is simple guesswork involved, then it's probably a sweepstakes. Skill requires the consumer to think, not to guess. A good example would be that rolling a pair of dice is a game of chance, while playing chess is a game of skill. In order to participate in a game of chess, a person must know how each chess piece moves. To be a good chess player, you must first learn how the game is played and then play often enough to learn what works and what doesn't. On the contrary, you could win at a game of dice just by rolling the right numbers—in other words, by *being lucky*.

While the extreme cases of chance versus skill are obvious, the more difficult gray area appears when there are elements of *both* chance and skill in a game. The rule of thumb is that as soon as the element of chance enters into the contest, the contest is no longer a contest, but a sweepstakes.

For example, let's say your contest is to play chess against a computer. At the end of a 6-week promotional period, you end up with 12 consumers who are able to beat the computer. If you then *randomly selected* a winner from those 12 consumers, you immediately turn your chess contest into a qualified entry sweepstakes. Even though the promotion started as a skill-based contest, the moment you decided to randomly select the winner, you introduced the element of chance into the promotion and turned the contest into a sweepstakes. However, if you took those 12 contestants and had them all play a tie-breaking game against the computer or, better yet, against each other for the championship, you keep the element of skill in your contest all the way through the winner selection process.

Earlier in this chapter, we discussed trivia questions as part of qualified entry sweepstakes. A question that often arises is, "Why aren't multiple-choice trivia questions considered skill questions?" The argument is that you must be knowledgeable about a particular subject matter in order to answer the questions. This argument does not hold if the answers to the questions are provided in multiple-choice format. The reason is that multiple-choice questions introduce the element of chance. That is, if promotion participants were provided with four answers to choose from, then they would have a 25 percent chance of being correct (with no skill at all).

But even after removing the multiple-choice answers, some would still argue that the trivia promotion is a qualified entry sweepstakes, unless the answers submitted could be judged by other criteria outlined in the official rules (such as time, creativity, uniqueness, or clarity of expression).

For example, if you asked the question, "What is the surface area of Lake Ontario?" the answer would be "193 miles by 53 miles." You could argue that there is skill involved in answering this trivia question, but how do you "judge" contest entries with the same exact answer? Television game shows overcome this by adding the elements of time and points. The skill is not just knowing the correct answer, but answering it faster than your opponents and building a score made up of correctly answered questions.

To copy this model on a Web site, the Internet version of a television game show must follow all the same rules and regulations. However, there is a key difference when you bring this game online—the issue of time.

For example, if three qualified entrants are playing from their home or work computers, it is likely that someone has an unfair advantage before the game even begins. Bill is playing from work on his company's network, which uses T3 lines for Internet access. Brian is also playing from work, but his company only has a single ISDN connection. And Elena is dialing in from home with her 56K modem connection. Even if you assume that all Internet traffic is constant once the three players send in their replies, Elena's response will always be slower because she has a slower connection. Bill's T3 network connection will likely give him the upper hand in answering questions the fastest. If you also factor in the processing speed of each computer, you have three people with three different speed abilities. Time can no longer be a valid criterion for this skill-based contest.

To avoid the time issues of answering questions across the Internet, some companies have built Java games that, once loaded, allow consumers to answer questions within the Java applet. That is, the game becomes a self-contained software program that essentially removes the Internet-related time issues. Once the program is downloaded to your computer, you are racing against a clock within the program itself, and not sending and receiving information across the Internet. After you have finished playing the game, the program automatically sends your score(s) back to the server from which the program came.

We'll discuss other examples of skill games later in this chapter. My point is that there are issues of skill and judging when running online contests. Each contest entry must be judged by predetermined skill-based criteria. Some of this judging can be automated as part of the program, but more often than not today's online contests require human judges that are experts in the subject matter—and this drives up the cost of contests.

In fact, contests are generally more expensive than sweepstakes. Official rules take longer to prepare and tend to include more detailed information than sweepstakes. Online contests often require more custom programming, so development costs tend to be higher. Additional costs are incurred with open-ended judging (you must judge each entry received, and each entry costs money to judge).

So Why Run a Contest?

Contests are more expensive, take longer to create and administer, and elicit a much lower response than sweepstakes. So why run a contest at all? Because, when done correctly, contests get inside the minds of your consumers in ways that sweepstakes cannot.

When consumers are asked to use 50 words to describe the perfect pint of Guinness beer, those who participate think long and hard about the Guinness product.

There is no question that Guinness will receive only a small fraction of the entries it would receive in a random sweepstakes. So why does Guinness repeat this essay contest year after year? Because the contest accomplishes three objectives that a sweepstakes can't. It

1. Gets consumers to spend time thinking about the product.

2. Provides qualitative information on how consumers think.

3. Gives ideas about product perception to the companies' agencies.

Contests get consumers to think, to play, to participate, and to create. They demand much more involvement than sweepstakes. While this involvement can become a participation barrier for your target consumers, the ones who do participate provide more of their time and intellectual property than you can expect from a sweepstakes.

Essay contests reward communications skills and give consumers an outlet to describe products that they would not otherwise spend time describing. Art contests encourage consumers to express their thoughts in nonverbal ways that can be even more inspiring and rewarding to companies. Competitive games are fun to play and encourage a healthy rivalry, which is a powerful tool for building and sustaining a community.

When you bring all of this online, you can do things that were never before possible. IBM continues to run its annual "Quest for Java" promotion that encourages programmers to come up with the best Java-based programs. When you submit your 50-word essay online, Guinness's program will tell you if you went over the 50-word limit (rather than simply disqualifying you). Microsoft created a virtual golf tournament where consumers played up to seven 18-hole golf courses and competed for the $100,000 grand prize (and bragging rights).

In short, contests are no better or worse than sweepstakes—they are different. Contests satisfy different marketing objectives than sweepstakes and can be an extremely effective tool when used correctly.

Essay Contests

Essay contests are one of the most popular forms of contests—online or offline. This is due to the fact that most consumers have the ability to write a short essay. Of course, having the ability to write does not mean that people will take the time to do so. Nor do I want to say that first-class writing is easy, as most will agree that it is not.

Essay contests appeal to the widest majority of consumers. Writing is a skill that most people have, and, therefore, essay contests tend to create less of a barrier than photo or art contests, which require a different kind of skill. This is an important consideration, because the more skill that your contest requires, the lower the number of consumers who can participate.

To create an effective essay contest, you must pick a topic or question that is compelling enough to motivate your targeted consumers to participate in your contest. Using my earlier example of Guinness's "Win a Pub" contest, the topic of the 50-word essay was to "Describe the perfect pint of Guinness." This topic has strong appeal among Guinness's core target audience, as most Guinness drinkers feel very strongly about their beer.

A compelling question or topic by itself, however, will not provide the necessary motivation. Unlike sweepstakes, essay contests require thought as well as time and energy to participate. This is where prize relevance comes into play. The prize (or prizes) must motivate consumers to take the necessary time to think through their essays and do quality work.

In the case of Guinness's "Win a Pub" contest, the grand prize was an operational bar in Ireland. This prize could not have been more relevant to Guinness's target audience. The uniqueness of the prize was not only motivating, but it generated a buzz among consumers and the media.

When done correctly, essay contests provide you with a better understanding of your consumers. Essay contests help companies get inside their consumers' heads. They provide a snapshot of how consumers think about a company or its product. Essay contests are especially helpful when you have a well-established brand and are trying to determine the best approach to an advertising campaign. The essay provides a forum for consumers to speak their minds and tell you what they think. Ironically, many companies have a difficult time believing what their customers tell them, but that's a whole different issue.

Essay Length

One question that often arises when creating an essay contest is, "How many words should my essay contest be?" While you might like to receive long essays on your particular subject matter, you must balance this desire with the reality and costs of having to judge each essay received. While each essay contest will vary, most stay between 25 and 100 words. Longer does not necessarily constitute better.

For a better understanding, try writing your own answer to the question or topic. Check the word count of your answer and see if you think the kinds of answers you'd like to receive would fit within this count or should be shorter or longer. If you don't think your answer is a good test, ask your colleagues to provide you with their own answers. Then confirm the costs associated with judging essays of the desired length and make sure you have enough money budgeted to cover judging all essays received. Remember, once the promotion begins, you must judge every entry—even if you receive more entries than you projected.

Online Advantages

There are some terrific advantages to running essay contests online, including:

- Accurate word counts
- Duplicate entry and geography checking
- Remote access for online judges
- Other cost-reducing factors

With traditional essay contests, it is costly to check word count up front. Most essays are scanned for length and only the obviously long ones are set aside. This creates a problem when judges select a favorite essay only to disqualify it later on in the scoring process because it's over the specified word count. Online, you have a choice: Tell consumers up front that their essays are over the specified word count, or automatically disqualify essays that go over the specified word count.

Most companies choose to tell their consumers up front that their essays are too long for the obvious reasons: It shows your customers that you care about their entries and that you want to give them every chance to succeed. The additional programming necessary to check for accurate word count is not difficult nor is it expensive. Companies looking to cut costs should consider automatic disqualification. Legally, it is the consumer's responsibility to provide an essay that has no more than the maximum word count. In roughly the same amount of time that it takes to program a check that alerts consumers that they went over the word count, you can simply thank the consumers for their entries and disqualify them on the back end. This cuts down the cost of judging all the entries received, as the official judges need not review these entries.

Online, you can also easily check for duplicate entries and the source from which the entries are coming. If consumers submit more than one contest entry, you can thank them for their interest, but tell them that you already received an entry from them (and that only one entry is allowed per person). Furthermore, if your contest is only open to residents of the United States, you can easily detect when consumers are coming from elsewhere and alert them that they are not eligible to participate in the promotion. (We will discuss the pros and cons of running international promotions in Chapter 4, "Protecting Yourself and Your Company Online.")

To some extent, you can prequalify most (if not all) of your requirements to be part of the contest. If your contest is only open to a specific age, occupation, or industry, you can prequalify the essays you receive. This front-end automatic checking of entries online saves you time and money that you would otherwise have to spend disqualifying these entries on the back end (people resources versus computers).

Remote access judging is another key benefit to holding your contests online. In the paper-based world, there is a cost to parsing and shipping out entries to qualified official judges if they are not within the same geographic region where the contest entries are collected. It is also more challenging to keep track of how many entries each judge scored. Online, you can allow judges to log in from their multiple locations to your central server. Judges can see how many entries they need to score, and you can keep track of how many entries each judge scores. This is important when it comes time to pay your judges based on the amount of entries they evaluated.

Other cost-reducing factors of online contests include the elimination of printing costs for entry cards and corresponding information about the contest. You still have to "promote the promotion" via advertising and, in some cases, in-store displays, but you eliminate the costs associated with paper-based entries. You further reduce (or eliminate) the shipping costs associated with collecting and judging the entries.

Beyond cost savings, you also reduce the time involved in the judging process. Now judges can log in and start scoring entries. Previously, there was significant preparation associated with providing the judges with the entries they needed to judge. If consumers sent in their entries via mail, there was time associated with opening all the letters, disqualifying entries that did not comply with the official rules, and sending off the entries to each judge. If consumers dropped their entries at a store location, there was a logistical nightmare associated with coordinating the shipments of each store location. If you've run traditional contests offline in the past, I'm sure you can think of many more issues than the few that I've presented here.

Photography and Art Contests

Wherever you find a specific skill that can be judged, you will find a contest waiting to happen. Photography and art contests follow the same guidelines as the essay contest except that the artist is using a different medium.

There are many reasons companies choose visual contests. Photography manufacturers and retailers use photography contests to sell more film. Schools will use these same contests to gather examples of their students' work. Companies that sell finished art and illustration use art contests to discover up-and-coming talent. Magazines will sometimes use art and photography contests to gather content. (Better content sells better advertising.) Web sites use visual contests for building community. By posting a picture of your dog to the "Cutest Dog Photo Contest" online, you're not only competing for the prize, but you're providing the Web site with reasons to keep you coming back (to check out the competition, show your entry to friends and family, and see who won, for example).

Advertisers use these art and photography contests to find the right visual representation of the product they are trying to sell. "Send us a picture of your child eating/using/wearing our product for a chance to win. . . ." Sometimes the "prize" is simply to have your child appear in the print ad, television commercial, or on the product packaging itself. In most cases, the winner will receive some tangible prize (such as cash, travel, or products), but sometimes the advertising and publicity are enough.

Today, more art contests are appearing online. Web sites targeting children are using Java programs that allow children to draw pictures and create their own designs and submit them electronically—all within the Web browser itself. Community Web sites, such as Netscape's Netcenter, fund Web site design contests where consumers are encouraged to create their own sites, and have a panel of experts judge their submissions.

As art and photography evolve, so too will the contests catering to these talents. As digital photography becomes cheaper and the quality/compression improves, more companies will encourage consumers to take digital pictures and submit them to their company-sponsored photo contests.

Games as Contests

As stated earlier in this chapter, there are legal considerations tied to games as contests. When video games are played in real time over the Internet, speed becomes an issue. If one player has a faster connection than another player, then the players are not on an equal playing field. That is, the contest is not only judging their skill, but their connection speeds as well.

But where there's a will, there's a way around the problem. Some companies are using downloadable games to be played against the computer for a score. Microsoft's Gaming Zone, for example, uses client-sponsored games that consumers can download, play, and then upload their scores. Usually, the consumer can play the game as often as he or she wishes, but will only get one chance to compete in the contest. Once the consumer switches to "contest mode," that score, which may not be that consumer's best score, is uploaded back to the Microsoft Gaming Zone Web server and compared against other scores in the contest.

Again, the key to having a legal contest is having skill-based criteria that can be judged. Many legal experts will argue that video games are not games of skill, but rather games of chance. The reason is that most games have a random component that does not allow contestants to be judged fairly. Other legal experts argue that because this random component is identical among all players, then the contest can be judged fairly. But even the most conservative lawyers will agree that there is minimal risk if the element of consideration is also removed. That is, if you're not charging for consumers to compete in the contest, then even if your contest is deemed a sweepstakes because of the random element of the game, you are not promoting an illegal lottery (defined as having all three elements of prize, chance, and consideration).

When done correctly, games can make wonderful contests. If your target audience enjoys playing games, you may even receive a higher number of entrants than is usually associated with contests. When participation in the contest doesn't feel like work, you tend to receive more contestants who want to compete with their friends and colleagues for the grand prize (and bragging rights).

Programming Contests

Programming contests engage a specific kind of consumer: programmers. If your target audience enjoys writing code, then a well-thought-out programming contest may be just what you need to satisfy your objectives. Programming contests, like essay or art contests, require a specific skill, but can be judged on the basis of creativity, ease of use, technical merit (such as advanced features), and even the quality of the documentation used to describe the program.

While programming contests have an extremely targeted audience, they can help build network relationships with the programmers who participate in the contests. The contests show the sponsor various ways in which programmers use code to help build their businesses. This understanding, in turn, helps the sponsor establish new ways to market software products and make improvements to the existing software.

Other Contests

Unlike sweepstakes that have specific categories of type, contests can be as varied as the clients who sponsor them. As long as the focus is on a set of skill-based criteria that can be judged, contests can be quite diverse. Some examples include audio contests, video contests, talent contests, and beauty contests.

Many of these contests are used to seek out talented individuals who specialize in a given field. An example is a record label looking for unsigned bands. In this type of audio contest, contestants are asked to submit a sample of their band's music to the official judging organization. The top talent gets invited to perform live in front of a studio audience and compete for the grand prize—usually some form of a recording contract.

Video contests are used to discover writers, directors, and actors, or sometimes to discover ideas for new television shows. When *America's Funniest Home Videos* hosts their contests, they ask us to send in a video usually centered on a theme such as funniest animals, wedding disasters, or babies. What you don't see on the show are all the hours of footage that the contest judges must view in order to find the 2-minute clip that will be awarded the grand prize.

Other Types of Promotions

As with any promotion, the most effective will be the one that satisfies your specific marketing objectives. This may be accomplished by utilizing a "tried-and-true" promotion such as the sweepstakes and contests described in this chapter, or you may want to try something else. Remember, the only way that a promotional tactic becomes "tried and true" is after innovative marketers have experimented with different ideas to see what works.

Although online sweepstakes and contests are extremely popular, there are many other kinds of traditional promotional techniques that marketers have found extremely effective when combined with the power of the Internet. Even as I write about these well-known promotional devices, there are many companies (both start-ups and established agencies) who are inventing new and better ways to use tried-and-true promotions online. In this section, I'll focus specifically on sampling, coupons, rebates, and loyalty programs.

Product Sampling

Sometimes the best way to acquire a customer is to initiate a trial of your product or service. This is especially true if your product is particularly unique or far superior to the competition. When the experience of using your product or service is the most effective way to capture your target's attention, then sampling programs will be far superior to any sweepstakes or contest.

Traditionally, however, product sampling has been extremely costly. The waste factor associated with most product sampling programs is astounding. The problem has been that when traditional marketers attempt to target specific consumers, the focused "direct" marketing program ends up more like a shotgun approach hitting only 2 percent of the targeted consumers. This stems from the fact that most companies who wish to implement a product sampling program buy or rent direct marketing lists that claim to contain the desired target market, but in reality contain numerous consumers who are not. Even if the list contains correctly targeted consumers, the direct mail containing the product sample is often overlooked or thrown out as "junk" mail because the consumer didn't ask for it.

To combat this problem, many marketers have deployed more grass-roots viral programs whereby samples are distributed in crowded malls and on street corners. While this approach appears to have less waste in terms of samples being thrown away, the marketer usually has no idea if the samples were distributed to the target audience.

The Internet helps solve this waste problem through self-selection. Web sites, such as FreeShop (www.freeshop.com), FreeSamples (www.freesamples.com), and FreeStuff (www.freestuff.com), allow their members to select from various free product samples. Marketers receive a database of consumers who have specifically asked for their product sample, and consumers receive products that they are interested in.

Some will argue that these sites attract "freeloaders," who are not interested in the product but only in the fact that it's free. While it is still too early in the online product sampling game to know for sure, early indications show that this is not the case. As with any promotion, there will always be some percentage of consumers who have no interest in your product or service and who are just there for the promotional benefits. As powerful as the Internet is, there are no technologies that will stop an avid (yet savvy) freeloader from participating in your offer.

But let's compare the waste. On the one hand, a company throws away up to 98 percent of its "targeted" consumers through traditional direct-mail sampling programs. In these programs, consumers who didn't ask for a product sample simply throw it away. On the other hand, a company sends out 100 percent of its samples *only to those who have asked for them*. While we can argue that some percentage of this list are unlikely to purchase your product, most would agree that the true waste is much larger when sending to consumers who do not self-select.

Imagine if you could control your physical mailbox in the same way you can currently control your in-bound email. Any "bulk" mailings would go straight into the trash, while only mail from known sources would reach your mailbox. Now reverse the analogy to understand the power of online product sampling. What if, in the real world, you could tell marketers what products are meaningful to you? That is, you'd never receive an unsolicited piece of junk mail again. Instead, you would only receive mail from companies that had relevant products that meet your individual profile. This is where online product sampling is headed. The power is in the self-selecting technology that allows end consumers to be in control of their relationships with companies.

Electronic Coupons and Smart Rebates

The good news is that price promotions work. The bad news is that price promotions are not a long-term strategy. Experienced marketers will tell you that nobody wins in an all-out price war. When Coke and Pepsi offer price discounts on their products, they don't steal each other's market share; they gain price-conscious consumers who aren't loyal to either company. Companies like Wal-Mart have already adopted a policy of "everyday low prices" that attempt to stop the price promotions altogether in an effort to sustain year-round price savings.

The trick is to create loyalty to your individual products and services—to reward your consumers for choosing your company, not for choosing the cheapest price. So how does the Internet help address this problem? First, it can help you by identifying your best customers. For years, marketers have talked about the 80/20 rule without much success. That is, 20 percent of your customers are responsible for 80 percent of your sales. This is helpful only if you can identify the 20 percent that are buying all of your products. With sales databases tied directly to your customer database, it becomes easy to see who's buying what (and how often).

Once you've identified your best customers, you can start marketing to them differently. You can send out specific offers that target them exclusively. By rewarding your best customers, you are likely to keep their loyalty and gain similar customers. That is, rather than increasing your overall number of customers, you can increase the 20 percent of customers responsible for 80 percent of your sales.

But this ideal scenario assumes that all your sales are completely traceable. This isn't always the case in the real world. Even without knowing all the details of your customers and their purchasing habits, there are smarter ways to take advantage of traditional price promotions.

This is where rebates come into the picture. You provide your customers with an official rebate form that they fill out and send in to receive cash back off the purchase price of your product. In the retail world, this is a preferred price discount because of slippage.

Consumers Who Redeem/Eligible Consumers = Slippage Percentage

Slippage is the difference between the total number of consumers who are *eligible* to receive money back versus the total number of consumers who *actually* send in their completed rebate form. Companies rely on the fact that only a small percentage of consumers who are eligible to receive money back will take the time to send in their paperwork. This allows companies to promote an overall lower price of the product in-store, without losing all the associated markup.

Smart rebates go a step further. Smart rebates do not send cash back to consumers. Instead, consumers receive checks good toward future purchases of the product. In this way, consumers receive a company-branded currency that is good only to purchase additional products. Most companies use this technique to cross-sell their other products. Cash back can be used to purchase anything and does not directly benefit the company providing the rebate (other than the initial sale, that is). With smart rebates, it's virtually a no-lose proposition for the company. If the consumer trades in a smart rebate, he or she will purchase additional products. However, if the consumer does not use the smart rebate, the company is no worse off than if it had received slippage from the customer eligible for the rebate.

Targeted electronic coupons are another smart way to take advantage of traditional price promotions. Electronic coupons can either be printed out or delivered via a URL string—depending on whether you want to have consumers redeem online or in a physical retail store. For online coupons, a dynamically generated URL string (for example, www.yourwebsite.com/coupon_code.html?454Q23RST55523XTV) can be sent directly to the email box of a consumer who has requested a coupon from your Web site or banner ad. Once the consumer clicks on the URL string, he or she will arrive at your "special offer" sales page and can proceed to purchase your product at a discount or receive any other kind of offer you are willing to provide (such as Buy One, Get One Free or Special Premium Offer). When combined with a sophisticated back-end targeting system, you can dynamically deliver different coupon offers to your best (read: loyal) customers versus comparison shoppers.

While there are different ways to deliver coupons online, the fact is that electronic coupons allow you to display various targeted offers at important decision-making time frames. For example, GotSavings.com hosts a massive database of manufacturers' SKU numbers that are linked to key e-commerce Web sites. When you go to make a purchase at Buy.com, participating merchants utilizing Got-Savings.com's back-end database are able to display electronic coupons and rebates right next to the product description that a consumer is considering. This is critical for manufacturers, as they can motivate a comparison shopper right at a critical decision-making point. This electronic version of a check-out counter display is changing the way that manufacturers are providing discounts and coupons online.

eCoupons.com has established a working relationship with MapQuest.com that is a win-win for consumers and businesses alike. Right now, when a consumer goes to MapQuest.com for driving directions, eCoupons.com is able to present targeted electronic coupon offers. One of the early pioneer partners to take advantage of this relationship was Jiffy Lube. As consumers are building their driving directions, they will receive a printable electronic coupon with pin-pointed directions to any Jiffy Lube within a few miles of the starting or ending point of their driving directions.

The one issue that many manufacturers and retailers face when delivering electronic coupons is the issue of overredemption. That is, if you can print one coupon off a Web site, what will prevent you from printing hundreds of them (or sending all your friends the digital coupon via email)? CoolSavings.com has a solution to this problem—proprietary software. With CoolSavings.com, consumers must download special software in order to receive the volume-sensitive coupons.

A perfect example is Blockbuster's "Rent One Movie, Get One Free" coupon. While Blockbuster wants to get you into the store, most of their consumers rent two to three movies on each visit anyway. If consumers could print out as many of these coupons as they wanted, Blockbuster would lose significant profit margins on their high-rent customers. Through CoolSavings.com, Blockbuster can ensure that each coupon that they send out to a customer will be printed only once. Additional bar-code programming also ensures that once a coupon has been redeemed, it cannot be used a second time.

Over the next few years, electronic coupons will continue to evolve and retailers will create new ways to get online customers into their retail stores. With more sophisticated back-end architecture, the best consumers will receive special offers that the less targeted consumers will not have access to. Nonloyal, price-conscious consumers may benefit from coupons in the paper world, but over time, they will be identified online and marketed to very differently than loyal customers (who represent a much bigger earning potential for companies).

Loyalty Programs

Imagine life before frequent flyer miles—a time before Marlboro Miles, Frequent Shopper Clubs, and credit cards that paid you back in cash, miles, or other perks just for choosing to pay by credit card instead of cash. If you wanted to go back to a time before loyalty programs existed, you'd have to go back to somewhere in the early 1800s.

Even in the mid-1800s, loyalty programs could be found in family-owned stores under the concept of "Buy 2, Get 1 Free." Early loyalty programs began as a simple way to reward frequent purchases at a specific location. The objective was to lure customers away from competitive stores that sold similar or identical products. This promotional concept was extremely effective in capturing what would be one-time (or random) customers, and encouraging them to return for future purchases in order to receive free product.

CASE STUDY: S&H GREEN STAMPS

In 1898, an entrepreneurial company called S&H took loyalty programs to a whole new level by creating a new currency that could be exchanged for multiple products. S&H created "Green Stamps," which retailers could buy and distribute to consumers who purchased from their stores. This allowed retailers to place a numeric value on their retail loyalty program such that the more money consumers spent at their stores, the more S&H Green Stamps they would receive.

Along with the stamps, consumers would receive a catalog (which was more like a list) of merchandise that could be acquired when enough S&H Green Stamps were collected. Physical S&H Redemption centers were also created so that consumers could physically browse through the available merchandise and determine the corresponding number of stamps needed. The concept was extremely well received, and as more and more consumers asked retailers for S&H Green Stamps, the loyalty program flourished.

What was truly amazing, however, was that this innovative loyalty program actually made it through the Great Depression. In October of 1929, the stock market crashed and many people lost their life savings. By 1932, approximately one out of every four Americans was unemployed. With such horrific economic disaster, you would think that a loyalty program that encouraged people to buy more would shrivel up and die. On the contrary, the exact opposite was true. In hard times, consumers scraped together what little money they had to buy the products they needed. S&H Green Stamps flourished, as consumers looked for anything that would stretch their dollar the furthest.

In fact, S&H Green Stamps successfully continued through World War II, and through much of the Baby Boom period. It was only after the United States had experienced its strongest growth periods in the 1980s that consumers paid significantly less attention to loyalty programs in general and S&H Green Stamps in particular.

In 1999, over 100 years after its founding, the S&H Green Stamps brand was repositioned as S&H Greenpoints.com, and is now a leading loyalty brand for both the online and offline markets. The Web site (www.greenpoints.com) allows consumers to make purchases online and via a growing number of physical retail locations. It is an extremely nostalgic Web site for anyone who remembers the good old days of licking S&H Green Stamps.

Like any promotions tactic, loyalty programs are most effective when they are used to solve the marketing challenge for which they were designed. Even the most effective loyalty program will not get customers to purchase additional products, if they are not satisfied with the product itself. That is, if your competition has a significantly better product, a loyalty program alone will not solve your problem.

Loyalty programs work best when you have a nearly identical product or service. Take the airline industry, for example. As a consumer, you have certain expectations about any airline that flies to destinations where you want to travel. Most people expect a fair price, a comfortable seat, reasonable care for their luggage, and to be fed if it's a long flight. In the past, when one airline changed their basic service by adding in-flight movies or telephone service, nearly all the major airlines followed suit. To a marketing employee of a major airline, a loyalty program like frequent flyer miles made a lot of sense—especially during a time when none of the other airlines had a loyalty program.

In its most simplistic form, a loyalty program gives *added value* to a purchase. In keeping with the airlines example, if consumers see the flight service of all the airlines as basically the same, then receiving frequent flyer miles from an airline encourages them to fly with that same airline again. Consumers are encouraged to build up enough *added value* on the flights they need anyway with the reward of exchanging these miles for upgrades, free hotel stays, and free flights.

Initially, when only a few airlines had frequent flyer programs, this was a distinct advantage over the competition. By offering these rewards, airlines had another tool in their marketing arsenal to use other than the standard price discounts. Business travelers would now use a single airline for all their travel—even if the flights were more expensive—as the company paid for the tickets, and the business travelers reaped the rewards.

After the huge success in the airline industry, many hotel chains and rental car companies started their own versions of loyalty programs targeting the business consumer, but the business consumer simply wanted more miles in the same program. The reason was all about simplicity. Very few people have the time to manage multiple loyalty programs. If multiple companies in different industries are targeting the same individuals, they will be far better off by combining their programs than by creating a new one.

Beyond Frequent Flyer Miles

With the success of frequent flyer miles in the airline industry, you might ask yourself if jumping on this bandwagon might be a good idea. While there are many advantages to joining an already successful program, it is important to consider your target audience for a moment. Just because frequent flyer mile programs are wildly successful, it does not mean they are the only answer to customer loyalty.

A good example of an alternative program is Marlboro Miles. When Marlboro decided to create its own loyalty program, it faced a similar scenario to the airline industry and could have easily tapped into the airline industry's success were it not for a few very important considerations. Namely:

■ The movement for nonsmoking flights

■ Purchase-to-point ratio

- Target audience considerations

- Financial considerations

As more and more airlines promoted smoke-free flights, it would have been peculiar for Marlboro to counter by giving its loyal smokers access to free flights that they couldn't smoke on. This would have sent a message that Marlboro was supporting an antismoking movement, which was entirely contrary to their business.

Even if the smoke-free movement had not been well under way, the purchase-to-point ratio would not have made much sense. Each pack of cigarettes costs only a few dollars whereas the purchase of an average airline ticket is closer to several hundred dollars. It already takes a fair number of flights to earn enough miles to receive a free airline ticket. Imagine how many cartons of cigarettes it would take in order to receive a free flight. Even when combining flights with cigarettes, the free flight would be gained primarily from previous flights, and not as a reward for loyal smoking.

More importantly, however, would be the target demographics of the customers. While frequent flyer mileage programs target frequent travelers (which, more often than not are business travelers), Marlboro's target was much broader. While some frequent travelers may be frequent smokers, the majority of frequent smokers may not be frequent travelers. It would be important for a cigarette company to find a reward program that was as broad as its target audience in order to be appealing—and an effective marketing solution.

With these and other considerations, there is little question as to why Marlboro decided to go on its own and create a new loyalty program. With Marlboro Miles, smokers can receive premiums as small as Marlboro-branded key chains and as large as an inflatable raft or mountain bike. With a focus on the outdoors, Marlboro successfully tied into the Marlboro Man theme, and created an extremely valuable database of its best (and most loyal) smokers. This allowed for follow-up direct marketing efforts and a way to communicate directly with the end-customer rather than with the retail chains that sold the cigarettes.

Before You Start Your Own Program . . .

If you are considering launching your own loyalty program, here are some things to consider. Everyone wants loyal customers, but a true loyalty program can be costly and overwhelming. Almost every company that started a major loyalty program now outsources the entire program. When loyalty programs flourish, they can become as important to the consumer as the core product itself. If the loyalty program is mismanaged, consumers will look toward competitive products and their corresponding loyalty programs.

Another consideration is that once you truly commit your company to a loyalty program, it becomes extremely difficult to end the program (or even modify it in any significant way). Targeted consumers come to rely on the loyalty program as part of their rationale for buying the product. If the loyalty program is changed significantly, consumers will reevaluate the product to determine if the new program fits their needs. If not, the change in the loyalty program will ultimately affect the loyalty of the consumer.

Online Loyalty Programs

While there are numerous companies that specialize in online loyalty programs, there are three major players in the industry: MyPoints (`www.mypoints.com`), Netcentives (`www.netcentives.com`), and S&H Greenpoints (`www.greenpoints.com`). Each has created its own loyalty program with its own specialty. MyPoints has focused on establishing a network of e-commerce partners (including Barnes & Noble, BMG Direct, Buy.com, Macy's, Microsoft, and Sprint) where consumers can both earn points and redeem the points that they have earned. Netcentives has based its point program around the major frequent flyer mileage programs. S&H Greenpoints has leveraged the household brand name "S&H Green Stamps" and is working to create its own network of retail partners—both online and offline.

MyPoints and Netcentives also have created "private label" versions of their main programs where your company can tap into their existing infrastructure, but with your own version of the program. That is, without leading your customers directly to MyPoints or Netcentives, you can take advantage of the back-end technologies that these companies have created and launch your own loyalty program.

Determining which program is best for you will depend on your target audience and specific needs. You can go online and investigate which program is right for you. You can also contact a sales representative from each of these companies and explain your needs. Each will be happy to explain how their solution can address the problems you've identified. You will then be able to make an intelligent decision as to which would work best for your company's particular needs.

How Do You Know When to Use What?

At last we reach the million-dollar question (literally). I'll begin here by saying that there is no substitute for experience. Effective promotional marketing agencies have little difficulty coming up with the right solution to the problem assuming that their client presents the right problem. In this section I will provide clear examples of when different promotional tactics work best, but understand that these are all just promotional tactics. While I have every confidence that these tactics work, the first question should not be "What works best when?" but rather "What problem are you trying to solve?" (see the section in Chapter 3, "Starting with a Clear Objective").

You will find a particularly strong theme throughout the remainder of this book. For successful online promotions (as with successful traditional promotions), you must begin with a clearly defined objective. Once you have identified the promotional objective, everything else will follow. The biggest failures I've witnessed have occurred because the right tactic was applied to the wrong objective.

Table 1.1 is a summary chart of preferred tactics based on the promotional objective. I use the word *preferred* because there are many factors that determine the ideal tactic. In many cases, more than one tactic could effectively satisfy the objective. The key is to truly understand why the preferred tactics are used with their corresponding objectives. Once the different promotional tactics are clearly understood, I believe the reason for their unity with the corresponding objective will become obvious.

Launching a New Web Site, Product, or Service

If your objective is to successfully launch a new product, then your primary goal is awareness. You need to find a way to break through all the noise in the marketplace. Of course, this is easier said than done. Every marketer faced with this exact same problem wants to come up with an "out-of-the-box" solution that will wow the target audience. The problem is that with so many marketers killing themselves to do something extraordinary, extraordinary has become the norm. In other words, as the box continues to grow and expand, it becomes more and more difficult to come up with that "out-of-the-ever-growing-box" concept. I believe it was Thomas Edison who said that there is no such thing as a truly original idea— just new applications of old ideas.

But while you are thinking up the perfect way to be heard above all the noise in the marketplace, here are some proven promotional tactics that will help you launch your new Web site, product, or service.

Random Draw Sweepstakes

Simple yet effective, a well-thought-out random draw sweepstakes can help you build awareness. With prizes that are compelling to your target audience, a random draw sweepstakes will help draw their attention. While the sweepstakes in and of itself should not replace the key marketing messages of your new product, service, or Web site, it will help to grab attention and give you a forum from which to tell the rest of the story.

Random draw sweepstakes are also extremely effective at building an initial database of your target consumers. In order to effectively launch your Web site, product, or service, you not only need to grab attention, but you need to get permission to provide your consumers with relevant offers and information. Random draw sweepstakes provide a compelling reason for a consumer to provide information about him- or herself. Once you have that information, you can begin to build a relationship with the consumer and move from your initial goal of awareness, into interest, desire, and action goals.

Instant Win

Similar to the effectiveness of a random draw sweepstakes, an instant win game adds a layer of instant feedback. An effective instant win game will have all of the plusses of a random draw sweepstakes, but then allows your target audience to find out immediately what they've won. When launching a new product, service, or Web site, instant win games are especially effective with a large number of lower-level prizes. The better the odds of winning, the more people will receive a small prize and have a positive experience with the promotion (and the Web site, product, or service).

Table 1.1 Promotional Objectives and Preferred Tactics

PROMOTIONAL OBJECTIVE	PREFERRED TACTICS
1. Launch new Web site, product, or service	Random draw sweepstakes Instant win Sampling programs
2. Build awareness/reinforce attributes	Qualified entry sweepstakes Promotional quiz Trivia game Treasure hunt
3. Drive sales	Automatic entry sweepstakes Rebates Smart coupons Premium offer Loyalty program
4. Drive traffic	Instant win with second-chance drawings Daily entry/prizes in random draw sweepstakes Preselected sweepstakes (via email)
5. Build brand loyalty/product preference	Loyalty program Daily instant win game Daily entry/prizes in random draw sweepstakes
6. Reinforce brand identity	Contests Tournament games Other kinds of contests
7. Generate ideas for an effective ad campaign	Essay contest Qualified entry sweepstakes
8. Collect demographic information and get permission for future marketing	Random draw sweepstakes Instant win game Premium offer Loyalty program
9. Increase memberships	Tell-a-friend sweepstakes Loyalty program Rewards/premium offer Sweepstakes
10. Initiate trial/create interest	Sampling programs Downloadable demos Smart rebates Tie-in sponsorship

Sampling Programs

When a Web site is fee-based or requires an extensive amount of time and/or information from consumers who would like to become members, a sampling program makes sense. This "try-before-you-buy" approach allows your target audience to determine if your Web site is right for them. If your site is selling exclusive content, then your sampling program could allow them to see some of that content via a trial subscription or a free area within the site. For financial institutions, it's important that targeted consumers are able to see the interface of what they will be using online and get a good feel for why they should be using the service provided. If your target audience is satisfied with the experience, then it will not be difficult to move them from the sampling program into the desired membership program or customer relationship.

Unique products and services require sampling programs to help educate consumers about the value that your product or service will bring them. If your product sells itself once it's in the hands of your target, then there is no promotional tactic better than a sampling program. In most cases, even when the product is not unique, an effective sampling program will have a truly positive impact on your desired customers because most everyone appreciates free stuff. While your advertising tells people why your product or service is the best, a sampling program allows them to experience it for themselves.

Build Awareness/Reinforce Attributes

After you've completed your launch programs, you'll need to continue your awareness-building efforts while reinforcing the features and benefits of your product. Each of the following promotional devices has something in common—they all require some thought and/or participation from your target audience. Unlike the random draw sweepstakes, instant win game, or sampling program, all of the following promotions require consumers to think before they enter. While they are thinking, you are planting the seeds of information about your product and reinforcing the key message you want to convey.

Qualified Entry Sweepstakes

In the most basic version, a qualified entry sweepstakes gets consumers to answer a question (or questions) before they can be entered into the sweepstakes. Remember that there is a fine line between education and annoyance. When a promotion is difficult to enter, people will think twice about how much they truly want to participate. That said, if you ask a relatively simple question, it will not be a deterrent to the entry process and you achieve your goal of getting people to think about what you're saying.

The right balance of simplicity and number of questions is something that you learn over time. You can experiment with a single simple question in your first promotion, and then add another question to a second promotion to see how your response rates are affected. If you can't afford to take this approach, you can reduce your own learning time by leveraging the experience of other companies and/or promotion agencies who have completed similar promotions targeting the same audience in which you are interested. In general, the more questions you ask of your consumers, the lower your response rates will be. Conversely, if you ask only a single question, then you will maximize the number of people who will enter your promotion.

Promotional Quiz

Sometimes in order to build awareness, you need to educate your target and a qualified entry sweepstakes just won't work. If you need to ask a lot of questions to determine if your messages are getting through, you can turn this requirement into a positive aspect of the promotion. With a promotional quiz, participants can receive instant feedback on the questions they answer (that is, which are right and wrong) and will be instructed to correct the wrong answers (usually with hints in the form of URL links). At the same time, you can analyze which questions are the toughest, and will know what information still needs to be reinforced in the marketplace.

Promotional quizzes are most effective when you're more concerned about the quality of the information you're trying to get across than the volume of people who participate. These quizzes help you determine the level of awareness that has been gained to date and what messaging still needs to be presented (perhaps differently) in order to achieve your awareness goals.

Trivia Game

Trivia is a great way to build awareness and reinforce your marketing messages. While trivia may not be exciting to everyone, many people enjoy showing what they know—especially when prizes are offered. By creating trivia questions that subtly tie back to your product or campaign, you can create an engaging promotion that reinforces what you've already told your target audience.

Oftentimes, the best trivia games pull in related content, but are not focused directly on a product or campaign. If you sell used cars on the Internet, then a trivia promotion about classic cars can be a great way to get car buffs to your Web site. If you're looking to attract sports junkies, there are volumes of statistics that can be utilized. There is trivia out there on just about any subject. When you find a good fit, you can continue to build awareness of your product while engaging your target audience in a compelling promotion.

Treasure Hunt

When your Web site is very large, one of the biggest challenges is building awareness of all the deep areas throughout the site. A treasure hunt can help. By alerting consumers that there are promotional icons throughout the site, they are encouraged to check out places where they may not have been before. If the prizes are worth the time commitments, consumers will spend more time than they normally would to get deep into the site in search of the icons that will help them win coveted prizes.

When consumers find the promotional icons, they can either receive a single entry into a random draw sweepstakes, or they can receive an instant win game piece. Perhaps there is a mystery to solve, and each promotional icon provides them with a clue to solve the puzzle. There are many ways to structure a treasure hunt, but they all accomplish the same goal: to build awareness of other areas within the Web site.

Drive Sales

This is the most common objective of them all. Every company needs to increase its sales efforts if it wants to continue to be in business. There is no problem having this as the primary objective of a promotion. However, it is important that the initial awareness goals have already been achieved in order to maximize the effectiveness of the following promotional tactics. It becomes much more difficult to create interest and desire when your target audience is not even aware of your product. If, on the other hand, your target consumers are well aware of your product, then it becomes easier to create effective promotions that will increase sales.

Automatic Entry Sweepstakes

The simplest promotional tactic that will help drive sales is an automatic entry sweepstakes. Here, consumers receive an automatic sweepstakes entry when they purchase your product. A compelling prize, such as a trip to Hawaii, cash, or a unique offering (such as a backstage pass to a concert), can provide an additional time-sensitive selling point that can motivate a consumer to purchase. An automatic entry sweepstakes works best to convert consumers who are already considering a purchase.

With enough advertising support, an automatic entry sweepstakes will help generate awareness of your product, although this is not its primary focus. The automatic entry essentially provides consumers with a reason to buy sooner rather than later. Assuming that consumers were already interested in the product in the first place, an automatic entry with purchase will convert them into purchasers.

Rebates

Rebates are often an abused promotional tactic because of their effectiveness at driving sales. Usually introduced at the point of sale, a rebate lowers the overall price of the product. Marketers depend on the fact that many consumers who buy the product and are eligible to receive money back in the form of a rebate do not take the time necessary to fill out the paperwork and send it in. This slippage provides the benefit of a perceived lower cost, but does not reduce the cost for those consumers who do not take the time to submit their rebates.

Better rebates are the ones that give consumers credit on their next purchase of your product (assuming that you have a line of similar products). This keeps the rebate money within the company and helps you cross-sell related products, thus driving sales on multiple products.

Smart Coupons

Coupons are a great promotional tool to help drive sales—especially during the off-peak sales periods. With a coupon, you can provide your customers a limited-time discount or offer that will entice them to purchase. As discussed earlier in this chapter, a smart coupon allows you to target consumers and provides them with an offering that is tailored to their specific need or previous buying patterns. Through learning about your consumers, you can provide them with special coupon offers that suit their specific buying habits and increase your sales. Smart coupons can be tied to specific products or can be linked from membership information. The more you know about the buying habits of your customers, the smarter you can be with your coupon offers.

Premium Offer

There is no better example of how a premium offer can drive sales than in the product Cracker Jacks. By inserting a small premium item, Cracker Jacks boosted their sales as children wanted the toys more than the snack. Similarly, cereal manufacturers have successfully followed this model for years, advertising their premium items on the front packaging of the cereal boxes. The right premium item can motivate consumers to purchase the product for the first time, or even motivate them to buy multiple products, in order to send in for the premium item.

In some cases, the premium item can become more valuable than the product itself. Take bubble gum and baseball cards, for example. Initially, the baseball card was used as a premium item of bubble gum (and cigars before bubble gum). Today, collectors of baseball cards couldn't care less about the bubble gum. When the premium is appealing to your consumers, it can be a powerful motivator for driving sales.

Loyalty Program

Retention of your current customers is one of the best ways to drive sales. There are all kinds of statistics (depending on your industry) that claim that it costs anywhere from two to eight times as much to acquire a new customer as it does to retain a current customer. Regardless of the amount, there is no question that your best customer is a loyal customer. A good loyalty program can encourage incremental sales—especially if your competitors offer a similar product.

Drive Traffic

If your product is content and you have created an advertising-based revenue model, then driving traffic to your Web site is most important. The following are promotional techniques that will help you drive traffic to your site (but can also be used to drive traffic to a retail store).

Instant Win with Second-Chance Drawings

As stated earlier in this chapter, instant win games are compelling because of their immediate nature. By providing your members (or even nonmembers) with the ability to play your instant win game on a daily basis, you encourage them to keep coming back to your site.

If frequency is not the issue, perhaps you are looking to get consumers deeper into the site's contents. Creating an instant win game where consumers must first find the relevant icons to play will encourage them to dive deeper into the content. This is more like a treasure hunt with an instant win overlay, but you get the general idea.

A second-chance drawing is recommended because no matter how many prizes you offer in your instant win game, the fact is that the majority of consumers will not be instant winners. When consumers don't win, at least they leave with the feeling that they have another chance.

Daily Entry/Prizes in Random Draw

If your marketing budget is sizeable, one great way to drive traffic is to award daily prizes. For example, "Every day we're giving away $1,000, so be sure that you keep coming back to enter for a chance to win." Webstakes (www.webstakes.com), FreeLotto (www.freelotto.com), and LuckySurf (www.luckysurf.com) all have done a terrific job of driving traffic to their sites by utilizing this technique.

If money is tight (and more often than not it is), you can pool your prize money and give your consumers an additional entry each day that they come back to the site. For example, "Each day you come to our site, be sure to enter for a chance to win our exclusive *Day of Beauty* package. The more times you enter, the better your chances are of winning." It's not as glamorous as winning a daily prize, but it's better than a single entry for a single prize.

Sweepstakes

The standard sweepstakes will drive traffic, but not nearly as well as some of the other techniques discussed previously. The good part about a standard sweepstakes is that it's the simplest to manage and execute. If time is not on your side, but you still need to get a promotion up and running quickly, you may want to consider a simple sweepstakes. You can always build on the first promotion with some of the other techniques when you have more time to plan.

Preselected Sweepstakes (via Email)

A preselected sweepstakes is a great way to drive traffic back to your site if you've already created a database of consumers who have granted you permission to market to them in the future. In other words, if you gave your target audience a check box on your last sweepstakes entry form that reads, "Yes, I would like to receive future promotional offers from *[your company]*," then this is a great way to drive traffic.

First, you send out an email to everyone with their own alphanumeric code. Then you tell them to come to your Web site to see if they've received the winning code. Ideally, you change the code every day and allow your consumers to dictate how often they would like to receive these promotional emails. If you're already sending out a newsletter, this is a great way to provide your sponsors with a way to ensure that their advertising gets read. "Your email code Q7R5668T has been brought to you by *[sponsor]*." Then, when they come to see if their number matches the one posted on your Web site, you can provide your sponsor with a full-page ad (with a relatively high click-through rate).

Build Brand Loyalty/Product Preference

No promotional tactic will help you sell a bad product successfully. Or, as David Ogilvy used to say, "Nothing kills a bad product like good advertising." I say this because if your product is inferior to your competitor's, it won't matter what your promotional technique is, consumers will choose the product that they like the most. Assuming that your product is *at least* as good as the competition, here are some promotional tactics that will help you build brand loyalty and product preference.

Loyalty Program

In a best-case scenario, a loyalty program will keep your satisfied customers coming back. Whether it is points, miles, or any other denomination, a loyalty program gives your customers that little bit extra that won't do much for them in the short term, but over the long run can add up to some nice perks in exchange for their loyalty. The one caveat here is that a loyalty program works best if your competitors don't have a competitive loyalty program or don't have a very good loyalty program. Loyalty programs are meant to be a differentiating factor between you and the competition. If your competitor already has a great loyalty program, learn from it and see what can be improved. If you can't beat their loyalty program, see if you can join an already existing loyalty program that is equally beneficial to your target audience.

Daily Instant Win Game

If you're building brand loyalty to your Web site, it should be noted that loyalty is built over time. Product preference is more immediate. The daily instant win game covers you on both fronts. The first time a consumer receives a game piece, he or she typically has a fun experience. If your customers are told that they can keep playing each time they come back, you can begin to influence their daily routines and eventually build loyalty over time.

If you're selling a product, an instant win game will not influence your customers to purchase something that they were not planning on buying already. However, the instant win game may influence them to buy a second time (assuming that they liked your product the first time). Depending on the prizes offered and the odds of winning, instant win games can influence consumer behavior and help build a purchase pattern. This pattern in and of itself is not loyalty. But, over time, what started as a carrot to get a consumer to purchase can lead to satisfaction with the brand (product preference) and ultimately build brand loyalty.

Daily Entry/Prizes in Random Draw

This is a different promotional tactic from the daily instant win game, but the logic is similar. While a daily entry and/or prizes in a sweepstakes in and of itself will not build product preference or brand loyalty, it will help create a pattern that can achieve the same result (assuming the consumer has a positive experience with your product). Daily prize drawings will provide a consumer with a reason to keep coming back to a Web site, or purchase a product a second time. Over time this will build the product preference and brand loyalty that are desired as long as the consumer has a good experience with the product.

Sweepstakes

A straight sweepstakes applies more to product preference than to brand loyalty (unless you have daily entries and/or prize drawings as stated previously). A sweepstakes overlay provides an additional reason to purchase your product or visit your site. Sometimes this is the only thing you need to establish a preference if your product or Web site is superior (or similar enough) to the competition. Granted, a sweepstakes by itself is not a very strong Unique Selling Proposition (USP), but, in many cases, sweepstakes have been known to give consumers that little extra they are looking for and can generate the desired sales.

Reinforce Brand Identity

Let's say you've been in the marketplace for quite some time, but you still need to drive home your brand identity. Here, the best promotional tactics will come in the form of contests—essay, photo, art, games, or another form of contest that makes sense to your brand. The right contest will not only engage your target audience but should help get your brand inside consumers' heads.

Tournament Games

If your brand is all about gaming, then there's no better way to reinforce brand identity than with a tournament game. Gamers can download a version of the game that is specifically geared to a tournament and then compete against each other for the grand prize. Scoreboards help promote the rivalry and encourage others to join in the competition.

These tournament games have also been used to reinforce brand identity of nongaming companies, but usually via the role of a sponsorship. The effectiveness of sponsoring a tournament game depends on the exposure and advertising support behind the tournament. In some cases, a sponsorship of a major online tournament can be much more effective than a straight online banner campaign or the sponsorship of a text-based content channel. In other cases where there is little to no advertising support behind the tournament, the sponsorship doesn't make much sense for the sponsor.

Contests

As stated earlier, contests do not generate as much response as sweepstakes. However, when your goal is quality not quantity, contests are an extremely effective promotional marketing tool. Nothing works better than contests when attempting to reinforce the product features and benefits of an established brand. Unlike sweepstakes, contests force consumers to take some action—not just provide you with their demographic information.

Choosing the right kind of contest is simple as long as you have a clear objective. If you are trying to come up with a new ad campaign, an essay contest will work wonders. If you're looking for real people to feature in your campaign, a photo contest is essential. Remember that the more you ask your consumers to do, the fewer entries you will receive. However, the entries that you do receive will have made a lasting impression on the target audience who took the time to participate.

There are other forms of contests besides the ones listed here. The best contest to reinforce your brand identity will depend on your brand and the attributes you are trying to reinforce. Perhaps a video contest is what your brand requires. Or maybe you're targeting programmers or developers and could construct a code-based programming contest. Maybe you're looking for the hottest new brands, so a streaming audio contest is what you need. The point is, there are many different kinds of contests and there is definitely one that is well suited for your brand. If you're not sure what makes sense for you, ask around the office or call your promotions agency for suggestions. Perhaps what you need has never been done before and could be a truly engaging contest.

Generate Ideas for an Effective Ad Campaign

Yes, this is what you pay your advertising agency good money for. Yes, they do have great ideas, but so do your customers. If you're looking for new ideas for an effective advertising campaign, qualified entry sweepstakes and essay contests can help. You will find that many of your customers fancy themselves as savvy marketers. Other customers may not see themselves as savvy marketers, but they may have had some great experiences that you can use as testimonials. Good promotions will entice your customers to tell their story and, in turn, help you to tell your story to other consumers.

Essay Contest

While you can certainly run a photo, art, or other visual contest where consumers can submit their experiences with your company (and/or its products), the written word will inspire a larger number of consumers who can and will participate. By asking your existing customers to describe how they use your product, what they like about the product, or any of a dozen similar questions, you invite consumers to tell their stories where the best story wins the contest (and ideally a wonderful prize).

A word of caution: Not all essay contests yield the desired result. In fact, if your products and/or company need serious improvement, these essay contests can give your consumers a platform to tell you what they truly think. Rather than compete in the contest, consumers know that you must judge every entry submitted and take advantage of this fact. Companies often find only a handful of entries that are truly worth the time and money of launching this kind of promotion, but not always.

Qualified Entry Sweepstakes

A qualified entry sweepstakes can be designed to look like an essay contest, but has one extremely important advantage: You don't have to judge every entry that is submitted. This is a key distinction if you are trying to generate ideas for an ad campaign, but you expect that you could receive tens of thousands of responses. You may prefer to sift through the entries at your leisure and figure out which ones are helpful and which are not. In order to do this legally, you must create a qualified entry sweepstakes where the actual winner is randomly chosen from all entries received. That is, in order to qualify, the entrant must provide you with a short essay (say, no more than 50 or 100 words), but the winner will be randomly selected and therefore all the entries received do not need to be judged.

Collect Demographic Information and Get Permission for Future Marketing

Seth Godin, Vice President of Direct Marketing for Yahoo!, conceived, developed, and published the Permission Marketing concept. To paraphrase, by getting permission from your customers to market to them in the future, you can begin to build a relationship with them over time. If you don't abuse the relationship and/or abuse the permission they have granted your company, you can create a long-lasting, profitable relationship. But in order to get there, you first need to get a consumer's permission. [For more on this subject, I strongly urge you to pick up a copy of Seth Godin's book, *Permission Marketing* (Simon & Schuster, 1999)—you won't be disappointed.]

The key question is, "How do you get permission in the first place?" The simple answer is, "You ask for it." The better answer is, "You create a compelling reason for someone to give you permission in the first place." The following are promotional marketing tactics that can be applied to get permission from your target audience to market to them—now and in the future. Please keep in mind that the promotional tactic is the *driver*—the motivating factor. For an effective campaign, you not only need a driver but you also need a compelling offer. The offer is derived from basic direct marketing. You create a "hook" that gets your target audience to take notice and participate. If you're an e-commerce Web site, perhaps your offer is in the form of a gift certificate, free shipping, or gift with purchase. The promotional tactic should be the overlay in this campaign—not the campaign in and of itself.

Random Draw Sweepstakes

Before the term *Permission Marketing* was coined, marketers were using simple random draw sweepstakes as the key driver to help create a database of both their target audience and existing customers. In order to enter into a sweepstakes, you need to provide your name, address, city, state, and zip code. Bingo, you've got your demographic information. But what about permission to market to them in the future? The simple answer was to add another question to the sweepstakes entry, "Would you like to be contacted by *[Company Name]* with special discounts and offers?"

This is where the whole issue of "opt-in" and "opt-out" began. Should we precheck the check box so that consumers must *uncheck* the box if they *don't* want to receive any communications from us? This approach became known as *opt-out* because consumers must uncheck a box in order to *not* be added to a list. Conversely, if the box was unchecked and consumers had to check the box to be added to the marketing database, this became known as *opt-in*.

Over time companies have come to realize that opt-out gives you inflated numbers, while opt-in provides a more accurate list of consumers who truly would like to receive special discounts and offers in the future. The reason is that a large percentage don't take the time to read the question and simply submit their entry after all the demographic info has been entered. Then, when opt-out consumers receive an email that they didn't feel they asked for, they would reply with either "Take me off your list" or something a bit more crass. This occasionally occurs with opt-in lists also, because consumers forgot that they granted permission when they entered the sweepstakes. Overall, there is a lot less confusion with opt-in than there is with opt-out.

Regardless of the method you choose, the random draw sweepstakes is one of the most popular ways to get permission for future marketing and communications from your target audience. Random draw sweepstakes became so popular because typically they were easier to create, develop, and manage than some of the other promotional tactics described later. The only downside associated with the relative simplicity of a random draw sweepstakes is their sheer volume online. Many companies have already discovered the effectiveness of this promotional tactic and tend to rely heavily on their proven success. The volume of these promotions makes it more difficult to distinguish yours from the others and, over time, such promotions will become less attractive to your targeted consumer.

Instant Win Game

As the market has become saturated with random draw sweepstakes online, instant win games have become increasingly popular. The immediacy of instant win games has driven up the success rates for collecting demographic information on consumers and getting permission to market to them in the future.

Similar to the random draw sweepstakes, instant win games typically ask consumers for their contact information up front. The chance to win compelling prizes instantly gives consumers a reason to exchange their information with your company. The immediacy of revealing their prize-winning status is a further reason to participate.

But what really drives the success of the instant win game is the game itself. Scratch-off games are fun to play online and because most people have played one in the traditional world, there is little to no learning curve in how to participate. And with Java, Shockwave, and other technologies, the kinds of instant win games that can be created are limited only by the imagination. Online, you can now grab your consumers' attention with compelling games and use them to capture important information about your existing and future customers. The instant win games will keep your target audience coming back to your site, and will provide you with an opportunity to not only get permission to market to them in the future but to do so during each new game play.

Premium Offer

If games of chance do not get the kinds of results you're looking for, then perhaps your target audience needs more of a direct benefit in order to participate. This is where the premium offer comes into play. Unlike the random draw sweepstakes and instant win games, with a premium offer, you're essentially buying your targets' information and permission directly from them. A premium offer becomes a direct exchange: Your consumers give you their demographic information and you give them something they value.

What premium works best? It depends on your target. For college students, T-shirts, hats, water bottles, and bottle openers are usually enough to get the information and permission you desire. For young adults, you may need to provide them with more "function" such as a calendar, watch, or flashlight. As you move into families you'll find that movies are extremely effective. And as you continue upward in the age and income categories, you may need to shell out more cash to get the right premium for your target. The good news is that there are hundreds of premium suppliers with catalogs full of items that range from 25 cents to $5 and up. These items have a highly perceived value that can be several times their actual cost (especially if you're buying large quantities). If this is a priority for your company, there are annual trade shows dedicated to premium vendors (such as the Premium Incentive Show).

Loyalty Program

A loyalty program is not necessarily the best way to collect demographic information and get permission for future marketing because by its very nature it is a *retention* program. When you try to use a retention program for an acquisition goal, you will not likely achieve your best possible results. However, once you've created your database and have received permission to market to your target audience in the future, a loyalty program is a great way to *increase* the amount of important information and permission you need. By the very nature of these promotional tactics, this information and permission gathering can be developed over time rather than in a single session, which can be overwhelming.

Obviously, you don't want to ask for more information or permission than you need. The point is that when you need to find out more about your customers in order to tailor offers to their specific needs, an offering of points, miles, or other perks can provide the right amount of motivation over time. Loyalty programs will further help you "test the waters" with your newly granted permission. As you create specific offers to those who have granted you permission, you can begin to determine which consumers will respond to specific offers. This information will help you segment your customers and market to them differently (not to mention more effectively).

Increase Memberships

Increasing membership is not entirely different from collecting demographic information and getting permission to market to your target audience in the future. The difference is more in the perception of immediate benefits to the member. Once a person fills out the membership information, he or she should immediately understand the benefits for taking the time to complete all the information required for membership. Ideally, there should be a close correlation between the amount of information the consumer is asked to provide and the benefit for providing the information. Otherwise, the new member may regret having given out so much information and may even ask that you delete him or her from your database.

Conversely, if you deliver quality benefits to your members, you will find that they will tell their friends about your membership program. As word spreads, your memberships will increase and the promotional tactics used will simply fan the fire. As with any promotional tactic, if your marketing proposition is sound, the promotion will help drive home the results you're looking for. If there is no true value to becoming a member, then the promotion will, at best, artificially stimulate your membership numbers. One way to confirm that your membership is valuable (and not artificially stimulated) is to determine how many "active" members you have. If the membership is worthwhile, your inactive membership numbers should be fairly low. If the majority of your members are inactive, then it is probably a result of not paying off the promised benefits.

Tell-a-Friend Sweepstakes

If membership to your Web site (or organization) has its own distinct privileges, then all you really need is a promotional tactic to help spread the word. Tell-a-friend sweepstakes are by far the most effective way to encourage the desired word-of-mouth advertising. By including a simple form and a robust back-end email server, you can empower and reward your existing members and get them to spread the word.

In most cases, the tell-a-friend sweepstakes provides the referrer with entries into a sweepstakes for each person they refer. More sophisticated sweepstakes track each referred individual back to the referee and reward sweepstakes entries for completed memberships. You can choose to allow the referrer to customize your marketing messages or only allow him or her to include a friend's email address. If you know what percentage of your target audience can receive HTML-formatted email, you may even be able to send out graphics and multimedia rather than straight text.

Regardless of the options you choose, the tell-a-friend sweepstakes will be most effective if membership is compelling. The more unique benefits you can offer, the more people (who receive an email from their friend) will bother to check out your site and sign themselves up for membership.

Loyalty Program

Perhaps your membership (at least as it stands today) does not attract enough attention. In this case, a loyalty program can actually *provide* a compelling reason to become a member. By offering points, miles, or other form of unique company-specific currency, you can convince your target audience to sign up and become a member to get free stuff. Becoming a member of a content-oriented Web site has the direct benefit of providing exclusive content to its members. But if your site is commerce-driven, the true benefits of membership are in the form of remembering previous orders, shipping addresses, and credit card information. While this may be compelling for some, others will require something extra before they become members of the site.

A loyalty program can provide that something extra to an otherwise "average" membership. By joining your site, customers will receive points every time they make a purchase (or visit your advertisers). Think about frequent shopper cards. There is very little reason to become a member of your local grocery store. But when they provide you with steep discounts and special offers on the products you'd normally buy anyway, your local grocery store just provided a compelling reason to become a member of their frequent shopping program.

Rewards/Premium Offer

In some cases, it doesn't make sense to set up an elaborate loyalty program just to convert existing customers into members. Perhaps you're experimenting with a pilot program and just want to get some research documented before you commit to a comprehensive loyalty program. In some cases, a single reward or premium item may be the only thing needed for conversion. "Become a member today and we'll send you *[insert valued premium item here]*" is a powerful message that may be all you need to drive membership.

If your desired membership form is lengthy, you may want to break it up into sections and give out special rewards for each section that is completed. These rewards can be offered all at once or over a specific period of time. As consumers provide the information you require for membership, you can distribute the initial reward. As more information is collected, further rewards are distributed until you receive all the information you need for full membership.

Sweepstakes

The most common way to drive membership is with a sweepstakes; it has advantages and disadvantages. On the plus side, sweepstakes are the least complex and are a promotional tactic with proven success. You would be hard-pressed to find someone who does not agree that a sweepstakes will increase membership. The major disadvantage, however, is that sweepstakes are the most common promotional tactic to drive membership, so there's a lot of noise and less punch. By offering prizes that are valued by your target audience, you can entice them to complete your membership application.

My suggestion is that you compare your results of a sweepstakes with that of a tell-a-friend or premium offer. With detailed analysis, you can quickly determine if the sweepstakes is the most effective tactic for driving membership or not. For many companies, it is extremely effective: Publishers Clearing House and American Family Publishers both built their magazine subscription businesses on their million-dollar (and multimillion-dollar) sweepstakes. A well-thought-out sweepstakes will work. It's just a question of how well a sweepstakes will work relative to other promotional tactics at your disposal.

Initiate Trial/Create Interest

When you launch a new product, your primary objective is awareness. At the same time you are building awareness, your secondary (and equally important) objective is to create interest in the product and ultimately initiate trial. If your product is desirable, once you get people to try it, they will want to keep coming back for more. This is why so many car dealerships want you to come in for a test drive. They know that if you're in the market for a new car, the simple act of driving a new car will get you thinking like a new car owner. This is why sampling programs are the most effective way to initiate trial for package goods products. If you're selling software, a downloadable demo version of the product is your best bet for gaining new customers. Smart rebates can help convert a consumer sampling your product into a sale, and tie-in sponsorships can provide the platform for your sampling programs.

Sampling Programs

When attempting to initiate trial, nothing works better than getting some version of the product into your target audience's hands—especially when the product is new or is being repackaged for use in a new or different way. Sampling programs are compelling because they distribute free products to your target audience. Earlier in this chapter, I discussed some of the ways that companies are getting smarter about how they distribute their product samples online. The key difference is that rather than distributing samples to everyone in a given area, you can target a specific group of individuals or allow self-selection of free product samples online. As sampling programs become more efficient, the cost of the programs is lowered and the conversion to follow-up sales increases. While I list other promotional tactics in this section, there is no question that product sampling is the most effective promotional tactic to create interest and initiate trial of new products.

Downloadable Demos

If your product is software, a downloadable demo can take many different forms. If the product is complex or could be confusing, a tutorial version of the product will likely be most effective at creating interest and initiating trial. By tutorial, I mean a canned presentation that provides the key features and benefits and walks a potential customer through how he or she could use your product.

If the product is straightforward and easy to understand, you may choose to provide your target audience with a 30-day trial version of the software (this is similar to a traditional sampling program). After 30 days, the program will stop functioning and the consumer can decide if he or she wants to purchase the product or not. I can't think of a single software company that doesn't have some form of this downloadable demo model incorporated into its core marketing efforts. It's the best way to allow your target audience to try before they buy. What's more, this promotional tactic is commonly included in an overall beta-test program, where targeted consumers test the product and help work out the bugs. This helps your target audience feel included because they are part of the development process of the product itself.

Smart Rebates

When you can't give some version of your product away, then smart rebates are the way to go. Rather than simply giving cash back, smart rebates give your target consumers a form of your company's currency that can be used to purchase more of the same product or for cross-selling complementary products. Smart rebates are a way of keeping the dollars allocated to help sell a product within the company. When attempting to create interest and initiate trial, smart rebates appear to lower the overall cost of the product being sold, but in reality earmark a specific dollar amount that can be used toward future purchases: a future discount that appears to be immediate. Smart rebates not only help create interest and initiate trial but they are a great way to ensure future sales of your products.

Tie-in Sponsorship

In and of itself, a tie-in sponsorship will help create interest but is unlikely to initiate trial. By identifying potential partners who are targeting the same consumers that you are, you can increase the overall impact of your promotion. That is, by combining your marketing dollars with those of partners attempting to attract your target audience, you will have a much broader reach and are more likely to create interest in your product. Depending on the partners, you may even be able to add a sampling component to the promotion. A good example would be creating a care package for freshman college students. If a few companies got together to create a tie-in sponsorship targeting college students, multiple companies could pool their resources to reach the same target audience and distribute their samples. I will go into more detail about this in Chapter 6, "How to Create a Multibrand Promotion."

Conclusion

This chapter should serve as a foundation from which the tools and techniques used in online promotions will be based. It is important to understand the fundamentals of what defines a sweepstakes versus a contest, as well as the various kinds of sweepstakes and contests. An illegal lottery has all three elements of prize, chance, and consideration. A sweepstakes, by definition, removes the element of consideration and contains only the prize and chance elements. A contest, on the other hand, removes the element of chance whereby all entries must be judged based on predefined skill criteria.

Additional promotional tactics include product sampling, electronic coupons, smart rebates, and loyalty programs. The key to successful online promotions is knowing when to use what. Without understanding the legal definitions and different variations, it becomes difficult to decide which promotional tactics would work the best given a particular marketing objective. Depending on the objective, some promotional tactics will work better than others. In the next chapter, I will explain the importance of starting with a clearly defined objective; this will make or break the success of your online promotions.

Why Online Promotions Work

There are actually two parts to this answer: (1) Why promotions work in the first place and (2) why promotions work extremely well over the Internet. The second part will be addressed in detail in the next section, "Overview of Online Advantages," but now I'd like to address why promotions work in the first place. Promotions are, by their very nature, action oriented. While advertising agencies build brands, promotions agencies get people to do stuff. All the various promotional tactics discussed in the previous chapter get people to take action and not be passive. Through advertising, you may be able to create an impression on a passive consumer (that is, generate awareness), but a promotion will either convert this passive consumer into an active one or it will leave him or her behind. Not everyone will respond to promotional tactics, but those who do are in an "active" state when they participate in the promotion, and companies catch them at a great time for conversion to sales.

Direct marketing firms and promotions agencies often approach the same objective with a different strategy and tactics. In fact, direct marketing firms and promotions agencies often work together in the pursuit of satisfying a client's objective. A direct marketing agency will help its client create a compelling offer that will encourage a consumer to "take action" by calling a toll-free number, sending in a business reply card, or accessing a particular Web site. The promotion agency will usually find a way to provide additional reasons to take action beyond the compelling offer that the direct marketing agency recommends.

At the end of the day, promotions work because they are an effective way to get a consumer to *take action*. The desired action to be taken will depend entirely on the objective of the promotion or marketing campaign. In Marketing 101, we learn that there are 4 Ps to marketing: Product, Price, Place, and Promotion. If you have a good product at the right price available at the right places, then all you need is an effective promotion to close the marketing loop and make the sale. This is why promotions work. Now, let's talk about why promotions work online.

Overview of Online Advantages

The Internet is a medium just like print, radio, or television. As with any medium, there are inherent advantages and disadvantages. Unlike other mediums, however, the obvious disadvantages of the Internet are being addressed every day. While there is no such thing as "the perfect medium," the Internet is on course to come really close to perfection. A few years ago, you could complain that, "Yeah, the Internet is great and all, but the audience isn't there, it's too slow, and it will never take the place of television." Perhaps these arguments still hold true today, but things are changing at an extremely rapid pace.

Every 6 months, technology improves drastically. Computer processing power becomes better, access to the Internet is faster, and more people get online. At the same time, more content is delivered via streaming audio and visual media and new devices are becoming Web enabled. Now you can access the Internet via your cell phone and a host of other mobile devices. Many futurists further predict that even our home appliances such as refrigerators and toasters will have access to the Internet.

Table 2.1 summarizes the advantages of online and offline promotions.

While the disadvantages of the Internet continue to shrink, there are many advantages that marketers can trigger right now, especially in the field of promotions. The following are very specific advantages to utilizing the Internet for promotional marketing:

Speed. Less time needed to create, launch, and manage an online promotion.

Research. Immediate feedback and response (quantitative and qualitative).

Technology. Ability to create tools and promotions that were never before possible.

Immediacy. Post immediate results in the form of a leader board, faster conversion to sales.

Viral. Spreading word-of-mouth has never been easier.

Environmental. Less paper and other waste on noninterested consumers.

Control. Ability to change creative and marketing messages on the fly.

Table 2.1 Advantages of Online and Offline Promotions

PROS OF ONLINE PROMOTIONS	PROS OF OFFLINE PROMOTIONS
■ Cheaper than traditional/ offline promos	■ Larger reach than online promotions/media
■ Real-time reporting	■ Less risk of technology failures
■ Can make creative changes on the fly	■ Less need for customer service/ support specifically for the promotion
■ Frequency costs are much lower	■ Easier to predict results (via past experience)
■ Higher degree of control	
■ No additional key punching required	■ More research/case histories
■ Faster (less time for implementation)	■ May be ideal for target audience (who may not yet have Internet access)
■ More highly targeted	■ Tried and true results
■ Can easily move consumers through the sales cycle (aware- ness, interest, desire, action)	■ Capture more sensory areas (for example, touch, smell, and taste)
■ Easy for consumers to participate	■ Can allow for face-to-face contact
■ More likely to get repeat visitors/ entries	
■ Technology allows for further innovations	

Permission. Consumers determine their own level of involvement and manage their own profiles.

Data and Information. Collect more data and information and use both more effectively over time.

Fun. Online promotions and games have brought the fun back into promotions.

Costs. Can be more cost-effective than other mediums.

Success. Meet and exceed clearly defined marketing objectives over time.

Participation. Audience is already engaged in a two-way medium (more likely to participate).

Email. Fast and effective follow-up marketing when consumers have given permission.

Integration. Can easily integrate into existing (or previous) promotional marketing efforts.

New. Constantly changing with new consumers, new technology, and new ideas.

Evolution. Continue success with small additions and changes based on research and feedback.

Mobility. New online devices allow consumers to participate from virtually anywhere.

Ongoing. Easier to keep consumers coming back to participate in daily programs.

Ideal. Most often the best medium to attract consumer participation.

Speed

One advantage of online promotions is speed. When comparing online promotions to traditional (brick-and-mortar) promotions, in general, less time is needed to create, launch, and manage an online promotion. For sweepstakes, there are still time constraints that are dictated by law. If the sweepstake's prize package is over $5,000, for example, then the promotion still must be registered in the states of New York (30 days prior to launch) and Florida (7 days prior to launch) or voided in these two states to be run legally. The point is that creating and posting HTML pages can typically be completed much faster than designing and printing point-of-purchase display units or creating advertising to be placed in newspapers, magazines, or on television.

Speed is addictive and is not always a good thing. Just because you can throw a promotion together in a matter of hours instead of weeks doesn't mean that you should. The best and most effective promotions are still given the right amount of time for planning, creation, and execution. Online, the time pressure isn't nearly as great as in traditional promotions. Rather than taking advantage of this leeway, however, many companies use it as a crutch and operate in a mode of chaos. Instead, speed should be used for testing, fine-tuning, and making adjustments. Rather than creating a single creative execution, why not test a couple of executions to see which ones work the best? As the executions are rotated, the numbers will reveal the most effective campaign. This is where the speed issue becomes important. As further knowledge is gained, creative fine-tuning can be made to increase the effectiveness of the promotion.

The management of the program is also faster, partly because of the database components. That is, where you previously would have had to key in sweepstakes entries and other promotional data, consumers do this themselves, and a database is created during the promotion (not at its conclusion). Daily trivia questions can be preprogrammed into a separate database and served up as new questions every 24 hours (or as needed). While the promotion appears to change daily, the majority of the work was completed prior to the launch and so the management of the physical execution can also be less than in traditional promotions. The exception to this is in the area of server management. If a Web or database server has problems or goes down altogether, then there is quite a bit of management necessary in a very short time frame.

Repeating online promotions takes further advantage of the speed focus. As you begin to understand which promotional tactics work best for your target audience, minor changes allow you to repeat successful programs, gaining even more time advantages. Anytime programs, databases, and creative assets can be reused, there are significant time savings and the speed to market is increased.

Research

Not just research, but immediate feedback and response occur with online promotions—both quantitative and qualitative. Quantitatively speaking, the numbers will tell you how compelling your promotion is, including the creative, offer, prize, and other promotional elements. From a qualitative perspective, even if you don't want to hear it, consumers unhappy with your promotion will find an email address and tell you what they think. Smart marketers take this a step further and invite feedback on the promotion once a consumer has submitted his or her entry. This can be in conjunction with an outside research firm such as QuickTake.com or can be integrated into the "Thank You" page at the end of the promotion.

Research and statistics may be the least of your concerns, but as the saying goes, Those who fail to learn from the mistakes made in history are doomed to repeat them. With traditional promotions, you can sit down and review the results at the end of the promotion, but with online promotions this can happen even while the promotion is taking place. Perhaps traffic from a link from a partner promoting the promotion is not bringing in the numbers as expected. Rather than talking about this when it's too late, the partial data can allow you to have an intelligent discussion while you can still do something about it (that is, before the promotion has ended). If very few of your targeted consumers are participating, you can find out why by simply asking them and perhaps save a potential disaster from happening.

Those with the most successful online promotions pay attention to the bottom line numbers along with consumer feedback and use their best judgment to make adjustments as needed. Perhaps it's simply a matter of consumers hearing about the promotion in the first place and more money is required to drive the right amount of traffic to the promotion. Online promotions allow you to take much of the guesswork out of the promotion and get back to problem solving.

Technology

Perhaps the most obvious advantage of online promotions is the technology itself. With the various programming languages available today, we have the ability to create custom tools and unique promotions that were never before possible. With the Internet, you truly are limited to your imagination. One man's crazy concept is another person's "big idea." I'm not suggesting that every crazy idea is a sound promotion waiting to happen, but all too often we fall into the tried-and-true methods and don't force ourselves to really come up with something unique and different.

Today we can integrate pictures, sound, video, and gaming into wild promotional concepts. Right now many of the "big ideas" are simply technical executions of tried-and-true concepts (online scratch-off games, scrambled image games, or lottery numbers, for example). Buried beneath all this hoopla are some really cool concepts—some that have already been explored and others that have yet to be developed. Over time, more and more companies will come up with killer concepts and then take the risk involved in trying something new.

While I truly believe that just about anything is technically possible, I will also caution that even if the concept is extremely cool, it must also satisfy the promotional objective to be effective. Technology is (and should remain) the icing on the cake, not the cake itself. A whiz-bang technology execution without a clearly defined objective, goals, or criteria is a problem waiting to happen.

Immediacy

Online promotions are immediate—even the simplest sweepstakes instantly confirms that your entry has been received. Consumers who participate in online promotions have come to expect immediate gratification. To this extent, instant win games have become increasingly popular and, in some cases, more effective than traditional sweepstakes. By allowing consumers to find out if they are an instant winner, the promotion takes full advantage of the immediacy aspect of the Internet. As long as consumers can play again and there are sufficient prizes to be won instantly, instant win games are a great online promotional tool.

Besides instant win, online promotions can post immediate results via email or in the form of a leader board. For sports or stock games, the winning status of contestants can be updated based on changes in the stock market or in relevant sports games. This can either be emailed out individually to each contestant, or posted on a leader board especially if the site already has a steady flow of Web traffic. Even for elements of the promotion that don't happen in real time, the Internet allows for immediate updates. Winner's lists, for example, can be posted the minute they have been cleared (that is, when the winners complete their affidavits).

This immediacy is not only an advantage of online promotions, but can assist with a faster conversion rate to sales. By reaching your target audience when it is no longer in "passive mode," but is actively participating with your company, you have a better chance to generate a sale. When you present a limited time offer to a consumer who just participated in your promotion, you're catching that consumer at a time when you have his or her full attention. The immediacy of the promotion can help contribute to the consumer's ultimate conversion from browsing to buying.

Viral

Viral marketing, also called *grass roots marketing*, is defined as marketing that encourages the word-of-mouth component among consumers. Rather than multi-million-dollar ad campaigns, viral marketing targets the local consumers on more of a one-to-one relationship. In the traditional world of promotions, viral marketing is launched in densely populated areas such as airports, malls, and college campuses. Online viral marketing can be as simple as providing your customers with tools to engage their friends.

Online viral marketing is not just email, but email is a significant part. Tell-a-friend programs are one of the more common viral marketing components that rely heavily on email. When consumers provide email addresses of their friends, they are rewarded with additional sweepstakes entries or instant win game plays. Trust and privacy are big issues that go hand-in-hand with tell-a-friend programs. In order for a tell-a-friend program to be successful, consumers must trust that you will not abuse the use of the email address they provide.

Free email services, such as Hotmail and Yahoo! Mail, use the signature line in the free email to send text marketing messages. When you send your friends an email using these free email services, your email includes a message from your sponsor (whether you know it or not). This is a great example of how viral marketing works. As your friends see the marketing message that reads, "Sign up for your own free email account," they may be encouraged to take action and sign up. This message would not have reached you had your friend not sent you an email from his or her free account.

Even when the promotion has nothing to do with email, email is often used for notification. Let's say that you entered your pet into a photo contest and you want to show your friends. The site that is hosting the photo contest will often provide you with the tools to email all your friends and provide them with an HTML link to view your submission. This not only exposes your friends to the contest but may also encourage them to participate and submit their own pet photos. This viral element contributes to the success of many online promotions—even if the site does not provide viral marketing tools. If consumers like the promotion, they're likely to tell their friends about it. The tools to do so simply encourage this behavior. With today's online promotions, spreading the word has never been easier.

Environmental

Even if you don't consider yourself an environmentalist, you will care about the cost savings associated with *not* printing unwanted coupons, samples, direct mail, and other materials for noninterested consumers. With many online promotions, there is a self-select criterion that allows interested consumers to participate and noninterested consumers to go about their business. E-coupons, for example, are only printed when consumers are ready to go to a physical location and therefore have much higher redemption rates. Sampling programs allow only consumers interested in a product sample to receive one. Opt-in direct-mail programs ensure that you only send out physical mail to consumers who have either prequalified or have requested that you do so.

I don't believe that we will ever live in a paperless world. Many successful online promotions are completely integrated into traditional offline promotional techniques. From counter displays, to free-standing inserts (FSIs) in the Sunday newspaper, there are many nonenvironmental aspects that are effective ways of driving consumers to online promotions. The difference is that online promotions have made, and will continue to make, a small dent in the amount of "junk" that we receive. As ebooks and enewspapers become more popular, it's possible that we will shrink the amount of waste that is delivered to us. While I am against unsolicited email (a.k.a. "Spam"), I feel much better about deleting unwanted emails (and even filtering unwanted emails directly into the "trash" folder) than I do about recycling all the unwanted junk mail I receive.

Control

Buddhists believe that control is an illusion. Perhaps they are correct, but the feeling of control is much stronger with online promotions because you have the ability to change creative and marketing messages on the fly. As I will detail in great length in Chapter 4, you should never change anything that affects the official rules of the promotion after it has launched (move the ending date, add or delete prizes, or change the odds of winning, for example). But, you can certainly test and change the look of the promotion and the marketing messaging used to engage consumers. By testing multiple versions of the creative and marketing messages, you can quickly determine which approach will yield the best results, and (unlike a traditional promotion) you have the power to change this while the promotion is running.

With partner promotions, you can quickly determine which partners are the most effective for your campaign. Online reporting allows you a quick summary of everything you want to know about the promotion—in real time. That means when another 200 entries are accepted during the time you're looking at the report, a simple "refresh" or "reload" will incorporate those entries into your report. If the promotion is an instant win game, you'll know which entries were winners, what prize was won, and who won it. If you suspect fraud, you can investigate while the game is still being played—not afterward when the damage is done.

I will caution you not to make the mistake of making changes "because you can." The element of control can be abused and the promotion can be changed so much that there is no consistency across the promotion. When this happens, you can negatively impact the promotion. As long as you have good cause to make changes, it's good to know that you have the ability to make them.

Permission

With online promotions, consumers can determine their own level of involvement with your company. You can engage your target audience with a sweepstakes, contest, game, or other promotional device and get their permission to market to them in the future. With a database back end designed to keep track of the information they provide, you can allow your consumers to indicate how often they want to hear from you and what will interest them the most. Advocates of your product may want to be contacted weekly via email about special offers and discounts, while less enthusiastic consumers may want biweekly or monthly notifications and may prefer traditional direct mail instead of email.

Permission marketing is not just the latest buzzword. It means that you can finally allow your customers to be in control of how much and how often they want to hear from you. As with any relationship, permission marketing is built on trust. Assuming that you do not abuse your consumers' trust, you can use online promotional techniques to build an on-going relationship with your customers and give them control of the relationship with online tools such as customer profiles. When consumers first give you information, you are essentially building a customer profile based on the information they provide. The best and most cost-effective way to keep this profile up to date is to allow the customers themselves to make updates and changes to their profiles. This can include information such as preferred way to be contacted, frequency of contact, special interests or hobbies (for comarketing opportunities), and even their birthday (so you can send them an exclusive birthday offer). I will go deeper into profiles and best practices in Chapter 8, "What to Do after the Promotion."

Data and Information

Online promotions collect both data and information. By *data*, I'm referring to all the raw numbers and statistics associated with an online promotion. This includes which pages were most frequently viewed, total number of unique entries, repeat entries, average number of entries per unique entrant, daily entry counts, hourly entry counts (if broadcast advertising is being analyzed), and so on.

Information is what all this data becomes when you place it into some context. While your data may show a sharp decrease in number of page views for the entry form page, the information you need is that there is a steep drop-off point right before the entry form page. This is information because you can now do something with it like change the number of pages or creative execution prior to the entry form. The information from the online promotion is essentially the data after it's been reviewed and analyzed.

This is a wonderful advantage of online promotions as it would be much more difficult to determine the drop-off points in a traditional promotion. Perhaps your target audience heard your radio commercial and went into their local supermarket to participate in your promotion. When they got there, however, they couldn't find the display unit you referenced in your commercial. It would be much harder to track this event in the physical world than in an online environment. Quite often, the numbers tell a good portion of the story. If there are no numbers, then there is an awareness problem. If there are significant drop-off points, then you can make the desired links more obvious and reduce the other noise in the promotion.

Over time, significant learning can be achieved from each online promotion. As the information is analyzed, online promotions can be fine-tuned both immediately and in the future. This kind of data and information would be significantly more expensive in the traditional world of promotions and, in some cases, just not possible.

Fun

This one is a personal favorite. Promotions by their very nature should be fun. I remember the very first time I experienced the Internet. I was blown away by the possibilities. When you combine the vast possibilities of the Internet with promotions, you should have an incredibly fun result. With online promotions, fun should be a requirement, and, for the most part, it is. Online promotions and games have brought the fun back into promotions. With chat, leader boards, interactive games, and a host of other programs, consumers not only have fun participating in the promotion, but they enjoy telling their friends about it (which adds to the viral marketing component). Online promotions will continue to be successful as long as the element of fun isn't lost in the details.

Costs

One of the reasons online promotions have become so popular over the last few years is because they are usually cheaper to execute than traditional offline promotions. While some costs, such as legal, fulfillment, and registration fees, are the same, online promotions significantly reduce the costs associated with development (no printing, for example), the processing of entries, and the creation of databases.

When you factor in all the costs of a traditional promotion versus that of an online promotion, the bottom line costs favor the online promotion. Even with all the development costs, database, and back-end programming requirements for a robust online promotion, the total cost tends to be much cheaper than all the traditional costs associated with printing (everything from entry forms, game pieces, and ad materials), postage for your direct mail, and converting your written responses into an electronic data file.

But there is a big difference between "cheap" and "effective" promotions. That is, just because the promotion is less expensive doesn't mean it's better. If an online promotion costs one-third of what a traditional promotion would cost, but does not yield the desired results, you've probably wasted your money.

With viral marketing, online promotions can ignite an effective word-of-mouth component that can far outweigh the cost associated with setting up the back-end email system. An online sweepstakes can help begin a custom database that would be significantly more expensive to purchase from a list company—-not to mention less effective when targeting the list. Online promotions lack many of the expensive printing costs.

The overall cost of the online promotion will be determined by the concept, but in many cases, the costs associated with an online promotion will be far less than if the same concept was executed in a traditional environment. Moreover, with the ability to target repeat customers and utilize specific profiles, the online promotion will usually have far less waste than a traditional promotion. This is a more difficult advantage to measure, as online and traditional promotions are usually not an exact "apples-to-apples" comparison. What I have learned, however, is that the cost of an effective online promotion *tends* to be less than the cost of an effective traditional promotion. I recommend that you do your own internal comparisons to see if you agree with what I have experienced.

Success

Currently, online promotions have a high success rate at meeting and exceeding clearly defined marketing objectives over time. This does not mean that every online promotion is successful the first time that it is launched.

Instead, online promotions tend to provide a clear picture of what works and what doesn't. Over time, marketers have a better opportunity for success by making adjustments to their original promotional ideas—even *before* the promotion has ended. That is, if the online promotion is closely watched, you can tell very early on if the promotion is *not* on track to be successful. By being proactive, problems can usually be addressed and true failures can be avoided. With many traditional promotions, you don't have the luxury of making changes once the promotion has launched—not without significant costs associated with the changes.

Participation

Online promotions receive a high degree of participation due to the fact that the entrants are already engaged in a two-way medium. Just by being online, consumers are in a more active mode of thinking than if they were in a passive mode watching television. If the online promotion is compelling, there are very few barriers to participation. Consumers wishing to participate simply use their keyboard and/or mouse and they receive instant gratification for doing so. They don't need to get in their cars and drive to a retail outlet or go to the post office to mail in their entry. They're online, they're already engaged, and the online promotion allows them to participate further. Participation is a great advantage of online promotions. Einstein said it best, "Things in motion tend to stay in motion." If consumers are already actively participating with your Web site (or your tie-in partner's), the right online promotion will simply focus their attention into an area that will help satisfy your marketing objectives.

Email

One of the best advantages of online promotions comes in the form of email. Email is an extremely cost-effective tool for increasing the success of your online promotions—especially when you avoid spam (unsolicited emails). Email can be used for verification, viral marketing, continuity programs, and traditional direct marketing efforts (without the traditional costs associated with those efforts).

Because of all the free email services available today, email is not a foolproof method of verification, but it is a good first defense against bad data. If an email confirmation is sent out and bounces back, then the entry data you received is likely to be bogus or at least inaccurate. By cleaning and purging inaccurate information from your database, the data that remains will become much more useful.

When creating the viral components of online promotions, email is one of the best tools for allowing consumers to tell their friends about the promotion. When an email is received from a known source, it is not immediately deleted. This helps spread the word about the promotion and increases the reach of the online promotion beyond the advertising that was paid for and other negotiated links or URLs.

Email also serves as a reminder or as follow-up marketing once a consumer has entered the promotion the first time. If the consumer asks to be included in the distribution of newsletters or special offers, email can be a wonderful way to pull nonactive consumers back into your promotional marketing efforts. For traditional direct marketing, there are multiple ways to use email effectively when consumers grant their permission, and I will go into more detail later in this chapter (see *Email Components: Why They Work*).

Integration

Some of the most effective online promotions are not stand-alone promotions, but rather are completely integrated with traditional promotions. Online promotions can truly extend your exiting promotional marketing efforts by allowing consumers to participate with your company in ways they were not able to previously. Supporting information and content for the promotion that would be much too costly to print and distribute in-store (or via direct mail) is only a link away. Interactive games and smart coupons can take your existing promotional marketing efforts further and increase their effectiveness.

Truly integrated campaigns utilize the best of both the online and traditional worlds of promotions. Traditional (offline) promotions, while more costly, have no technology requirements (that is, computer and Internet access) and a much larger audience base that can be tapped into. By integrating your traditional promotions with online promotions, you can identify consumers who are willing to participate in online promotions and you can begin to shift your more costly offline marketing efforts to less expensive online efforts. At the same time that your costs are being *reduced*, your level of interaction with your consumers *increases*, and you can begin to build more loyalty toward your products and services.

Meanwhile, you are not excluding consumers who are unable to participate in your online promotions. This is important because although the rate of adoption for the Internet is the fastest in U.S. history (according to Bill Gates), not everyone has Internet access at the present time. If you question whether or not your target audience is connected, it is important that you not abandon all your traditional promotional marketing efforts just because of all the unique advantages to online promotions.

New

Sure the Internet medium is new—so what? Just because online promotions are relatively new is not an advantage. What *is* the advantage is that with a new medium comes new customers, new technologies, and a new way of looking at the world. With all these new things being added to the marketing mix, new ideas are developed—better ideas that couldn't be done before this medium was discovered and truly utilized. The newness is exciting because the Internet has been around for decades, and we're still finding new ways to use it every day. With each new company that is formed and each new idea that is tested, we are changing the traditional world of promotional marketing. With all this newness, there are wonderful opportunities that simply weren't available a few years ago. New, in and of itself, is not necessarily cool, but whenever you change your perspective and get out of your old habits, you can reach new levels of success.

Evolution

By evolution, I mean change for the better. As new ideas are tested, some fail and some succeed. Those ideas that fail are never heard from again. Those ideas that succeed are touted in the press and repeated by all the "me too" companies that find new applications for what was a new idea. A wonderful advantage of online promotions is this process of evolution. As individual companies go out on a ledge to try something new, the entire promotions industry is better for its efforts. As the research, feedback, and results are measured and analyzed, online promotions evolve from guesswork to more of a science. The optimum promotional tactic is identified for each objective that a company is trying to achieve. With each failure and each success, companies hone in on the most effective ways to reach their objectives. And rather than taking years to build up this knowledge base, companies are gaining this knowledge in a matter of months.

Mobility

Online promotions are not just for personal computers any more. With Web-enabled phones, Personal Data Assistants (PDAs), and more wireless devices still in development, online promotions are not confined to the Web, bulletin board systems (BBSs), and email. Now you can enter to win on your Palm Pilot, cell phone, two-way pager, and other handheld devices. As the mobile market grows, so do the possibilities for online promotions. New online devices allow consumers to participate from virtually anywhere. This industry is red hot and is showing no signs of slowing down.

Ongoing

Your promotion is only a click away. This is both the good news and the bad news. On the positive side, online promotions can easily keep consumers participating in daily programs such as trivia games and continuity programs. With daily newsletters, pop-up windows, and other proactive tools, you can easily remind your target audience to keep participating in your promotion and give them a link to get there. Unlike direct mail, print, or broadcast, when your messages begin in the online space, they can easily push and pull consumers into your promotions. By clicking on the link that accompanies your reminders, consumers are instantly taken from their email or other software program directly to your promotion.

On the downside, if your online promotions are not compelling, then your consumers are gone with a click of the mouse. If your promotion is buried, the majority of your consumers will *not* take the time to look for it. They will simply go about their business and seek out information and offers that are easier to find. If you keep your online promotions compelling and easy to take advantage of, then you will have much more success than your competitors.

Ideal

In many cases, the Internet is the best medium to bring consumers into for participation in your promotions. There are many reasons why promotions are ideal in an online environment. In addition to the advantages outlined in this chapter, there are simple things like efficiencies and participation. Much efficiency can be gained when your promotions are brought into an online environment, and the two greatest efficiencies come in the form of cost and timing. Because of the immediacy of feedback and confirmations, participation levels increase in an online environment.

The sum of the advantages of an online promotion is far greater than any individual advantage unto itself. While you can look at specific reasons why you should utilize the Internet for your promotions, the biggest reason may not be fully understood until you try it. With each marketing objective comes a specific need that a promotion must satisfy in order to be successful. Sometimes, other advantages of being in an online environment are not obvious until you get there. In my view, the Internet is an ideal place for promotions, and the advantages of online promotions are still being discovered with each new online promotion that is launched.

Instant Win Games: Becoming More Interactive

If you spend a good portion of your time online experimenting with current online promotions, you'll see some familiar trends, namely, lots of standard random draw sweepstakes that collect data on consumers in exchange for a chance to win. The prizes offered, creative (look and feel), copy, and official rules may change, but the process of entering information and getting a "Thank you for your entry" page is quite standard.

The problem is that these standard random draw sweepstakes are missing the whole interactive nature of online promotions. The Internet has always been a two-way medium, and the traditional random draw sweepstakes smacks of the old one-way mass media approach. Don't get me wrong, traditional random draw sweepstakes continue to be extremely effective at accomplishing their goals (that's why they are so prevalent throughout the Internet). I'm saying there is a better way that's more fun.

Why Instant Is Better

With a traditional random draw sweepstakes, consumers fill out their entry forms, click the Submit button, and get some sort of confirmation that their entry was received successfully. On the positive side, they don't know if they lost, but they also don't know if they won either. There's very little that is compelling about hitting a "Submit" button. Let's face it: It's not fun.

But when you find out immediately if you're a winner or not, you're more likely to come back a second or third time—especially if the promotion has good odds of winning. Even if you receive the "Sorry, You're Not an Instant Winner" message, at least you found this out immediately and are invited to try again. When there are compelling prizes on the line, consumers have the sense that even though they didn't win this time, there are still more chances to be taken and more prizes to be awarded.

This works even better when there are numerous "small" prizes up for grabs. By adding T-shirts, hats, mugs, phone cards, and gift certificates in large quantities and establishing a realistic number of actual game plays, you can increase the odds of winning a prize, and promote this fact throughout the promotion. That is, if you expect that you will receive 100,000 unique game plays, you can build your prize pool such that there are 25,000 prizes in total and the odds of winning instantly are 1 in 4.

Some companies go so far as to promote how many prizes are left in the promotion on the results page. By telling consumers what's still available in this promotion, you are encouraging consumers to keep trying because all these prizes must be awarded. Also, with decent odds of winning, as more consumers actually win during the promotion, you receive the added component of word of mouth. Everyone loves to win prizes when playing an instant win game and most people like to tell their friends about it when they win. While you can promote your random draw winners *after* the promotion has ended, it's much more effective to show off your winners during the promotion and keep the momentum going.

Taking Full Advantage of the Medium

With instant win, you add another dimension to the promotion—gaming. While determining if you're an instant winner is at some level more satisfying than waiting to be notified that you're a winner some six or more weeks later, the real advantage is in the *way* consumers find out if they are instant winners. From virtual slot machines to scratch-off games, color decoders to sports games, there are all sorts of fun and unique ways to convey your winning (and losing) messages. There is no limit to the creative ways to convey an instant win game, except maybe our own imaginations.

Scratch-Off Games

One of the earliest forms of online instant win games, Internet scratch-off games have been around since before the right technologies existed. In 1995, early pioneers used .gif animations to "fake" the actions of a consumer scratching off a game piece. That is, consumers would receive a game piece that looked like a scratch-off card, but rather than using their mouse to scratch off the concealed gaming part of the card, they would simply click on the image and this action would replace the first image with a second animated image that would appear to scratch itself free of the concealed gaming area.

When Macromedia's Shockwave appeared on the scene, companies could create more realistic scratch-off games that took full advantage of a consumer's mouse movements as well as adding audio components. Now with sound and more user control, the scratch-off game was much more compelling to consumers, but there was still one drawback: You had to first download a Shockwave plug-in to participate. Requiring this action meant further delaying consumers' ability to participate in the online promotion.

Sun Microsystem's Java programming language solved that problem. With Java, marketers had fewer concerns about plug-ins, downloads, or version control. While Java was by no means foolproof, it was much easier to ensure that the majority of the target audience could take advantage of richer multimedia capabilities without downloading the required (time-consuming) plug-ins. Java applets also allowed the program to be broken up into smaller pieces that could be downloaded faster, thus creating a better user experience.

Today, Macromedia's Flash and Shockwave come prepackaged with the latest versions of both Netscape's Navigator and Microsoft's Internet Explorer Web browsers, but there are still version control issues to be concerned about. The bottom line is that while technology isn't perfect, the developments have come quite a long way and the best online promotions take full advantage of what is available today.

Scrambled Image Games

Another traditional-technique-turned-online-promotion comes in the form of scrambled image games. These games were highly popular as children's cereal games. The colored images appeared as little more than a colorful mosaic until you held colored cellophane (usually red or blue) over the image to reveal a secret message or cartoon character. These games were often included in or on the cereal box to entertain kids while they ate the cereal.

Promotions companies, such as Marden-Kane and WebDecoder, have taken these entertaining concepts online in different ways. Marden-Kane chose to create solid-color decoders that consumers would use to go online, hold over their computer monitor, and reveal scrambled images that would appear as part of the promotion. Conversely, WebDecoder used the concept to print scrambled image game cards that, when held up to a computer monitor broadcasting a specific color (as part of the promotion), would reveal a hidden message on the plastic game card itself.

As a result of creating these games, these companies have discovered a unique way to solve the integrated media puzzle: "How do you ensure an offline connection to the Internet (or vice versa)?" By providing scrambled images in one medium (either printed or online) and then providing a means to decode the scrambled image via a specific color via the opposite medium, these games ensure a completely integrated marketing circle.

In Marden-Kane's case, consumers receive a printed decoder offline which they bring to a designated Web site to determine their winning status. When consumers receive their scrambled image online, they simply hold their physical game piece over their computer monitor to see if they are an instant winner. Moreover, the same decoder can be used several times throughout the promotion. That is, the online images change, but the same colored cellophane game piece can be used over and over to determine winner status.

With WebDecoder, consumers can play only once per physical game piece. Here, consumers receive a printed translucent scrambled image game piece that they then take to the designated promotional Web site to see if they are an instant winner. By holding the printed game piece up to their computer monitors, the color projected from the monitor will display a hidden message on the game piece itself.

Once this message is revealed, no further game plays are possible without new printed game pieces.

Clearly, there are advantages to using both. In some instances, it is more important that consumers receive a reusable game piece since the objective is to build traffic and keep consumers coming back to a Web site. In other instances, it is more logical to have the consumer visit the promotional Web site only one time, say after they have become a member of the site, signed up for a promotional offer, or responded to a direct-mail piece. Both methods excel at bridging the gap between online and offline promotions.

"Free" Lottery Games

In the real world, the most popular form of legalized gambling (nationwide) is the lottery—either the state lottery or, in some cases, a multistate lottery. With millions of dollars on the line, everyone dreams of what life would be like if he or she won. But as was discussed in Chapter 1, a true lottery (having all three elements of prize, chance, and consideration) is illegal if hosted by your company.

So how do online companies, such as FreeLotto.com, LuckySurf.com, and a slew of others, get away with it? They remove the element of consideration. By providing people with free methods of entry into these lotteries, they avoid all the currently legislated legal pitfalls associated with illegal lotteries and, instead, make their money on advertising revenue.

While copying this model is probably not your most economical solution to use for your next online promotion, many of these companies provide "private label" versions of their major promotions. In this way, you can leverage their game, including the technology, database tools, and (in some cases) even their large prize pools to provide you with a first-rate online promotion for a fraction of the cost to recreate all this yourself.

Casino-Styled Games

If lotteries are not exactly in line with your marketing objectives, then perhaps a casino-styled game is more up your alley. In truth, you can easily integrate a roulette wheel, slot machine, and other forms of casino games as the front end of your instant win game. It's a lot easier than you might think. Rather than using your mouse to scratch off a game piece, or reveal a scrambled image, you pull the arm of a slot machine, spin a roulette wheel, or roll the dice. The only things that change are the front-end actions of rolling dice, spinning a wheel, or spinning multiple wheels (in the case of a slot machine) to simulate the game play.

In reality, your odds of winning are determined before you ever receive the casino-styled game. That is, the back-end database determines (based on the total number of prizes and game plays) if your pull on the slot machine will prove to be a winner or not. The animation simulates what you're used to in a casino, but the truly random part of the game happened before you even received the image of the game itself.

This is why it is not difficult to add fun and familiar front-end components to an instant win game. Once the back-end database has been created (including the tracking of game plays, number of prizes, and total game plays allowed), what is displayed to the consumer is simply a matter of preference.

Knowing who your winner is even before he or she play the game also helps increase the security and integrity of the game. For security purposes, this simple database design can help you avoid lesser forms of fraud during your online promotions. Of course, a truly determined hacker will find loopholes in any system. The real question is, are your instant win prizes worth the time it would take to hack into your online promotion? I will dive further into this issue in Chapter 4, "Protecting Yourself and Your Company Online."

Match-and-Win Games

The next most obvious instant win gaming technique comes in the form of match and win. Prior to the launch of scrambled image games, match-and-win games were the most logical connections between printed materials (including direct mail) and a Web site. Rather than receiving any kind of physical game decoder, you simply were issued an alphanumeric code that would be typed into an HTML entry form to determine instant winner status. These codes could be issued in any medium—television, radio, print, outdoor, or email, for example—and would further verify where the consumer came from and which advertising medium was most effective for reaching the target audience.

When issued in electronic mediums, match-and-win games are simply faster. Consumers can cut and paste the digital number into the entry form (or, in the case of email, just click on a link) and they are instantly told if they are a winner or not. Meanwhile, on the back-end side, companies are using these codes to determine the effectiveness of the campaign—not just which medium, but from which email list, Web site, or pop-up banner.

Match-and-win games can also be played entirely on a single Web page, using the traditional card game. In this implementation, consumers receive multiple squares that all appear to be the same. Consumers simply attempt to match two pictures (or numbers) in order to win instantly. The more squares to choose from, the more difficult it becomes to choose two of the same object.

Collect-and-Win Games

Collect-and-win games are exactly as they sound. Rather than simply playing a single time to determine if you are an instant winner, you can collect game pieces that together allow you to win a specific prize. That is, rather than receiving a "Sorry, You're Not An Instant Winner" message, you receive the letter "R." If you also collect the letters "C" and "A," you can spell the word "C-A-R" and win the automobile prize.

In the traditional world, I would venture to say that the most famous collect-and-win game is McDonald's Monopoly game, which is promoted annually. Each year, the prizes change (slightly), but the game stays the same. You peel off game pieces from your Big Mac, Large Coke, or Large Order of French Fries to see if you are an instant winner. If, however, you don't win instantly, you receive a game piece on McDonald's Monopoly board. If you collect "Park Place" and "Boardwalk," you win a large cash prize ($25,000 or more). If you collect all four railroad station game pieces, you receive a travel prize.

Online, the major difference is that consumers no longer have to keep track of their own game pieces. When consumers create a user name and password, the back-end database remembers what game pieces the consumer had previously along with what the consumer needs to win. Each time the game is played online, the game pieces that are received are automatically added to the consumer's game board. This is a compelling reason for consumers to play these games online versus the traditional world, but that's not the only reason. Online, you can also create more compelling interactive components. Beyond the traditional image files, you can add animations and audio components to make the resulting game board extremely fun and interesting.

From an administrative perspective, online collect-and-win games allow you to know which consumers have collected which game pieces—a task that would be nearly impossible in the physical world. You can also build in "red flags" when specific game pieces are awarded. In this way, you can keep track of who won the most coveted game pieces and protect yourself (at least at the most basic level) against players attempting to fool the system.

Beyond the Traditional

According to every book I've read about the Internet, it has significantly impacted every major business paradigm—and the world of promotions is no different. While there is no cure for a vastly changing industry, there are applicable solutions. The primary solution to an industry changing at the speed of light is the ability to break out of the traditional techniques to get ahead of the technology curve. The following are a few examples based on the known universe, but, as the Buddhist saying goes, "Do not seek to follow in the footsteps of a master, seek what he sought." That is, apply the *thinking* for breaking out of the mold of traditional promotions refurbished online rather than duplicating these specific examples.

I believe that streaming audio and video are *great* vehicles for nontraditional online promotions. Normal radio and television spots have a call-to-action such as "visit our Web site," "call our 800 number," or "come into our store." Streaming video and audio, however, can go much further. By combining the online promotion with the streaming content, consumers have an extremely rich media experience and an engaging way to participate in online promotions. Within the streaming content, you can build hooks (specific links to Web pages), such that your online promotions can grab consumers' attention during the streaming advertisement, and literally pull them into designated Web pages or promotional games.

Besides streaming content, there are a multitude of ways that companies can integrate their own look and feel into online games (including the creation of new online promotional games altogether). Package goods companies, for example, can use their own product packaging to reveal instant win messaging. You can virtually "unscrew" the top of a bottle and look under the cap. You can peel off a label and look at a soup can. You can rip open the top of an envelope and have messages pop out. You can pop bubble gum bubbles, and let the explosion form the winning message. Best of all, you aren't even confined to reality. If you want your consumers to pull a giant elephant out of a thimble, it can be done. You can add audio components to any of these actions that respond to the movement of your consumers' mouse. As they click, drag, open, turn over, and perform any action to determine their instant winning status, you can set their actions to music or specific sounds.

Admittedly, there haven't been many companies who have taken instant win games this far, but it's certainly not the technology that's stopping these things from happening—it's simply a matter of breaking out of the traditional mold and taking advantage of what the Internet has to offer. This takes time and money, but the results will far outweigh the cost of putting these innovative programs together.

Interactive without Instant Win

While instant win games are far more interactive than standard random draw sweepstakes, they are not the only interactive promotions that take full advantage of the medium. Trivia games online provide a game show feel to the promotion and can generate a ton of excitement. Online stock market games can be played in real time, providing instant updates and leader boards. The same holds true for sports tournament games like the NCAA tournament. In fact, any kind of prediction game can be made much more compelling by taking advantage of the real-time nature of the Internet.

Trivia Games

When trivia games were first played on the Internet, the nice feature was instant feedback. Immediately, you would find out if the answer you provided was correct or not. This provided a game show atmosphere without the game show. Trivia game promotions could attract a large audience and have them compete against each other to see who could answer the most trivia questions correctly.

The introduction of programming languages, such as Sun Microsystems's Java and Macromedia's Shockwave and Flash, helped add a timing element that was previously missing. Now when trivia questions were served up to contestants, they could be awarded points for both speed and accuracy. It was no longer simply a matter of who answered the question correctly, but who could supply the most correct answers the fastest. Then when you added features like chat, players (and spectators) could talk to each other before, after, and between the questions being asked.

As gamers continue to refine the best ways to serve up trivia games, the user experience will continue to improve. But even by today's standards, trivia games have become quite interactive and can offer an attention-getting online promotion for your company (without the elements of instant win).

Stock Market Games

Just about every stock-related company has used a stock market game to promote its online presence. Even companies who are not in the business of buying and selling stock, but provide information about stocks have (at one time or another) used a stock market game to promote their services. While the premise of the game is the same (that is, to reward those who pick the highest-performing stocks), the methods of playing the game can be quite different.

In the most basic version of the game, consumers simply pick five or ten stocks from a specified list that they think will perform well during a specified period of time. At the end of the specified period, the person with the best-performing stocks wins. Variations on this concept include: (1) the ability to buy and sell as many stocks as you want during a specified period but with limited funds, (2) not limiting the list of stocks available, (3) choosing a set number of stocks each week, and (4) "Beat the Experts" where you're simply trying to score higher than stock experts.

There are numerous ways in which to structure the game, and on top of all these choices is how the leaders are tracked. That is, some games simply announce the winners at the conclusion of the specified period while others have complex leader boards that display the top scoring players based on the real-time performance of the stock market. Others include your own individual ranking against everyone else who is playing. These levels of complexity are based on what kind of information you have at your disposal and how much time and money you have to put toward the promotion. Obviously, the more compelling the online promotion, the more word-of-mouth attention you will receive, but it's not necessary to have the most high-tech game in order to have an effective online promotion.

Sports Tournament Games

Online sports tournament promotions have been around since the first online promotions. My then company, Modem Media, built the earliest NCAA tournament that I'm aware of for CBS in February 1995. This was a simple 64-grid team selection application where you would choose which college basketball teams would beat their competitors—all the way to the final four and final tournament game. Points were awarded for each correct game identified, and the further you got into the tournament, the more points each game was worth. This basic premise is still used today. Simple, yet effective, these selections (in essence) provide a large-scale office pool feel to your online promotion.

Using JavaScript, the tournament grids can be preprogrammed so that they are all displayed on a single page. Rather than selecting round 1 teams and submitting the selections, then selecting round 2 teams and submitting the new selections all the way to the final games, the program logic will allow all these game selections to happen in a simple one-page interface. It just makes for a better user experience (not to mention less stress on the Web servers).

Similar to the stock market games, the sports tournament games can have leader boards to display the top players based on their team selections as well as provide your consumers with their individual rankings. The only challenge with these leader boards is that in the initial rounds there will be a number of people tied for the same ranking. As long as the program is designed to handle this issue, you can have several individuals tied for first, second, and third place—all the way down the scoreboard, in fact. If, at the end of the promotion, there are still ties, then tie-breaker questions like "What will be the final score of the championship game?" or "What will the half-time score be at the championship game?" can be asked. Or, the grand-prize winner can be determined by a random drawing, based on all individuals with the top score—it just depends on how you structure the game in the official rules of the promotion.

Other Prediction Games

Over the past few years, I've seen some really cool prediction games. Everything from "Who will be nominated for [*insert famous award show here*]," to "Which movie will gross the largest this summer?" There are even Web sites dedicated to a stocklike trading game of famous movie stars. As movie stars in your portfolio get signed to the next biggest box office smash, the value of your portfolio increases. When your stars are in a box office flop, your portfolio decreases. I believe this has also been done using public relations ratings. As famous individuals are hailed by the public, their public relations value increases along with your portfolio, while their public relations disasters decrease their ratings and your portfolio accordingly. Bizarre? Perhaps, but the point of all this is to underline the fact that with the right ideas and the right technology, just about anything is possible. The next successful online promotional ideas will simply take a common interest or desire and build an engaging promotion around that idea. If you can tie in your products and services around that idea, so much the better.

Email Components: Why They Work

Even with all the technology advances online, sending and receiving email is still the number one use of the Internet, according to most online research groups. Email comes directly to your "in-box." While it's much easier to hit the Delete key or filter "junk" email into the trash can, opt-in email can be extremely effective at generating awareness, creating interest and desire, and driving action. Email is personal. When you are addressed by name, email can catch your attention. If the email sounds like a marketing pitch (it doesn't sound like it was written by a human), it is more likely to be deleted. But if the email was requested in the first place and it's compelling, it will be read and acted upon. If your offer is too good to pass up, it will also be forwarded to family, friends, and coworkers.

With the addition of hyperlinks, your email has a call to action and can be tracked for effectiveness. If it's not effective, it will become obvious immediately as reporting is instant and on demand. As more and more email software supports HTML-formatted emails, messages have become visually compelling and appear more like Web pages than text-only email. And just when you thought you knew everything you needed to know about email marketing, new mobile devices provide more applications for *where* consumers can receive your email.

There's no single reason why email components work, as the whole is greater than each individual component. Personalization, in and of itself, is not a good rea-

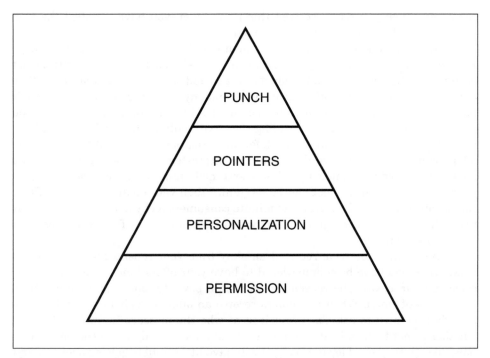

Figure 2.1 Email hierarchy: permission, personalization, pointers, and punch.

son. If personalization were the only reason that email worked, then every Web site you visited would ask for your name so that it could personally greet you the next time you visited the site. Email works because of all the reasons email is what it is: direct, personal, portal, easy to forward, easy to manage, and can be received just about anywhere.

In this section, I will dive deeper into each of these reasons so that it will become clear why adding an *optional* consumer-driven email component to any online promotion is a good idea. Because of the effectiveness of email, there continues to be more and more legislation about what you can and can't do with email and what defines opt-in. I will address the current state of email legislation in Chapter 4.

Figure 2.1 illustrates the email hierarchy that should be followed to ensure effective email marketing programs. Starting with getting permission to send the email in the first place, the elements of personalization, pointers, and punch all build off each other. While you might think it's important to provide pointers or build in punch to your emails, these elements will be less effective or ignored unless the foundations of permission and personalization are first put into place.

Permission to Send Email

Permission is the foundation of an effective email hierarchy. By permission, I'm not talking about leveraging someone else's opt-in email distribution list. True permission is granted directly and solely from your target audience to your company. When you have received this permission, you have satisfied the first requirement of an effective email campaign.

When consumers allow you to send them email, you have received a privilege that should not be abused. If your consumers only signed up for a newsletter, don't assume that they want special product offers in addition to that newsletter. If they agreed to receive product offers from your company, it's not okay to forward their names to strategic partners or sell their names to a list brokerage service. You must maintain their trust by providing them with only what they have asked for. Once that trust is gained, you can ask for authorization to take additional steps to offer them what you believe they would be interested in. If they agree, then you have maintained your integrity. This is extremely important, because as long as your communications are not viewed as "junk," then your email marketing efforts can be quite effective. However, the minute consumers feel you have violated their trust, they will ask to be removed from your list and/or simply filter your messages directly to the trash.

Assuming that you have received an okay from your consumers to send them email, then you have been empowered to have your offers land directly into your consumers' in boxes. The reason this is such a powerful opportunity stems from the nature of email. When consumers receive an offer in their in boxes, they are already prompted to act. They first look at who the message is from and decide whether or not to open it. If you have sent out email to only those customers who have specifically asked for it, then you will have little trouble getting over the first hurdle: getting your email read.

By the sheer fact that your target audience has asked for the email, it is likely that they are already interested in what you have to offer. If you can provide a compelling offer through a discount, premium, or sweepstakes to your target audience, they are likely to respond—especially since they are reading their email with the mind frame of clearing out their in boxes. Think about your own email in box. When you start your day, you take care of the most urgent emails first, but you usually look at everything that doesn't appear to be unsolicited (spam).

With email, your customers don't have to remember to visit your Web site or come into your physical retail store. When they get their emails, they receive that reminder and can act immediately. While some may save your email or place it in a "to-do" folder, the majority of your respondents will act immediately. Thus, you can know if your email was compelling or not right away. This is the power of the in-box immediacy.

Adding Personalization

In my hierarchy of email requirements, the first requirement is getting permission. The second is adding personalization. Getting personal helps with the relevance factor and can help save your emails from being deleted. There are varying degrees of personalization. At the most basic level, you can add a person's name. Rather than beginning the email with, "Dear Friend," you can start with "Hi Bill," and do a better job of grabbing attention. But for true relevance, you want to include something as relevant as a bank statement. Imagine if you could begin every email with, "Hi Bill, you have $12,347.52 in the bank and, when you c bine your stocks and mutual funds, your total net worth is . . ." I don't know a you, but I'd not only welcome that email, but I would begin to depend on it and even get angry if it didn't show up one day.

If you're not in the financial industry, however, you need to strive toward something that is on the same plane of relevance. If your email is a follow-up to your online promotion, you can begin with, "Hi Bill, you currently have 12 sweepstakes entries and, if you continue to play every day, you can receive an additional 35 entries." Okay, it's not as significant as your total net worth, but it's a lot better than not having any level of personalization other than a first name. If you have a loyalty program, an excellent way to begin your emails is with the total number of points or miles the consumer has earned to date.

Outside of the promotions realm, you can thank the consumers for their recent purchases or ask them why they have not visited your site in a while. The point is to add relevance to the emails so that they do not have the feeling of being the broadcast messages that they most likely are. The more you can get personal (without stepping over the clearly defined privacy line), the more likely consumers will take your email seriously. For your top customers, perhaps the best approach is to assign a real person to the task of creating and answering the email. That is, let your top customers know that you care about them and if there's anything that they need, they can email (or call) a specific person. While not everyone will call, your customers will be happy to know that their business is significant enough to warrant personal attention.

Pointers: Adding Links to the Email

The third level in an effective email hierarchy is the inclusion of links from your email to the appropriate Web pages. At the most basic level, this should include links to opt out of the emails that are being received and to respond to your offer. There's no use telling someone about a great offer if he or she can't use the email to get to the offer directly. An effective email will allow a consumer to get right to the heart of the offer from a single mouse click. If there are multiple offers, each offer should have its own link; consumers can then go directly to what is relevant to them.

For reporting and measurement purposes, each link should be tracked, so that you know which email was the most compelling and which offer motivated the majority of your target audience. The links can be assigned dynamically as part of the personalization if the corresponding Web page will again greet the consumer by name and other relevant information. Otherwise, alphanumeric codes can help you identify the specific email that was sent out and answered.

I'm assuming that the email address being used for the email campaign actually works. That is, if someone replies directly to the email, they will not have their email bounce, but will receive a personal reply to their message. While the cleanest way to add or delete someone from a database may be through HTML links, the consumer should also be able to reply directly to the email received and either unsubscribe from your newsletter or ask not to receive messages in the future.

Punch: Adding Creative Design

In the fourth hierarchy, the element of "punch" is added with as much creative as not to jeopardize the reading of the email. At a minimum, this means coming up with a catchy subject line that is informative and provides yet another reason for your target audience to open the email. Once into the email, the copy should be clear and to the point. An email that is longer than it needs to be may be discarded before it is ever read.

From a design perspective, I will speak to the pros and cons of HTML-formatted emails (see Table 2.2). If the email software of your target audience is not known, it is safer to design the email as straight ASCII text rather than using any HTML formatting. The reason is that if you send HTML-formatted emails to non-HTML-compatible email programs, the email software will simply display all the HTML source code in the body of the email. That is, consumers will actually see the <HTML> tags. This makes for a horrific user experience, and this is much worse than not including some nice graphics within the body of the email.

However, if you know what email program your customers use, then you can segregate HTML-compatible programs with non-HTML-compatible programs. There's no question that an HTML-formatted email looks much better than a text-only email (at least when it is viewed through an HTML-supported email program). When you're used to seeing text-only messages, the graphic emails certainly grab your attention and can be more effective at getting the point of the email across visually. HTML-designed emails can also better incorporate hyperlinks, such that actual key words are linked rather than displaying the entire URL. For example, the straight ASCII text email might read: "To take advantage of our buy one, get one free sale today, visit http://www.yourwebsite.com/buyone.html?advcode=12345"

On the other hand, the same offer using HTML-formatted text could have a "Buy One, Get One Free" graphic button right next to the offer, or include the link as part of the text. In this case, the link would be placed around the words, "buy one, get

Table 2.2 Advantages and Disadvantages of HTML-Formatted Email

PROS OF HTML-FORMATTED EMAIL	CONS OF HTML-FORMATTED EMAIL
■ Provides color and design where these elements are usually lacking.	■ HTML source code appears when viewed through an email program that does not support HTML-formatted emails.
■ Can visually represent what would be more difficult to explain with words.	■ Can take longer to display the email if large images are referenced as part of the email.
■ Provides better incorporation of hyperlinks on both text and graphic buttons.	■ Appears more like an "ad" than normal ASCII text emails would.

one free" in the following manner: "Take advantage of our <u>buy one, get one free</u> sale today."

The two other cons of HTML-formatted emails are that: (1) they can take longer to display because the HTML code is pulling graphics from the Internet into the email and (2) the email will appear more like an ad for the simple reason that only a small percentage of emails sent out take full advantage of HTML formatting. While the first few HTML-formatted emails might be appealing, over time they run the risk of becoming associated with advertising, as most consumers will not take the time to create HTML-formatted emails to each other until doing so is as simple as creating a signature file with all your contact information.

If It's Good, It Will Be Forwarded

The viral marketing impact of email may be its biggest success driver. Simply put, if the email is truly compelling, it's incredibly easy for your targeted consumers to click the Forward button on their email programs and forward the email to as many of their friends and family members as they choose. It doesn't get any more grass roots than this. As your email gets forwarded to others, you are not only receiving additional exposure at no additional cost but you are also receiving a stamp of approval from a known source to the people who receive the forwarded email.

While this feature of email is usually a blessing, it can sometimes be a curse. If your offer has been highly targeted, you may want to discourage your consumers from forwarding the offer. While this is rare, it does happen. If you are concerned about having a highly targeted email forwarded, then you can provide a single-use hyperlink. That is, once the link has been used, it will not allow others to take advantage of the same offer from the same link. But if you're really smart, you'll find a way to encourage (rather than discourage) consumers to tell anyone they know about your offer. Even if you can't make their friends the exact same offer, it's usually possible to provide the referred friends a way to receive an offer that is equally rewarding.

Mobile Devices

The more recent addition to the email phenomenon has been the inclusion of mobile devices. Today you can easily receive emails via cell phones, pagers, wrist-watches, and handheld devices such as the Palm Pilot. As the number of devices where you can receive email increases, so too does the importance of email as a component of your online promotions, especially if the mobile device has instant access to the Internet.

Email on mobile devices also presents a different design challenge. While it is always recommended to be as much to the point as possible, some of today's mobile devices have strict character restrictions, limiting the length of the email. Most pagers, for example, only allow the first few lines of an email to be sent. If your email marketing strategy includes (or specifically targets) mobile devices, extra care should be taken with the content of the email message.

Beyond email, mobile devices themselves are changing the world of online promotions. More and more companies are looking to the wireless and mobile marketplace as the next big Internet push. From the perspective of online promotions, mobile devices present a perfect opportunity to market differently to consumers and to provide online promotions that are applicable to how consumers use their mobile devices. With cell phones, online promotions can provide on-demand information regarding products and services and use a coupon or discount offer to convert an information inquiry into a sale. Pagers can be utilized so that your consumers can remind themselves to participate in your upcoming promotion or purchase your product the next time they are in a supermarket. Online promotions can also provide an enjoyable distraction on a handheld device taken into a meeting or onto an airplane. As marketers continue to learn about how their customers prefer to interact with them, new promotional ideas will be created and tested. Successful online promotions for the mobile marketplace will flourish, as this relatively new marketing medium becomes a standard communications vehicle.

Immediate Feedback and Response

Perhaps the most unique and important aspect of online promotions comes from the real-time reporting and the ability to respond to feedback *during* the online promotion. This is completely standard in the online promotions industry but is quite different from the traditional world of promotions. Normally, once a traditional promotion is launched, reporting happens weekly (at best) and results are not truly learned until the end of the promotion when an analysis is completed. In other words, by the time you figure out that something better could have been done, there's usually not much time to do anything about it.

This is not true for online promotions, unless you are speaking about the prizes, official rules, or odds of winning. These (as I will discuss in detail in Chapter 4, "Protecting Yourself and Your Company Online") legally cannot be changed. The official rules state that the promotion begins on a specific date and ends on a specific date, and if there are any changes to the official rules, prizes, or odds of winning, the whole promotion can be deemed invalid and shut down (not to mention the fines and, in extreme cases, the potential jail terms associated with the changes).

On the positive side, the creative, media, technology, and support can all be changed and adjusted after the launch of the promotion. Commonly, creative is the element most often changed after the launch of the online promotion. Through online media tests, it is determined that specific creative is far more effective than the alternative creative, so the effective creative is used and, in some cases, additional creative is developed in conjunction with the work that is pulling the best results. Media placement is another area for tweaks and adjustments after the launch of the campaign. If one site is generating much better response rates, media dollars can be added to one site and removed from another (depending on who was used for the media buy). If additional Web servers are required to support unexpected traffic after the launch of the promotion, the hosting and the programming around the hosting can all be modified. If there is an overwhelming email response, outside email marketing support groups can be deployed to deal with the volume of emails received.

The real trick, of course, is knowing: knowing what to look for when you receive your real-time reports and knowing what is worth responding to in real time versus what elements will ultimately play themselves out.

Real-Time Reporting

Assuming that you started with a clear objective and took time to plan, your needs for real-time reporting should be obvious. If your objective was to increase Web site traffic and you are using a sweepstakes or instant win game to accomplish this objective, the most important report you will want to see is how your Web site traffic has been affected by the online promotion. In addition to your traffic numbers, you will most likely want to review real-time reports on the sweepstakes itself, including:

- Total number of sweepstakes entries

- Total number of unique contestants

- Average number of entries per contestant

- Total number of contestants from each media vehicle or Web site

- Number of consumers who responded to an email invitation

With each promotion, specific reporting needs will be a direct result of the kinds of information that need to be tracked and analyzed. If peak Web traffic is a major concern, the maximum number of simultaneous entrants will need to be identified and monitored. If there are a limited number of customer service representatives who are answering email inquiries, then it will be important to monitor the total number of emails received each day and the efficiency of each customer service representative.

Analyzing Results

The only way to successfully analyze results is to first know what you are looking for and, second, to have the right kind of information from your real-time results that will alert you when the event you are looking for takes place. Take Web traffic, for example. If you are concerned that your online promotion will spike your Web traffic beyond what your servers can handle, the critical information you need is an alert when a single Web server has reached 80 percent capacity or the network is significantly above the normal range of Web visitors.

If you are attempting to determine whether consumers will respond better to creative treatment A or B, then you need real-time feedback on the number of consumers who have responded to each of the creative treatments. The creative treatments might also work differently depending on where they are shown, so it also becomes important to see the results of the creative treatments relative to the Web sites on which they are displayed. Perhaps one Web site is a little more rough or edgy than the others. It may make sense that one specific creative treatment would work better in the rough or edgy environment than in the rest of the Web sites.

To effectively analyze results of your online promotions, you need only have the right information from your real-time reporting. As long as you have determined the critical reporting needs ahead of time, the analysis becomes a cinch.

Responding in Real Time

For best results, responding in real time requires a dedicated team of individuals with the right skill sets. While minor changes to an existing promotion can be done without a dedicated team, the changes that matter require knowledgeable people with the time and ability to make changes on the fly.

If you have already created three separate creative treatments, deploying one treatment or the other is not difficult. If, however, you find out that none of the creative treatments appears to be working, then the problem may be with the communication of the offer and additional work may be required. When real challenges occur, it is important to be able to assemble the team that created the promotion to discuss what can be done. If additional media support is needed, it is important to first understand *why* the original media buy isn't working before additional time and money are spent fixing the problem.

Sometimes flukes occur, and it is important not to overreact to minor setbacks. As you review the results of your online promotions, enough time must pass to allow the results to be meaningful. Perhaps the first day of the promotion was slow due to the fact that not all media was placed on time. By the second day, the additional information will begin to show early signs of what's happening. In general, it is important to allow a week to pass so that the real-time reporting has enough opportunity to provide meaningful information. Once the first week's reports are understood, then creative, media, and technology changes can be made if needed.

Responding in real time is most critical when disasters occur. Perhaps a promotional Web server crashes or the router that directs your traffic blows up. These incidents are rare, but they do happen. Online, you have the ability to make quick fixes so that your consumers need not feel the full impact of the disaster. A quick fix for a crashed promotional Web server might be to reroute the traffic to a different server that was not being used for the promotion or temporarily capture the entries via a flat text file rather than the robust database you were using. With the right people on your team, you can quickly brainstorm and figure out the best way to avoid a potential disaster.

A final word on the subject of responding in real time is that the more experience you have with online promotions, the better off you will be in an emergency. The first time you encounter a crashed server, it feels like the whole world has come to a grinding halt. But, contrary to the feelings you have at that moment, the major problems are where you learn the most about the challenges of online promotions. When you come to a resolution, you not only feel good about solving the problem but you also have a much better understanding of how to avoid that problem in the future. While it would be nice to avoid the problems altogether, the ability to react quickly and steer clear of a potential disaster is one of the strengths of online promotions. Beyond solving the problem itself, you gain quite a bit of knowledge when things don't go as planned, and end up that much more prepared for your next online promotion.

Conclusion

Promotions work because they are action oriented. While advertising agencies build brands, promotions agencies get people to do stuff. Online promotions have even more advantages, including cost efficiency, real-time reporting and adjustments, more control, faster time to market, technology innovation, and the ease of consumer participation. This chapter outlined some 20 distinct advantages of online promotions, but any one of these should be sufficient to consider the inclusion of online promotions as part of your integrated marketing tactics.

Online instant win games are better than random draw sweepstakes because of their immediacy—a core advantage of the Internet. Win or lose, consumers want to know immediately and instant results will encourage consumers to come back and try again—even if they didn't win. There are various kinds of instant win games, and new games are continually being developed. Scratch-off games, scrambled image games, match-and-win games, and casino-styled games are all different forms of instant win games. Each is compelling for its own reasons, but all are interactive and provide immediate gratification.

Email is still the number one use of the Internet. As long as this is the case, email components will continue to be an important and effective part of online promotions. Effective email marketing programs begin with getting permission to send the email in the first place, then add the elements of personalization, pointers, and punch. This email hierarchy is important as personalization will not be effective without first receiving permission to send the email. Likewise, punch will be more difficult to achieve without personalization or pointers. By following the email hierarchy, you ensure that targeted consumers receive relevant emails that encourage them to take action.

Perhaps the most unique and important aspect of online promotions comes from real-time reporting and the ability to respond to feedback *during* the online promotion. Although prizes, official rules, or odds of winning cannot be changed, creative, media, technology, and support can all be changed and adjusted after the launch of the promotion. Responding in real time is most critical when disasters occur and while it's no fun to have a disaster on your hands, it's good to know that potential damages can be limited by moving quickly to solve problems. Many disasters can be avoided altogether with proper planning, which is the topic of the next chapter.

3

Planning an Online Promotion

Online promotions follow a circle made up of four distinct parts: Planning, Production, Execution, and Conclusion (see Figure 3.1). This chapter will focus on planning. It is important to understand that while this book must have a starting and an ending point, a true circle does not. After the first time around the entire circle, what was learned from the first online promotion is used to plan the next online promotion. So although this chapter will focus exclusively on planning, Chapter 8, "What to Do after the Promotion," will also discuss planning—but from the context of what was learned from a previous promotion.

This chapter assumes that you are planning your first online promotion. Without having completed a previous online promotion, you're starting with a deficit. From the start, you're missing the distinct benefit of having valuable insights and learning from a previous online promotion that can be applied to the current objectives you are attempting to solve. If you are, in fact, planning your very first online promotion, this deficit can be overcome with the help of more experienced individuals (such as research organizations and promotional marketing agencies) that can lend you their insights and experience to help you avoid common mistakes. In addition, you'll have a much better sense of what to watch out for if you finish reading this book *before* launching your first online promotion.

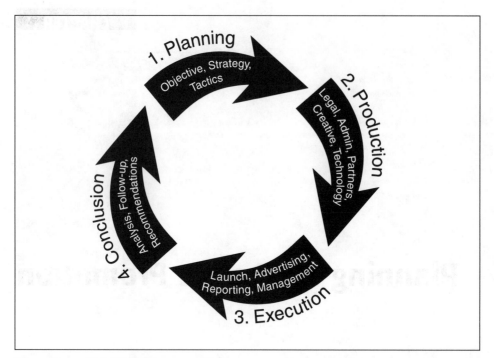

Figure 3.1 Circle of online promotions.

This chapter will also touch on the initial phase of building your own database through promotional data collection. While the topic of databases will be referenced throughout the remainder of this book, this chapter will focus on the preliminary planning process that will impact the data collection efforts of future online promotions.

In subsequent chapters, the production aspects associated with creative, technology, partnership selection, and legal issues will be discussed. The execution components of the launch, advertising, and ongoing management, as well as the conclusion components of analysis, follow-up, and recommendations, will likewise be investigated and explored. For now, we will focus on the objective, strategy, and tactics associated with an online promotion. Elements from this chapter will be built upon in subsequent chapters until the topic of planning brings us full circle back to the beginning.

Starting with a Clear Objective

So far we've defined sweepstakes, contests, and other promotional marketing tactics. We talked about the advantage of online promotions and described the best promotional tactics to use given diverse objectives. But I haven't truly stressed the importance of starting with a clear objective. In my opinion, starting with a clear objective is the single most important thing you can do prior to the launch of your promotion (be it online or offline). Without a clear objective, you'll never know if your online promotion was successful or not. Your objective serves as your blueprint from which all your resources are focused. Without this blueprint, much of your time and money will be wasted on an execution-focused approach that lacks direction.

To put this another way, just because the Internet allows us to create and launch online promotions in a matter of hours doesn't mean we should. Speed and effectiveness are not the same thing. While there is something to be said for experimentation (that is, trial and error), you still need a clearly defined objective to see if your test was successful.

It's extremely easy to get so wrapped up in the details of the execution that we forget to ask a simple question: Why? More to the point, "Why are we doing this promotion in the first place?" If you don't know, chances are that you're about to run an objectiveless promotion, which is actually a contradiction in terms, since a promotion without an objective is not a promotion—it's a waste of money.

So why do people waste their promotion dollars? Here are some common answers that are *not* good reasons for running a promotion:

"Because my competitor is doing one."

"It's a cool concept/technology/idea."

"It's got great PR value."

"We've got an approved budget."

"It came down from the President/CEO."

"We did it last year."

"We've got an opening in our calendar."

(This list of excuses could go on for several pages, but you get the idea.)

Life is too short for objectiveless promotions. I realize that it's a common mistake, but it is one that can easily be rectified without much additional effort. The promotion industry is booming right now and there's already a ton of noise competing for the attention of your target audience. "Me too" promotions are not the most efficient use of an online promotion's budget. Having money is not an objective and while technology continues to advance at a tremendous pace, we should all be past the "BYC" (Because You Can) rationale for launching cool and nifty promotions.

Solving the objectiveless promotion problem is simple and takes very little time. When you stop to consider *why* you're doing something, the decision-making process throughout the remainder of the promotion becomes much simpler. If the option that is presented is on strategy (that is, meets your objective), then it makes sense. If not, then it's detracting from what you're trying to accomplish and should be discarded.

Starting with a clear objective up front also helps you determine later if the promotion was successful or not. That is to say, in order for an objective to be clear, it must include some measurable criteria in a given time frame. If the objective of the promotion is "To increase sales of product x by 3 percent in the fourth quarter," then it should be easy enough to measure the success of the promotion when it's over.

Before you spend any money on the promotion itself, a clear objective will allow you to conduct research up front and quickly determine what parts of the promotion are compelling and what needs help. Concept testing and other forms of primary research can be accomplished very quickly online, but only if you have a clear objective from which to start. It is not possible to determine if a promotion is compelling unless you have some basis by which you can measure its potential impact (sales, traffic, awareness, or memberships, for example).

Even if the promotion is unsuccessful, having a clear objective will help you determine what aspects of the promotion failed and what you can change in the future to make it a success. If you didn't start with a clearly defined objective, it will be extremely difficult to determine what went wrong. As the saying goes: "If you don't know where you're headed, you'll never know if you actually get there."

Avoid Multiple Conflicting Objectives

At the other end of the spectrum lies a promotion with multiple conflicting objectives. Let's say, for example, you have identified all the key objectives that you want to achieve. If you decide to use a single promotional technique to satisfy them all, you run the danger that your messages will conflict with each other and end up as noise rather than as an effective promotion. Having multiple objectives isn't bad per se, but you must use caution. More often than not, when a promotion has multiple objectives, it shows.

It's difficult to effectively "increase sales" when you're also trying to "create awareness," "drive traffic," or "reinforce brand identity." When you have multiple objectives, one objective usually takes precedence, and when it does, the others suffer. This is assuming that the promotion works at all. Often when there are multiple objectives, the promotion ends up being a muddled mess, contradicting itself, and ultimately it doesn't succeed.

In many cases, when one objective doesn't take precedence over the others, the promotion has a serious identity crisis. This identity crisis usually leads to an unrealistic expectation that the target audience is willing to jump through all the necessary hoops to participate in your promotion—they won't.

I don't want to imply here that a promotion can't have multiple objectives—it can. The key is ensuring that the objectives don't conflict and that they follow the logical marketing flow of first creating awareness, then stimulating interest, cultivating desire, and then driving action (see Figure 3.2). If these goals are accomplished in their proper order, the promotion can have multiple complementary objectives and still work out just fine.

For example, if you have an established product in the marketplace, but your two objectives are to "initiate trial" of your product and "increase sales," you might create a sampling program to help initiate trial and include a coupon or rebate to help increase sales. These objectives are complementary and therefore achievable via the same promotional tactics. When you distribute the product sample, you also include a coupon for the purchase of the complete product. If the product sample is satisfactory, then the consumer is likely to go the next step and redeem the coupon or rebate offer.

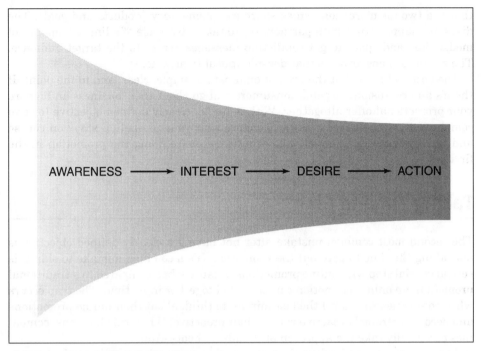

AWARENESS ⟶ INTEREST ⟶ DESIRE ⟶ ACTION

Figure 3.2 Logical marketing flow.

Let's take another example. If you were launching a new product, one objective would certainly be focused on generating awareness while a second objective would be to drive sales. While sales are obviously the ultimate objective, without awareness, sales-driving promotional tactics will not be effective. The danger here lies in putting the cart before the horse. If sales-driving efforts, such as coupons, rebates, or premium offers, are the main driver of the promotion, the awareness goal is lost (or downplayed) and a very important step is skipped. While some percentage of your target audience might take a chance on your product without knowing anything about it, the majority of your target will first want to find out about the features and benefits of your product before they decide to buy it.

To avoid conflict, a logical flow must emerge. The awareness goal must take the priority (even at the risk of downplaying the sales-driving efforts) and promotional techniques geared toward generating awareness take the forefront. Let's say that a qualified entry sweepstakes is used to drive home key features or benefits of the product. As consumers are drawn into the sweepstakes, they can quickly be moved from their initial awareness of the product into a product sample offer or coupon. In this scenario, the first objective of awareness is accomplished before moving the consumer into the interest/desire phase of the program.

In Chapter 6, "How to Create a Multibrand Promotion," I will further discuss the kinds of complementary objectives that can work and also talk about the complex issue of two companies who are interested in the same target audience. In essence, when multiple products or brands share similar objectives, the promotion can satisfy more than one company's marketing objectives. The key, however, is that the two (or more) companies share complementary products and goals. The disasters happen when both partners try to take advantage of a limited amount of media time and space to get conflicting messages across to the target audience. The result is chaos or noise that doesn't appeal to anyone.

The bottom line is that the promotion must be simple, clear, and to the point. If there's any confusion, targeted consumers will go about their business and ignore your promotional offer altogether. With a single, clearly defined objective (or two complementary objectives), you will ensure that your promotion stays on course and you'll never find yourself wondering why you're doing the promotion in the first place.

Taking Time to Plan

The second most common mistake after not having a clearly defined objective is not taking the time to plan out the promotion. It's a common mistake to skip this second crucial step with online promotions because when compared to a traditional promotion, an online promotion can be pulled together in no time. The trap occurs when companies wait until the last minute to think about their online promotions and become extremely reactive rather than proactive. When this happens, companies essentially take the approach of "Ready—Shoot—Aim."

In the early days of online promotions, this approach actually worked sometimes because online promotions were so new. Now that the newness factor has worn off for much of the online marketplace, planning becomes a much more important element to creating successful online promotions.

Obviously, most people do not intentionally skip the planning process, it just happens when a sense of urgency overpowers common sense. When this happens, the original objective of the promotion takes a back seat to the directive to hurry up and get it done. To avoid this common mistake, ask yourself this simple question: "Who do I work for?"

At first thought, this question seems simple enough. Initially, you might answer, "Myself" or you might name a person in your company who is higher up on the corporate food chain. But then, you might think about the question a little bit more and answer, "My customers."

The truth is that you work for the people who pay your bills. While the paycheck may come from the company itself, the people who truly pay your salary are the people who buy your products and services. So what happens when you discover that few of these people have any loyalty or preference to your company?

This is a hard pill to swallow, but one that helps keep things in perspective. When this realization sinks in, the important things that need to be accomplished tend to rise to the top. Short-term gains become much less important than accomplishing the long-term goals and objectives.

Avoiding Less Important Short-Term Gains

In today's "Hurry-Up-and-Inflate-My-Numbers-for-Wall-Street" mentality (courtesy of your neighborhood dot coms and venture capitalists), I believe that many companies have traded in their long-term plans for short-term gains. These short-term gains come in many shapes and sizes; they include everything from inflated Web traffic and overstated membership numbers to sales figures based on price discounts so deep that they result in a loss for the company.

It's not difficult to create a free-for-all when you give away your products or pay off your target audience to become a member of your site. But then what? Smart marketers know that artificially jacking up these measurement criteria in the short term will only cause more problems later on—and yet they do it anyway. Why?

Many of today's online marketing promotions are a direct reflection of the internal chaos that many companies are going through. Brainstorming concepts developed in a Monday morning status meeting are expected to be live by the next week's status meeting (if not sooner).

Marketers reacting to this kind of demand for immediate results are rarely given the chance to take a step back and build their long-term strategies. There's a huge difference between flexibility and chaos. Reacting to demand without a well-thought-out strategy is like rolling the dice and hoping for the best.

From Chaos to Smart Marketing

The irony of all the internal chaos is that much of it is self-imposed. By not taking the time to build a long-term plan (even for the next 12 to 18 months), you are forced to react to what the competition is doing and to what other people within the company tell you.

As my handyman grandfather used to tell me, "Measure twice. Cut once." Those four little words are extremely powerful. They boil down all the issues related to not taking the time to plan. If carpenters cut their wood before they were confident of their measurements, they risked wasting more wood and adding their work to the scrap pile. Marketing (online or offline) is no different. If you don't take time to plan up front, then you end up wasting a lot of time and money doing things that probably will not work. Without proper plans in place, you might as well be shooting at a moving target. It's extremely difficult to tell what works because satisfying your immediate objective may actually move you farther away from your long-term goals.

The Right Customer at the Right Price

Creating a 12- to 18-month plan forces you (and your colleagues) to agree on your long-term goals and the best course of action to accomplish those goals. Moreover, these goals may conflict with your short-term inflation strategies, as giving away your product or paying off your customers could ultimately be counterproductive in the long term.

Bill Fritsch, Executive Vice President of FreeShop.com, spoke at an International Quality & Productivity Center conference called, "Converting e-Browsers into e-Buyers" in Chicago, Illinois. During his presentation, he put up a slide that talked about three different customer acquisition strategies, which included:

1. Any customer at any price

2. The right customer at any price

3. The right customer at the right price

Short-term gains usually fall in the first and second categories of getting customers at any price (targeted or not). But to get the right customer at the right price, you must develop a plan that will create awareness, interest, desire, and action all for the right cost of acquisition.

Although plans will differ from company to company (based on their individual long-term objectives), the commonality among all these plans is the roadmap that is created at the end of the day. While developing this roadmap, the actual plan will *force* people with conflicting views to sit down and discuss their differences. As long as everyone is willing to listen to those with opposing opinions, these early discussions help solidify what the company is truly trying to achieve and, more importantly, how it should do it.

Once all the meetings have taken place, the plan that emerges will identify key issues, including how much the company is willing to spend to acquire and retain customers. Knowing this will help you identify the "right price" that should be spent to get and keep the right customers. This will help streamline your marketing efforts, rather than wasting money on a shotgun approach to get any customer at any price.

Long-Term Benefits of Planning

Once a plan has been developed, it's okay to be flexible—especially when new information has been added or discovered. Building the plan will provide a roadmap to which everyone can return. This does not mean that you must stay the course, but there should be strong rationale for diversions.

While long-term plans do not provide "quick-fix" results, they have long-lasting staying power from which marketers can reap the benefits. Well-thought-out marketing and promotions not only capture the attention of the target audience but they stay rooted in the minds of consumers. They have the best referrals because people actually think about the promotion and tell their friends about it.

The bottom line is, when you take time to plan, it shows. Your programs are more effective because you've had time to think through the various angles and potential problems. When immediate action is needed, the plan provides a well-constructed starting point. But the biggest benefit of planning is the avoidance of costly mistakes and the elimination of counterproductive marketing efforts.

When Online, Do as Your Users Do

Creating effective online promotions means understanding the best ways to market online. This seems simple enough, but when you don't spend a lot of time online, it shows. While the Internet is another medium to market your products and services, to be effective you must take advantage of what this unique medium has to offer. The only way to do this is to keep abreast of the changes in technology and community online. As technology continues to move at breakneck speeds, it becomes more and more important to go online and experience what your customers are experiencing.

Online promotions do not need to be strict translations of what you've done in the offline world. With the advent of each new medium comes an experimental phase that evolves over time, pushing the limits of the medium itself. Movies, for example, first began as recorded theater shows. The cameraman would sit in the audience and film the theatrical performance just as if you were sitting there in the theater. Then came the evolution as filmmakers experimented with camera angles, editing, and eventually sound, sound effects, and making the surreal seem possible.

Television began in a similar fashion, copying the format of radio broadcasts. Early television simply added the visual element to what had become standard entertainment via radio programming. Over time, these programs evolved to take advantage of the medium and all kinds of new programming emerged.

The Internet is no different. In its early stages, people took their printed brochures and distributed them online. From a business perspective, the Internet provided a cost-effective way of distributing sales collateral and information. Then the experimental phase began and email, bulletin boards, chat, and newsgroups were utilized in an effort to take advantage of a new two-way interactive medium. Rather than just blasting out marketing materials, companies began to listen to their consumers and to welcome feedback from them.

Online promotions evolved from these early phases of the Internet. Because of their early success, some of the first online promotions have been repeated time and time again without much evolution. Each year you can still find basic college basketball NCAA tournament grids that are little more than HTML forms where you can select teams you think will win. The majority of sweepstakes entry forms are fundamentally the same, collecting entry data via simple scripts and databases. But these tools will continue to evolve and become more engaging and, in turn, become more effective at accomplishing the desired goals.

The key here is that if you *don't* go online enough, you begin to miss out on the evolution. If you're not participating in online promotions yourself, you gravitate to what you know or have done in the past. This becomes dangerous as your competitors continue to experiment and try new ways to accomplish their marketing objectives. In other words, you're either part of the evolution or outside of it. If you're evolving then you're trying new things and checking out what others are doing online. If you're on the outside looking in, then your online promotions will become stale and ineffective. Sorry, the truth hurts sometimes.

How to Be a Good Consumer

The biggest challenge most marketers face when attempting to "do as their users do" is to take off the marketing hat and just have some fun. Admit it, you feel guilty when you come to work and "goof off." But here's the secret: That's what your target audience is doing when they stumble across your online promotion. Perhaps they were simply doing some research for a company report, doing a competitive analysis, or on an assignment to find out what's new and cool. Whatever they were doing, they most likely were *not* looking for your online promotion and yet they stopped and participated. Why? Because online consumers cannot live on information and research alone.

Everyone has a basic desire to be happy and enjoy him- or herself. When online, the information is everywhere you look. New search engines are launched every few months with different ways to index the same information. But just because the Internet provides information faster does not necessarily mean that people will be more efficient. Along with all that information are great distractions. Let's face it, you're trying to create one of those great distractions. So to do that effectively, you must key into which distractions grab your attention the most and (most importantly) *why*.

In my opinion, "Why?" is the most important question in the English language. *What, Where, When,* and *How* all ask for specific facts and details, but *Why* beckons a basic understanding. To answer the question "Why?" means to have the knowledge that is necessary to answer the question in the first place (not just the facts). That is to say, the facts are the dots while the understanding is the connection between the dots. Have you had enough of the Zen Buddhist approach to online promotions yet?

To be a good consumer, you must understand *why* successful online promotions work. The only way to gain that knowledge is to go out and play. I admit it, it's not easy to sit in a business environment and have a truly good time. We are conditioned to believe that work is painful and we are constantly reminded that "If work was fun, they wouldn't have to pay you to do it." But in order to create effective online promotions, we must forget our conditioned guilt and have some fun. We're in the promotions industry, after all. It's all about creating behavior change through compelling (read: fun) techniques. If your promotion isn't fun, your distraction will not be very good and consumers will go do what they were intending to do in the first place.

So loosen up. Take that suit jacket off (if you wore one in the first place), shut your door (if you're lucky enough to have a door), and spend some quality time online just goofing off. If your CFO forces you to fill out timesheets, record your goofing-off time as "Online Promotions Research." And the best part is that when you take this advice, you're likely to win a bunch of prizes. Talk about a win-win scenario: First you begin to enjoy your job a little more and on top of that, you might win some prizes too. Is the online promotions industry great or what?

Finding Online Promotions

Are you with me so far? If you've heeded my advice, you are in the right frame of mind. You're willing to stop playing "know-it-all" marketer, and you're going to roll up your sleeves and have a good time participating in online promotions. But one simple problem stands between you and having a good time: "Where do you find good online promotions?"

If this were 1994, you'd have some problems. Online promotions were few and far between, but even then you'd find them in the same places you'll find them today: search engines, information sites, and just about anywhere companies are vying for your attention. In fact, online promotions have become so popular that they are usually found on the home page of most major Web sites (some Web sites are built exclusively around online promotions).

Let me be more specific. Webstakes.com (`www.webstakes.com`) is *dedicated* to online promotions. If you go there, you will find literally *categories* of promotions. That's all this Web site does: It attracts consumers who want to participate in online promotions. Type the word "Sweepstakes" in your favorite search engine (Yahoo!, Excite, Lycos, AltaVista, or Snap, for example), and you'll not only find online promotions but also *directories* of online promotions such as Sweepstakes Advantage (`www.sweepsadvantage.com`), Sweepstakes Online (`www.sweepstakesonline.com`), and AtWinBig.com (`www.atwinbig.com`), whose sole purpose is to direct you to some of today's hottest online promotions—not just sweepstakes, contests, and games, but sample offers, coupons, discounts, and the works. At any given time, there are hundreds (if not thousands) of online promotions listed in these directories.

There are also Web sites dedicated to online promotions such as Lucky Surf (`www.luckysurf.com`), Free Lotto (`www.freelotto.com`), and IWON (`www.iwon.com`), which are not directory Web sites of online promotions, but year-long destination sites where you can participate in a huge ongoing online promotion.

Still not satisfied? Then it's time to simply fish where the fish are. Start out by going where your targeted consumers are likely to go. Would they usually start with a search engine? If so, then that's where you should begin. Think like your target audience and go to the Web sites they would go to. But when you get there, pay slightly more attention to those banner ads and pop-up windows. See if there's a compelling online promotion staring you right in the face. If so, check it out. This is only the tip of the online promotions iceberg. There are tons of industry-specific Web sites from information to commerce, from hobbies to auctions. If you don't know where your consumers hang out, it's high time you asked them.

I know this will sound absolutely crazy, but what if you simply had a link on your site that read, "What other sites do you like to visit?" Hey, that's crazy enough, it just might work. Or, if you don't have the power or ability to make that simple change, then hire a research company like QuickTake (`www.quicktake.com`) that can help you post your questions in the morning and have answers for you by the afternoon of the same day.

How Do You Know What's Good?

Now that you've seen a plethora of online promotions, it's time to start distilling effective from noneffective online promotions. Start with the very same question you'd ask yourself, "What is the objective of this promotion?" Is it clear and obvious or does it seem pointless? Try looking at the promotion from various perspectives. As a consumer, does the promotion appeal to you? If so, why? As a marketer, does the promotion appear to be satisfying the apparent objective?

I like to compare test-driving other people's online promotions to that of wine tasting. The first time I visited a wine-tasting cellar, I had no idea what I was doing. I simply went with some friends and let the taste-tester do his thing. The first wines were difficult to tell apart. I wasn't sure what I liked, so I tried a whole bunch of wines. As the day went on, I became both drunk and knowledgeable about wine (no coincidence, I assure you). The second time I went out with some friends to taste wines, I had a much better idea about what I liked. I enjoyed red more than white, spice more than subtle, Merlot more than Cabernet. I was by no means an expert, but I had a very good idea of what I liked and didn't like.

Going online and experiencing different promotions won't give you the euphoric sensation that wine brings to the experience, but the end result is quite similar. The more online promotions you check out, the better feel you get for what you like and what you don't. Soon, you become a self-proclaimed expert who can spot a good promotion from a disaster a mile away.

But let's separate the forest from the trees. If you're looking for specific measurement criteria on what defines a "good" online promotion, I define it in two ways:

1. Is it compelling?

2. Is it effective?

By compelling, I mean, "Would the target audience stop what they were doing to participate in the promotion?" By effective, I mean, "Did the promotion satisfy its objective?" Without being on the inside track for the promotion, it's difficult to determine if it was truly effective—some promotions are more obvious than others.

But even if you answer "No" to either or both of these criteria, it doesn't mean you can't learn something from the online promotion. Many promotions have some element about them that is compelling, even if you wouldn't consider the promotion "good." If you come to the conclusion that the promotion is lacking an objective, is not compelling, or if you find some other reason you don't like the promotion, you can usually manage to find something about the promotion that you can use in your own future efforts. Perhaps the creative caught your eye, or maybe the offer was unique (even if it wouldn't necessarily compel you to act). The point is that "good" comes in many different colors. Even if the promotion as a whole is not necessarily "good," there may be good elements contained within the promotion that can be used in your own efforts.

Data Collection: Building Your Own Database

By now, you should have a good idea of the kinds of online promotions you would like to use so let's look at two of the more practical issues you will face online: specifically, collecting data through your online promotions and what to do with the data you collect. It should be noted that privacy and security issues will *not* be addressed in this section. If this is your chief area of concern, please skip to Chapter 4, "Protecting Yourself and Your Company Online."

In this section, the focus will be on the database: from the initial plan, to the design elements, to the kinds of information you should collect, to the management, to the ongoing use. This is not intended to be a crash course in becoming a database administrator (DBA), but more of a marketer's guide to databases and what they can do for you.

Begin with a Plan

As with any aspect of marketing, your database components are only as good as your plans. The more planning you do up front, the less time you will waste when you get into the design, development, and execution of the database. The plan should encompass everything from the objective of the database to what kind of data you wish to collect and how you will or might use that data.

Although each company's needs will vary, there are some common elements across any database plan. In essence, you are trying to market smarter to your target audience. By asking the right questions, you will be able to determine the kinds of people who are coming to your site and which people are most likely to be your best customers. As you build the plan, it's important to think about the process through which you want your target consumers to go. From best case to reality, it is important to understand how you will identify your customers' needs and their identity.

Online promotions provide a compelling reason for consumers to provide their demographic information, but there is a limit to what they are willing to tell you about themselves. I like to think about the first contacts you have with your customers as "Consumer Dating." That is, with each contact you have with your target audience, you have a chance to exchange information about your company for information about your customer. While the end goal is to sell your products or services, the best sales will come from long-term customer relationships, which are developed over time.

This is an important aspect to developing the plan, because if you ask too many questions up front, you are not likely to receive the kind of responses you seek. Most of your target audience will not see the benefit of providing all that information, and will choose not to provide it. Or perhaps your promotion is compelling enough to get them to complete your lengthy questionnaire, but the hesitation to answer all the questions is channeled into providing wrong or inaccurate information. I would argue that having inaccurate information is much worse than having no information at all.

Your database plan should strike a balance between the minimum amount of information you need from your first encounter with a consumer and your desire to market to him or her in the best way possible. It's true that *if* you knew every essential piece of information about your target audience, you could provide them with the solution that is right for them. However, asking some of the more pertinent questions may drive your target audience away from you. Perhaps the best approach is to begin by explaining the benefits of what you can do with the consumer information provided. Once it is understood why you are asking for specific information, consumers can decide if your proposed benefits are worth the price of their private information.

Designing the Database

Once you have decided the best approach to asking for the desired information, the next step is to map out the database itself. Essentially, this step identifies what information will go into the database and what information needs to come out. For example, for your first online promotion, let's assume that you are asking basic demographic information (Name, Address, City, State, and Zip) and an opt-in question such as, "Would you like to receive special discounts and offers via email?" To account for this information, the database must be set up so that you can easily distinguish those who want to receive the special offer emails and those who do not. While this first example is quite straightforward, as you begin to ask more specific questions, you will need the ability to separate consumers into different categories (for example, working mothers with a yearly salary of over $50,000 who drive an American car and have at least one child under the age of 5).

Long-term database design is not for the faint of heart, nor is it likely to be your primary responsibility. Once you have determined what information you will need to execute your online marketing efforts, it is then best to speak with a database administrator about what your project needs are. The database administrator will help you identify the kind of database that you need based on: (1) the estimated number of people who will be participating in your program, (2) the data that will be collected, and (3) what needs to happen with that data. The more you can think through the answers to these three key questions, the more accurate the database administrator can be with his or her recommendations.

Database design is a critical aspect between effective online promotions and your direct marketing efforts as it is the link between the information you receive from your target audience and how you can respond to that information and market to them as individuals. Without a well-designed database, the data that is being captured during your online promotion is likely to be wasted or used ineffectively.

Collect Only the Data You Plan to Use

As you begin your online promotions, it is important to collect only the data that you plan to use immediately. Even if you plan to use some of the information "down the road," leave off as much of the futuristic questions as possible. The more questions you ask, the less likely you are to receive accurate information from the majority of your target audience. Instead, take a minimalist approach and make sure your target audience knows why you're asking the specific questions. Let them know what immediate benefit they will receive by answering the important questions.

If you have tailored product offerings, use your database to provide the right offer to the consumers who answer the qualifying questions. If you provide immediate feedback and responses, people will be more likely to give you additional information.

Effectively Use the Database

When done correctly, what began as a database built from an online promotion will quickly transform into a central database from which all major marketing efforts will take advantage. With each new marketing campaign, the consumers contained within the database will provide valuable information and feedback that will help drive your sales efforts. To use the database effectively, it is important to keep the information accurate and up to date. With each new product offer, you will receive feedback on how the offer was received in the form of response rates and sales data. If you take advantage of this information, you will quickly know what offers are most effective within your key audience segment. As you begin to learn more about your customers, you can become more personal and your offers can become more relevant.

With respect to online promotions, your database will keep track of the most active consumers. It will be easy to determine which consumers are most interested in your promotions based on their frequency of participation. There are few more ideal times to speak to your consumers than when they are engaged in your online promotion. Because you can't always be there at the exact moment your customers are in the decision-making process, your online promotions are an effective way to help keep your company in their minds. By knowing who's most active in your promotions, you can tailor special offers to these individuals and channel their receptive energy toward your products and services.

The most effective use of your database is to find ways to market smarter and with more relevance to consumers. The sheer act of building a database means you are attempting to separate your target audience from the entire population of consumers. Once this first step is taken, you can continue to find ways to extract information from your database to help further your relationship with your customers.

Managing the Data

It's important to clean out the database from time to time so that the information will continue to be relevant. Inactive consumers should be flagged and marketed to differently from the active ones. If a consumer has not responded to any of your product offerings, try to find out why. Perhaps he or she was only interested in your promotion and does not wish to be contacted any further. Or perhaps the offers you have been providing are not relevant because the consumer provided inaccurate information initially.

Ideally, consumers should have the ability to make their own updates and changes to your database. If they are no longer interested in receiving information from you, it should not be difficult for them to tell you that and stop you from continuing to market to them. If you have a strong ongoing relationship with your customers, it should be easy for them to update their contact information when they move or change jobs (or email addresses). Without providing your consumers with an easy way to make changes to their own records, you cause a significant amount of additional work for your company.

Managing your database should not be a difficult task if the database was well designed in the first place. If you can easily determine the last time a consumer contacted you, made a purchase, or responded to an email campaign, then it will not be difficult to segregate your database to focus on your top customers. Database marketing allows you to market to your customers differently and to identify the 20 percent of your customers who are responsible for 80 percent of the sales. With ongoing management of the data, you can keep a close watch on the top 20 percent and make sure that they are happy with your products, services, and company as a whole. Any research that will affect key decisions made by your company should include this top 20 percent. *These* are the customers you want to keep for life and upon whom you should spend the bulk of your marketing dollars.

Conclusion

Effective planning starts with a clearly defined objective. If you don't know where you're going, you'll never know when you get there. Objectiveless promotions waste time and money. But even promotional failures are better when they have a clearly defined objective because you are not doomed to repeat the same mistakes. With a clearly defined objective, you're more likely to know about problems when they arise and, more importantly, how to solve these problems now and in the future. Multiple objectives for a single promotion should be avoided when at all possible. Otherwise, one objective usually gets precedence and the others are not likely to get accomplished.

Taking time to plan pays big dividends. Long-term plans should not be exchanged for short-term gains. Smart marketers know that artificially jacking up the measurement criteria in the short term will only cause more problems later on. Well-planned online promotions target the right consumer at the right price (as opposed to any consumer at any price or the right consumer at any price). Once a plan has been developed, it's okay to be flexible—especially when new information has been added or discovered. When immediate action is needed, the plan provides a well-constructed starting point. But the biggest benefit of planning is the avoidance of costly mistakes and the elimination of counterproductive marketing efforts.

Creating effective online promotions means understanding the best ways to market online. This is accomplished by seeing what else is out there. The best way to do this is to act like your targeted consumers and just explore the kinds of promotions that are screaming for attention. Online promotions do not need to be strict translations of what you've done in the offline world. Experimentation with the Internet can be fun and, at the same time, lead you to a compelling new online promotion. If you're looking for specific measurement criteria on what defines a "good" online promotion, ask yourself: Is it compelling? Is it effective? Even if a competitive promotion as a whole is not necessarily "good," there may be good elements contained within the promotion that can be used in your own efforts.

As with any aspect of marketing, your database components are only as good as your plans. Database design is a critical aspect between effective online promotions and your direct marketing efforts as it is the link between the information you receive from your target audience and how you can respond to that information and market to them as individuals. Online promotions provide a compelling reason for consumers to provide their demographic information, but there is a limit to what they are willing to tell you about themselves. If you ask too many questions up front, you are not likely to receive the kind of responses you seek. The issues of privacy and security are important considerations when building your database, and both of these issues are discussed in detail in the next chapter.

Protecting Yourself and Your Company Online

This chapter is intended to provide you with detailed information about the legal aspects of online promotions. The information contained in this chapter should help you focus your online promotional efforts so that they stay within the boundaries of current state and federal legislation. While this chapter is intended to help you protect yourself and your company against common legal pitfalls when launching online promotions, the best way to stay out of legal trouble is to hire a law firm or promotional agency that is expert in this area of the law. This is not a new business pitch. The laws and regulations that affect online promotions are constantly changing. Even as I write this chapter, there are new laws pending or going into effect and old laws are being reinterpreted by state and federal legislators. While I provide current examples of this changing legislation, as soon as this book is printed I'm sure there will be new laws passed that may affect your upcoming online promotions.

So if the legal aspects of online promotions are constantly changing, why read this chapter?

The truth is that while new laws are being passed and new interpretations of existing laws will affect how the official rules of online promotions are written, the legal foundations generally remain constant. By understanding the basic premise of the laws that affect your online promotions, you will spend less time on the clock with your lawyers and more time thinking up new and better ways to legally accomplish your marketing objectives. Furthermore, as new laws are passed, they often reflect or are based on the premises or intent of prior legislation. By understanding the base legislation, the new laws will make more sense than they would if you didn't already understand their basic underlying premise.

I would like to take this opportunity to thank Ken Florin, who is both an attorney for Loeb & Loeb and a close personal friend of mine, for reviewing this section of the book. I have worked with Mr. Florin for the past four years, and he continues to keep me informed and out of trouble. While neither Ken Florin nor Loeb & Loeb is responsible (read: cannot be held liable) for this chapter, I feel more confident about sharing what I have learned about the legal aspects of online promotions when my own legal counsel has reviewed my work product before it was printed.

Privacy and Security Issues

Let's cut to the chase. Privacy, security, and the Internet will continue to be hot topics in the years to come. Today, even with the explosion of legislation and consumer advocacy groups, there are still a lot of gray areas with respect to privacy and security issues, which can be both a blessing and a curse. The good news is that because the market is still evolving, the governmental bodies that legislate privacy and security issues have, to a large extent, allowed companies to come up with their own best practices in many areas. The bad news is that if you don't use good judgment or understand the issues associated with privacy and security, you may end up becoming a "test case" and the subject of regulatory scrutiny.

In this section, I will speak to the broad issues of privacy and security and then dive deeper into specific legislation such as the Children's Online Privacy and Protection Act (COPPA) and recent email legislation.

Privacy: What's Your Customer's Information Worth?

Before jumping into all the issues that surround privacy, the first question is, "What information should be kept confidential?" First, anything you declare will be kept confidential (via your privacy policy) should always remain confidential. Also, any specific information about a consumer that was provided by the consumer. That is, even demographic information, such as the name, address, phone and email address of a consumer, should not be used for any purpose other than what it was collected for in the first place.

The underlying issue behind all the debates over privacy is the conflict between a marketer's desire to provide relevant product offerings by knowing as much as possible about an individual versus the individual's desire not to share his or her personal information with companies who may or may not abuse the privilege of knowing personal information. It's important to consumers that they are able to identify the kinds of companies that they wouldn't mind sharing personal information with in exchange for relevant product offerings, deep discounts, and other marketing perks. The problem is that once personal information is shared with an *irresponsible* company who abuses their trust and shares this personal information with others without consent, it is difficult (if not impossible) to stop the sharing of this personal information with other companies.

The issue of privacy becomes crystal clear if you place a value on your personal information and treat it like a competitive advantage and a well-kept secret. When you begin to think of your personal information as a form of a secret, you can see what all the fuss is about. If you were to tell a close friend a secret about yourself, you would trust that your friend would not blab that secret to other people. If your friend protects your secret and doesn't share it with anyone, then the bond between you and your friend becomes stronger. The more secrets you tell your friend, the tighter the relationship and the more trust your friend earns, the more likely you are to tell more secrets to your trusted friend. But when your friend (either out of anger or bad judgment) breaks your trust and tells others about your secrets, then the relationship is soured and difficult to repair. Once your secrets are out in the open, then it's very difficult (if not impossible) to stop the secret from spreading and becoming common knowledge.

When companies treat private information like a rare and precious diamond, then they would be foolish to give it away (or even sell it) for short-term gains. In the long run, the companies that succeed will hold on to the precious information that they are given by their customers and will find ways to use the information without abusing trust. That's the key to successful privacy management.

In essence, a customer's private information is a competitive advantage. What many companies don't realize is that if the information is shared, it becomes common knowledge and is of much less value to the few companies with whom it was shared in the first place. It seems only logical that a company would do its best not to share private information about its customers, but the financial temptations to do otherwise are great.

One temptation is to provide customers' private information to partner companies in a related field (that often copromote their products and services) to increase sales. This level of information sharing can have negative results if your customers are not first made aware of what you want to do and grant you permission to do so. It is wrong to share your customers' private information with your partners and expect that your customers will be comfortable with this practice. Those who did not want their private information shared will be upset and, at the very least, discouraged from providing any further information to your company—not the place you want to be for a long-term relationship. If consumers are angry enough, they may write to the FTC or commercial privacy organizations that will, in turn, investigate claims against your company. This could result in a loss of time and money during the investigation, and could even result in a lawsuit, causing your company financial losses and negative publicity as well.

Because information is valuable, it is tempting to sell information to companies outside your business model and even data warehouses. Here again, there are certainly short-term profits to be made by selling private information, but the practice usually ends up backfiring in the long run. Besides upsetting consumers who will distance themselves from your company, there is the danger of your customers' private information falling into the hands of your competition. Even though you didn't intend for this to happen, by selling information, you lose control over it and it is now up for the highest bidder.

The bottom line: Your customers' information is extremely valuable, but only if you keep it in strictest confidence and use the information they have provided you only within your company. If you absolutely must share some information about your customers to your partners, you can generally do so without breaking your customers' trust by providing information in the aggregate (that is, general information about *all* your customers). If your partners want to leverage the information you have accumulated, it should *only* be with the express permission of your customers. Only after presenting your customers with this option will you and they remain in control of their personal information and continue to trust your company with that information.

FTC: Self-Regulation and Privacy Online

Before jumping into what the Federal Trade Commission (FTC) has to say about privacy online, I want to point out that the law firm Loeb & Loeb has produced a comprehensive white paper on how the United States and the European Union deal with privacy issues online. If you'd like to learn more, send an email to Ken Florin at kflorin@loeb.com.

To see what the FTC thinks about online privacy, you can download a report from the FTC Web site at www.ftc.gov/reports/privacy3. The latest report provides a summary of what the FTC is currently faced with and how they are dealing with privacy issues online. According to the July 1999 report, the FTC's conclusion was the following:

> The self-regulatory initiatives described above, including the guidelines adopted by the OPA and seal programs, reflect the industry leaders' substantial effort and commitment to fair information practices. *They should be commended for these efforts.* [Emphasis added]. Enforcement mechanisms that go beyond self-assessment are also gradually being implemented by the seal programs. Only a small minority of commercial Web sites, however, have joined these programs to date. Similarly, although the results of GIPPS and OPA studies show that many online companies now understand the business case for protecting consumer privacy, they also show that the implementations of fair information practices is not widespread among commercial Web sites.
>
> Based on these facts, *the Commission believes that legislation to address online privacy is not appropriate at this time.* [Emphasis added]. We also believe that industry faces some substantial challenges. Specifically, the present challenge is to educate those companies which still do not understand the importance of consumer privacy and to create incentives for further progress towards effective, widespread implementation.

In essence, the FTC has decided to take a "wait-and-see" attitude toward online privacy. The FTC recognizes that this is a huge issue and that the online industry itself is, at least for now, in the best position to develop its own practices, policies, and procedures for addressing online privacy. Over time, the FTC will watch the development of online privacy initiatives and will ultimately decide if governmental legislation and regulation are necessary.

This is great news for marketers that adhere to best practices of information gathering and sharing. If you're not sure what best practices your company should take, the FTC recommends TRUSTe (www.truste.org), BBB*OnLine* (www.bbbonline.org), CPA WebTrust (www.webtrust.org), and industry-specific organizations such as the Interactive Digital Software Association (IDSA) and the Entertainment Software Rating Board (ESRB).

TRUSTe is credited as being the first online privacy seal program. It launched on June 10, 1997, and is an independent, nonprofit organization founded by the CommerceNet Consortium and the Electronic Frontier Foundation. Among other things, TRUSTe is a third-party monitoring service that requires its members to write an official privacy statement, and then audits its members for compliance with its own statement. TRUSTe will, for example, check to make sure that your company honors its promise to remove members from databases and email lists. TRUSTe also acts as a consumer advocacy group to whom consumers can submit complaints and concerns.

BBB*Online* is an online subsidiary of the Better Business Bureau, which launched its privacy program on March 17, 1999. BBB*Online* requires that its seal recipients comply with BBB*Online*'s own information practice principles as well as agree to participate in a consumer dispute resolution system and third-party monitoring by BBB*Online*. By taking the BBB*Online*'s "Compliance Assessment Questionnaire," you identify your privacy practices, which will allow BBB*Online* to assess if your practices are in line with their seal requirements. Similar to TRUSTe, BBB*Online* acts as an advocacy group where consumers can submit complaints and concerns, and BBB*Online* will investigate and work with corporate seal recipients to resolve disputes and complaints.

The third group, the CPA WebTrust, was created by the American Institute of Certified Public Accountants and the Canadian Institute of Chartered Accountants in September 1997. The CPA WebTrust consists of certified public accountants who conduct quarterly audits to confirm that seal recipients stick to stated business practices, including the adherence to transaction security and privacy controls. In essence, the CPA WebTrust tells consumers that the Web site they're on has taken precautions not only to protect consumer information but also to protect credit card information and transactions as well.

And finally, there are industry-specific organizations, of which the earliest is the Interactive Digital Software Association (IDSA), which was launched in October 1998. The ISDA established the Entertainment Software Rating Board (ESRB) on June 1, 1999, to focus on a ratings system for entertainment software and interactive games. To find organizations specific to your industry, you can do an online search, check out your competitors' Web sites, contact any of the previously mentioned organizations or the FTC directly. As the FTC mentioned in its report, there are several industry-specific organizations that have been developed or are currently under development. Chances are, there's a specific organization that can help you create your ideal privacy statement and help you practice what you preach.

Children's Online Privacy Protection Act (COPPA)

While there continues to be industry self-regulation and ongoing debates about how best to require companies to protect the private information that they collect from their consumers, the first step has been made with respect to children under the age of 13. In October 1999, the Children's Online Privacy Protection Act was passed and in April 2000, COPPA's legislation became active. COPPA is the first act in the United States specifically targeted to protect children's private information. COPPA focuses on consumers that the government and several advocacy groups feel are most likely to be in need of protection: children under the age of 13.

Even if you don't specifically target children under the age of 13, you should be aware of COPPA if your company collects, manages, or maintains information from (or about) the people who visit your Web site. If you don't collect any information about your customers online, then COPPA does not apply to you— although I will say that you probably have bigger issues to worry about like, "Why do you have a Web site in the first place?" For everyone else, COPPA is specifically targeting the collection and management of information about children under the age of 13. Conservative companies are using the COPPA regulation as a guideline to address data collection for *anyone* under the age of 18, although children between 13 and 18 years of age are not covered by COPPA.

At the Promotional Marketing Association's Law Conference in November 1999, Ronald Plesser and James Halpert of Piper & Marbury, LLP, wrote an extremely informative document called, "Internet Legislation in the 105th Congress," which specifically addresses the Children's Online Privacy Protection Act. In this document, they provided:

1. A clear scope of the COPPA act

2. The regulation of collection and use practices

3. Safe Harbors (that is, specific protection and exceptions from COPPA), along with several other sections pertaining to COPPA.

For a full disclosure of the act, request this document via email at `lawfirm@ pipermar.com`.

In this section, I will provide a top-line summary of COPPA, taking excerpts from the Piper & Marbury document and address what companies and agencies are doing to protect themselves during these early formative years as COPPA is regulated and enforced.

Scope of the Act

The scope of the act applies to any Web site that targets children under the age of 13 that collects personally identifiable information (Name, Address, Email, or Phone, for example) or allows a child under the age of 13 to post such information (through a bulletin board, chat, or creation of a home page). Targeting is determined by the nature of the Web site content and if the site has actual knowledge that it has collected information from a child under 13. Information that is collected in the aggregate (that is, not personally identifiable) is not covered under the scope of COPPA.

Ronald Plesser and James Halpert specifically write:

[COPPA] applies to the "collection, use and disclosure" of information collected online from a child under 13 years of age. §§ 1303 (b) (1)(A)(ii), 1303 (a) (1). The term "disclosure" is defined to include both: (1) releasing information to others (not providing internal support for the same company), and (2) providing a forum in which children may post individually identifiable information (such as an Internet home page, pen pal, e-mail, bulletin board, or chatroom service). § 1302 (4). The Act applies only to communications in interstate or foreign commerce, and does not apply to non-profit organizations that are otherwise exempt from the Federal Trade Commission Act ("FTCA"), 5 U.S.C. § 45. §§ 1302 (2) (A) & (B).

The Act applies to individually identifiable information collected online from a child, including both a first and a last name, address including street and city/town, email address, phone number, social security number, or any other identifier that the FTC determines permits the physical or online contacting of an individual. It also covers other information that a web site collects online from a child and combines with one of these identifiers. § 1302 (8). Information in aggregate form is not covered.

The Act covers a commercial website or online service, or any portion of a commercial website or online service, that is targeted to children. §§ 1302 (10) (A) & 1303(a) (1). Whether a site is targeted to children is determined in light of its subject matter, visual content, age of models, language, offline advertising for the site, and other features of the site. Bryan Statement at S11657. The Act also applies where a site or service has actual knowledge that it is collecting information from a child under 13. § 1303 (a) (1). However, the Act does not apply to sites merely because they refer or link users to different sites that are directed to children. § 1302 (10) (B).

As stated earlier, more conservative companies are also using the COPPA regulations as a guideline for all children under the age of 18, although this is outside the scope of COPPA at this time. While this section identifies who COPPA is targeting, the next section speaks to the specific responsibilities of companies who are targeting children under the age of 13.

COPPA Regulation

The FTC created clear-cut guidelines to avoid misunderstandings as to the regulation corresponding to COPPA. Included in the FTC's regulation guidelines are terms like, "available technology" and "reasonable efforts," which the FTC will define further over time. The FTC clearly demonstrates its understanding of how quickly technology evolves, and has made an honest effort to set forth legislation that can adapt to an evolving environment. As things like digital signatures become more prevalent online, so too will the definition of "available technology."

There are five parts to FTC regulation of COPPA:

1. Notification

2. Parental consent

3. Parental disclosure

4. Limitation of enticements

5. Security

Notification

The first part of FTC regulation comes in the form of notification. In order to be in compliance with the FTC, you must declare what information is being collected from children under 13 and how that information is being used. This declaration must be clear and cannot be a bunch of gibberish meant to confuse someone who is attempting to determine what information is being collected. The notification must also be prominently displayed so that a parent could easily find the notification without spending a lot of time searching for it.

So if you are targeting children under the age of 13, it's important to explain—up front—what information you are attempting to collect and for what purpose. The FTC mandates that you must make "reasonable efforts" to present these disclosures using "available technology." The point here is that you don't need to spend a fortune to build a complex notification system using leading edge technology to comply with this mandate. The FTC uses the term *reasonable efforts* to allow interpretation of its mandate. So while you can't simply bury your notification so that it's difficult to find, you don't need to make your notification the most technically advanced part of your online promotion either. Within the next few years, the FTC will more clearly define what "reasonable efforts" covers and will be more specific about what "available technology" is preferred.

Parental Consent

Beyond posting clear notification of what information you're collecting from children under 13 and for what purpose, you are also mandated to get *verifiable parental consent* through "reasonable efforts" using "available technology." That is, it's not enough to simply post notification, but you must go to the next step and get permission from the child's parent (or legal guardian) to collect and use information about the child under the age of 13. Here again, "reasonable efforts" is loosely defined, but it is clear that the FTC is looking for *verifiable parental consent*.

Many will argue that the only way to satisfy this requirement is to get the parent's signature either through the U.S. mail or via fax machine. While some companies are experimenting with digital signatures and pens that will allow parents to send their digital signatures, these newer technologies are not yet readily available to the average parent. Some companies have interpreted this mandate to mean email confirmation. That is, when a child is asked to provide information about him- or herself, he or she must first provide a parent's email address. In this case, the company can send an email to the parent requesting permission to collect data on the child under the age of 13 and stating for what purpose. Opponents of this approach argue that the child could avoid parental consent by simply providing a fake email account such as a free email address from Yahoo! or Hotmail. Proponents counter this argument saying that the child could easily do the same thing in writing. Most agree, however, that the confirming email approach should only be used when you're collecting only the most basic information from the child (for example, email address) and have no plans to disclose that information to any third party.

According to the *Privacy White Paper*, published by the law firm Loeb & Loeb, there are five generally accepted practices for getting verifiable parental consent. They are:

1. Getting a signed form from the parent via postal mail or fax machine

2. Accepting and verifying a credit card number

3. Taking calls from parents through a toll-free telephone number staffed by trained personnel

4. Receiving an email accompanied by a digital signature

5. Receiving an email accompanied by a PIN or password obtained through one of the other four verification methods

At this juncture, the FTC has not yet weighed in on what "available technology" is acceptable and what would be defined as "reasonable efforts." There is also no clear definition of verifiable parental consent. If you're unsure about what makes the most sense for your upcoming promotion, I urge you to seek out a promotion agency or law firm that can provide you with the most current rulings and accepted practices. Regardless, you must make "reasonable efforts" using "available technology" to get parental consent allowing you to collect, use, and disclose the child's information.

Parental Disclosure

The next regulation comes into play when the parent contacts your company directly for further information. Obviously, you must first verify that the person contacting you is, in fact, the parent of the child in question. Once you have received suitable identification, there are three things that you must do:

1. Explain the specific types of information that you have collected from the child online.

2. Give the parent the chance to opt-out their child from any further collection of personal information, use of existing information, or maintenance of existing information (note that some practitioners prefer requiring parents to opt-in their child).

3. Supply a reasonable means for the parent to find out about the personal information that has been collected from his or her child (and delete that information if requested to do so by the parent).

In other words, if a parent wants to find out what information you have collected on his or her child under the age of 13, you should have a reasonable means of disclosing what information has been collected and allow the parent to opt-out the child from any further use of the information that has been collected. Furthermore, if a parent decides to opt-out his or her child from your marketing efforts, this decision overrides any previous consent given. Parents, in other words, have a right to change their minds and should not have to live with a previous decision to allow their child to participate in your program.

It is extremely important that permission be as easily revoked as it is given. If permission is abused, then it will most certainly be reversed, and this is no different for a parent of a child than it is for customers over the age of 18. That said, a parent opting-out his or her child from one program does not prevent you from seeking permission in the future if a new request is received from the same child. The parent does not have to grant permission, but if the child makes an additional request to participate, a parent's previous decision to opt-out the child doesn't necessarily mean that he or she will choose to opt-out the child in your new program. Perhaps you have learned from the previous program and have made additions that specifically address the parent's concerns. As long as you respect the wishes of parents and provide them with the information and ability to make the decision that is best for their children, you will demonstrate to the FTC that you have made reasonable efforts to comply with their disclosure regulation.

Limitation of Enticements

The fourth regulation states that you may not lure a child into providing more personal information than is reasonably necessary to participate in a promotion, win a prize, or participate in another activity. You may want to know everything under the sun about your customers, but when you're getting your information from a child under the age of 13, you must stick to the requirements of the program— nothing more. In a sweepstakes, for example, you may need the child's home address for the sole purpose of delivering a prize. You may want additional information such as "Do you have any brothers or sisters?", but this request for information is not vital to the sweepstakes and would therefore be deemed an enticement to capture more information than is necessary.

If detailed information is desired about the family, then it's best to communicate with the parent. Let the child provide only the information that is absolutely necessary to participate in the promotion. Beyond that, contact the child's *parent* to request additional information and allow the parent to decide if he or she feels that providing you with additional information is "worth it" (based on the direct benefit of providing the information).

Security

This should go without saying, but the FTC requires that you take reasonable steps to ensure the confidentiality, security, and integrity of personal information collected online from children. Without this regulation, what good would the first four regulations be if the personal data collected from the child could easily fall into the wrong hands (for example, deceptive marketers)? Without taking the proper precautions to ensure that information collected is secure against unauthorized use, all the other FTC regulations become less meaningful. This final regulation in the Children's Online Privacy Protection Act makes a lot of sense.

Again, the FTC uses the word *reasonable,* which means that you must be able to demonstrate what steps you took to ensure the confidentiality, security, and integrity of your data collection. If you do not have an Information Technology (IT) department at your disposal, my recommendation is that you speak with your

Internet Service Provider (ISP) about what security measures make the most sense for your program. In most cases, your ISP has already taken preliminary precautions to protect the integrity of their Web servers. If you explain to your ISP what you are doing with your promotion and that you need to ensure the security of the data you collect, the ISP can recommend a solution that makes sense.

While your ISP and/or IT staff will recommend a *technology* solution that may include things like a firewall, encrypted File Transfer Protocol (FTP) access, and other security measures, it is equally important that you create a *people* solution as well. By people solution, I mean a list of authorized personnel who will be accessing the data collected. This is important because each person on your list must be fully aware of the sensitive nature of the data you are collecting. If the database administrator (DBA) is unaware of the sensitive nature of the data, he or she may not use the necessary precautions to ensure the highest level of security. Firewalls and encrypted FTP access are a good start to a technology solution, but without alerting and keeping track of the people using the system, you can leave holes in your security strategy. I will speak further about creating a secure environment later on in this chapter.

COPPA Exceptions

As with any regulation, there are exceptions to the rule. Specifically, nonprofit organizations, and other companies that are otherwise exempt from the Federal Trade Commission Act, are likewise exempt from COPPA legislation. Even if your company does not fall into this category, there are other event-specific exceptions that do not require parental consent such as the following.

Single-Use Requests

The first event-specific exception comes into play if a child's information is in response to a specific request. That is, if you are not maintaining the child's information, but are simply collecting information on a one-time basis (for example, to deliver a premium item), then you are not required to receive parental consent to fulfill the child's request, although you should *attempt* to get parental consent.

You should still use caution when collecting information from a child under the age of 13 so that your one-time data collection is carefully destroyed after its one-time use. For example, if you start out with a request for information for the sole purpose of delivering a premium item, but the data collected is stored at your fulfillment house, then what started out as a single-use request has the potential to be used a second time and would therefore require parental consent.

As long as the data collected is destroyed after its initial use, then your program does not require parental consent according to COPPA legislation. The minute you keep and maintain the child's data for further use, you must get parental consent.

Contacting the Parent

It's okay to collect the parent's name and online contact information from a child under the age of 13 for the sole purpose of seeking parental consent. If, however, the parent does not respond to your request for permission in a "reasonable" time, the parental information must be destroyed. If no permission was granted, then it's not okay to maintain the parent's contact information and/or use it for any purpose other than for seeking parental consent and it's not okay to collect information from that parent's child.

Responding to a Specific Request

You are not required to get parental consent if you are responding more than once to a specific request from the child as long as the child's information is not used for any other purpose beyond the specific request. An example of this would be an email newsletter. If a child under the age of 13 subscribes to a weekly, biweekly, or monthly newsletter delivered via email, you are not required to get parental consent to deliver that email as long as the child's information is not used for any other purpose. It is recommended, however, that you obtain the parent's consent prior to sending that first (and certainly the second) newsletter.

Note that you *would* need parental consent if you collected information on the child that was used to target the child for special offers within that newsletter. So while it's okay to ask for the child's email address to deliver the newsletter, you would need parental consent to target the child with special offers.

Child Safety

If the only reason that you are collecting information on the child under 13 is for the child's own protection, then you are not required to get parental consent as long as the information collected is not disclosed. An example of this would be if a child is participating in a chat group and your Web site flagged children under 13 to identify them and help protect them against strangers who attempt to arrange meetings with them. In that case, you would not need parental consent to protect children on your Web site. The purpose of COPPA is to protect children under 13. If the reason you are collecting any information about children under 13 is to help protect them, then the FTC does not require that you get parental consent to do this.

When in Doubt, Ask

When in doubt, it's always better to ask for parental consent than to be accused of deceitful marketing practices to children. These exceptions were made so that companies with good intentions would not be penalized by COPPA legislation. But it's still a good idea to get parental consent whenever possible. Marketing to children under the age of 13 is challenging, but if this is your core business, then it would make sense to speak with a law firm or promotions agency to ensure that you are staying within the bounds of COPPA legislation.

European Union Data Protection Directive

The Internet is global, so shouldn't your promotions be? No, unless you know the rules internationally and it's worth the money to keep abreast of the changes in international privacy laws. Similar to the FTC, the European Union (EU) published a directive on October 25, 1998, on the protection of personal information.

The text of the directive is available at `http://europa.eu.int/eurlex/en/ lif/dat/1995/en_395L0046.html`. This directive was created to regulate the collection of personal information and how that personal information is used within the European Union.

While the scope of this directive goes beyond the scope of this chapter, I mention it as an example of some of the international legislation that your online promotions are subject to if you intend to go international. Usually, when a company wants to go international, it's because they have offices in other countries that would like to take part in the online promotion. If this is the case, then the best thing to do would be to clear the promotion with legal counsel residing in the countries outside the United States. I will talk about international promotions online later in this chapter.

Tell-a-Friend Emails

Are tell-a-friend emails information or are they spam? (Okay, I'm sure you know what spam means, but for those of you who are new to the Internet, let me explain that *spam* is slang for unsolicited email. The term comes from an old Monte Python spoof.)

The success of tell-a-friend emails is amazing. By simply allowing consumers to email their friends about an online promotion, online marketers have discovered a way to capitalize on word-of-mouth advertising and actually help spread viral marketing—isn't the Internet the greatest medium? But because of the success, government agencies are beginning to take a closer look at what constitutes spam versus "information." Using a literal definition of "anything that wasn't asked for is spam," it's clear that tell-a-friend emails are just as much unsolicited email as the "Follow me to financial freedom" email that I get about three times daily. But the key difference is that someone you know actually thought you might want to receive the tell-a-friend email, and so email marketers are arguing that tell-a-friend emails are *not* spam. While I'm not aware of any specific antispam legislation that has passed, a number of states are currently considering such legislation.

So, to protect your company from pending antispam legislation, the following sections discuss four consideration points to help keep you on the straight and narrow when adding a tell-a-friend email component to your online promotion.

One-time Mailing

If a consumer submits his or her friend's email address for notification to your online promotion, this should be a one-time mailing to the friend. Since the email address was not provided by the owner of the email address, it should not be used for any purpose other than to send notification of the online promotion. At the top or bottom of the email, there should be a clear notice to the effect that this is a one-time mailing and that no further emails will be sent.

It's common "netiquette" to include opt-out information at the bottom of email newsletters and other ongoing emails. This is of particular importance if the tell-a-friend email somehow signs up the referred friend to an ongoing email list. While intentionally having a friend sign up another friend for an ongoing email subscription is clearly not wise, accidents do happen and data collected from one program sometimes ends up being used for purposes that were never intended. To minimize damage from accidental email subscriptions, it is critical that your email lists clearly define how a consumer can opt-out of the subscription.

Follow Your Own Privacy Policy

Your tell-a-friend email campaign should *not* in any way violate your existing privacy policy. This should be obvious, but some marketers believe that their privacy policy only applies to membership or sales data collected on their Web site when, in fact, it should apply to any information collected or disbursed. The tell-a-friend program should be carefully reviewed to confirm that it stays within the boundaries of the existing privacy policies, and should not be treated as an exception.

Full Disclosure

This is a bit trickier. You have two options with tell-a-friend emails: Make the email appear as if it's coming from your company or make the email appear as if it's coming from your friend. The technology exists so that the "From" line of the email can be made to appear as if the email was sent directly from the friend's own email program, when, in fact, it wasn't. If you've ever experimented with these two options in tell-a-friend emails, you know that if the email appears to be coming directly from the friend, the response rates will generally be higher.

The problem lies in what could be construed as a deceptive practice. When something appears one way but, in fact, it isn't, it can be considered deceptive by government authorities. Right now, there is no clear-cut legislation on this issue, but most law firms are pushing for full disclosure from whom the email was sent. Specifically, if the email was sent from a company, then it should look like it was sent from that company and not from the friend who provided the email address. This is not just a legal issue, but is sound business practice. Your tell-a-friend emails should not have to disguise themselves as coming from the referrer—even if the act of doing so provides a higher response rate.

Higher response rates are one good reason why the direct-mail sweepstakes companies have been involved in numerous class action lawsuits claiming unfair and deceptive marketing practices. "Congratulations, you've just won a million dollars" had a much better response rate than "Enter for a chance to win a million dollars," even though the former statement wasn't true.

Limit Additional Entries for Referrals

This one will cut right to the heart of the tell-a-friend email component. The very reason that most consumers are compelled to refer their friends and family members is for the increased chance of winning. This is fine as long as there is a write-in method or "free" method of entry that allows consumers not referring friends an equal number of entries into the sweepstakes. The argument here is that a friend's email address has value, and it could be argued that it constitutes consideration if the act of giving the friend's email address allows additional entries that could not be received elsewhere in the promotion. Going back to Chapter 1, "Promotional Marketing Basics," if the sweepstakes has all three elements of prize, chance, and consideration, then it is not a sweepstakes, but an illegal lottery.

To avoid this problem, give a limited amount of additional entries for referrals, but be sure to include a write-in method of entry or alternate online method of entry where consumers who do not provide their friends' email addresses can receive an equal number of "extra" sweepstakes entries. As long as all the methods of entry are equal, referring a friend will not give consumers an advantage, and you should stay within the confines of the law as currently interpreted.

As I stated previously, there has been no legislation that specifically and solely deals with tell-a-friend emails to my knowledge, so this information is proactive and attempts to steer you clear of perceived risk. As I tell all my clients, I take the conservative route when it comes to legal matters because I never want either my client or my agency to be part of the "test case" that helps *define* current legislation. Along these same lines, the larger your company is, the more likely it is to appear on the radar screen of legislators. If you're a small company that is willing to take risks, you should seek legal counsel to clearly define what those risks are (for your specific requirements) and decide if they are worth the potential benefits.

Security: Creating a Safe Environment

One hundred percent security is an illusion. While many will strive for perfection, the fact that a human hand touches the system makes the system less than perfect. People make mistakes. Besides that, the only way to guarantee that your information is secure against unauthorized use is to not let anyone else have access to your information, and this simply isn't practical.

In February 1995, my friend Chan Suh, cofounder of Agency.com, taught me a valuable lesson about security. He was working with me on a project for one of my client's Web sites. I was having trouble with some HTML code and I asked for his assistance. He called me back and asked me to check out the page that I had been working on. He had fixed the problem. At first I was extremely thankful that he had been able to fix the HTML problem, but then it dawned on me—I hadn't given him access to the site. How did he upload the HTML page?

I asked him about it and he told me it was an old programmer's secret and he'd have to kill me if he told me. After much prodding, he finally explained that he had simply used a WHOIS search to determine the hosting facility and then he called the tech support line of the hosting facility, explained who he was and that he had a deadline to fix a problem, and just like that, they gave him access to the server. The security of the Web server had been compromised not by finding a coding error but by finding a weak link in the people chain. There was no harm done, but from that point on I was much more aware of the security measures of my hosting facility as well as my internal team. What good is a firewall or encryption program if a simple phone call could usurp the whole security system.

I seriously doubt that you could accomplish the same trick with the standards of today's hosting facilities, but most Management Information Systems (MIS) managers will tell you that many breaches in security happen when the wrong person is trusted with sensitive information. Security begins internally at your company. Before designing a comprehensive technology plan, it may behoove you to create a simple flowchart of who has access to what information. By identifying who has access to what, it will become easier to recognize the potential weak links in the security system.

Ethical Hacking

What? That's what I said when I first heard this term at one of Penton Media's Internet World shows a few years ago. Just about everyone has heard of hackers. The media plays them up to be evil programmers who lurk around every company's Web server room waiting to steal access codes so they can take down your Web site. When a major Web site gets hacked, all the newspapers and magazines do a story on the latest security issues on the Internet.

But in the same way that the *The Wizard of Oz* had both "good" witches and "bad" witches, there are both *good* hackers and *bad* hackers on the Internet. The unfortunate thing is that only the bad hackers appear to get any media coverage. The main difference between good and bad hackers is ethics. Just about all the same techniques are used, but the main difference is to what end. A bad hacker's objective is some form of personal gain from the disruption of service or theft of information or passwords. A good hacker's objective is professional gain through identifying the most common tricks of a malicious hacker, and plugging the security holes as well as possible.

For example, an ethical hacker might use the same software program built to gain unlawful access to a Web server, but with the express purpose of *fixing* the security holes for the company who has retained his or her services. So while a malicious hacker might use a software program to break into a Web server or database, an ethical hacker will use the same program to stop a malicious hacker. The important difference is that ethical hackers get a company's consent before hacking away.

Think of ethical hackers as security experts who have been trained in the art of hacking, but have chosen to put their knowledge to good use—to help companies *identify* their security problems before they become security nightmares.

Choosing the Best Technology Solution

Go to ethicalhacking.com and you'll get a company called EVINCI, whose entire business is built around Internet security. They are not alone. The International Computer Security Association (ICSA) (www.icsa.net) boasts 2,785 members in its Alliance for Internet Security (AIS) alone, representing 7,391,590 "nonaggressive" systems. B2Bnow (www.b2bnow.com) and AllBusiness (www.allbusiness .com)—not to mention all the search engines—provide listings of Internet security companies that can help you determine what security measures are best for your company.

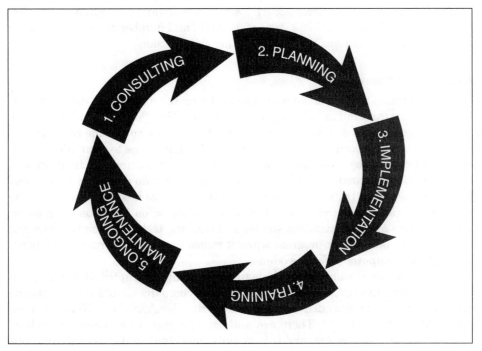

Figure 4.1   Technology solution.

As Figure 4.1 illustrates, there are five components of any technology solution:

Consultation: When you hire an Internet security specialist, he or she will evaluate your existing security from both an internal and external vantage point.

Planning: Together, you will develop a plan with your security specialist that will balance ideal security measures with the realistic needs of your company. Security risks will be identified and recommendations will be made.

Implementation: After a security plan has been created (and approved), your Internet security specialist will help you implement the plan, adding additional technology and people processes to your existing corporate infrastructure.

Training: Along with implementation, education and training will be required for key personnel as well as documentation for any employee that is identified as a link in the security chain.

Ongoing Maintenance: Once your technology and procedures have been implemented, there should be ongoing maintenance of your new technology solution so that both your technology and people resources stay current and aware of new security threats and overall risk management.

While every company's ideal security solution will vary depending on key factors such as the kind of business, type of network, and number of employees, there are some basic precautions that any company should take.

AntiVirus Software

Computer viruses are, unfortunately, one of the most common and damaging pitfalls that companies fall into. Deadly computer virus like "Melissa" and the "I Love You" viruses can wreak havoc not only on your computer but on the computers of your friends and coworkers. Viruses can attach themselves to your files, delete critical operating files from your computer, and cause a tremendous financial loss because of the destruction of your documents and the time necessary to disinfect your computer. I am truly surprised at how little progress has been made over the years at knocking out a virus's ability to wreak havoc on a person's computer. While we have made tremendous strides at advancing technology on the Internet, we have made only minor progress when it comes to stopping viruses from penetrating basic computer defense systems.

To avoid common viruses sent via email attachments, corrupted files, and downloads from the Internet, each computer in your company should have antivirus software from companies such as Symantec (Norton AntiVirus) and Network Associates (McAfee VirusScan). There are antivirus programs for servers as well as desktop personal computers, and it is equally important that this antivirus software be installed on the network as well as individual computers.

Beyond initial software installations, it is important to keep your antivirus software programs current. New viruses are developed all the time, so it is important that your antivirus software have the ability to incorporate new virus definitions and fixes into its software so that you are protected. Most of today's antivirus programs provide these updates from their Web sites, whereby your software can be automated to download patches and updates on a regular basis. While antivirus software will not protect your system 100 percent of the time, it will provide you with the bare minimum of protection against common viruses.

Backups

What if every file on your computer was damaged beyond repair? I shudder to think what a loss that would be for most of us, but if you haven't experienced this hardship, you are lucky! Depending on what's wrong with your computer, it is possible to spend large amounts of time and money to repair your system, but there are some problems that simply can't be fixed. In either event, your hardships would be significantly reduced if you had a tape drive or writeable compact disk backup with all your important files.

With the cost of writeable CD-ROM drives going down, along with the decreasing cost of tape drives, there is no reason not to have an automated back-up procedure in place. With a network, this can be as simple as having your employees leave their computers on overnight so that the server can back up critical files and important information on a daily, weekly, or biweekly basis. If you are a sole proprietor just starting your new company and only have one computer, consider buying a machine with a writeable CD-ROM drive that will automatically back up your files.

Even if you don't have the right hardware to do automated backups, manual backups are worth the time spent when you consider the importance of your electronic files. Also, you should be sure to test the backups from time to time to ensure that there are no problems with the system. You could be doing everything right but if your back-up system fails, you may be more vulnerable than you think.

Firewalls

Think of a firewall as a virtual gatekeeper for your computer network. The firewall acts much like customs officials for international flights, checking to see who is attempting to access your network and whether they are authorized to do so. This happens before you ever receive a login page where you would normally enter your username and password. Using the customs official analogy, let's say you want to use your Automated Teller Machine (ATM) bankcard in a foreign country. While your bankcard may work in another country, if you don't have a passport, you are not allowed into the country. It doesn't matter if you have an ATM bankcard and a PIN number; if you don't have a passport, you will never reach the ATM machine to withdraw funds from your bank account.

In general, firewalls are used to permit and deny different kinds of traffic to get in and out of a company's network. That is, even if you are sitting at your desk at work and logged onto the network, if a Web site has been deemed unsafe or inappropriate for a work environment, you will be denied access to that Web site. Conversely, if your competitors are attempting to access your company's Intranet (your internal Web site), they will be denied.

Contrary to popular belief, firewalls are not ideal for every company. Your company may not require firewall security, and you should check with an Internet security professional before you invest in firewall protection.

Encryption

Encryption is used to scramble private information (credit card numbers, for example) that is being passed through "unsecured" networks, such as the Internet, or while it is being stored in a database (and is not being accessed). Encryption allows you to use codes or algorithms that essentially turn numbers and text into gibberish until the same code or algorithm is used to decrypt the gibberish back into meaningful information.

For example, I could set up a formula so that when I sent the number "123456" over the Internet, it would appear as "QEMPE432DKPE6859ANE23." If a hacker intercepted my transmission, the information would be useless without the formula to decode the string of alphanumeric text back into the numbers "123456."

There are many forms of encryption software, including PGPfreeware, which is free encryption software for your email. If memory serves, PGP stands for "Pretty Good Privacy," which made me chuckle when I first heard it. The point is, even encryption is not 100 percent secure, but it's *pretty good*. For a comprehensive list of encryption software, I recommend going to CNET's Web site, Download.com (www.download.com). There you will find roughly 350 different kinds of encryption programs—some free, some shareware, and others that are 30-day evaluation copies. After evaluation, you can purchase the full version.

Additional Security

We are now stepping outside the bounds of the intended scope of this book (it's supposed to be about online promotions, after all), but if you're hanging on to my every word about security, you really should check out the International Computer Security Association Web site (www.icsa.net) to learn more about things like:

- *Intrusion Detection Systems,* which alert security administrators of suspicious activity on their networks and computer systems *in real time*!

- *IPSec,* which is comprised of the latest in Internet Protocol (IP) security and specifically designed for electronic communications over the Internet.

- *Internet Service Providers Security Consortium,* which is an organization created specifically for the support of the growing security demands of ISPs.

- *Public Key Infrastructure,* which helps companies take advantage of a secure infrastructure so that there is confirmation that the person (or company) with whom they are communicating on a network is who he/she says he/she is.

There are some additional precautions that you can take in addition to the software you buy and the network that you set up within your company. These precautions include:

Passwords: The use of password protection is not enough. The passwords themselves should not be obvious such as the person's name, phone number, date of birth, or a common word from the dictionary. Alphanumeric passwords (including text and numbers) are the best. Even with an alphanumeric password, passwords should be changed from time to time to ensure maximum security.

Server access: Nowadays, hosting facilities come standard with required sign-in authorization and identity checking. Take heed of their attention to the physical security of their Web servers. A firewall is no good if it can be turned off and the Web server accessed directly. Your own network should likewise be stored in a locked room to avoid unauthorized access. Only people who really need to use the server should have access (physical or virtual). You will maximize security if you go the next step and keep track of who is accessing the server and deleting user names that are no longer being used.

Network administrators: Even if you don't have one, make sure someone is completing the tasks of a network administrator. This includes standard maintenance of the server (making up dates for peak performance); downloading and installing software patches for the operating system, database, and other software programs; checking log files for suspicious activity; and analysis and removal of unused programs such as sendmail, gopher, NFS, finger, PERL, and other standard Web server programs that could provide a backdoor for unauthorized users.

All this information on security is meant to alert you, not to scare you. Fifty percent or more of this material may not be necessary for your business—especially if your company would not be an obvious target for a hacker. But knowing what's out there is important as your business grows and you begin to do more and more of your business online. Knowledge of a particular subject should not frighten you. If you suddenly feel unprotected, then consult with a professional and find out if your concerns are unfounded or realistic.

Overview of the Legal Aspects of Online Promotions

Now I'd like to get into the heart of the legal aspects of online promotions. You hear those disclaimers during the very last few seconds of a radio commercial, "No purchase necessary. Must be 18 years of age or older. Void where prohibited. Blah Blah Blah!" You know you need those disclaimers, but the legal aspects of online promotions are usually the very last thing online marketers think about when preparing a sweepstakes, contest, or game. Unfortunately, the legal aspects will make or break your promotion (be it online or traditional).

In the next chapter, I will talk about when to call a promotional marketing agency versus when it's okay to run online promotions in house. Specifically, I will go into how best to determine if your in-house legal counsel is sufficient to protect you and your company when conducting online promotions. The purpose of this chapter, however, is to provide you with a basic understanding of the legal aspects of online promotions so *you* can better protect yourself and your company.

To begin, the legal aspects of online promotions are similar to that of traditional promotions. A sweepstakes by any other name is still a sweepstakes. While there are additional laws, such as the ones discussed earlier in this chapter, that specifically apply to the Internet, basic sweepstakes and lottery laws that were created for traditional promotions are essentially the same laws that must be adhered to online. In other words, traditional sweepstakes laws still serve as the basic foundation for online promotions. To date, very little legislation has been passed that focuses specifically on online promotions. Instead, the governmental bodies have applied current legislation to activities on the Internet. Interpretation of existing laws via court findings and actions by regulators create legal precedent, which in turn is incorporated into the verbiage of an online promotion's official rules and legal disclaimers.

There are three basic principles to keep you and your company out of trouble:

1. Know the laws.

2. Stay within the laws.

3. Expect the unexpected.

In this chapter, I will attempt to help you better familiarize yourself with the laws that pertain to promotions—online and off. Please note that this will be a summary of the basic foundation of the laws and is not intended to prepare you for the bar exam.

Knowing the laws is truly half the battle. Staying within the laws is only possible if you have a clear understanding of where the boundaries lie. Once you know what can and cannot be done, it's much easier to stay within the confines of what's legal. Most companies are not willing to take major risks when it comes to breaking the law. So if you come to a point where you recognize that what is desired from an online promotion is not legal, your explanation of the law will usually help put the promotion back on track. Other people within the company may want to confirm your opinion with outside legal counsel, perhaps, but they will certainly not ignore your concerns.

Finally, expecting the unexpected means taking the time to think about what could possibly go wrong. It's much easier to "put out fires" when something goes wrong with your online promotion if you've already thought about the potential problems and have a good idea of how you would react. What if a state legislator asks you to explain how you selected the grand prize winner? What if the printer mistakenly prints the "Congratulations, You're an Instant Winner" message on all the packaging instead of the "Sorry, Please Try Again" message? What if a hacker takes down your server? What if your database is compromised? For every question listed here, there are probably five more that would directly apply to your next online promotion. The more time you spend up front thinking about worst-case scenarios, the less chaos you will face when your worst nightmare becomes a reality. (I'm not usually a pessimist, but I've seen enough online promotions disasters to think through as many potential problems as I can fathom.)

Illegal Lotteries

In Chapter 1, "Promotional Marketing Basics," I described in detail the differences between sweepstakes, contests, and other forms of promotions. The big legal issue that was discussed was that of *consideration*. If your sweepstakes has all three elements of prize, chance, and consideration, it is not a sweepstakes, but an illegal lottery. Illegal lotteries are a criminal offense in most jurisdictions. The act of running an illegal lottery is punishable by fines and, in rare but possible circumstances, jail time. That's right. If you knowingly conduct an illegal lottery, you could go to jail. Gambling is illegal and addictive. The state and federal governments will do everything in their power to ensure that illegal lotteries do not happen.

Consideration

As stated in the first chapter, the topic of *consideration* is a much-debated issue. Consideration is not just about money, it's about value. Time can be construed as consideration. Detailed personal information can be construed as consideration. And even requiring access to the Internet has been debated as a possible means of consideration.

When putting your online promotion together, you should be mindful of common consideration pitfalls:

1. *Television, radio, print, direct mail, outdoor, and/or other forms of traditional media are used to drive traffic to an online promotion.* Although most regulators have not weighed in on the subject, requiring Internet access could potentially be construed as consideration. There are several ways to address this potential problem to reduce your risk:

   ■ State in the eligibility requirements of the official rules that consumers are required to have had Internet access *prior* to the start date of the promotion. By clearly stating this as an eligibility requirement, no argument can be made that consumers were induced to purchase Internet access for the sole purpose of participating in the online promotion.

   ■ Provide an alternate "free" method of entry via mail. Even though the cost of postage is usually more than the time a consumer would spend online, legal precedent has shown that using a mail-in method of entry (requiring one stamp) is not construed as *consideration*. It is not necessary to require that consumers have Internet access prior to the launch of the online promotion if an alternate "free" method of entry exists.

   ■ Provide an alternate "free" method of entry via toll-free phone number. While the costs associated with a toll-free number may or may not make sense for your online promotion, it is certainly a viable alternative.

2. *You want to require that consumers complete a detailed survey or lengthy membership form in order to enter your online promotion.* The potential problem is that detailed surveys or membership forms require a time commitment from your consumers. It could be argued that the consumers' time to complete the survey or membership application and the information they provide could be consideration. The best ways to avoid this problem are:

   ■ Provide an alternate "free" method of entry via mail. In the mail-in method of entry, do not require that consumers complete the membership application or survey. In this way, even if the time or information is deemed to be a consideration, there is still a "free" method of entry available.

   ■ Offer a sweepstakes-only entry form. If you do not wish to offer a mail-in method of entry, you can provide an alternate online method of entry that does not require the consumer to complete the survey or membership information.

   ■ Make the survey or membership questions optional. If you don't require the survey or membership information, then it cannot be deemed consideration. Those who wish to complete the information will do so and those who do not can simply enter the sweepstakes.

3. *You want to provide additional entries for consumers who provide the email addresses of their friends and family members.* The problem with giving additional entries for email referrals is that an advantage is given to those who provide the information. If the only way to get more entries is to provide email addresses of friends and family members, you may have a consideration issue. Here's how to avoid this problem:

    ■ Cap the number of additional entries that can be received for referring friends and family members. If the number of additional entries is limited, then it is possible to provide additional entries to those who enter via mail or online without referral. As long as there is a way to receive the same number of maximum entries without referring friends and family members, you can sidestep the whole consideration issue.

    ■ Provide the total number of additional entries that a consumer would get for referrals via an alternate "free" mail-in method of entry. If, for example, you could get a maximum of six entries per day online (one for the daily entry and five more for up to five email referrals), then provide the same six entries for a single write-in entry.

    ■ Allow the consumer to enter the maximum times online without referring friends, so they will receive as many entries as they would for the referrals. Again, using the example of six entries per day, you would allow a consumer to enter up to six times per day from the online entry form without referring friends or family members' email addresses.

4. *You want to reward consumers for downloading your software program by entering them into an exclusive sweepstakes.* The problem is that if the file is large and it takes a long time to download, the time spent downloading the program could be construed as consideration. To avoid consideration issues:

    ■ Allow sweepstakes entry without the download. By allowing consumers to enter into the sweepstakes without downloading the software program, you can avoid the consideration issue altogether.

    ■ Offer an alternate "free" method of entry via mail. In this case, the mail-in entry would not require the software download and there would be no consideration issue.

5. *You want to offer an automatic entry into the sweepstakes when consumers buy something from your online store.* If the only way to enter the promotion is to purchase a product, then this is by far the most clear-cut issue of consideration. Any payment to participate is a clear issue of consideration. Avoiding consideration with automatic entries is simple (and should sound familiar by now):

■ Provide the standard "free" method of entry via mail. In this case, consumers who purchase online will receive an automatic entry into the sweepstakes, but without purchasing they can decide to write in for an entry form. Here again, the entry process cannot favor purchase. Write-in entries must receive the same amount of entries that a sale would receive.

■ Offer an online method of entry without purchase. As long as consumers do not have to purchase your product to enter into the sweepstakes, you will avoid the issue of consideration. [Keep in mind that this is only possible if you're not advertising (or not greatly advertising) offline and you're not an Internet Service Provider.]

6. *You want to give out 50-percent-off discounts as a "prize" in your sweepstakes.* This is perhaps the least obvious of the bunch, as there are postconsideration issues associated with discounts or coupons as prizes. The issue here is that to take advantage of your offer, consumers must make a purchase. That is, to claim their "prize," they must make a purchase (therefore, consideration). To avoid consideration:

■ Don't do it. Providing a discount or coupon as a prize in your sweepstakes or instant win game is something you should typically try to avoid. At the very least, it should not be your only prize offered (and even then you'll have some risk).

■ Provide everyone who enters with the same discount or coupon just for entering. That way, your coupon or discount is not a prize but simply an added bonus just for participating. If you can't offer the same discount or coupon to everyone, then either come up with an offer that can be universally distributed or remove the sweepstakes altogether.

With these few examples, I have covered some of the more common consideration issues that come up with online promotions. But as I tell my clients, "When in doubt, check it out." If you're not sure if your promotion could run into some consideration (or postconsideration) issues, ask a professional. In the case of online promotions it definitely is *not* easier to apologize than ask for permission.

Sweepstakes Registration

If the *total* prize package in your sweepstakes is over $5,000, you must register with the states of New York and Florida if you want your promotion to be open to residents of these states. Some people mistakenly think that a single prize must be $5,000 or greater, but this is incorrect. If *all* of your prizes added up together come out to exactly $5,001, you must register the promotion if you want to run the promotion in New York and Florida. At $5,000 you do not have to register, but at $5,001 you do. (Hey, the line had to be drawn somewhere.)

You must also provide surety bonds or a trust account for the total prize structure for each registration. If your total prize package is $250,000, then you must provide a surety bond or trust account for the same amount for each state in which you are registering. Bonds can be obtained from your promotion agency or insurance brokers. In either case, you are required to pay a small nonrefundable fee, which is usually between 1.5 and 3 percent of the total prize package for each bond. (Discounts are given on larger prize packages.) Trust accounts are essentially certificates of deposit that are specifically designated for the promotion. In other words, if your company is cash rich, you can legally designate funds to cover the total prize package in lieu of a bond.

New York and Florida require these bonds or trust accounts because of an old scam where a company would promise to give away $1 million, collect as many sales as possible, and then declare bankruptcy and therefore be unable to award the $1 million prize. By requiring surety bonds or trust accounts, if the company goes out of business before the promotion has ended, all prizes will still be awarded. This means that the surety bond or trust account will be used to cover the prizes that were promised in the promotion.

New York requires that you register your promotion *at least 30 days* prior to its launch. While this is the law, New York is not known for enforcing this 30-day requirement. I'm not saying that you should deliberately ignore the 30-day requirement, I'm just saying that if you find yourself closer to the promotional launch date than the required 30 days, you may choose to register rather than voiding New York residents from participating in the promotion. I can tell you that in the four years that I have been creating and managing online promotions, there have been several promotions that did not make the 30-day window, and no fines have been imposed from the state of New York. Your results may vary.

Florida, on the other hand, will fine you without thinking twice about it. The state of Florida requires that you register your promotion *at least 7 days* prior to the launch of the promotion. If you fall one day short, be prepared for a fine of around $2,000 *per incident* (although the fine could be higher). In other words, if your registration is late and your bond forms are late, then you could be fined $4,000 or more. Thankfully, there is FedEx and UPS overnight delivery. If it comes down to the wire, you're better off delaying the launch date or voiding the residents of Florida from participating in the promotion. If you're late, there's a pretty good chance Florida will fine you. If you choose to run the promotion without registration in Florida or New York (and without voiding these residents), you are risking serious fines. They don't catch every promotion, but yours could be the one. Better to play it safe than sorry.

Also, if you're offering a sweepstakes through retail establishment, and the total prize value is in excess of $500, registration in Rhode Island will be required (although that state does not have a bonding requirement).

Contest Registration

Remember that a sweepstakes is *not* a contest. If you're running a skill promotion where official judges will be scoring every entry, then you do *not* have to register with the states of New York and Florida (even if your prize package is $5,000 or more). Instead, you may need to register with the state of Arizona if you wish to include Arizona residents. Arizona does not require surety bonds or trust accounts for the prize package, but does require that you complete their official registration form and submit it along with the official rules of the promotion.

1099 Filings

Any prize winner who has won a prize valued at $600 or more must be issued a 1099 tax form at the end of the year. This form is used to track "income" that has not already been taxed and alerts the government of the prize value that has been awarded and to whom. The prizewinner is responsible for including a copy of this 1099 in his or her tax return and for paying the applicable tax based on the gross income of the household.

DISCLAIMER **Please note before you read any further that I am not a certified public accountant (CPA) and this discussion should only be taken in the context of a 1099 filing—not as my rendering tax advice. If your Chief Financial Officer disagrees with any of this, do yourself a favor and follow his or her advice.**

For cash prizes, the amount that is included on the 1099 is obvious—whatever cash was awarded must be declared. For prizes other than cash, the amount can be a bit trickier. Take a car, for example. If your company has purchased a new car as a prize in the promotion, then the amount that was used to purchase the car should be the actual value of the prize and what is included on the 1099 form (even if the car is "worth" more than your company actually paid). But what if the car was provided by another prize sponsor (in exchange for the car company's logo on all the promotional advertising, for example)? Usually, the company providing the car can provide you with the cost of the automobile, but, if not, you should use the average retail value (ARV) of the car or blue book value if one is available. Generally, I recommend providing the ARV as the taxable sum.

The same goes for computers and electronics equipment. If you bought the equipment from a retailer or wholesaler, the 1099 should be for the amount that was paid for the equipment. If the equipment was provided, you must use the average retail value for the prizes (if the company providing the equipment cannot provide you with the cost).

This becomes a bigger issue when winners don't agree with the value placed on the prize they won. Because they are required to pay taxes on the value of the prize (whether it is cash or not), they may choose not to accept the prize because of the tax implications. Let's take the extreme case of giving away a Ferrari. The value of the car may be $175,000 (or more). If the winner is in a high-income tax bracket and must pay 33 percent on his or her income, that $57,750 must come out of pocket at the end of the year. Suddenly when reality strikes, this fabulous prize isn't that attractive. When the winner weighs the cost of insurance on top of the tax that must be paid at the end of the year, the first thing he or she will ask you is can they take a cash alternative instead. This is why the awarding of the prize must be crystal clear in the official rules of the promotion. If there is no cash alternative, then the rules must state this (along with the fact that the consumer is responsible for all taxes related to the prize won).

Let's say that you recognize this hardship, but still want to give away the Ferrari. You could throw in $60,000 in cash to help cover the taxes. But now the prize is no longer valued at $175,000 because the cash bumps it up to a grand total of $235,000 and the taxes will now be $77,550 (assuming a 33 percent tax bracket). There's no question that the addition of the $60,000 helps, but the winner will still be responsible for an additional $17,550 out of his or her own pocket. As you can see, your company can never truly take care of the tax burden unless a significant portion of the prize is cash.

This becomes even more of an issue with obscure prizes. I came across a British company that wanted to give away predominantly British prizes in a promotion in the United States. One of the prizes was an original British Telecom phone booth worth roughly $10,000. It sounded great initially, until winners realized that they would have to pay a few thousand dollars in taxes for this phone booth. Then they began to ask themselves, "What would I do with it anyway?" For over a year, this company disqualified potential winners who declined the prize because of not wanting to pay the taxes. I believe the only way they could ever resolve the issue was to offer a cash alternative to the prize (or perhaps they are still attempting to award the prize to this day).

If you want to promote a bunch of funky obscure prizes, I recommend that you do *not* buy those prizes until after you have selected your potential winners and determined if they can and will pay the taxes. Cash alternatives to the obscure prizes are your best bet. And, of course, if the prizes are under $600, then you need not worry about issuing a 1099. Consumers are on their honor to identify the prizes they won and claim them on their next tax returns.

Official Winners List

Because you are promoting that you are giving away prizes in your sweepstakes and contests, you are required to have an official winners' list at the conclusion of the promotion. This official winners list is your declaration of who won the prizes in your promotion. Consumers wishing to inquire about the winners in your promotion should be able to send you a self-addressed, stamped envelope and get a list of the prize winners.

For privacy and protection of your winners, you are only required to provide the first initial, last name, city, and state of the winners along with the prize won. If I had been fortunate enough to win the grand prize of a trip to Hawaii in your promotion, my listing would look like this:

[Your Company's] "Hawaii Getaway Sweepstakes" Official Winners List

WINNER	PRIZE WON
B. Carmody, Santa Rosa, CA	Grand Prize Trip to Hawaii

Your official winners' list should be available via mail. Many companies will choose to post the official winners' list on their Web site in an effort to promote the fact that, "Yes, people really do win in our promotions." While this is a good habit to get into and will help increase the participation levels in your online promotion, it will not satisfy the legal requirement to have an official winners list available via mail. Even if your promotion is an online-only promotion (that is, not advertised via traditional mediums such as TV, radio, print, outdoor, or direct mail) you still must have a Post Office box or business address where consumers can write to receive the official winners list. New York has recently rejected registrations that do not include this Post Office box or mail-in address.

Ending the Promotion

Your sweepstakes isn't over until the prizes are awarded and, if the entire prize package was over $5,000, the official winners list has been sent to New York and Florida to release the bonds (or trust accounts). Awarding all the prizes can be tricky with online promotions—especially if you've only collected an email address as the consumer's sweepstakes registration. The problem with using email as the only contact information is that most consumers don't believe their official prize notification emails. They are inclined to think they are bogus emails and delete them—even though they registered for your promotion.

If the potential winners that you have selected and contacted fail to respond to your official winner notifications, then they must be given a final notice and disqualified. New potential winners must be notified and the whole process repeated until all prizes over $25 have been awarded. At this point, it should be noted that many sponsors have taken the position not to award unclaimed prizes with lesser values.

Once this is done, you must make a different version of your official winners list that is sent to New York and Florida. The main difference is that for official notification to state governments, you must include complete name and contact information along with the value of the prize and the date won. Also, this official winners list must be *notarized*. Using the earlier example of winning the Grand Prize Trip to Hawaii, your official winners list to state governments would look like this:

[Your Company's] "Hawaii Getaway Sweepstakes" Official Winners List

WINNER	PRIZE WON	VALUE	DATE WON
Bill Carmody 543 Lewrosa Way Santa Rosa, CA 95404	Grand Prize Trip to Hawaii	$5,000	September 3, 2000

This additional information helps New York and Florida determine if the prizes you declared in your official rules match those that were awarded and when they were won. If any consumers complain about the promotion or suspect fraud, this detailed information will help the states determine if the winners declared in your official winners list actually won the prizes they are listed for, or if further investigations are required. Since the states typically correspond via mail, they require that you provide the complete addresses of your winners.

Once New York and Florida have received your notarized official winners list, they will release the bonds or trust accounts used to secure the prizes for your promotion. When you receive the official letter from New York and Florida that the bonds have been released, then the promotion is officially over (until December 31 when you issue all the 1099s to the winners).

Preparing the Official Rules

In this section, I will review the importance of the official rules and why they are one of the most critical aspects of your promotion—online or off—and the issues associated with changing official rules after the promotion has launched. I will provide a checklist for especially important areas that must be considered when preparing official rules. If writing rules is not your idea of a good time, I will provide resources for some professional help. And, finally, I will discuss some of the basic requirements for disclaimers and abbreviated official rules.

As stated previously, this information should be used only as a guide because every online promotion is different and has its own requirements when it comes to the official rules. Even if your online promotion remains constant from month to month, new laws will continue to be passed that will affect the legal aspects of your online promotions. This said, if you understand the basics, the changes in the laws should be fairly easy to apply and with each new online promotion you will gain experience and knowledge that can be applied to your next promotion.

Why Are Official Rules Important?

The official rules of your sweepstakes or contest act as the contract that you are bound by and by which your consumers are bound through participation in the promotion. The official rules spell out every aspect of the promotion and the requirements of someone who wants to participate. The official rules will protect your company if a hacker penetrates your online promotion and jeopardizes the integrity of the promotion. The official rules will ensure that only eligible consumers who abide by the rules will win the prizes set forth in the promotion.

Your official rules tell consumers what prizes are available, the value of the prizes, when and how winners will be selected, the start and end dates of the promotion, and a host of valuable information to protect your company against mistakes or foreseeable problems that can occur. Without the official rules, there would be no guidelines as to how the promotion should be conducted or restrictions on who may participate. Disputes regarding prizes or winners would be much more difficult (not to mention costly) to resolve without these clearly established rules and regulations.

If your promotion is ever investigated by a governmental agency, you wouldn't have any defense without having official rules. Unhappy consumers would have a much easier time bringing lawsuits and creating negative publicity against the "unfair and deceptive practices" claims against your company if there were no official rules that clearly state the quantity and value of the prizes in the promotion and the odds of winning a prize.

For every reason that I can think of why official rules are important, there are likely to be several more that I can't even imagine because they haven't happened yet. That is, without official rules for your promotions, you are entering unexplored territory where, in all probability, there are new ways to destroy your company financially as well as its image and reputation that have yet to be examined or documented. Even with official rules, legal problems can occur, but you will be much better off if you have already declared the rules and regulations of your online promotion.

Can Changes Be Made to Official Rules?

No. Under no circumstances should your official rules be changed after the promotion has been launched. That's like trying to unilaterally change a signed agreement. It can also be deemed false advertising, among other things. In other words, if you change your official rules after the promotion has started, you could be in serious trouble.

This is especially true when you have a promotion with a total prize package of $5,000 or more and you have registered with the states of New York and Florida. All that a consumer needs to do is send a copy of your "revised" official rules to a New York or Florida regulator and the investigation will begin. Changes in prizes, eligibility, method of entry, and completion dates are especially problematic.

Instead of changing your official rules, find some other way to deal with the problem. If a prize that was originally offered is no longer available, you can offer the winner a cash alternative. Just make sure you've allowed yourself this option in the official rules. If your promotion was so successful that you want it to continue for another month, then launch a second promotion that builds off the first promotion and has its own prize package. If you're finding too many consumers who are not in your target area entering your promotion, learn from this and apply it to your next promotion.

The challenge with online promotions is that your ability to make changes "on the fly" tends to encourage you to make changes in real time. While this is fine when it comes to the creative execution or technical demands (increasing the hosting requirements, for example), it is not okay when it comes to the official rules. Note your desired changes and save them for the next online promotion. If you take the risk and make changes, they will usually come back to haunt you.

Checklist for Chance Promotions

You should use care when drafting the official rules. Avoid any misrepresentation by using clear language in both your official rules and any copy or verbiage that references the promotion (this is particularly true if minors are eligible). If your ads speak to the promotion, be sure that what they say is consistent with your official rules. By supplying clear and adequate instructions for your consumers, you can steer clear of any consumer confusion or frustration in a consumer's desire for participation.

Now let's move into the details. While this checklist will provide some of the more important aspects required in preparing the official rules, there will always be project-specific requirements that should be addressed. If your promotion in any way involves alcohol, for example, or another regulated industry, there are industry-specific rules and regulations that will be applicable. In some states it may be flat out *illegal*, while others have specific requirements such as registration. This checklist will provide you with the foundation for your official rules, but is not industry-specific. If you suspect you need more help, I strongly recommend seeking professional help (which I will cover in the next section).

1. Start and End Dates

Every promotion must have an official start date and end date. This defines the promotional period by which all entries must be received. Once the promotion has begun and the official rules have been published—either online or via traditional media—these official start and end dates cannot be changed. If the promotion is doing extremely well, a second promotion should be added that plays off the first promotion. Regardless, the promotion *must end* when it was originally scheduled to end.

2. No Purchase Necessary

If your promotion is a sweepstakes, there must not be a purchase requirement. If the sweepstakes requires a purchase to enter, then it is not a sweepstakes, but an illegal lottery (having all three elements of prize, chance, and consideration). This "no purchase necessary" statement is extremely important to your official rules as it declares that this is a legal sweepstakes and that you may enter it without purchase. It should be clearly stated how a consumer can enter the promotion without purchase (through a Post Office box address or online at a specific URL).

If your promotion is a contest, you may (except for a few states) need a purchase requirement if there is no chance element within your promotion. If you have an essay contest, for example, you may require a purchase because all essays will be judged using a predetermined skill-based requirement.

3. Number of Entries and Facsimile Entries

There should be a statement about the number of entries that are allowed in the promotion. If you are allowing consumers to enter once per day, then your official rules should reflect this requirement. By limiting the number of entries per person, you can void additional entries by the same person over that limit. This is important if a person sends you 300 entries in a single day. If you combined all those entries with everyone else's, then he or she would have greater odds of winning. By limiting the number of entries per person, you can ensure that everyone who enters has an equal chance at winning.

You should also have a statement about entries that are copied. In general, if you are allowing write-in entries into the promotion, you do not want someone to reproduce mass quantities of these entries and send them in. You can state that facsimile entries (photocopied entries) will not be accepted. If someone decides to mass-produce a bunch of write-in entries, you can simply disqualify them.

In the online world, this is especially important if a consumer finds a way around your automated duplicate checking program. If you are checking for duplicates via email addresses and the consumer enters with multiple email addresses, then this verbiage will protect you against multiple entries by the same individual.

4. Random Drawing or Judging of Entries

You must declare how winners will be determined. If the promotion is a sweepstakes, you will make a statement that winners will be selected randomly from among all eligible entries received. The official rules will outline when the official drawing dates are scheduled to occur. This may be only once at the end of the promotion or may be daily or weekly, depending on the number of prizes and frequency of winners desired.

If the promotion is a skill-based contest, all entries must be judged in accordance with objective criteria. This judging requirement must be detailed and explain the criteria that will be judged. For example, in an essay contest, there are usually points assigned to a few different categories such as Originality, Clarity of Expression, Appropriateness to Brand Image, and Humor. The official rules must detail how many points are available for each category so that entrants know how their entries will be judged. If the contest is ever audited, you must be able to show that your entries were judged according to the official rules (and were not a random drawing as in a sweepstakes). You should also have a way of breaking any ties (a different criterion or an additional judge, for example).

5. Geographic Coverage

The geographic coverage verbiage protects you by keeping the promotion within the geographic boundaries of the laws by which you are abiding. If you do not declare the geographic boundaries of the promotion, then you are declaring that the promotion is open to everyone worldwide and that you are liable to every country's international regulations of promotions. This is not recommended.

In general, your promotion should be open only to legal residents of the United States unless you have cleared your official rules with lawyers in the countries you also wish to include. While you would like your online promotion to attract as many people as possible, you must weigh the benefit of international participation with the risks associated with running your promotion in foreign countries where you are not aware of the legal implications. I will speak more to the international issues later in this chapter.

If your grand prize is a travel prize, some companies choose to void Hawaii and Alaska to avoid the increased cost of airfare. If your total prize package is worth $5,000 or more and you were not able to register in New York and Florida within their respective 30-day and 7-day requirements, you may want to void these states to avoid fines and other potential liabilities.

6. Odds of Winning

The number of entries received and the number of prizes available determine the odds of winning in a random drawing. In an instant win game, however, you must predetermine a set universe (number) of game pieces from which all your prizes will be seeded. In this way, you can show that if there are a million game pieces and only one grand prize trip, then the odds of winning that trip are 1:1,000,000. If there are other prizes besides the grand prize, then you must calculate the odds of winning the other prizes based on the total number of game pieces *and* the total number of prizes. For example, if your prize package also had 10,000 T-shirts, your odds of winning a T-shirt would be 1:100. If you had a total of 100,000 prizes in all that you were giving away, you could state that the odds of winning any prize would be 1:10.

There are no odds in skill-based contests as all entries must be judged.

7. Prizes

Your official rules must list the total quantity of each prize along with a description of each prize and its estimated retail value. It's a good idea to include any part numbers on merchandise and version numbers on any software prizes. The more you detail your prizes, the less likely that there will be any confusion from consumers who win the prize.

I once had a client who had 20 Palm Pilots as prizes, but neglected to include the model number. During the promotion, a new version of the Palm Pilot was released. When the time came to award the prizes, a few consumers complained that they were receiving an older model. You wouldn't think that a winner would "look a gift horse in the mouth," but it happens more often than not. This problem could have been avoided altogether if the model number was included in the official rules.

When your prize descriptions are not detailed, you leave yourself open to liability. You must say exactly what you are giving away and what you are not responsible for. Travel prizes, for example, should detail everything from transportation to and from the airport, to rental cars, hotels, meals, and spending money. If all you are giving away is the flight and the hotel, you must state that the winner is responsible for travel to and from the airport, all meals, associated taxes, and other expenses not expressly identified. There can then be no confusion or argument of misrepresentation when it comes time to award the prize. For travel prizes, it is also important to require that the winner (and guest) not only sign an affidavit of eligibility but also a travel release form so that you and your company are not liable if a tragedy should strike and the plane crashes or the winner is involved in an accident.

8. Affidavit of Eligibility and Travel Release

The affidavit of eligibility confirms that the potential winner of a given prize has complied with the official rules and is eligible to win. Winners of prizes valued at $600 or more are required to sign an affidavit of eligibility to ensure that they are in compliance with the eligibility requirements of the promotion. It is a good idea to require affidavits from all major prize winners so that there is no question that the potential winners in the promotion are eligible to win the specified prize. For prizes under $25, it is usually not worth the time to get an affidavit signed by each winner (especially when there are hundreds or thousands of winners), but having the requirement in the official rules gives you the option if you ever suspect that a potential winner is not eligible to win the prize.

By requiring that winners of travel prizes complete and sign a travel release form, you are limiting your liability if anything should happen to the winner during the travel portion of the prize. If a potential winner refuses to sign the travel release form, then you can disqualify him or her in accordance with your official rules. This protects you on both fronts. If the potential winner signs the release and accepts the prize, your liability is limited if anything should happen. If he or she refuses to sign the release, you can disqualify him or her and find an alternate winner who will comply with the release requirement in your official rules.

9. Notification of Winners

Your official rules should state how winners will be notified. If you have only collected their email address as part of their sweepstakes registration process, then you should state that winners will be contacted via email. You should also provide a time requirement for response. That is, if you send out multiple email notifications to the winner with no response, then you should be able to disqualify him or her and select an alternate winner. By stating that potential winners have 5 or 10 days to reply to your notification, there will be fewer problems if no reply is given and the winner is disqualified.

This becomes critical if the grand prize is something like a trip to the Grammy Awards where the date is fixed and the prize must be awarded. While there may be many people who want to go to the Grammys, as the date gets closer, it becomes more difficult to award the prize as people make other plans and don't respond to your official notification right away.

Whenever possible, it is best to get physical mail addresses from your sweepstakes entrants. Awarding prizes via email is a difficult task as very few consumers actually believe that the email notification is real. Even with multiple notifications, the consumers tend to think the email is spam and that there must be a catch. Awarding prizes via overnight delivery such as FedEx or UPS provides urgency and gives the impression that the notification is much more official and realistic.

10. Minors as Winners

Not all promotions target adults 18 years of age or older. Children are an important market to many companies. While it's okay to have promotions in which the winner can be under the age of 18, there are special considerations when marketing online promotions to children. First of all, the minor's parent or legal guardian must cosign the affidavit of eligibility and other legal documents such as travel release forms. A child under the age of 18 does not have legally binding signing authority and therefore requires the participation of a parent or legal guardian in order to award prizes. It is important to have this language included in the official rules if the age requirement is under 18.

There are other considerations that need to be reviewed such as COPPA, which was discussed earlier in this chapter. Marketing to children is similar to alcohol promotions in that there are different laws that will affect the online promotion depending on the objective and how the promotion is being advertised. It's best to review any promotions targeting children with a promotional law firm or promotions agency that will indemnify you against potential risk.

11. Disqualifications

The official rules should cover the different ways that a consumer could be disqualified. The more obvious disqualifications include:

- Not meeting the specific eligibility requirements

- Not responding to official winner notifications

- Not completing the required affidavits of eligibility or travel release forms

Other disqualifications should include:

- Any deliberate attempts to damage or spoof the entry process

- Inaccurate, mutilated, or illegible entries

- Mass-produced entries or reproduction

- Sponsor-related entries

Employees and immediate family members of your company or your promotion agency and those living in their households should not be eligible to enter the promotion.

12. Free Entries

If the main point of entry is via a purchase, online registration, survey, or other entry process that could be construed as consideration, there must be a "free" alternate means of entry. This is usually accomplished via the U.S. mail. If the promotion is an instant win game, free game pieces must be made available either at the point of sale (without purchase) or via U.S. mail. These free entries must be limited to the same number of entries that a person can make with purchase or via online registration or survey. If it's one entry per person for the entire promotion, this should be clearly stated. If consumers can enter once per day per person, then this too should be clearly stated. If instant win game pieces are being requested, the request should include a self-addressed, stamped envelope in which one free game piece is provided per envelope per person per day. Also, free entries should be available for the same period of time as the other method(s) of entering.

Regardless of how you structure your "free" alternate method of entry, it should be clearly stated and detailed information provided as to where to send the entry (or request) and how often this can be done.

13. Tax Liability

A statement should be made in the official rules that all taxes related to the prizes awarded are the sole responsibility of the winner. In this way, you cannot be held liable for paying the taxes for the prizes that you award to your winners.

14. Separate Addresses

In your official rules, you should have separate addresses for your alternate "free" write-in entries, winners' list requests, and official rules requests (if applicable). While this is not a legal requirement, it is important that each of these three functions be kept separate and unless you want to sort through all the mail and separate out entries from winners' list requests and requests for official rules, it's more efficient to have three separate Post Office boxes to handle the different kinds of requests.

These addresses should not be the same address as where you receive your orders or sales. Again, this is not a legal requirement, more a matter of logistics. If your promotion receives a large volume of mail, you may have a difficult time sorting out orders from promotions elements—each having its own time-sensitive requirements.

15. Reservation of Publicity Rights

If you plan on releasing the winners' names on your Web site or via a press release, it's a good idea to include a reservation of publicity rights in your official rules. In other words, by entering, a consumer agrees to allow the sponsor to use his or her name and likeness in advertising and publicity without additional compensation. This should also be in the affidavit of eligibility, but you have a stronger case if you also include this in your official rules in case a consumer refuses to go along with this and has to be disqualified. If the statement was not in the official rules, then a consumer can argue that he or she did not agree to this when entering the promotion and therefore cannot be disqualified by refusing to agree to this in the affidavit of eligibility. Remember, your official rules act as your contract with your consumers. The more you protect yourself up front, the fewer headaches you'll have at the conclusion of the promotion.

16. Deadline for the Receipt of Entries

Your promotion must have a deadline for the receipt of all entries *in addition to* the end date of the promotion. In the case of online entries, this is usually midnight (either Eastern Standard Time or your local time zone). But when you're dealing with the mail, you must provide a few extra days (usually five) for the mail to arrive. In other words, if the promotion ends on Friday, the 15th, an entry mailed on that day will not arrive until the following week. By setting a deadline for the receipt of entries, you remove your liability for problems with the mail.

With a deadline for the receipt of entries, you are not responsible for lost, misdirected, or late entries (also covered in the next section, Disclaimer of Sponsor's Liability). It's up to the consumers to get their entries in on time.

17. Disclaimer of Sponsor's Liability

Disclaimers are where you really attempt to cover yourself for all the potential problems that you can foresee with the promotion. As stated in the previous section, this will include things like not being responsible for lost, misdirected, or late entries due to problems with the mail. But you can also cover yourself for things like a Web server going down, the Internet backbone dropping its connection, the destruction of a database, hackers destroying entries, phone lines being disconnected, and a host of potential technical problems.

If you are running an instant win game, you can protect yourself against printing errors such as the printer mistakenly prints millions of "Congratulations, You're a Winner" messages instead of the "Sorry, Please Try Again" message.

The disclaimer of sponsor's liability is where you include every conceivable problem that could possibly go wrong with the promotion so that you will not be held liable if any such disasters occur. Remember, the liability issue does not mean the problems go away or that consumers will like your company any better if mistakes are made; it simply means you limit your liability from a legal perspective. Public relations and smart marketing are a whole other ball game.

18. Void Where Prohibited

Ah, yes, the real "catch phrase" in promotions. In other words, if this promotion is prohibited for some reason that we may or may not be aware of, then it is void according to the official rules. Not only is this an important part of the official rules, but it is a critical element to the abbreviated rules and disclaimers that are featured in all advertising and promotional-related copy on the Web site.

19. Tampering with Online Promotions

If someone hacks your online promotion, you not only want to void his or her entries, you also want to take legal action—so say that in your official rules. Put contestants on alert that if they mess with your online promotion, you will pursue legal action to the fullest extent. Not that this will stop someone who is determined to hack your online promotion, but you have provided a warning as part of your contract with consumers. Once you have identified who has tampered with your online promotion, you can then take legal action against them.

More important to the promotion itself, however, is your ability to take action once you have determined that someone has interfered with the integrity or fairness of the promotion. If you don't say what you can or will do at this point you are again sailing into uncharted waters. By identifying up front your intentions to suspend, modify, terminate, and/or cancel the promotion if the integrity of the promotion has been breached, you are within the boundaries of your own contract to take action if online tampering is suspected or has, in fact, occurred.

20. Dispute of an Email Address

What happens if two or more people use the same email address to enter your promotion? This could be problematic when attempting to award the prize *if you don't deal with this in your official rules*. One way to avoid this potential problem is to define in your official rules who will be deemed the legitimate owner of the email address and awarded the prize. The language usually used is "authorized account holder" and is defined as the person who is assigned the email address by an Internet Access Provider or other organization such as a business or school. You can further require proof of the status of the account holder at the time of entry.

Again, the more potential problems you can think of ahead of time, the better off you will be by covering them in your official rules.

Disclaimers and Abbreviated Rules

From your official rules, you will need to develop disclaimers for your television and radio spots. Disclaimers are the "short" version of the legal verbiage that is required when publicizing the promotion. While it would be unreasonable to expect that the entire commercial be made up of an announcer reading the full official rules on a radio spot, or showing the full official rules in a television ad, you are required to provide the bare minimum information so that interested consumers will know where to find the complete version of the official rules (and whether or not to bother doing so in the event that they are ineligible to enter).

While the specific language will change from promotion to promotion (and all disclaimers should be reviewed by legal counsel or your promotions agency), here is the basic foundation from which all disclaimers are built:

No purchase necessary: If the promotion is a sweepstakes, you must include the fact that no purchase is required—even if you are advertising entry with purchase. For example, "Look inside specially marked packages of XYZ product" can be the main message, but you must include the fact that no purchase is required to participate in the promotion.

Void where prohibited: You must make your audience aware that the promotion is not valid anywhere that it might be illegal. With broadcast, you don't always have the luxury of pinpointing your audience's location and must make this broad statement to protect yourself in the unlikely event that your promotion is prohibited for some reason. Also, if you are voiding any particular states (such as New York or Florida), this must be identified as well as any U.S. territories (such as Puerto Rico).

Eligibility requirements: Any eligibility requirements must be made clear. If a contestant must be 18 years of age or older to enter, then say so. If he or she must have Internet access prior to a specific date, then this must be identified. Anything that would prohibit someone from entering (or to be disqualified for entering) must be declared in the commercial.

Start and end dates: You must provide the time period for the promotion. In this way, you are not asking someone to participate in a promotion that has ended or hasn't started yet. This is especially important, as commercials don't always air when they are scheduled to do so. By having these dates in the disclaimers there is less chance that a consumer will mistakenly attempt to participate in a promotion that has ended or has not yet begun.

Subject to official rules: You need to alert consumers that there are more legal requirements than those being broadcast. Moreover, you must tell consumers where they can go to get a copy of the complete official rules. This is usually in the form of a Post Office box, but can sometimes be a URL link to the promotional Web page or (even better) the official rules Web page. When telling consumers to write in for official rules, be sure to provide the last date by which you will send them a copy of the official rules (usually a week prior to the end date).

Total prize value: You should also include the approximate value of your total prize package.

Usually, for print ads, you can include similar disclaimers, but most law firms and promotions agencies would recommend that you include abbreviated rules (unless your promotion includes Florida residents, in which case they'll insist on full rules). The difference between disclaimers and abbreviated rules is that abbreviated rules provide just a bit more information than disclaimers would. How much more? It depends on who you're talking to. In general, you would include all the information from the disclaimers above as well as the following:

How to enter: Usually with abbreviated rules you will provide the points of entry. This is usually part of the commercial itself, but in the fine print you include all methods of entry (write-in, online, in-store, for example). This would also include a statement about entry limit (such as one per person per day).

Odds of winning: This is usually a statement such as "odds of winning will depend on the number of entries received" unless the promotion is an instant win game where the actual odds of winning are known prior to the launch of the promotion.

Description of prizes: Again, with more room, you want to cover a bit more. Rather than just the total prize value, you would provide a brief description of the prize(s).

Winner selection and notification: This includes a statement about how winners will be selected and notified and the approximate dates when this will occur. This is also a good place to add the fact that winners must complete an affidavit and publicity release (and in what time frame) as well as limits of liability.

Official winners lists: Tell consumers when the list of official winners will be made available and how to get a copy (usually sending a self-addressed, stamped envelope to a separate Post Office box).

As I said, the exact language for each promotion will vary depending on the specifics of the promotion. If your promotion includes alcohol, there will be additional disclaimers to satisfy the legal requirements of alcohol promotions. If you are giving away a car or travel vacation as a prize, there are sometimes additional limits of liability statements that lawyers prefer to include.

Getting Professional Help

The information in this chapter should save you some time (and money), but I do not recommend using your own recipe for writing official rules or disclaimers without consulting a professional. Laws change and are constantly being reinterpreted based on decisions from court cases.

Don't be alarmed if all this is a bit overwhelming. The official rules and other legal verbiage are extremely important aspects of the promotion and should not be taken lightly. A common mistake that marketers make is to attempt to create or use a template for official rules and/or disclaimers. This is a big mistake, as each set of rules and legal copy requires its own verbiage that is tailored to the specific promotion. While there will be similarities between promotions, new legislation beyond your control may require that new language is added or old language be modified to work within existing legislation or recent rulings.

In the next chapter, I will help you determine if your in-house resources are sufficient or if you should seek outside resources and for what specific areas. I will also make recommendations on the best resources to use for getting professional help. This book is meant to help you better understand the different aspects of online promotion, *not replace* your law firm or promotions agency.

Cautions for Legal Compliance

In addition to the official rules and legal disclaimers, there are general principles and practices that should be noted to protect yourself and your company online. This section will cover these specific areas that are not necessarily associated with the official rules of a promotion, but which can have a significant legal impact. When you combine these principles and practices with a good set of official rules, you will be well on your way to protecting yourself and your company when conducting online promotions.

Avoid Deception

This should be obvious, but deception is still a huge complaint by regulators and consumers with respect to promotions (online or off). States are cracking down on companies that put out false or misleading statements and have started to legislate very specific requirements for the kinds of things that can be said—especially in the world of direct mail. It's sad that government bodies have had to put into legislation things like you can't tell someone he or she is a winner if he or she is not a winner. That would seem to be common sense, but Publishers Clearing

House and American Family Publishers have been accused of (and have been sued for damages over) sending misleading direct mail to consumers.

You can't use words like "Official Sweepstakes Notification" if it isn't. You can't say things like "Congratulations, Bill Carmody, You've Won $10 Million" in 48-point type and then in 8-point type say, "That's what we'll say if you return your sweepstakes entry and it has the grand-prize-winning number." This is deceptive and misleading, and you shouldn't do it. If you do, not only will you get into trouble with the government but you will also experience a ton of negative publicity and/or negative word-of-mouth discussions from your consumers who are duped into believing they've won something when they really haven't.

Sweepstakes are a powerful marketing tool, but when you abuse the tool, government regulators and consumer advocacy groups will come down hard and make you regret, retract, and pay for any misleading statements you made. Deception may help short-term profits, but will destroy your long-term credibility as a respectable company (not to mention your long-term profitability).

Use of the Word *Free*

When you use the word *free* in conjunction with your promotion, you subject yourself to special regulations. Specifically, you must disclose the exact terms by which a consumer will get something for free in immediate proximity to the word *free* and in the same prominence and no less than half the size. Very few people still believe in the concept of a free lunch, and those few remaining do not include state regulators. When you say something's free, there is almost always a catch such as "Buy one, get one free," or "Sign up for a year's worth of service, and get something free." These catches must be crystal clear or you will be in violation of many states' statutes regarding the use of the word *free*.

If there are limitations on the frequency or duration of the free item or offer, these limitations and time limits must also be disclosed. There are many other restrictions applicable to using words like "free" so be sure to consult your legal counsel or promotions agency when embarking on a "free" offer promotion.

Equitable Means of Entry

Your methods of entry must be equitable. That is, there can be no discrimination between people who purchase your product, become members of your site, fill out the survey, and so on, and those who simply write in and take advantage of the "free" method of entry. If consumers can purchase unlimited products, then there can be an unlimited amount of write-in entries. Most companies want to limit the number of entries per consumer, so this limit must be across all methods of entry. The point is that consumers must not feel that they will have better odds of winning if they purchase a product or jump through a bunch of hoops. More than the perception, the reality of equitable means of entry must be true. If the people who purchase your products have a better chance of winning because there is an element of consideration in your promotion, then it quickly becomes an illegal lottery rather than a chance promotion. By providing equitable means of entry, there is no discrimination between the methods of entry and therefore, the "no purchase necessary" requirement is upheld.

Investigation of Official Winners

For smaller prizes, an affidavit of eligibility should suffice. But if you are planning on announcing the grand prize winners with some publicity, it would behoove you to do some additional checking to make sure that your winner is not a convicted felon or someone who could embarrass the company. This can be accomplished with simple character references from friends and family members, or a more comprehensive background check can be completed by a private investigator.

Just because the person turns out not to be a desirable winner doesn't mean you can disqualify him or her. (You must adhere to your own official rules.) But, knowing up front that publicizing the winner could cause more problems than goodwill for the company can be quite advantageous. The caution here for legal compliance is not to break any privacy rules or laws when investigating the winners. There are plenty of public records that will tell the story of your winner. It's not worth an illegal investigation that will come back to haunt you.

Enforcement

Lottery laws are criminal statutes. Breaking these laws risks the penalty of both fines and imprisonment. A common mistake is to assume that a company will "get away with it" because consumers will not care enough (or know enough) to report a violation. This simply isn't true. Consumers who feel duped or misled tend to go out of their way to correct the injustice. Life isn't fair, but when consumers feel that they have been lied to or cheated, they will do everything in their power to make it right.

Besides, even if your consumers do not report the violation, don't you think your competitors will? Think of your own marketing department. Part of its job is to check out the competition and see what they're doing. If you noticed they were doing something illegal, it would only take a phone call to tip off government regulators and make their lives much more difficult. Competition is fierce. It's not smart to assume that cutting corners will go unnoticed when it comes to online promotions. And when it comes to the legal aspects of online promotions, the risk is definitely *not* worth the potential reward of a little time or cost savings.

International Promotions and Foreign Laws

The Internet is virtually worldwide, so shouldn't your online promotions be? Not really. In the world of online promotion, it's best to stick to the old saying "When in Rome, do as the Romans do." Each country has its own government, its own laws, and its own regulatory practices that affect online promotion. In Canada, for example, sweepstakes *are illegal*—all sweepstakes, not just certain types. Contests, on the other hand, are acceptable (at least for the most part). So to legally

Figure 4.2 Promoting overseas—what's legal and what's not. (By permission *PROMO Magazine*)

COUNTRY	PREMIUMS	HOME-DELIV. COUPONS	MAIL-DELIV. COUPONS	GAMES	CONTESTS	SWEEPS	REBATES/ REFUNDS	GIFT W/ PURCHASE	DATABASE MARKETING	PRODUCT SAMPLING
Argentina	Legal	Not in use.	Not in use.	Legal	Legal (if proof of purchase is required, free option must be fixed)	Legal	Legal	Legal	Legal	Legal
Australia	Legal	Legal, but third parties cannot put together coupon books or coupons from groups of companies.	Legal, but third parties cannot put together coupon books or coupons from groups of companies.	Legal	Legal	Permit sometimes required. All states require compliance with special laws.	Legal	Legal	Legal, but state privacy laws shortly anticipated.	Legal, except therapeutics.
Belgium	Legal, but with many restrictions. Value may not exceed 5% of the main product value.	Legal	Legal	Legal, but not when linked with purchase.	Legal, but not when linked with purchase.	Usually not allowed.	Legal, but with many restrictions and conditions.	Legal, but with many restrictions and conditions.	Legal	Legal
Brazil	Legal, very popular.	Legal, but not popular.	Legal, but not popular.	Legal, very popular. If requiring purchase or based on chance, approval from Consumer Defense Dept. required.	Legal, very popular. If requiring purchase or based on chance, approval from Consumer Defense Dept. required.	Legal, very popular. If requiring purchase or based on chance, approval from Consumer Defense Dept. required.	Legal, but not popular.	Legal, popular.	Legal, very popular. Mail must be discontinued at receiver's request.	Legal, very popular.
Chile	Legal	Not in use.	Not in use.	Legal	Legal	Legal	All consumers must have the same discount based on volume bought.	Legal	Legal, but consumers can request to have names removed from database.	Legal
Colombia	Legal	Legal	Legal	Legal, but games based on chance or luck require authorization.	Legal, but contests based on chance or luck require authorization.	Legal, but sweeps based on chance or luck require authorization.	Legal, but not popular.	Legal	Legal	Legal
England	Legal	Legal	Legal	Subject to compliance with Lotteries & Amusements Act.	Subject to compliance with Lotteries & Amusements Act.	Subject to compliance with Lotteries & Amusements Act. Free prize draws & instant win may allow free entry.	Legal	Legal	Legal	Legal, but some restrictions on alcohol, tobacco, medicines, solvents and some foods.
Finland	Legal, if gift has small value or there is an evident material connection between the goods or services offered.	Legal, except coupons having a combined offer or connected to purchase, or containing illegal sweeps or lotteries.	Legal, except coupons having a combined offer or connected to purchase, or containing illegal sweeps or lotteries.	Legal, when based on skill, purchase can be required. When based on chance, free method of entry is required.	Legal, when based on skill, purchase can be required. When based on chance, free method of entry is required.	Legal, when based on skill, purchase can be required. When based on chance, free method of entry is required.	Legal	Legal, if gift has small value or there is an evident material connection between the goods or services offered.	Legal, with many restrictions.	Legal, some restrictions.
France	Legal, if gift has a very small value or is identical to the good purchased. Usually not allowed when the premium is free.	Legal, but only when offering discount on same product. Cross coupons forbidden.	Legal, but only when offering discount on same product. Cross coupons forbidden.	Legal, but must be absolutely free and not connected to a purchase.	Legal, but prize promotion must be skill, absolutely free, and not connected to a purchase.	Legal, but must be absolutely free and not connected to a purchase.	Legal	Legal, if gift has a very small value or is identical to the good purchased. Usually not allowed when the premium is free.	Legal	Legal
Germany	Buy one get one free not allowed.	Legal, only for product samples. Price-off coupons not allowed.	Legal, only for product samples. Price-off coupons not allowed.	Legal, mechanics must be checked before practiced.	Legal, mechanics must be checked before practiced.	Legal, should be checked with lawyer.	Legal, only to 3% maximum.	Usually not allowed. Some small-value give-aways are allowed, lawyers usually can find a way around the law.	Legal, but consumer must consent first.	Usually legal when only samples are used. No regular or original retail products.
Holland	Legal	Legal	Legal	Prize value not to exceed US$2,500. Regulations currently under review.	Prize value not to exceed US$2,500. Regulations currently under review.	Prize value not to exceed US$2,500. Regulations currently under review.	Rebates - Legal. Refunds - price restrictions.	Legal	Legal, with some restrictions. Consumer can request to have name removed from database.	Legal, except for alcohol, drugs and pharmaceuticals.

ON-PACK PREMIUMS	ON-PACK COUPONS	IN-PACK PREMIUMS	IN-PACK COUPONS	NEAR-PACK PREMIUMS	SELF-LIQUID. PREMIUMS	BONUS PACKS	FREE IN THE MAIL	CONTINUITY/ LOYALTY	PHONECARDS	FREQ. SHOP. CARDS
Legal	Not in use.	Legal	Not in use.	Legal	Legal	Legal	Not in use.	Legal	Not in use.	Legal
Legal	Legal, third party trading stamps not a problem.	Legal	Legal	Legal	Legal, but exact nature of offer must be revealed (closing date, # of proofs required, etc.)	Legal, but some packaging restrictions.	Legal, except therapeutics, alcohol, cigarettes.	Legal, but many restrictions.	Legal	Legal
Legal, but with many restrictions.	Legal, but only when offering discount on same product. Cross coupons forbidden.	Legal, but with many restrictions.	Legal, but only when offering discount on same product. Cross coupons forbidden.	Legal, but with many restrictions.	Legal, but with many restrictions.	Legal, but with many restrictions.	Legal	Legal	Legal	Legal
Legal, popular.	Legal, but not popular.	Legal, popular.	Legal, but not popular.	Legal, but not popular.	Legal, popular.	Legal, very popular.	Legal, but not popular.	Legal, popular.	Legal, but not popular.	Legal, popular.
Legal	Not in use.	Legal	Not in use.	Legal	Legal	Legal	Legal	Legal	Legal	Legal
Legal	Legal	Legal	Legal	Legal	Legal	Legal	Legal	Legal	Legal	Legal
Legal	Legal	Legal	Legal	Legal	Legal	Legal	Legal	Legal	Legal	Legal
Legal, if gift has small value or there is an evident material connection between the goods or services offered. Restriction when directed to children.	Legal, if the good being offered free or at a discount has very small value and there is an evident material connection between the goods and services offered.	Legal, if gift has small value or there is an evident material connection between the goods or services offered. Restriction when directed to children.	Legal, if the good being offered free or at a discount has very small value and there is an evident material connection between the goods and services offered.	Legal, if gift has small value or there is an evident material connection between the goods or services offered. Restriction when directed to children.	Not in use.	Legal, as long as offer is not connected to a purchase.	Legal, as long as offer is not connected to a purchase.	Legal	Legal, but not in use.	Legal, as long as offer does not contain illegal benefits.
Legal, if gift has a very small value or is identical to the good purchased. Usually not allowed when the premium is free.	Legal but only when offering discount on same product. Cross coupons forbidden.	Legal, if gift has a very small value or is identical to the good purchased. Usually not allowed when the premium is free.	Legal but only when offering discount on same product. Cross coupons forbidden.	Legal, if gift has a very small value or is identical to the good purchased. Usually not allowed when the premium is free.	Legal	Legal	Legal, if gift has a very small value or is identical to the good purchased. Usually not allowed when the premium is free.	Legal	Legal, if gift has a very small value or is identical to the good purchased. Usually not allowed when the premium is free.	Legal
Usually not allowed.	Retailers cannot make price reductions. Consumers must collect an on-pack code and mail it directly to the manufacturer.	Usually not allowed.	Usually not allowed, must be checked with a lawyer in every case.	Usually not allowed.	Legal	Legal, but many restrictions. Must be checked with a lawyer in every case.	Usually not allowed.	No special refunds except a maximum discount of 3% when paying with cash.	Legal, but can't be combined with purchase.	Legal, members can buy exclusive offers. Advantages such as reduced prices only for members are not allowed.
Legal	Legal	Legal	Legal	Legal	Legal	Legal	Legal	Legal, with some restrictions. Must conform with the Privacy Law.	Legal	Legal

continues

Figure 4.2 *(Continued)*

COUNTRY	PREMIUMS	HOME-DELIV. COUPONS	MAIL-DELIV. COUPONS	GAMES	CONTESTS	SWEEPS	REBATES/ REFUNDS	GIFT W/ PURCHASE	DATABASE MARKETING	PRODUCT SAMPLING
Hungary	Legal, but only used between trade companies.	Legal, usually used in connection with fragile or large products.	Legal, must contain information as to where the advertiser's office is located.	Legal, must get approval from Gambling Supervision.	Legal, must get approval from Gambling Supervision.	Legal, must get approval from Gambling Supervision.	Legal, but only used between trade companies.	Legal, as long as gift has a very small value.	Legal, consumers can request to have names removed from database.	Legal, except pharmaceuticals, tobacco, alcohol, weapons or explosives.
Ireland	Legal	Legal	Legal	Legal, if based on chance free entry required. If winner is determined by skill, purchase can be required.	Legal, if based on chance free entry required. If winner is determined by skill, purchase can be required.	Legal, but purchase cannot be required.	Legal	Legal	Legal	Legal, but tobacco is prohibited.
Israel	Legal	Legal, but not popular.	Legal, but not popular.	Legal, but proof of purchase may be required.	Legal, but proof of purchase may be required.	Legal, 180 days must be between each sweeps from the same company.	Legal, but not popular.	Legal	Legal, but can't use private data such as credit card, bank, healthcare info, etc.	Legal
Italy	Legal, 20% tax on prize value. Government notification required.	Legal	Legal	Legal, 45% tax on prize value. Government notification required.	Legal, 45% tax on prize value. Government notification required.	Legal, 45% tax on prize value. Government notification required.	Illegal	Legal, 20% tax on prize value. Government notification required.	Legal, but with use of personal data, written permission of consumer required.	Legal
Japan	Legal, but very strict restrictions apply.	Legal	Legal	Legal, but very strict restrictions apply.	Legal	Legal, but very strict restrictions apply.	Legal	Legal, but very strict restrictions apply.	Legal	Legal, except medicine.
Malaysia	Legal	Legal	Legal	Legal, but prize promotion must be skill, not chance.	Legal, but prize promotion must be skill, not chance.	Illegal	Legal	Legal	Legal	Legal, except alcohol, cigarettes, to Muslims.
Mexico	Legal	Legal	Legal	Legal	Legal	Legal	Legal	Legal	Legal	Legal
New Zealand	Legal	Legal	Legal	Legal	Legal	Legal	Legal, with restrictions.	Legal	Legal, but protected by consumer privacy act.	Legal
Poland	Legal	Legal	Legal	Legal, but games of chance restricted by Law on Games of Chance & Mutual Bets.	Legal, but games of chance restricted by Law on Games of Chance & Mutual Bets.	Legal, but restricted by Law on Games of Chance & Mutual Bets.	Legal, but rebates are not in use.	Legal	Legal, but significantly limited by the Law on Protection of Personal Data.	Legal, except pharmaceuticals and alcoholic beverages.
Singapore	Legal	Legal	Legal	Legal, may require permission from authorities.	Legal, may require permission from authorities.	Legal, with many restrictions, and may require permission from authorities.	Legal	Legal	Legal	Legal
Spain	Legal, but you must ask for permission.	Legal, but you must ask for permission.	Legal, but you must ask for permission.	Legal, you must register with the government.	Legal, you must register with the government.	Legal, you must register with the government.	Legal, you must register with the government.	Legal, some restrictions.	Legal, you must register database with data protection agency.	Legal
Sweden	Legal, but exact details of offer must be revealed (closing date, conditions, value, etc.).	Legal, with some restrictions. Illegal to send to persons under age 16. Restrictions when sending to parent of newborns, relatives of deceased persons.	Legal, with some restrictions. Illegal to send to persons under age 16. Restrictions when sending to parent of newborns, relatives of deceased persons.	Legal, but government permit required.	Legal, but promotion must be skill, not chance. Some restrictions to connect to a purchase. Exact details of offer must be revealed (closing date, conditions, value, etc.).	Legal, but promotion must be skill, not chance. Some restrictions to connect to a purchase. Exact details of offer must be revealed (closing date, conditions, value, etc.).	Legal, but exact details of offer must be revealed (closing date, conditions, value, etc.).	Legal, but exact details of offer must be revealed (closing date, conditions, value, etc.).	Legal, with some restrictions and a permit to maintain list. The marketing offer must state where the address was obtained.	Legal
United States	Legal, but all material terms and conditions must be disclosed.	Legal, with restrictions on alcohol, tobacco, drugs.	Legal, with restrictions on alcohol, tobacco, drugs.	Legal, but on-pack games subject to certain restrictions.	Legal, some states prohibit requiring consideration. Bona fide skill must dominate and control final result. Various state disclosure requirements.	Legal, no consideration. Significant disclosure requirements by states. Some states prohibit everybody wins, direct mail sweeps subject to stringent disclosure requirements.	Legal, must not be coupons.	Legal, but cost of gift may not be built into cost of purchased product.	Legal, consumers may request to have name removed from industry, state, and company lists.	Legal, with restrictions on alcohol, tobacco, drugs and some agricultural products.
Venezuela	Legal, some restrictions when with food. Must register with the government.	Legal, but only in use by very few retailers.	Legal, but only in use by very few retailers.	Legal, must register with the government.	Legal, must register with the government.	Legal, must register with the government.	Legal	Legal, some restrictions when with food. Must register with the government.	Legal	Legal, except cigarettes and alcohol to minors. Must register with the government. Some restrictions when with food.

ON-PACK PREMIUMS	ON-PACK COUPONS	IN-PACK PREMIUMS	IN-PACK COUPONS	NEAR-PACK PREMIUMS	SELF-LIQUID. PREMIUMS	BONUS PACKS	FREE IN THE MAIL	CONTINUITY/ LOYALTY	PHONECARDS	FREQ. SHOP. CARDS
Not in use.	Not in use.	Not in use.	Not in use.	Not in use.	Illegal	Not in use.	Legal, except pharmaceuticals, tobacco, alcohol, weapons or explosives.	Not in use.	Legal for use as a surface for advertising, very popular. If used as a credit card, many restrictions.	Legal, not very popular.
Legal	Legal	Legal	Legal	Legal	Legal	Legal	Legal	Legal	Legal	Legal
Legal	Legal, but not popular.	Legal	Legal, but not popular.	Legal	Legal	Legal	Legal	Legal	Legal, but not popular.	Legal
Legal, 20% tax on prize value. Government notification required.	Legal	Legal, 20% tax on prize value. Government notification required.	Legal, but cross coupons not permitted; 20% tax on redeemed value of coupon.	Legal, 20% tax on prize value. Government notification required.	Legal, but price of purchase must be more than price of base product alone.	Legal	Legal	Legal, 20% tax on prize value. Government notification required.	Legal, 20% tax on prize value. Government notification required.	Legal, 20% tax on prize value. Government notification required.
Legal, but very strict restrictions apply.	Legal	Legal, but very strict restrictions apply.	Legal	Not in use	Legal, but very strict restrictions apply.	Legal, but very strict restrictions apply.	Legal	Legal, but very strict restrictions apply.	Legal	Legal, but very strict restrictions apply.
Legal	Legal	Legal, must comply with safety requirements.	Legal	Legal	Legal	Legal	Legal	Legal	Legal	Legal
Legal	Legal	Legal	Legal	Legal	Legal	Legal	Legal	Legal	Legal	Legal
Legal	Legal	Legal	Legal	Legal	Legal	Legal	Legal	Legal	Legal	Legal
Legal	Legal, not in use.	Legal	Legal, not in use.	Legal	Legal	Legal	Not in use.	Legal	Not in use.	Legal
Legal	Legal	Legal	Legal	Legal	Legal	Legal	Legal	Legal	Legal	Legal
Legal, some restrictions.	Legal, you need permission from data protection agency.	Legal, some restrictions.	Legal, you need permission from data protection agency.	Legal, some restrictions.	Legal	Legal, some restrictions.	Legal	Legal, you need permission from data protection agency.	Legal	Legal, you must register database with data protection agency.
Legal	Legal	Legal	Legal	Legal	Legal	Legal	Legal	Legal	Legal	Legal
Legal, with restrictions on alcohol, tobacco, drugs. Premium must be appropriate to targeted age group. Certain restrictions apply to premiums directed to children.	Legal, but all material terms must be disclosed. There must be a minimum six-month redemption period.	Legal, with restrictions on alcohol, tobacco, drugs. Premium must be appropriate to targeted age group. Certain restrictions apply to premiums directed to children.	Legal, but all material terms must be disclosed. There must be a minimum six-month redemption period.	Legal	Legal	Legal	Legal, unordered merchandise considered free gift.	Legal, but all terms and conditions must be clearly disclosed and consumer expressly consents to join plan.	Legal, cannot be used to change customers' long distance service without written authorization.	Legal
Legal, must register with the government.	Not in use.	Legal, some sanitary restrictions when with food. Must register with the government.	Not in use.	Legal, some restrictions when with food. Must register with the government.	Legal, some restrictions when with food. Must register with the government.	Legal, some restrictions when with food. Must register with the government.	Legal, but not very common. Some restrictions when with food. Must register with the government.	Legal, but not very common. Some restrictions when with food. Must register with the government.	Not in use.	Legal, but not very common. Some restrictions when with food. Must register with the government.

have an online sweepstakes in Canada, a skill-based question must be asked (more as a formality than anything else) if a Canadian resident is selected as a winner. Also, did you know that if your online promotion includes Quebec residents, the entire promotion must be made available in French? Or that you must pay a fee to the Reggie de Lotteries for the province of Quebec?

I am only scratching the surface to be sure. Every country has its own rules that your online promotion must adhere to in order to be legal. Official rules written in the United States will not necessarily meet the requirements of every other country. There are tons of potential pitfalls that you can unknowingly lead your company into, and they are different for each country.

That said, there are different risks depending on the size and location of your company. If you own your own business and are running it off your laptop in the second bedroom of your house, then your liabilities are much less than a company like IBM with offices in 72 countries (approximately). While IBM must face the fact that it has offices in several different countries where the local government can literally shut them down for violations in an online promotion, a start-up company with barely an official office space risks being barred from doing business in that country (and possibly extradition if the office is significant enough). In other words, big companies with multiple locations outside the United States have much more to worry about than their smaller counterparts, but there *are* risks involved for both.

Country-Specific Guidelines

In the August 1998 issue of *PROMO Magazine*, Douglas Wood and Linda Goldstein, two partners in the New York City law firm Hall Dickler Kent Friedman & Wood published an article called, "A Lawyer's Guide to Going Global." It is by far the most useful article I have ever read in *PROMO Magazine* and I'm not just saying that because Linda Goldstein is a personal friend. I keep a copy of their four-page chart on my wall that outlines "What's Legal and What's Not" internationally.

This chart is shown in Figure 4.2. While this chart is somewhat dated, it is the only resource that I know of that is this comprehensive in nature. This will give you an idea of just how complex international promotions can be. If international promotions are critical to your Internet strategy, I recommend seeking out country-specific legal counsel, or the support of a company like Hall Dickler Kent Friedman & Wood, to get country-specific legal counsel on your behalf.

Translating Your Promotions into Multiple Languages

In addition to all the legal aspects covered in the previous section, there is the practical issue that your international consumers do not all speak and read English. If you are truly attempting to attract international consumers to your online promotions, it would be a wise move to get your international promotions translated into the appropriate language most widely used in the country you are targeting. This shows that you are interested in attracting consumers living outside the United States and are willing to take the steps necessary to market to them *in their own language*.

The challenge is keeping this translation all the way through the promotion and including multiple languages in the responses to email questions and in general support. The key is to weigh the overall costs of going international with the benefits of increased participation. Translation is a big cost consideration in addition to the international legal clearance of the official rules and legal disclaimers. As these factors are weighed on a country-by-country basis, many online promotions stay inside the United States or travel outside only to key international markets.

Avoiding Cultural Blunders

The one caveat to translation is that you should make sure that you have checks and balances built into your conversion from English to other languages. Some of the most famous case studies in international cultural blunders occurred as a direct result of translation mistakes. These include the Chevy "Nova" automobile, which translates to "No Go" in Spanish. Without knowing this, Chevy marketed its car in Mexico without much success. Purdue Chicken had an advertising slogan, "It takes a tough man to make a tender chicken," which was badly translated to "It takes a sexually erotic man to make a chicken affectionate." The phonetic translation of Coca Cola in Japan literally meant, "Bite the wax tadpole." We learn about these cultural blunders in our international marketing classes, but the key is not to become the next case study.

To avoid translation errors, it's a good idea to have different companies (ideally) or at least different people write and review the translations. With more than one person or a group of people working on the translations, there is less chance of a major cultural blunder. It also helps to include some native speakers from the countries you are targeting to ensure that the language used would be the best choice for the region.

Conclusion

This chapter provided information on privacy and security issues as well as a comprehensive look at the legal aspects of online promotions. While you may not be able to pass the bar exam and get your law degree, this chapter should serve as a solid foundation from which to build your online promotions. Regardless of how well you understand the legal aspects of online promotions, it is a good idea to work with either a promotions agency or outside law firm to review the legal aspects of your online promotions. Even if you're confident that you've followed all the right steps to protect yourself and your company online, it never hurts to get a second (outside) opinion.

One hundred percent security is an illusion. By the very nature of human involvement with the security aspects of an online program, security itself can never be completely foolproof. People make mistakes. The key is to find the best ways to eliminate potential human error and supplement these security policies and procedures with the right hardware and software solutions that meet your security needs. An ethical hacker is a security expert who has been trained in the art of hacking, but has chosen to put his or her knowledge to good use. Ethical hackers can help find security holes and make recommendations on the best ways to fill these holes.

There are three basic principles to keep yourself and your company out of trouble: Know the laws, stay within them, and expect the unexpected. The legal aspects of online promotions can be quite daunting at first glance, but after a few promotions have been completed with the help of a good promotions agency or outside legal partner, the legal aspects become clear (and somewhat straightforward). Sweepstakes and contests each have their own registration requirements, which must be closely followed to avoid fines and other potential problems.

Just because the Internet is international doesn't mean your online promotions should be. Each country has its own government, its own laws, and its own regulatory practices that affect online promotion. While a country-specific guideline was provided in this chapter, you are strongly urged to seek support from international promotions experts before jumping into online promotions that are open to countries outside the United States. In addition to the legal challenges, most international promotions also require translation and a solid awareness of cultural differences to be successful (and to avoid cultural blunders).

With all these requirements still fresh in your mind, we move to the next chapter, where we will review the pros and cons of outsourcing versus using your in-house resources to plan, produce, execute, and measure your online promotions. There are definite advantages and disadvantages to both, so the key is to understand what works best when.

Outsourcing versus In-house Resources

Should you build an online promotion *internally* or *seek outside help*? That is the question we will address in this chapter. Whether it is better to save a few bucks by using your in-house talent or to send the project to outside experts for new ideas or to save time and minimize risk, this chapter will help you decide what makes the most sense for your particular situation. I will start off with some common questions you can ask yourself to see if you have the right in-house resources you'll need. If not, I will show you the best way to find the resources you need and how to determine the best fit.

In addition to providing information on how to find and interview resources, this chapter will cover the difficult topic of when and how to fire your promotions agency should the need arise. And finally, I will outline the specific areas that you need to cover should you decide to start your own in-house promotions group.

The overarching issue of keeping projects in house versus outsourcing tends to be a sensitive area for most companies regardless of size or the number of years in business. Companies as large as Coca Cola have spanned both extremes; at one point, it created virtually all its marketing and promotions in house, while at a different phase of the company's life cycle, it outsourced just about everything. I use the symbol of the Ying Yang to represent the balance between both of these perspectives (see Figure 5.1). And, as you will see, it is the balance between both extremes that most companies strive to maintain.

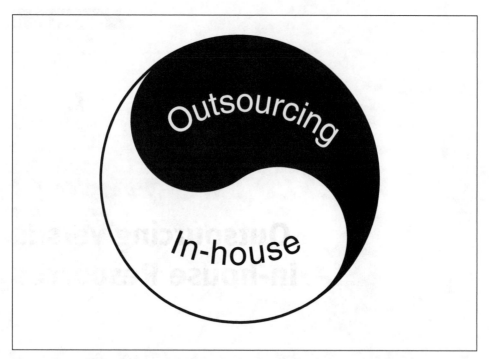

Figure 5.1 Striking a balance between outsourcing and in-house resources.

Without skipping too far ahead, I bring up the concept of balance because, in my opinion, life is more about balance than about absolutes. While most of us strive for perfection, we learn early on that perfection is impossible to achieve. What does this have to do with online promotions? Everything. There is no perfect solution to any given problem—there are usually numerous solutions, each of which will address certain aspects of the problem better than the others. The trick is to find the solution that works best for you.

There will be times when outsourcing entire projects will be the best solution, other times when outsourcing only part of the project is ideal, and still other times when the best thing to do is to keep the project completely in house. While this chapter help you find answers to questions like "Do we need to staff up more or get more suppliers?", my recommendation is to seek the best solution for *each* online promotion that you are planning. Even with the best possible in-house resources, there will be times when outsourcing will be critical to finding a new perspective. Conversely, there will be times when it is completely inefficient to outsource a project, and you may need to hire in-house talent that you don't currently have. *Seeking balance* will help you avoid the frustrations of taking only one side or the other and attempting to force every online promotion to fit a high-level directive to either work in-house or outsource. So when you read this chapter, please try to keep an open mind. When you catch yourself gravitating to one view or another, try to remember balance—there are situations when the opposite preference is the best choice.

When to Call a Promotional Marketing Agency

From the title of this section, it may appear that I'm already starting out biased. Please be assured that this is not my intent. The fact that I have my own integrated (online and offline) marketing and promotions agency does not mean that I think every online promotion requires calling in the experts. You may be surprised to learn that I have turned away business and recommended to potential clients that they handle their own online promotion. I believe that if you make the right recommendations to your clients (even if it means not getting the business), you will be rewarded with the more valuable long-term relationships that most agencies seek.

That said, there are some initial questions that can help you identify the basic resources needed for your online promotions and help you decide if your in-house resources will satisfy those needs or not. I have broken online promotions down into the following 10 categories:

1. Strategy

2. Legal

3. Technical

4. Creative

5. Media

6. Partnerships

7. Customer support

8. Administration

9. Fulfillment

10. Research/analysis

Each category has its own requirements, so let's take a look at them individually and review the pros and cons of keeping each category in-house or outsourcing it to the right partner.

Strategy

While each of the 10 aspects of online promotions is important, I believe that the right strategy is a cut above the rest. The right strategy for your online promotions comes from a combination of knowledge and experience. *Knowledge* includes the facts and research that have been gathered in support of the online promotion objective. *Experience* is having tried different online promotions to see what works best in a given situation. While each online promotion is different, the right knowledge and experience will guide you to make the best decisions and to create the correct strategy that will ultimately satisfy the promotion's objective.

Your strategy is more than just the "brains" behind the online promotion. Your strategy incorporates both the strengths of your company and the current events that are affecting the market. When the right strategy is used to meet the online promotional objective, success is nearly guaranteed. Conversely, the wrong strategy usually becomes apparent the minute the online promotion is launched. While strategies can be tweaked somewhat after the online promotion has launched, the core strategy will ultimately make or break the promotion and cannot be easily changed or adapted once the promotion has launched.

Keeping Strategy In-house

With something as important as strategy, you might think it should be completed internally. On the one hand, no one knows your products or the competitive environment in which you compete better than you do. But, on the other hand, you may be too close to your products to be able to see them clearly. You might not agree with the perceptions of your customers and, inadvertently, dispute or ignore the research that is gathered. Or your perceptions may be accurate, but you may not have any "fresh" ideas. When you've tested various online promotions, you may know "what works" but may have a difficult time coming up with a new way to keep "what works" appealing to your customers.

Pros

You are in the best position to know your products and the industry. No one lives and breathes the day-to-day challenges of your industry as much as you do (except for the competition).

You know the political environment of your company and can work within the boundaries defined by its leaders. No time will be lost educating outside resources about the company itself and its long-term goals and objectives (that is, outside of the specific online promotion).

Learning opportunity. By keeping the brain trust in-house, you (and your employees) will become online promotions experts over time and will eventually have enough experience to know what works and what doesn't.

Cost. Money is saved by not retaining an outside agency to develop the online promotional strategy.

Speed to market. Sometimes it's faster to come up with the strategy internally and avoid the time necessary to educate an outside agency on the problems you are facing (depending on the complexity of the problems and complexity of your industry).

Cons

You may be too close to your products. You might know what you *want* your customers to believe about your products, but your perceptions may not be in synch with the marketplace.

You may lack the experience necessary to create an effective strategy. If online promotions is not your area of expertise, you will stumble through trial and error before you discover what really works to satisfy your objectives.

You might suffer from "Been There, Done That" syndrome. If all your online promotions ideas look the same, then it may be time to get a fresh perspective.

You may be penny-wise and pound-foolish. If saving money on the strategy results in a less than effective online promotion, more money is ultimately lost than saved.

Outsourcing the Strategy

Does this idea appeal to you or make you cringe? While most can envision outsourcing almost every other aspect of online promotions, there is either a sense of pride or guilt attached to the strategy component. For some, the idea of outsourcing the strategy gives a feeling of relief—"It's okay, I can outsource strategy and still maintain control." Others go into a flurry of justification, feeling threatened if outside thoughts are solicited.

When your focus is laser-sharp, you tend to see only the tree in front of you and not the entire forest by which you are surrounded. Soliciting outside resources to help you come up with strategic recommendations should not be viewed as a weakness, but a strength. By recognizing that you may be too close to a project or the industry to come up with the best strategy, you allow yourself to step back and take a broader look at the problem. Even if your outside vendors do not come back with something earth-shattering, the act of taking a step back and looking at the problem from a different angle will certainly provide you with long-term value.

Pros

Fresh perspective. Outside agencies and resources can often come up with ideas that you might not have because you are too close to the problem.

Experience. Agencies that are dedicated to coming up with strategies that work for their clients have lots of experience upon which they can draw to help solve your problem. Perhaps a similar online promotion that worked in a different industry might be applicable to your specific problem. While it's new to your industry, it may be "tried-and-true" elsewhere.

No baggage. By starting with a blank slate, outside resources will come up with their best ideas without the constraints that you may knowingly or unknowingly place upon yourself or your company.

Time savings. By relying on an outside source for strategy, you may avoid the time associated with developing the strategy internally—especially if your products and industry are *not* overly complex or do not require a lot of background and education.

Cons

   Lack of product-specific or industry-specific knowledge. Outside
   agencies will require additional research and understanding about your
   specific industry and products. This may be a significant disadvantage if
   your products and industry are difficult to understand.

   **Opportunity for internal brain trust is lost when an outside agency is
   relied on**. While knowledge will be gained from the ultimate strategy that
   is conceived, the act of not coming up with this strategy internally may
   mean slower growth for the internal team.

   Cost. The cost of retaining an outside agency may not be feasible based on
   internal budget parameters.

Recommendation

Since your strategy is one of the most critical aspects of your online promotion,
evaluate the pros and cons and identify opportunities to experiment with both.
Perhaps hire an outside agency to help you determine your overall strategy and
then hire in-house resources to apply the recommended strategies to specific promotions. Or maybe the reverse makes more sense for your industry. Overall, you
must determine if your needs gravitate toward a fresh perspective or internal
experimentation.

   Oftentimes, this corresponds with your company's current life-cycle phase (see
Figure 5.2). If, for example, you are part of a start-up organization, you may not
have the financial resources available to hire outside consultants and instead need
to develop an internal brain trust. Alternatively, at the growth phase you have
plenty of money, but not enough internal resources (or new ideas), to meet the
demand. When the company reaches its maturity, in-house resources may be all
that is needed for ongoing maintenance marketing. When a decline becomes obvious, a fresh perspective from an outside agency may help you get back on track.

Legal

"I'm not a lawyer, but I play one on the Web." Sound familiar? The legal aspects of
online promotions have been covered at length in the previous chapters, and for
good reason. While promotions can fail and mistakes can provide great learning
experiences for future efforts, the legal aspects of online promotions are one area
in which you don't want to be wrong. Not being a legal expert yourself, however,
it's sometimes difficult to accurately judge your in-house legal capabilities or identify the areas for which you should seek outside help.

   I don't believe that many companies *intentionally* break the laws pertaining to
online promotions. Instead, I believe that most companies suffer from incorrectly
assessing their knowledge of the laws or from relying on in-house counsel to perform all legal duties. While in-house attorneys can certainly save companies significant money when it comes to their own areas of expertise, in-house attorneys
are often burdened with the unrealistic expectation that they are specialists in "all

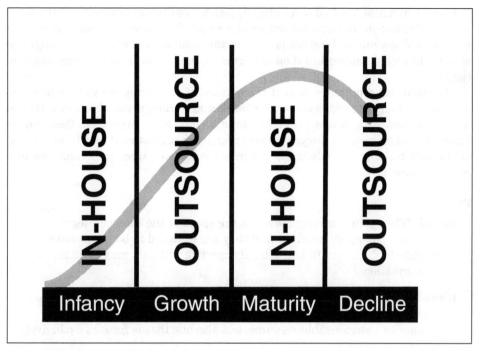

Figure 5.2 Company life cycle.

things legal." To illustrate this, I will borrow an example from the medical profession. While your general practice doctor is great for helping you stay healthy and identifying potential health risks, you would never expect that same doctor to perform heart surgery or attempt to remove a brain tumor. If you had a serious health risk, you would receive a referral from your doctor to see a specialist who has received extensive training in a particular medical field.

The legal profession is not much different. Some lawyers are specialists in contract law, others focus on copyrights, and still others are trained in the art of promotional law. Don't assume that your in-house counsel is a specialist in all things legal. Usually, the first person to address this issue is the in-house counsel—that is, unless he or she is trying to live up to the company's unrealistic expectations. The next issue is to decide whether or not it is worth investing in an in-house promotional lawyer or to consult with outside legal experts on an "as needed" basis.

In-house Legal Expertise

The main factors to consider when deciding to use in-house legal counsel are the size of the company, the expertise of the in-house counsel, and the volume of promotions. If your company is relatively small, the cost of hiring an in-house legal expert may not make sense—especially if legal needs are not great. Large companies, on the other hand, tend to have more legal issues that need to be addressed in a timely manner, so in-house counsel may make sense.

Even if in-house legal counsel already exists, you must determine if the legal aspects of online promotions are within the scope of the attorney's comfort zone. If promotional law and/or Internet law is not the main area of expertise, it might be smarter to seek outside counsel on important issues (or at least to verify assumptions).

The third factor is the volume of promotions. If your company uses online promotions as a main tactic to meet your marketing strategy and objectives, then it may make sense to develop in-house promotional legal expertise. This can be accomplished by hiring a lawyer whose specialty is promotional and Internet law, or through training and educating a current in-house lawyer to become the promotional expert.

Pros

Speed. When your company moves at the speed of the Internet, legal questions pop up in meetings and they are expected to be answered immediately. Having in-house legal expertise will help maximize the speed of information.

Knowledge and expertise. If you have a lawyer who is primarily (or exclusively) focused on promotional law and Internet law, not only will you develop an indispensable resource, but also one that is focused exclusively on your business.

Cost savings. If the volume of online promotions is large, there are significant cost benefits to having in-house legal expertise.

Cons

Training and development. Having a reliable in-house legal expert is incredibly valuable, but building that resource may require significant training and development time. This long-term goal must be backed up with sufficient time and money devoted to creating this in-house expert.

Cost efficiency. If your volume of online promotions is on the low side, the cost associated with in-house legal counsel may not be worth it. Hospitals require specialists, your general practice physician does not. If online promotions are used only sporadically to help specific objectives, then an in-house resource may not be cost-effective.

Perspective. If online promotions are not your company's focus, an in-house resource will eventually see everything through an "industry filter." That is, if you are in the automotive industry, the focus will be on promotional law and automobiles or the Internet as it pertains to automobiles. Sometimes this industry filter can prevent a more general (unbiased) approach.

Outside Legal Counsel

Sometimes you just need a little help with promotional legal disclaimers or the writing of the official rules. If online promotions are not a core part of your business, then outsourcing your legal needs makes sense. Or perhaps your company is still growing and the short-term needs do not necessitate in-house counsel. Even if having in-house legal expertise in the areas of promotional law and the Internet is part of the long-term plan, you may need help today while you're building the internal resources. Outside legal expertise makes a lot of sense in these situations.

Pros

Per-project costs versus long-term commitments. While using outside legal counsel may be more expensive than an in-house resource, there are usually no long-term commitments. Therefore, outside counsel can be used on an "as needed" basis and actually reduce overall costs in the long run.

Detachment. With outside legal counsel, there is no fear of sugar coating associated with "telling it like it is." If there's a legal problem, outside counsel will usually be blunt about it, whereas an in-house resource may be more mindful of the business problems associated it.

General knowledge, not industry-specific. Outside counsel typically deals with a variety of companies and industries. The lack of industry focus can sometimes be helpful as rulings from one industry can be applicable to another industry.

Cons

Slower responses. Outside legal counsel must "catch up" on internal meetings and discussions. You must also coordinate schedules and consider the other priorities of an outside agency instead of an assigned internal resource that is more likely to be available more often.

Missed learning opportunity. With each online promotion that uses outside legal expertise, there is a missed opportunity for developing the internal knowledge and experience of an in-house resource.

Inefficient for a large volume of online promotions. If online promotions are a big part of your business, you may be better off with in-house counsel.

Recommendation

If you can afford in-house legal counsel, it's usually a wise investment. The challenge will be to assess just how many in-house legal resources you require. If online promotions are a small part of your overall marketing strategy, then it is not necessary to have dedicated in-house resources for your online promotions. Instead, engage outside legal counsel either directly or through your promotions agency on an "as needed" basis. It's important to have resources available for the legal aspects of online promotions (such as official rules, disclaimers, privacy, and a general understanding). But if this isn't a core part of your business, you're better off hiring legal counsel when you need it and not having to justify the cost of a dedicated resource that is underutilized.

On the other hand, if online promotions are a large part of your marketing strategy, then in-house resources may make sense. Depending on the size of your company, you may still want outside legal counsel for a second opinion and indemnification (if nothing else).

Technical

Few will argue about the tremendous speed with which today's technology is moving. The challenge is determining just how far your company should go down the technology path before that path leads you outside your core business goals. Let's say you're in the research industry and you have developed your own online applications to address the needs of the research industry. At what point does the company cease to be a research organization and become an information application service provider (ASP)? There is a fine line between creating and developing the right technology solutions in support of your business and reengineering your entire company so that it is technology focused—which brings us full circle back to the question of how much technology you should keep in-house versus outsource.

I realize that this is a much bigger issue than just the technology associated with your online promotions, but perhaps by reviewing relevant pros and cons associated with the world of online promotions, the bigger issues of how technology is affecting your business will become apparent. In general, the efficiencies are determined by the volume and kinds of work that the company does. If technology is a big part of the existing company, then carving out online promotions responsibilities is probably a natural fit. Conversely, if technology is only a drop in an otherwise large bucket of your company's infrastructure, then outsourcing may be the way to go. The key here is to measure the pain of the up-front costs and maintenance with the long-term benefits.

In-house Technology Staff

There are real advantages to having dedicated internal technology resources. Similar to the legal resources, in-house technology personnel are extremely focused on your business. They will keep up on the latest and greatest technology trends and apply them to your company's individual needs. When something breaks, only an in-house technology staff will be able to address the problem as quickly as you would like. When new developments arise, an in-house technology staff can guide those developments into the existing infrastructure much better than any outside organization. The major challenge of an in-house technology staff is justifying the costs associated with these highly skilled professionals. Technology is such a booming field that *keeping* your in-house technology staff is one of its biggest challenges. If you take junior people and train them to be in charge of your technology applications, the minute they have completed their training they will likely have other job offers for *two or three times* what you originally paid them.

Eventually, the marketplace will level out, but today the Internet is a mission-critical part of everyone's business, and companies are willing to pay through the nose for top talent. If you can afford to keep your in-house technology staff happy, it's usually a wise investment over time (assuming that technology is a significant portion of your business model).

Pros

Quick response time to problems. Even a highly paid Internet Service Provider (ISP) will not respond as quickly as in-house resources can. They know your system better than anyone.

More tightly integrated programs and applications. Outside vendors all have their own ways of coding and integrating their code. If the majority of your applications are built internally, the entire system will be much cleaner than the hodge-podge approach of multiple outside vendors all trying to use legacy systems and previous applications.

Experts focused on improving your business over time. With in-house talent, you have experts who are staying abreast of the latest and greatest technology advancements and thinking of ways to incorporate the new technology into your business.

Keep ahead of the technology curve. Your in-house knowledge, when applied, will keep your company ahead of the technology curve. As advancements occur, your in-house team will experiment and incorporate them into your existing systems.

Cons

Expensive to retain top talent. With a little experience, your top programmers and technologists will be courted (rather overtly) by placement agencies and your competitors. Top talent is expensive and may not be worth the overall cost to your in-house technology solutions. If technology is only a small part of your business, then in-house resources will not likely be cost-effective. Besides, without much work to give them, your in-house resources will spend more time becoming "highly desirable" to other technology companies in an effort to maximize their salary potential.

Difficult to set technology boundaries or limitations. Once you start down the technology path, it's difficult to put limitations on how much you are willing to spend. When the system requires upgrades and maintenance services, it's virtually impossible to stop the money flow. As the system becomes larger, more staff is required to maintain and manage it. Make sure you have a good technology plan before you jump in with both feet.

Outsourcing Technology Requirements

The good thing about a booming technology industry is that you have options. With more and more ISPs (Internet Service Providers) becoming ASPs (Application Service Providers), there are many choices for outsourcing your technology needs. The biggest advantage to outsourcing is usually cost. If your company is not focused on technology as a core part of your business, then outsourcing can help you get what you need when you need it—most of the time.

The main disadvantage of outsourcing is that you're now on another company's timetable. During the sales period, your outside vendors will swear up and down that if you ever need them they are available (in most cases 24 hours a day). What they don't tell you is that only the most junior-level technologists get stuck with the after-hours shifts and any major problems will have to wait until the next business day (or when the senior programmers are not busy or away on vacation). Also, if you have multiple outside vendors, you leave yourself wide open to the "it's not my fault" game, where fingers are pointed everywhere but at the problem.

Pros

Huge cost savings when compared to in-house resources. This is not only with respect to people resources but software as well. Database software and most server software can be expensive. With outside resources you can pay for what you need, usually over time, instead of incurring the massive up-front costs associated with building an internal system and staffing up to maintain it.

Specialists are available when you need them. Perhaps you need a database programmer, but only to set up your tables and do the initial installation. You can pay as you go, and you don't have to retain expensive talent during the time when you don't need it.

Cons

Time is *not* on your side. With outside resources, you are relying on their availability and this is especially painful when you have a technology meltdown or emergency. Most technology companies will not guarantee more than a 24- to 78-hour time frame to identify or fix problems. Tell that to your irate customers who don't care about your internal problems.

Unclean code. With multiple vendors come multiple styles and approaches to problem solving. Even if you use the same vendor, there is no guarantee that the programmer you used last time will be available for your current need. Pretty soon your technology system looks like a giant quilt with multiple designs stitched together.

"It's not my fault" becomes a running theme among your vendors. With multiple hands touching your system, it becomes difficult (if not impossible) to identify the origin of breakdowns and system crashes. While you just want things fixed, you are forced to play along, trying to determine which vendor caused the problem and should be responsible for the fix.

More difficult to stay on top of technology advances. If you're not in charge of updating and evolving your technology solution, who is? Without in-house resources, it's difficult to stay on top of the latest advances in technology and their applications to your business.

Recommendation

Bring your technology in house if you can afford it. Even if you can't afford a number of technologists, it would be wise to keep a well-paid vice president (VP) or chief technology officer (CTO) on staff. This way someone is responsible for managing the outside vendor relationships and keeping abreast of technology advancements and how they affect your business. Without in-house technology resources, it will be difficult to stay competitive in this day and age (and that goes for just about every industry).

If you can't afford in-house technology, then do your best to keep a variety of vendors available, but channel them all through your main resource (your ISP, ASP, or main technology vendor). The trick is maintaining a balance between having all your technology eggs in one basket and keeping back-up resources at the ready when emergencies take you by surprise.

Creative

In the first three elements of strategy, legal, and technology, I laid out the pros and cons of keeping these elements in house or outsourcing them. With creative, I recommend outsourcing with very few exceptions. In-house creative teams are a real challenge, because individuals all have their own styles that they bring to any assignment they work on. While it is important to keep consistency across your marketing efforts, creative is the one area where I feel an outside perspective is critical for success. This is especially true if your company is new, in its growth phase, or on the decline. Mature companies that have stood the test of time can experiment with in-house creative resources, but even then I recommend an outside perspective to help keep the marketing messages fresh and relevant.

Effective creative executions mix the extremely challenging element of humor into the marketing messages. When done correctly, campaigns can outlast their creators and sometimes will be brought back after years of using less effective campaigns. When using outside agencies for creative executions, you can usually get a good feel for the kind of campaign you are interested in, based on that agency's portfolio. Perhaps elsewhere they have done something that is a breakthrough in your mind and could be applied differently to *your* industry. The best ideas tend to be modified slightly and then recycled over time.

In-house Creative

It is difficult to be objective with an in-house creative team. You become accustomed to their work and even the best ideas may feel familiar and be challenged. One advantage of an in-house creative team is the consistency of work. If you're happy with a campaign and plan on using it for some time, an in-house creative team can make the minor tweaks to apply that campaign to various mediums and help take the campaign international (if that is one of the goals).

When launching your online promotions, in-house creative resources will help with the speed of developing and launching the required HTML pages. Ideas from brainstorming meetings can quickly be mocked up and posted to an internal Web site. Once the creative is approved, the promotion can be launched quickly. Also, if creative changes are required during the promotion, an in-house creative staff can address those needs quickly and help monitor the results of the changes as they relate to the campaign.

Pros

Speed to market. An in-house creative staff can quickly develop ideas and post them to an internal Web site for quick reviews, approvals, and deployment.

Quick changes during the promotion. If creative needs to be modified or changed during the promotion, an in-house team will quickly make those changes and can help monitor the effectiveness of the different creative treatments.

Consistency. An in-house team will provide a level of consistency that is unparalleled in the marketplace. Without agencies vying to place their own signatures on campaigns, your creative will become a standard that your consumers can rely on.

Little to no education required. Your in-house creative requires very little briefing or background in order to go to work. This is the only account these people work on, so very few directions or instructions are necessary.

Cons

Stale concepts and innovation. With an internal team working on the creative components, a box will quickly be formed (based on approvals and feedback) that will be difficult for the internal creative to break out of. Breakthrough ideas will be few and far between.

Lack of fresh perspective. When creative people are working on a multitude of products in multiple industries, they are constantly researching different creative executions and ideas for different clients. The opposite is the case for in-house resources. Tunnel vision tends to prohibit the fresh perspective that is required for killer creative concepts.

Results are likely to be flat. An internal creative team will gravitate to what is most effective and then keep tweaking the concepts. Unless the campaign has a killer concept, the long-term results are likely to become flat and/or depreciate over time.

Outsourcing Creative Needs

In my opinion, this is the only way to go. By outsourcing your creative, you are guaranteed fresh ideas. As long as you keep an open mind and allow the research to help you make your decisions, outside resources will keep your creative fresh and effective—the only way to be.

While things like timing and consistency will be more challenging for outside resources, the ideas themselves more than make up for any challenges you will find when working with an outside resource. What benefit is the ability to make changes on the fly if the ideas are not as effective as they could be? While outside resources may take longer to get up to speed or to make changes, the overall result is well worth any additional time required.

Pros

Killer concepts. Need I say more? All the other challenges of outsourcing are well worth it if, at the end of the day, you have awesome creative that works.

Fresh perspective. Outside creative resources don't work at your company. They will only concern themselves with the politics that you force on them. Without a giant box around them, outside creative resources will come up with great ideas that take a fresh perspective on the company as a whole.

Measurable results. Who cares about the creative awards if you don't generate results? You can hold outside agencies more accountable than you can in-house resources. If the in-house resources fail, they try, try again. If you're not happy with your outside creative support, you have the option to allow them a second chance or simply move on.

Cons

Timing and responsiveness. You might want the concepts yesterday, but that's not how it works with outside resources. If you allow the creative process to take its course, you will be much happier with the end result. This means allowing the outside resource to provide you with more realistic deadlines for their deliverables.

Getting up to speed. With outside resources, you must help educate them on the important aspects of your business. This takes more time than telling someone who works with you to simply "get to work."

Inconsistency. Especially when you have multiple outside creative resources, it becomes a full-time job keeping your brand identity. With each creative resource's own signature on its own campaign, it becomes a challenge to keep your own look and feel consistent (and recognizable as your brand identity).

Recommendation

Outsource. For all the reasons previously stated and more that you will experience if you don't. It's okay to have in-house resources that coordinate the outside efforts, but if you're attempting to do all your creative in-house, it's time for a fresh perspective. Not convinced? Allow your internal resources to compete with an outside agency for an upcoming project and shop and compare. See what ideas come out of your internal group versus those of an outside agency. For best results, make sure your outside agency has a portfolio of work that interests you. If it has work that appeals to you, it is more likely to come back with recommendations that will satisfy your marketing objectives.

Media

Similar to the creative elements (but for different reasons), I recommend that an outside media specialist buy media on your behalf. When it comes to buying media and making media recommendations, the more experience and dollars behind your company, the better the deals and negotiation power. Media-buying agencies leverage their core experience and multiple clients to get the best results for all their clients. While you can hire experts from these agencies to create an in-house staff of media buyers, you will still be missing all the clout that comes with multi-million-dollar media buys. Let's face it, if the media agency places millions of dollars of media each year, your buy will do much better as part of *that* placement, rather than by itself.

The other major advantage to a media-buying service is its knowledge about all the extras that go along with the media buy—this is especially true when it comes to radio and promotional media. Beyond the traditional buys there are extra mentions, on-site participations, radio giveaways, and all sorts of other extras that the right media placement agency can help you get to add to the overall value of the buy. When it comes to buying media, it's best to leave this job to the experts.

In-house Media Buys

In-house media buys don't really save you much time or money. Typically, the 15 percent (maximum) commission associated with media buys is not refunded or applied back to a company that isn't using an outside agency to place the media. While there is always room for negotiation, most media companies charge clients without an agency the same price as they would charge an agency that has built the commissions into the buy. In other words, most media companies do not give a 15 percent discount to companies usurping their agency and buying direct. In fact, when David Ogilvy was first starting out, this was a main argument to companies who were placing their own media. Since there is no major cost savings for placing the media directly, why not let an experienced agency handle the buy and make its commission?

The one area that is an advantage for an in-house media person is knowing the industry media vehicles inside and out. Internally, an in-house media person knows what the company is after (their marketing objectives) and has the time to research the best vehicles to utilize for media buys. In general, however, this keen knowledge is not worth the in-house expense.

Pros

Extremely knowledgeable about your industry. Having a media specialist in-house will provide you with someone who is an expert in placing media in your industry.

An in-house media person can sometimes barter for media exposure with partner companies or with media vehicles that are willing to work with a nontraditional media buy in exchange for services or a free product for the target audience.

Cons

Lack of negotiating power. Without large media dollars, an in-house media buyer will have a difficult time competing with full-time media placement agencies.

Not likely to be notified of "deals" that come up with media companies. That is, when extra inventory exists, media placement agencies are the first ones to be notified of the surplus and are offered deals way below market value for excess inventory.

More difficult to keep current. Media placement agencies have a better knowledge base as they are armed with all sorts of research and trends analyses, whereas your in-house media resource would have a difficult time justifying the cost of such information.

No real cost savings. In general, there is no real cost savings to having an in-house media person. If anything, you have the extra expense of his or her salary, which would be difficult to apply toward any cost savings generated on a particular media buy.

Outsourcing the Media Buys

Outsourcing the media buys is the only way to go. Again, an outside media placement agency has much more financial clout than your individual media buy. Outside agencies know the tricks and all the extras to ask for and can leverage their experience to benefit your company. While an outside media resource will not be as knowledgeable about your specific industry, what it lacks in individual knowledge it more than makes up for in research and media reports that are at its disposal.

The money associated with retaining an outside media agency is covered by the commissions associated with the buy. In other words, you don't really lose anything by using the outside resource. The media-buying agencies make their money through the actual placement and the commissions that the media company provides. Although your in-house resource may be able to negotiate for some of this commission to be rebated to the company directly, in most cases this will be negligible unless the buy is a multimillion-dollar deal that is only being funneled through a single media vehicle (network radio, national broadcaster, or cable station, for example).

Pros

Financial clout put to work for your business. Especially with the larger media placement agencies, the incremental dollars placed through the various media companies will help your individual media buy, as agencies have significantly more negotiating power than your in-house resource.

Up to date. When buying and placing media is the main focus of your company, you are armed with all sorts of research and analysis that only makes sense for a media-buying company. These reports show where the consumers really are and help identify potential buys that can be extremely helpful to your company.

No out-of-pocket costs. Media placement agencies work off commissions that they receive from the media companies themselves. In most cases, you will not have to pay for the media agency's service directly—payment will come in the form of a commission from the placement itself.

Special offers. Media placement agencies are the first ones contacted when there is a surplus. In some cases, this could positively impact your media buy if the timing works out (especially if your buy is somewhat flexible).

Experience is king. When it comes to media, I say leave it to the professionals. Even if you recruit your own in-house professional, the minute you take him or her out of the agency, he or she is disconnected from all the reports and information that would add value.

Cons

May not be industry-specific. The media agencies are typically not specialists in all industries. They may need some additional time to research your industry before making their recommendations.

May be able to negotiate back part of what would have been the agency commission. Again, this is not the standard, but a good in-house resource may be able to extend the media buy by negotiating back part or all of the agency commission (usually if the media buy is large and with a single media outlet).

Recommendation

Outsource. It's not worth the cost of an in-house media expert unless your company is so large that its own media buys alone provide significant financial leverage for negotiations. In other words, unless you're a *Fortune 100* company planning to spend tens or hundreds of millions of dollars on media, engage someone who is planning to spend tens or hundreds of millions of dollars via all of its clients.

NOTE If you don't want to manage multiple outsource partners, the right promotions agency can do this for you with its own internal resources, partnerships, and alliances. While you can certainly retain a media agency directly, it may be easier to retain a single agency that can handle all of your outsourcing needs. I bring this up because outsourcing to multiple companies can itself become a full-time job. If you prefer not to become a "producer" of your online promotions, then you can hire a capable promotions agency (or internal promotions resource) to handle all your outsourcing requirements.

Partnerships

I used to hate it when people would tell me that "it's not what you know, it's who you know." But when it comes to partnership marketing, this is 100 percent correct. If you're well connected and know all the top VPs and executives of all the companies you'd like to partner with, then you will not need any outside resources to help find partners. If, on the other hand, networking and passing out several hundred business cards annually is not your idea of a good time, then perhaps an outside promotions agency would do you some good.

Companies seek out partners for their online promotions when the target market is roughly the same and two or more companies have the same (or similar) marketing objectives. Usually, partnerships are formed to decrease the overall cost of the promotion while, at the same time, increasing the overall effectiveness. There are a number of challenges with partnership marketing, which I will discuss in more detail in Chapter 6, "How to Create a Multibrand Promotion."

Negotiating Partnerships In House

The main advantage of negotiating partnerships in house is the relationships themselves. When you or your colleagues broker a partnership for an online promotion, it's usually a test case for future marketing opportunities. These can either be long-term strategic relationships or simply a way to decrease costs while increasing reach and frequency through a partner. If you can take the time necessary to network and meet with all the right people at potential partner companies, then it makes a lot of sense to keep this function in house. The fewer people in between you and your partner, the better.

On the other hand, if you don't spend a lot of time networking and you don't have an internal resource who enjoys the networking aspect of the job, then outsourcing is the way to go. It really is that simple.

Pros

More control of the partnership. By controlling the negotiation in house, you have the ability to cultivate a new relationship with a potential partner. This is a wonderful opportunity, especially if you plan on utilizing this new partner for future marketing efforts.

Better long-term strategy. If you are the one networking with potential partners, you will have a better chance at cultivating a long-term strategy with each partner. This long-term strategy will also help your partners identify what you can bring to the table now and in the future and why it is important for them to join marketing efforts with you.

No financial cost to creating the partnerships. If you have more time than money, this is another good reason to create the partnerships yourself. The only costs associated with creating the partnerships are phone calls and any travel arrangements that may be necessary to meet face to face (to finalize the negotiations).

Sharpened networking and negotiating skills. Seeking out partnerships and then negotiating the deals are actually extremely valuable skills that can be used in other facets of your job. If this interests you, then it makes sense to handle these negotiations internally.

Cons

Time constraints. Partnership negotiation takes time. If this is not your core responsibility (or that of your colleagues) and you do not see the long-term value associated with the partnership, then the job may be better off in someone else's arena.

Lots of rejection. Let's face it, creating a partnership is just like selling a product. You must be able to handle rejection if you're going to be good at it. If not, then taking on this responsibility will lower your morale (or that of your colleagues).

Outsourcing Partnership Negotiations

Companies outsource their partnership negotiations for two main reasons: to save time and to leverage existing relationships with the agency. Outside promotions agencies are constantly networking (for new business if for no other reason). Companies wishing to save time can simply engage a promotions agency on their behalf to work out the details of the partnership. When a promotions agency identifies the right opportunity, it will present it to your company for final approval. This saves you loads of time in the whole negotiation process.

Also, if the promotions agency is already working with companies that you would like to partner with, the promotions agency already has the advantage of existing relationships. In this case, sometimes a simple introduction is all that is needed to establish a working relationship for a massive online promotion effort.

Pros

Saves time. If this is not your core responsibility, then the act of identifying the right potential partners and then the whole negotiation process may require more of a time commitment than you can make. If you have more money than time, outsourcing is the way to go.

Leverages existing relationships. An outside promotions agency already has a number of existing relationships. If you are interested in any of these relationships, then the partnership negotiations should be much faster and easier with a promotions agency.

Provides realistic expectations. An outside agency will provide you with an initial reality check if the "gives" and "gets" are not realistic. That is, if you want a multimillion-dollar media buy in exchange for some free product, an outside agency can provide an initial reality check before potential bridges are burned by unrealistic expectations.

Experienced partner works on your behalf. This is especially important if you're new to partnerships. If you've never completed a partnership negotiation, be prepared to be "taken to the cleaners" if you're not careful. An experienced partner will help you avoid that.

Acts as a mediator or middleman. Why is this an advantage? Because any problems or difficulties will be handled by the agency. In other words, being once removed helps create a buffer when challenges arise.

Cons

Additional engagement costs. Promotional agencies are "for-profit" and therefore require additional compensation for the negotiating process. This is usually quite reasonable, as this negotiation practice will help the agency on its search for new business opportunities as well.

Once removed from the partnership. If you engage an outside agency on your behalf, you're once removed from the entire process. This can be both an advantage and disadvantage. The disadvantage is that you are once removed from the partnership itself. This makes it more difficult to leverage in the future or to jump in if there's a problem.

Less control. Without doing the partnership negotiating yourself, you have less control over the entire process. Certainly, the promotions agency is working on your behalf, but you're still once removed and have less control because of that.

Less opportunity for long-term relationship. This doesn't mean it can't be done, just that it's more difficult to leverage a partnership that was not introduced or cultivated by you. For future relationships, you may require the ongoing services of the promotions agency you used to create the partnership in the first place.

Recommendation

Go through your contact list and see if any obvious partners pop out at you. If not, then seek out a promotions agency that either already has the partner you'd like to be working with or has the skills necessary to get you that partner.

In general, if you have more money than time, use an outside resource. If you have more time than money, cultivate the relationship yourself. While it's better to create partnerships yourself when you can, you may not have the luxury of time or the necessary skills. If this is the case, it is better to call in the experts to help negotiate the best deal for you and your company.

Customer Support

Why is this promotion void in Puerto Rico? Where do I write in for a free entry? When I clicked Submit, I received a server error. What do I do now? For every question that I could list here, there are probably four more that are particular to your individual promotion. Online promotions have their own unique challenges. It's not a good idea to run an online promotion without having *at least* an email address where customers can ask questions and get answers in a reasonable time frame.

With a few exceptions, I highly recommend that customer support be handled in house. While there are a number of customer support organizations that would be happy to assist you, you are much better off being in control of the customer contact. Not only can you ensure quality answers, but you might just learn something when you listen to what your customers have to say.

In-house Customer Support

It just makes sense. When customers call or email, they want to speak to a representative of *your* company—not someone else who is paid to act like a representative. The biggest challenge I get when I make this recommendation is that "our customer service people don't know how to deal with promotional questions." To this, I recommend that the promotions agency prepare a frequently asked questions (FAQ) document that outlines the most common questions and their appropriate answers. Not only can this FAQ document be posted to the Web site, but the customer support people can keep it handy in case they receive online promotions inquiries. Also, I recommend that the customer support group forward to the promotions agency any emails with questions that they are not sure how to answer. The agency will then formulate an official reply and add it to the FAQ document for later use.

If you don't have a customer support center already in place, this should become your next priority. There are very few companies that don't have a specific need for customer support. Your 800 number and support email address are your lifelines to your customers. If you don't have a clearly defined way for customers to reach you to deal with questions or problems, they will go somewhere else that does (usually your competitor). If you can't justify the cost, you should examine ways to create an in-house customer support center in conjunction with a partner who also has minimal needs for customer support. Together, you can balance the cost of the call/email support center, but under very few circumstances should you ever *not* have one.

Pros

First line of defense. You are going to receive the calls/emails whether you want them or not. Even if you attempt to outsource customer support, many consumers will prefer to come to you first rather than use the special 800 number or email address you've created for the promotion. Take advantage of this opportunity to help your customers.

Learn about other sensitive customer problems or issues. While you're responding to an email or phone call about the online promotion, you will often learn more about how your customers feel about your company, its products and services, and their sensitive problems or issues. This is an added bonus. It's free research.

Easy extension to your existing call/email center. Providing customer support for the online promotion should simply be an extension of your existing infrastructure and should not be a significant increase in costs or internal resources.

Increase in response time. By keeping the calls and emails internally, you can keep track of the average response times, which will usually be much faster than if the calls or emails went to an outside resource (unless, of course, you're understaffed).

Encourages increased customer loyalty. When you do answer questions and help solve problems, your customers feel better about your company. This is a golden opportunity to increase the brand loyalty of your customers. If you help solve a problem for your customers, they are much more likely to come back to you (versus your competitors) the next time they are faced with a problem.

Positive customer impact. When you keep customer service in house, you have a much better chance for positive customer impact. This is because you have demonstrated your ability to answer questions and provide real support for customers who need help. When you do this, the customer feels much more positive about your company.

Cons

Increased call/email volume. Heavily advertised promotions will undoubtedly increase the volume of calls and/or emails you receive. If you are unable to handle this additional volume, you may have no choice but to outsource the additional demand.

Lack of promotions knowledge. The people in your customer service group are not promotions experts. While the FAQ provided by the promotions agency will be helpful, there are likely to be questions that the group just can't answer. While the promotions agency can help solve these problems, there will be a few cases when the call operator (or person emailing) will need to admit that he or she doesn't know the answer and will have to get back to the customer.

Lack of an established call/email support center. If this is true, then you probably have more problems to deal with than you are aware of. The easy answer is to outsource the customer service part of the promotion, but the better answer is to address the larger problem and establish a support center.

Outsourcing Customer Support

This is not the preferred approach, but there are many companies out there willing to take on your customer support requirements. For minimal monthly fees and per-call or per-email costs, you can outsource your customer support with very little up-front time required. I do not recommend this approach. It is much better that *you* keep abreast of the problems and concerns your customers have. The minute you outsource your customer support, you are redirecting your customers outside your company and outside your immediate control. It is much better to keep the customer support requirements in house until you can no longer handle the volume of calls or emails. Then, and only then, do I recommend that you seek outside help.

Pros

Unlimited call/email volume. If your internal resources are not sufficient, you can outsource as many emails or phone calls as your customers demand.

Relatively inexpensive to outsource customer support. Once you've provided the basic FAQ, your outsourced customer support will document any additional questions that customers have and relay the responses you provide. In this way, you tell one person an answer that is then disseminated across the whole team.

Perhaps faster than setting up or training an existing internal call/email center. This, of course, depends on the state of your existing in-house call or email center. If you don't have one, or if the one you have is ineffective, then outsourcing to the professional call/email center can be much faster because it has trained professionals awaiting your instructions.

Cons

Lost learning opportunity. You don't know what your customers are saying about your company or its products. When you outsource your customer service, you are allowing another company to speak on your behalf and you lose the opportunity to deal with related problems or learn from your customers (stuff not necessarily related to the online promotion).

Customers still come to you first. Even if you outsource, if there is an existing phone number to call or contact email address on your Web site, the calls and emails will come to you first, thereby slowing down the outside agency's ability to respond quickly.

Outsource agency may be slower. Even if there are no delays in getting the calls and emails, the outside agency may not be as fast as your internal standards. You must trust that it is, but unless you call or email yourself, it will be difficult for you to know if it is responding in the time frame your company would prefer.

Loss of control. Customer contact is the one area where you want to stay in control. Whenever possible, you should retain control of the communications with your customers.

Recommendation

Keep customer support in house if at all possible. Do whatever it is you have to do to keep the calls and emails coming. They are your lifeline to your customers and should not be handed off to an outside organization. There are additional comments that are usually included with questions about the online promotion. This is your chance to satisfy your customers and keep them coming back for more. If you have to outsource, make sure your partner lives up to the standards that you have set for your own call/email center.

Administration

Successful online promotions, like any marketing endeavor, require attention to detail. Promotion administration is where all the details are identified, organized, and completed, and then double-checked. If the administration of the promotion is poorly executed, then even the best ideas are not likely to catch on or be successful.

The administration of the promotion includes everything from the writing of the official rules, filing and bonding the promotion with the appropriate states, paying insurance premiums for million-dollar skill contests, producing legal disclaimers for the advertising copy, opening Post Office boxes, managing write-in entries and requests, and managing every other detail that is required for a successful online promotion. The questions to ask when deciding if the administration should be kept in house or outsourced are:

- Are your in-house resources detail-oriented?

- Do your in-house resources have the knowledge and experience to handle all the details?

You can develop your own in-house promotions experts through the sheer volume of online promotions that your company may handle. After you've completed a few different kinds of online promotions, the similarities become fairly obvious, and the differences can be easily identified and dealt with. If you have a large volume of online promotions, then it may make sense to keep the administration duties in house for cost and efficiency purposes. However, many companies prefer to place a promotions agency on retainer to handle the large volume of promotions to achieve the same cost reductions and efficiencies.

In-house Administration

The decision to bring the administrative duties in house will depend on the volume and type of online promotions you are interested in managing. There are a number of advantages to having an in-house administrative staff to manage your online promotions if you plan on handling several online promotions each year (that is, at least one a month) as part of your overall marketing plan. By keeping the administrative duties in house, you can establish your own way of handling the online promotions responsibilities that are required for each promotion. With your own internal system established, it is much easier to standardize the way the online promotions are handled. Furthermore, your own internal process will help you educate all your employees who are interested in becoming involved with online promotions (even if they are not directly responsible for them). An internal staff will keep itself up to date on the latest legal and administrative requirements. In short, you'll have more control over your online promotions by managing all the details internally.

On the downside, if you make mistakes, those mistakes are your own responsibility. You may need to take out "errors and omissions" and other kinds of insurance to protect your company against possible mistakes. This will help you reduce the amount of risk you take on, but not remove the risk entirely. Also, if you decide to do your own internal judging (sweepstakes drawings and contest judging), you lose the element of an unbiased, independent third party whose decisions are final. In other words, consumers who question your internal group's decisions have a better chance of bringing their claims to court than they would if an independent third party were used. Finally, the time and costs may not justify the needs—especially if you don't plan on a lot of volume with your online promotions. If you are considering an in-house staff, it is important to weigh both sides and determine which will work best for you.

Pros

Creates a tightly integrated companywide process. By developing an internal team, you can create your own way of doing things and incorporate that process throughout the rest of your company. In this way, even your employees who are not directly involved with online promotions are aware of how online promotions are handled.

Develops a knowledgeable internal staff to handle the details. Even if you only start with a single knowledgeable employee who is responsible for the details, that person can help develop an internal team and help educate the rest of the company about online promotions requirements.

Keeps you up to date with the latest administrative requirements. By handling the online promotional administrative duties internally, you will be kept up to date as the requirements change and evolve. If, for example, a state passes new registration requirements, you will be made aware of those requirements via your legal resource or promotional association, such as Promotion Marketing Association.

Encourages better understanding of the legal requirements. As the official rules are developed internally, the people who develop those official rules will become more knowledgeable about the specific legal requirements associated with the online promotion. The more online promotions developed internally, the better the knowledge base of the legal requirements.

Increased control over the details. You have more control of the details if they are handled internally. In this way, you can ensure that the details of the promotion are handled appropriately and to your satisfaction.

Cons

No third-party unbiased judge involved in the selection of winners. If a consumer questions the validity of the sweepstakes drawing or contest judging, the integrity of the promotion is more likely to be questioned without an outside, independent third-party involvement. Third-party judging decisions are "final" according to recent court findings, while internal decisions are more likely to be questioned in a courtroom situation.

No scapegoat if administrative mistakes are made. In other words, if there are problems with the administration of the online promotion, there's nowhere to look but inside the company. Not that a scapegoat would be needed, but if problems occur, it's nice to know that someone outside the organization is working to take care of those problems.

Extra insurance may be needed. The company may need to purchase "Errors and Omissions" and other insurance (or a larger policy) to cover the risk of online promotions mistakes. This is especially true if large prizes (or a large volume of prizes) are being given away. If, for some reason, the database of winners gets switched around or the instant win game pieces award too many prizes, you may be liable for the mistakes and this type of insurance can prevent the company from going under because of the mistakes.

Lack of cost justification. Cost of additional internal resources may not justify the need if the number of online promotions is relatively small. While you may prefer such internal resources, if you don't conduct a large number of online promotions, these internal resources may be overkill.

Wasted time requirements for administrative duties. If online promotions are not a core part of your business, the time of your internal resources may best be spent elsewhere to increase efficiency and profitability.

Outsourcing Administration

When companies outsource the administration duties of online promotions, it's usually because the volume of online promotions is not sufficient to justify dedicated internal resources to handle the promotional needs that crop up from time to time. Even if the volume of online promotions is relatively high, companies may not want to be responsible for all the details or the liability associated with online promotions. The administration duties reflect the attention to detail and the focus of the company itself. If it doesn't make sense to train an internal team to be detail-oriented with respect to the execution of the online promotions, then outsourcing is a good option. With outsourcing, you can usually accomplish your online promotions objectives without getting sucked into all the details.

The loss of control and integration are really the biggest downside of outsourcing. When you choose to outsource, you lose control of all the details to your vendor. Many companies are delighted that they do not need to be in control of the details, but others have a difficult time letting go. Also, the outside organization will likely do things differently than you may want and this makes it harder to integrate the outside resources with your internal resources. By outsourcing, your internal team will also be less knowledgeable about the changing online promotions' requirements. Without being involved in the online promotions, your internal team may learn of changes in the rules and administrative requirements, but without completing these requirements internally, the knowledge will be little more than a cursory overview.

Pros

Third-party intervention. With a third-party organization, you insert an unbiased, independent organization between your promotion and your consumers. Unlike internal judging decisions, a third-party's judging decisions are final (and are less likely to be challenged by a state legislator or by a courtroom judge).

Indemnification. In most cases, your outsourced agency will indemnify you against problems or mistakes made in the promotion. Most promotions agencies carry liability, errors and omissions, and other insurance to protect against mistakes or potential liabilities that crop up from time to time. This reduces your risk in your online promotions.

Maintains high-level control. By working with an outside agency, you can stay in control of the strategic and high-level aspects of an online promotion without getting sucked into all the details. While the details are an important aspect of online promotions, most companies do not enjoy being responsible for them and prefer to maintain a high level of control instead.

Usable on an "as needed" basis. With an outside promotions agency, you do not incur any expense during the down time in between your online promotions when you do not have any administrative needs.

Reduces the overall cost for a low level of online promotions. Outsourcing helps reduce the overall cost associated with the administrative aspects of the online promotions, especially if your online promotional needs are sporadic. With outsourcing, you can use what you need when you need it, or you can retain an outside agency to provide ongoing support at a reduced cost.

Cons

Loss of control. By outsourcing your administrative details, you are no longer in control of how those details are completed. For some, this is important, because outsourcing means it is difficult (if not impossible) to micromanage all the details.

Timing not always in synch. You may have administrative details that you need help with, but your preferred agency may not have the right amount of resources at the exact moment you need them (especially if the agency is given very short notice). In this case, you either need to find another outside resource or delay the online promotion by a few days.

Less integration within the company. Outside resources have their own way of doing things and they do not always line up with your company's internal process. If you're looking for seamless integration, you may not be happy with outsourcing the administrative details.

Internal resources not as knowledgeable about online promotions. When you outsource, you are looking to the experts to handle the details of your promotion. While the outside resource will be required to stay up to date on changes in administration requirements, your internal resources will be less knowledgeable than they would be if they handled the requirements internally.

Recommendation

Unless you are completing a large number of online promotions or need to be in control of all the details, most companies prefer to outsource the administrative duties of online promotions. While you may have specific reasons to bring your administrative duties in house, most companies prefer to leave the details to the promotions agencies that have the necessary expertise to handle all the details. Even companies with a large volume of online promotions tend to weigh the cost of internal staffing versus a retainer that would provide a better cost efficiency through an outside resource. While outsourcing is not always the best solution, most companies find that they prefer to focus on their core business rather than bring in the necessary resources to handle administrative duties.

Fulfillment

The art of "pick and ship" is not as easy as it might seem. Companies such as Amazon.com have learned that the extremely important aspect of having good fulfillment resources is a critical component to successful online marketing. If consumers go online to make a purchase, they expect that their purchase will be delivered immediately and without problems. Fulfilling orders successfully while maintaining a reasonable cost for doing so is the challenge of the fulfillment industry.

Online promotions are no different—especially when it comes to instant win prizes. The Internet is immediate, and consumers expect that your business uses the speed and immediacy of the Internet in everything you do. If you plan on giving away several thousand prizes in your instant win game, consumers expect that when they win, they will receive their prize immediately (and not have to wait the traditional 4 to 6 weeks for delivery).

Similar to the administrative duties, fulfillment is quite detail-oriented. If the prizes are kept track of poorly, then mistakes are bound to happen. If fulfillment requirements are organized and detail-focused, then there is less of a chance for breakdown. If fulfillment is a big part of your current business, then extending the fulfillment of prizes and other promotional offers should not be much of a challenge for you. If fulfillment is not your main focus, then it is unlikely that you will start getting involved in it for the sole purpose of your online promotions. The challenge for outsourcing then, is identifying the right partner that suits your needs.

In-house Fulfillment

Unlike many of the other aspects of online promotions, in-house fulfillment is really only an option if fulfillment is already part of your existing business or makes sense as part of your vision for the future of the company for reasons other than online promotions. It is very unlikely that you would create an in-house fulfillment center solely to support the needs of your online promotions. Fulfillment requires significant physical space where the items can be stored, weighed, and properly packed to avoid damage during delivery. Fulfillment requires ongoing inventory so that the promotion runs smoothly and all prizes or premium items that are awarded can be sent out immediately.

The main advantages of having fulfillment in house include your ability to micromanage this component, to set up an integrated process, and to respond to problems or mistakes. The downside is mostly the cost factors and true viability if fulfillment isn't already part of your existing business.

Pros

Micromanage the fulfillment process. With in-house resources, you have a much better chance at ensuring quality control measures than with an outside partner. With in-house fulfillment, you can set expectations and then manage the back end if those expectations are not met.

Tightly integrated process. The process of a consumer winning a prize (or the awarding of a premium item) to the fulfillment of the prize can be completely integrated if kept in house. A tightly integrated process means less chance for breakdowns.

More seamless transition between the promotion and fulfillment. This is more of a result of the first two, but it is important to point out that with an in-house fulfillment resource, the hand-off, from the capturing of the promotional data to the fulfillment of the items associated with the promotion, is more seamless.

Quick response to problems or mistakes. When problems or mistakes do happen, an in-house team can respond faster (and even have possible problem scenarios mapped out) because the fulfillment team works in tangent with the promotion administrators or managers.

Cons

Extremely expensive if not already established. Again, an in-house fulfillment resource for the sole purpose of online promotions will rarely make financial sense. The cost of designating sufficient space to house all the prizes, purchasing and storing the packing materials, setting up the postage meters, and staffing requirements will rarely justify an in-house need for online promotions.

Overkill if fulfillment is not already part of your business. Beyond the costs, there is the question of being practical when setting up an in-house fulfillment center. Generally, the needs are not as great as they may seem, unless fulfillment is already a large part of your business.

May be cheaper to outsource to a different labor/real estate market. Most fulfillment centers are in remote areas of the Midwest, Mexico, or

Canada. These more remote areas have lower costs of storage and a cheaper labor market that will reduce the costs associated with fulfillment.

Outsourcing Fulfillment

Again, if you don't have an in-house fulfillment center, it doesn't make sense to start one solely for the purpose of online promotions. How do you identify a good outsourcing center? In the next section, I will talk about how to identify good outsourcing partners. With respect to fulfillment, there may be some initial trial and error—even if you've checked out their background and have spoken with previous clients. Like many outside partners, good fulfillment centers are difficult to find. That said, the search for a good fulfillment partner is well worth the time when one is found.

In general, the costs associated with outsourcing are much lower than starting your own in-house fulfillment center. You can use them only when you need them and can even have several different outsource partners, depending on the needs of the promotion. If, for any reason, you are not satisfied with your outsource partner, you can discontinue the relationship and find another partner. On the downside, outsourcing leaves you with less control over your back-end fulfillment. You can't always react as quickly as you would like to problems that arise with your fulfillment partners (since they have to do their own internal investigations before confirming problems and providing potential solutions). Overall, outsourcing is the only option if you don't already have and use a fulfillment center of your own as an integral part of your existing (or future) business.

Pros

Much lower costs than starting your own in-house fulfillment center. Even if you're completing online promotions all the time, it's usually much cheaper to outsource than store prizes and packaging materials and pay for the labor involved in packing and shipping.

Used on an "as needed" basis. With outside fulfillment partners, you incur no costs when they're unused. You can set up a project just as easily as you can terminate one with an outside partner.

Different partners satisfy different needs. Some fulfillment centers are much better at large volume. You may have one partner for large volume, another for smaller volume, and yet another for unique requirements.

If you're not satisfied, you can use someone else. Outside fulfillment partners are judged on their performance. If you're not happy with their performance, you can easily choose another fulfillment center.

Cons

Less control over your back end. When you outsource, you're giving part of your responsibility to an outside party. Clearly, you do not have as much control over your outside resources as you would with internal ones.

Less integration with the rest of your company. Beyond control, it will also be challenging to integrate an outside partner into your own process. Fulfillment centers tend to have their own way of doing things, and you will more than likely need to adjust your projects to meet your partner's requirements.

Reduced ability to react to problems quickly. When a problem is identified, you have an outside company that is also involved and that must do its own investigations into the problems identified. This reduces your time to react to the problems, which may be a problem in itself.

Recommendation

If you have an in-house fulfillment center already in existence, then use it. It should not be difficult to extend the existing internal resources so that they can work within your online promotions requirements. If, however, you do not have an in-house fulfillment center, it will probably *not* make sense to create one solely for the purpose of online promotions. Outsourcing is the right answer if fulfillment is not already part of your existing business model or is unlikely to be part of your future model.

Research/Analysis

Research and analysis will bring us full circle back to the strategy that drives the promotion. Before you decide the best strategy to accomplish your objectives, it's a good idea to utilize research and analysis to help you make the right decisions. While there's no substitute for experience, research can help provide the knowledge that is required for successful online promotions. Research can include elaborate studies or quick validations of your assumptions. It's best to ask the very customers you're targeting. If you have a membership database, you can invite your existing customers to participate. If not, you can set up a random capture from the homepage of your Web site that will pull in every "nth" person (depending on the number of surveys you require).

I'm grouping the research and analysis functions together because of their interdependence. Each is important as a separate component, but neither is very significant without the other. Research requires good analysis to weed through the data and turn it into usable information. Without good research, the analysis is not worth much. While I tend to lean toward outsourcing the research and analysis components for third-party objectivity and experience, the best research and analysis utilize in-house lists and databases. The combination of in-house customer lists and outside research organizations tends to be the best approach for optimum learning and improvement of your online promotions.

In-house Research/Analysis

You should know your customers better than anyone (even your competitors). This is both a blessing and a curse. On the positive side, you know what your customers respond to and what they tend to ignore. The problem is, you may rely too heavily on this knowledge and miss some great promotional opportunities by dismissing ideas before you test them. It's a good idea to have an outside research organization help you validate your assumptions and/or test the new ideas. While you can most certainly accomplish this with an in-house group, the challenge is to keep objectivity within the internal research group to avoid using internal buzzwords that have little or no significance to your customers.

When bringing the research and analysis functions in house, the major upside is the contact and control of your existing customers. You can easily incorporate your research needs into the rest of your business. Many companies combine their registration of products with research requirements. Others tie research to the tail end of the online sales process (the thank you/confirmation page, for example). While this can certainly be accomplished with an outside organization, it's usually easier to incorporate all the research requirements into the rest of the sales process when the team is part of the internal organization. With research and analysis, you'll likely find that a combination of in-house and outsourced resources is the best approach.

Pros

Builds and utilizes your customer database. With an internal team, you are more likely to develop an internal customer database from which current and future research will be drawn. This internal database will both encourage your existing customers to share their opinions with your organization directly and help provide you with a good sales-leads database for future marketing.

Provides more seamless integration into the rest of the sales process. With an internal team, you are more likely to make research and analysis of projects an integral part of your company. While there may be resistance to including an outside organization as part of your internal sales process, an internal team will have fewer hurdles to jump over.

Allows speed of research deployment. As soon as research criteria are agreed on, your internal team can immediately deploy it. Over time, this speed of research and its corresponding analysis can provide a competitive advantage—especially when combined with the speed of the Internet.

Develops intimate understanding of ongoing research and analysis needs. With a dedicated team, you will develop a deep understanding of not just the individual research projects but also the overall trends company-wide.

Creates and utilizes a research database. Beyond the customer database, a research database will be developed where past studies and analysis will be stored and used for baseline studies and changes in trends and research findings.

Lowers costs on a per-research basis. If research is a core part of your operations, the individual cost of a specific research project will be much lower than if a third party were used.

Cons

>   **Lacks third-party objectiveness**. Internal research teams develop company biases (for better or for worse). The tendency is to gravitate toward the information that is known and the testing of existing practice. It becomes more and more difficult to look at problems objectively over time.

>   **Lacks the experience of a dedicated research organization**. Dedicated research groups conduct research on a multitude of different topics and for a variety of companies and industries. This expertise will be lacking from an internal team of research experts.

>   **Induces industry-specific tunnel vision**. While the internal team will become experts on your industry, it will usually lack the broader trends from other industries that are directly applicable to your company.

>   **Allows misleading analysis of research**. The same research may draw different conclusions from your internal team versus an outside research organization. Your internal team is likely to draw on additional information and research that is not part of the current project.

>   **Is expensive if not properly utilized**. If the internal team is not incorporated into the ongoing process of your company, its overhead may be more expensive than using an outside research organization on an "as needed" basis.

Outsourcing Research/Analysis

An outside research organization is dedicated to the field of research. While it may not be as intimately involved in your specific industry, its advantages come in the form of experience and objectivity. While an internal team may soften the blow of research, an outside organization is more likely to "tell it like it is." Moreover, an outside research organization can utilize relevant research from other industries to identify patterns and trends that are likely to affect your company.

The downside with an outside research group is that it may require additional information about your specific company or industry before a research project can be deployed. As an outside organization, it is less likely to be completely integrated into your company's process. But perhaps the biggest problem is that an outside organization is unlikely to create a research database for future cross-reference and baseline understandings. The research itself could be less expensive if the company is not interested in ongoing research but simply in need of specific information.

Pros

>   **More objective perspective**. An outside research organization is more likely to come up with an accurate picture of what the research says. Little to no sugar coating will be added to even the most dismal outlook. This objective perspective will allow for more factual information that can be acted on.

Cross-references other industries for relevant information. Because the outside research organization is not industry-specific, it is likely to spot trends in other industries that are directly applicable.

Pay as you go: There are no long-term overhead costs associated with using an outside research organization. In most cases, you can simply pay for the research that you need when you need it.

Experienced in the latest research trends, tools, and techniques. Perhaps the best part of using an outside research organization is that it is current in the latest research trends (how to ask questions, get incentives, and boost response rates, for example) and is likely to have developed its own tools and techniques for administering the research and corresponding analysis.

Cons

Much less background and focus on your specific industry. Research on your specific industry will require that your internal team review the questions to ensure that the right information is being gathered and that obvious questions are not part of what you are paying for.

May require more background and debriefing. It will be up to you and your team to educate your outside research organization on specific trends and information that are "common knowledge" in your industry. Don't expect that your outside partner will be as knowledgeable as you are about your company or industry.

Less integration into your companywide process. As an outside organization, it will have a more difficult time integrating within the company. This may prevent the true integration of research throughout your organization or simply require more time to accomplish the integration.

Slower deployment of research and analysis. Once your internal team has agreed on the research requirements, the briefing of the outside organization must occur before the research begins. This slow-to-market approach may not work for quick information requirements.

Research database unlikely to be developed or utilized. Unless your internal team creates a database or the outside organization is given this task, a research database is unlikely to be developed. The lack of this tool will result in less trends analysis and reduce the ability to track and measure changes and trends that are specific to your company.

Recommendation

Overall, most companies gravitate toward a combination of internal and external resources when it comes to research and analysis. The internal developments are things like the customer database, research database, and companywide integration, which can be accomplished much easier with in-house focus and representation. Outside research groups are used for the deployment of broader (less time-sensitive) studies that require objectivity and little or no industry-specific requirements. Companies pick and choose the type of research that is best developed and managed internally versus the studies that require a third-party organization to help ensure objectivity in the research and analysis.

Summary of Recommendations

Table 5.1 lists the 10 promotional components and corresponding recommendations.

Finding Vendors, Consultants, and Other Resources

Once you've determined your outsourcing needs, the next big question is, "How do I find the vendors I need?" In the world of online promotions, there are a number of options for each component. This section will give advice on how to find resources for each of the 10 promotional components outlined in the previous section. In general, however, if you plan on outsourcing more than one or two components for your online promotions, you may want to consider outsourcing all your needs to a promotions agency. Even if your online promotions agency does not handle all the components you need to outsource, it will have its own partnerships and vendor relationships, which it will manage on your behalf.

Online Promotions Agencies

For every business need there is a directory, and online promotions agencies are no different. The main magazine of the promotion industry, *PROMO Magazine*, has its own directory of promotions agencies, which includes online and integrated promotions agencies. In addition, *PROMO Magazine* has an annual review of the top 100 promotions agencies and ranks them based on criteria such as revenue, company size, and amount of time the company has been in business (to name a few). If you're not sure what kind of promotions agency you should hire, *PROMO Magazine* is a good place to start.

In addition to *PROMO Magazine*, you can find other listings of promotions agencies in publications such as *Incentive Magazine*, *Brand Week*, *Ad Age*, and *Ad Week*. Online marketing publications such as the *Industry Standard*, *Interactive Week*, and *iMarketing News* do not currently have listings of online promotions agencies, but do have listings of Internet marketing agencies (who often partner with and/or can recommend online promotions agencies). Very soon, you will also be able to get listings of online promotions agencies from the more popular online marketing magazines.

I wouldn't be doing my job as Chief Marketing Officer for Seismicom, if I didn't recommend my own company for consideration. Seismicom is one of the top

Table 5.1 Promotional Components and Recommendations

PROMOTIONAL COMPONENT	RECOMMENDATION
1. Strategy	Corresponds directly with the phase of the company life cycle you are currently in. If you're a start-up, keep the strategy in house. If you're in the growth phase, you should outsource. If the company is mature, keep it in house. If the company is in a decline, then outsource.
2. Legal	Bring legal in house if you can afford it. Also depends on the volume of online promotions. If small volume (only a few a year), then outsource. If large volume (at least one a month), then bring it in house. Even with in-house counsel, it's a good idea to get a second opinion when necessary.
3. Technical	Bring your technology in house if you can afford it. You need someone who is responsible for managing the outside vendor relationships and keeping abreast of technology advancements and how they will affect your business.
4. Creative	Outsource. It's okay to have in-house resources that coordinate the outside efforts, but if you're attempting to do all your creative in house, it's time for a fresh perspective.
5. Media	Outsource. It's not worth the cost of an in-house media expert unless your company is so large that its own media buys alone provide significant financial leverage for negotiations.
6. Partnerships	If you have more money than time, use an outside resource. If you have more time than money, cultivate the relationship yourself.
7. Customer support	Keep customer support in house if at all possible. Do whatever it is you have to do to keep those calls and emails coming. They are your lifeline to your customers and should not be handed off to an outside organization.
8. Administration	Outsource the administrative duties of online promotions unless you are completing a large number of promotions or need to be in control of all the details.
9. Fulfillment	Outsourcing is the right answer if fulfillment is not already part of your existing business model or is unlikely to be part of your future model.
10. Research/ analysis	Use a combination of internal and external resources when it comes to research and analysis. Pick and choose the type of research that is best developed and managed internally versus the studies that require a third-party organization to help ensure objectivity in the research and analysis.

integrated marketing and promotions agencies, which includes both online and traditional promotional marketing capabilities. In addition to Seismicom, you may want to check out Promotions.com and RealTime Media.

Strategy Consultants

For the purposes of online promotions, there are two kinds of strategy consultants: online marketing strategy consultants and advertising and promotions agencies that include strategy. When it comes to strategy, it truly depends on how far you want to go. Some companies turn to groups like Anderson Consulting to handle some of their corporatewide strategy initiatives (which include online promotions), while others have their corporate strategy figured out, but need help with online promotions only. If you're looking for online marketing strategy consultants, you can turn to any of the agencies listed in *Brand Week* or *Ad Week*, with complete quarterly reviews of the top interactive marketing agencies as part of their "IQ" section.

Online marketing strategy consultants include companies such as Saturn Networks, Oven Digital, Agency.com, RazorFish, Blue Marble, and Modem Media. Each of these companies has its own unique specialties from production to programming, but they all focus on Internet strategy as a core component of their respective business.

Advertising and promotions agencies (be they online or traditional) all include strategy as part of their business offerings. In addition to the online promotions agency listings previously discussed, there are similar listings for advertising agencies in publications such as *Ad Week* and *Ad Age*. While advertising agencies can help companies establish their overall marketing objectives, they will usually work with direct marketing and promotions agencies to develop a strategy that aligns a company's brand objectives with its sales goals. If you choose an advertising agency to develop your overall strategy, you may also need other promotional support to go beyond brand development and into specific promotional goals and objectives.

Legal

Outsourcing the legal aspects of your online promotions can be accomplished via your online promotions agency or specific outside legal counsel. An important consideration when choosing outside legal counsel to oversee the legal aspects of your online promotions is that the law firm you designate must be proficient in promotional law, which is different from contract law, business law, and other forms of legal practices.

There are numerous law firms that can help you with the laws associated with your online promotions, and most of them are members of the Promotion Marketing Association (PMA). In fact, one of the best investments you can make is to attend the annual PMA Law Conference, where you will find some of the best promotional law firms in the business. If you're not able to attend, simply go to the PMA Web site (www.pmalink.org) for a listing of promotional law firms.

Seismicom retains the services of the law firm Loeb & Loeb (www.loeb.com) and also uses Hall Dickler (www.halldickler.com) and Field Fisher Waterhouse (www.ffwlaw.com) for support with international promotions.

Technical

Outside technical support can be challenging for small to medium-size businesses. If you're willing to spend hundreds of thousands of dollars on your technology support, there is no end to the number of technical resources you can find. Pick up a copy of the *Industry Standard* magazine (or go online to www.thestandard.com) and you can search through numerous technical support organizations. There are also regional magazines such as the *Silicon Alley Reporter*, which covers the technical market in New York. Technical organizations for large enterprises include Oven Digital, Agency.com, RazorFish, IXL, and Modem Media. With the right budget, you can accomplish just about anything.

If money *is* an object, however, you may be better off with a smaller technical organization that has lower overhead costs to cover. These smaller organizations also have high-caliber programmers, but not as many of them and usually not in the highest-paid technology markets (such as New York, San Francisco, Boston, and Houston, for example). Good technical resources for small to medium-size businesses include WIT, WebJones, Blue Marble, Promotions.com, and Acid Tested. Many times, your ISP can provide recommendations for small to medium-size programmers and/or may be able to satisfy your technical requirements.

If you're simply looking for turnkey technology for your online promotions, be sure to check out application service providers such as IQ.com and the sweepstakes division of banner advertising agency DoubleClick (http://sweepstakes.doubleclick.com).

Finally, if you need to *hire* a technical resource for your company, there are a number of placement agencies including Hot Jobs (www.hotjobs.com), TechieGold.com, MonsterBoard (www.monsterboard.com), and a host of recruitment agencies that can be found in just about any resource book.

Creative

For creative resources I recommend that you use your advertising or promotions agency. For best results, the group that is developing your strategy should also be allowed to execute the creative aspects of your online promotions. If you are developing your strategy in house and outsourcing the creative aspects, then I would still recommend that you use an advertising or promotions agency. Whether or not the agency is focused on online or offline marketing is less important than the creative strategy itself. Even if your agency is traditionally based, it can usually adapt its creative concepts to the Internet.

To find an advertising or promotions agency, check out the previous section, Online Promotions Agencies. In addition to the advertising and promotions resource listings already mentioned, creative boutiques can be found via your local chapter of the American Advertising Federation (AAF) and/or Ad Club. There are also creative publications such as *Creativity*, which can point you in the right direction.

To truly find the right creative resource, however, you should simply become aware of the kinds of promotions that *you* like. Watch out for the kinds of creative work that you respond to, and then call up the company doing the promotion to see which agency it used. Really good current or previous work is usually a good indicator of future performance.

Media

Promotional media is different from traditional media in that you can usually find creative ways to utilize inventory that ties back to the broadcaster or publication. Radio, for example, lends itself to numerous opportunities to tie in your online promotions directly to the local radio station or national syndicate. For best results, you should use a promotions agency or media-buying company that truly understands the nature of promotions. Kelly, Scott & Madison (KSM) continuously demonstrates its ability to "go the extra mile" with promotional media dollars and finds creative ways to get more bang for your buck. Similarly, Promo TV utilizes spot cable television to cost-effectively enhance most promotional media buys.

Companies such as Initiative Media have the advantage of being extremely large, so their biggest advantage is not their knowledge of promotional media, but the sheer volume of media that they place every year. The publication *Media Week* is similar to *Ad Week* and *Brand Week*, but with a focus on the issues that affect media buying and selling. *Media Week* publishes its own agency listings for buying media.

Partnerships

There may very well be companies that are compensated solely for their ability to create partnerships, but I'm not aware of them. If you're looking to outsource your partnership negotiations, I'd recommend using your promotions agency (see the previous section, "Online Promotions Agencies," for information on how to find a promotions agency).

Customer Support

As stated previously, I believe that customer support should be handled in house. The reason is that your customers are the lifeblood of your company and should not be given to an outside resource. When customers call or email to complain or ask questions, they usually will share invaluable information about your company that you can use to improve your operations and overall success.

However, there are times when keeping customer support in house simply isn't an option. Call volume may increase beyond the point where internal personnel can handle it. Rather than staffing up with less than satisfactory employees, outsourcing becomes a necessity. Beyond the usual call centers, there are a few online companies that handle email and online support quite efficiently. After a brief training period, you can outsource all or most of your customer support requirements to these companies. Two companies that I recommend are People Support and Live Person. These companies completely understand the importance of online integration into customer support and have done a tremendous job of providing on-demand customer support.

Besides these two companies, you may find that many of the traditional call centers offer online customer support as well. That is, traditional call centers have upgraded their internal systems to include email and instant message capabilities. I'm not aware of any listings of higher-tech call centers, but it's easy enough to determine if a traditional call center has what you're looking for.

Administration

The administration of online promotions should be handled by your promotions agency. If you are looking to outsource the administrative duties of your online promotions, you should find a good promotions agency that can handle these administrative responsibilities. (See the earlier section, "Online Promotions Agencies," for information on how to find a promotions agency.)

Fulfillment

There are a number of fulfillment companies. *PROMO Magazine* has a full listing of fulfillment companies via their resource book, and you can find similar listings in *Incentive Magazine*. For companies focused on online fulfillment, just do a search via your favorite search engine for "Fulfillment" agencies. In most cases, if the fulfillment agency has taken the time to build a Web site and list itself with the search engines, it also has online fulfillment capabilities.

Fulfillment agencies (like other companies) have their own specialties. While one may be great at one type of fulfillment job, it may be horrible at another. There are a few fulfillment companies that seem to do a good job overall. Arrowhead Fulfillment (www.apfco.com) is a good resource that seems to work across multiple kinds of fulfillment jobs. Another fulfillment company that is extremely responsive is United Marketing Services (www.umspromo.com). You may find that various fulfillment companies will suit your needs differently depending on their own specialties. In other words, you may need a few different fulfillment agencies to use on different projects.

Research/Analysis

When it comes to online research and analysis, there are a few companies that are the leaders in this category. If you're looking to do your own research and you need it done yesterday, QuickTake.com and Greenfield Online are your best choices. If you need more general information, but you need it to be current and cutting edge, then check out Forrester or Jupiter. Find/SVP is great for finding information that already exists elsewhere and getting the secondary information you need at an extremely reasonable cost. And then you have access to all the industry trend data from Media Metrix to Nielson to NFO's online panel reports.

While there are no ratings systems or listing services currently in place for research and analysis in the online marketing sector, these are the major players you should look into to satisfy your outsourcing requirements.

Asking the Right Questions to Determine a Good Fit

Using an outside resource does not necessarily require a period of trial and error, although you never truly know how good your outside partner will be until you put him or her to the test with an actual project. Although the trial period cannot be avoided, it is possible to reduce your risk of "error" by asking the right questions up front. By knowing what to ask before the project begins, you are less likely to be disappointed when you actually put your outside resource to the test.

In general, questions are for the purpose of learning about your outside resource's strengths and weaknesses. No company wants to advertise its faults, but smart companies will not attempt to hide their weaknesses when asked directly. If your needs require something that your outside resource is not proficient in, it's better for you to know this up front rather than when it comes time for the outside resource to deliver on its promises.

In the sections that follow, I have outlined specific questions to ask, depending on your company's needs. While these questions are by no means comprehensive, they will give you a general guideline to work from when interviewing your outside resource.

Strategy

Because strategy is so important, the questions you'll need to ask with respect to strategy are all about the success of previous strategic recommendations. Even when a recommended strategy doesn't work, a good agency will have a reasonable explanation as to why their recommendations failed. It's important for a strategic agency to have good referrals from current and past clients because that will help make your decision to hire them that much easier. Here are a few good questions to ask when interviewing an outside strategic resource.

Is strategy your core focus? If not, what is?

Find out if strategy is the key driver of your outside resource. You don't want to hire an outside resource for something that is not its core competency. If strategy is not its main focus, then you will want to keep looking for a resource that does have a chief strategic focus.

Can you provide a list of companies for whom you have provided strategic services?

The list doesn't need to be long, but you should be able to recognize some of the companies on the list. If a list cannot be provided, then it probably means that the resource you're looking into does not place strategy in its core competency. While some companies may require your strategic resource to sign a nondisclosure agreement (NDA), there should be at least a few good companies that don't mind if other companies know that they have received strategic services from them.

Do you have referrals of satisfied companies who used your strategic services?

Positive referrals from satisfied clients are even better than a list of companies for which the strategic resource has rendered services. These can be in the form of a "thank you" letter from the client, the agreement to allow the strategic resource to have prospective clients call them, or press clippings in which positive things were said about the company's strategic recommendations.

Do you have examples of past strategic plans?

Strategic companies can't usually provide the whole plan from a previous client, but they can remove some of the more sensitive information from a previous plan and provide you with an example of past work. You can then evaluate the format in which your strategic recommendations will be presented back to you. If you're not happy with the way the strategic resource presents its findings, then chances are you will not be satisfied with the plan either.

What research companies are used to support strategic recommendations?

Good strategic recommendations are backed up with research. It's all well and good to have a fair amount of experience with similar marketing challenges, but in today's information age there's no excuse for not verifying assumptions and doing background reality checks. A good strategic resource should have a few different research companies that it relies on to help support its recommendations and verify assumptions.

Can you execute on your strategic recommendations?

In other words, can you walk the walk or simply talk the talk? If the strategic resource you're considering is only able to identify the problem and make a recommended solution (read: talk the talk), then chances are when you go to execute its recommendation (read: walk the walk) with someone else, that someone else will usually have alternative strategic recommendations. In the best-case scenario, if you're not planning to do your own executions, you should find an outside strategic resource that can both make the recommendations and then follow through with the execution of those recommendations. If its strategy is on target, its execution will yield the very results you're looking for.

Legal

You need to find out if an outside legal resource can handle all the legal aspects of *online promotions*, as opposed to contract law, corporate law, or other forms of business law. It's of little use to have an outside legal resource working on your online promotions that doesn't understand the intricacies of promotional lottery laws and Internet law. These are some of the questions you can ask to make sure you're hiring the right kind of legal resource for your online promotions.

Would you consider your company to be online promotions legal experts?

Be blunt. It will help you in the long run. The legal resource should be proficient in the laws associated with sweepstakes, contests, and games as they pertain to the Internet. If the legal resource is not familiar with COPPA or not comfortable with state and federal lottery laws, then you should ask for a referral to a legal resource that can better satisfy your online promotional needs.

How much of your legal practice is focused on promotional law?

Find out if online promotions represent a good portion of the legal resource's business or if it's only a small fraction of what it does. Does it have specific legal experts who focus on online promotions? Just online? Just promotions? Do they write official rules? Do they review advertising copy for legal compliance? Do they think that a sweepstakes and a contest are the same thing? If promotional law is a significant part of their business, they will be able to answer just about any promotional question you have (although not usually for free). If promotional law is one of their specialties, then you've come to the right place.

Do you have other online promotions–related clients?

Find out who else the legal resource represents. If it has examples of current online promotions for which it provided legal support, so much the better. The more clients and/or referrals you can get your hands on, the more comfortable you will feel about choosing it to handle your online promotional legal needs. If, on the other hand, it does not have other online promotions–related clients, it's probably not a good idea for you to become its guinea pig. Better to go with experts in the field than help a struggling legal resource change its company's business focus.

Is your company an active member of the PMA?

If not, was it *ever* a member of the Promotional Marketing Association? Memberships do lapse, but this is an important question because many of the online promotional case studies and much of the current information is shared through this organization. While your legal resource may have its own way of getting updated on new laws pertaining to online promotions, the majority of the resources you should be considering are already part of the PMA (and in some cases may even include board members).

Technical

Asking the right technology questions can be tricky. Technology is such a booming part of the new economy that finding the right technology resource can be quite challenging. The main things you need to know, however, have to do with the reliability of the network you're on (if you're in need of hosting services), the kinds of programmers it has on staff, the kind of access you have to the programmers, and any code ownership issues you may have.

What kind of redundancy, backup, and guaranteed uptime does your facility have?

When you're talking to representatives of an ISP, they will be most happy to provide you with an on-site visit to show you how they spent money on their "state-of-the-art" facilities. But these facilities will mean very little to you when your Web site is down and you need someone to help you get it up and running. Forget the "gee-whiz" stuff related to the facility and get back to basics. If you're on a shared Web server, how often is it backed up? Is there a mirrored Web server that will keep your promotion running if the main server goes down? What is the facility's guaranteed uptime? That is, if the server goes down, how long do you have to wait until it's back online? What do you get if it doesn't make the time limit it promised?

What is your priority escalation process?

In other words, how many layers do you need to go through to get to a technical contact? When there's a problem, it's usually extremely difficult to get to the right person who can help solve the problem. Before you sign on the bottom line, find out how many "monkeys" (nontechnical contacts put in place to field your calls) you have to go through to get to someone who can answer your questions. On a daily basis this is not important, but when things go wrong, you need to know that someone is on top of the problem besides you.

What kind of monitoring do you have in place?

Most technical resources have a pinging service similar to Red Alert (www
.redalert.com). Every 15 minutes, your online promotion is "pinged" to ensure that the Web pages are reachable. When the server goes down, the pages become unreachable and the monitoring service will either email or page you (depending

on how the service is set up ahead of time). If your technical resource has this in place, ask to be included on the list of contacts when the server goes down. This way, you'll be the first to know when there's a problem and won't have to wait until your customers complain.

What are your in-house programming capabilities?

When hiring a technical resource, you need to know if it is farming out your job to outside vendors. Whenever there are third-party programmers, it becomes more difficult to keep on schedule. Find out how many programmers your technical resource has in house. Then try to determine the breakdown of the kinds of programmers that are in house. Does your outside resource have database administrators? If so, for what database platforms (that is, Oracle, SQL, Informix, etc.)? How many HTML programmers? Java programmers? CGI and Perl programmers?

If you don't know what you need, it will be more difficult to determine if you have a good fit. Perhaps you may need to have your technical resource help you identify your needs and then determine what percentage of them can be satisfied by your outside resource directly versus its third-party resources.

What kinds of training programs do you have in place for your technical staff?

The next most important thing is to find out how well your technical resource keeps its programmers trained and up to speed. It's no use having programmers who are not familiar with the latest programs and technology advances. If their programmers haven't been inside a classroom for several years, chances are that they are using their old familiar programs, which may not be as efficient as today's software programs and the latest code libraries. This doesn't mean that older technology can't be useful, but the more advanced the technical resources, the better off your online promotions will be.

Are new programs built on a "work for hire" basis? Who owns the code?

This becomes a very important consideration if you plan on running a similar program in the future. Sometimes it's worth it to pay the extra premium to own the code if you have a long-term basis for your online promotions. Other times, it's better to test your online promotional strategy to see if it works. In either case, you should know up front who owns the code associated with the program. If you want code ownership, be prepared to pay extra. Not all programmers will charge a premium for a "work for hire" contract, but reusable code is where many programmers make their highest profits. If you don't want them using your code on other projects, you'll usually be charged extra for this part of the contract.

Creative

When it comes to the creative aspects of your online promotions, it's all about the ideas and the work. You're looking for examples of past creative that demonstrates their creative strategy, ability to think, and their ability to express their ideas with words and graphics. The examples need not be in line with what your current needs are. Usually, a good creative team will come up with totally new ideas to address your current problem, so past work should be used in general, not as a specific application to the problem you're working on. Here are some questions to lead you in the right direction.

Do you have a portfolio of work and/or an agency reel?

Seeing is believing when it comes to creative work. A good portfolio of work should be somewhat diverse, covering different markets and areas of expertise. If all the work is centered around a particular industry (and not yours), the agency may have problems adapting to your specific creative needs. When looking at the portfolio of work, try to remove yourself from your own creative challenges and look at the work from the eyes of the target audience. "Would this appeal to me if I were shopping for a new car?" If you can focus on the strategic objective, you're more likely to see the creative strategy that the agency used to satisfy the objective (and then be in a better situation to evaluate the agency on its past work).

Can you provide an example of past creative brief and/or case history?

Try to go beyond the actual creative deliverable and see how the work evolved. If the agency can provide you with a creative brief to a corresponding example of work, you can get a good feel for what the directives of the project were and if the resulting creative satisfied those directives. Similarly, a case history will tell you what the client was looking for and what was delivered. Again, these more detailed examples will help you understand how the agency thinks and if its creative strategy will satisfy your needs.

Do you have referrals from satisfied clients?

While the work may speak for itself, the client may have a different story to tell. Try to get the names and numbers of a few past clients so you can do your homework and see if the clients are truly as happy as the agency claims they are. From past clients, you can find out how easy the agency is to work with, if the project was delivered on time or was delayed, and a host of other valuable information that can only be learned from actually having worked on a project.

Have you received any creative awards? If so, which ones and for what categories?

Does your agency resource have "award-winning" creative? If not, I wouldn't necessarily discount them. Many agencies simply do not take the time necessary to submit their work to the appropriate judges for these awards, but those that do will be happy to share with you any awards they have won. Find out in which categories their work was entered and in which categories they took home awards. This may tell you something about their creative strengths.

What is your approach to creative strategy?

Every agency has its own unique way of handling creative problems. By understanding the process that an agency goes through to develop its creative, you can see how it works and if its methodologies are likely to satisfy your requirements. You may need to be more hands-on with the creative process than the agency is comfortable with, or perhaps the reverse is true. By knowing how often it wants you involved, you can see if its approach to the creative strategy is what you are looking for.

How does creativity integrate with the rest of the agency?

This is the million-dollar question if you plan on using a single resource for all or most of your online promotional needs. In some agencies, there is an ongoing battle between strategy, account, and creative resources. In others, the creative component is an extension of everything the agency does. The more tightly integrated the creative work is to the entire agency, the better the chances your online promotion will be successful.

Media

Not all media-buying agencies are the same. This is especially true when it comes to promotional media. While it is not *critical* to find a promotion-focused media-buying agency, you'll find that it helps to have someone who understands your promotional needs. Here are some questions to help you find out if the media-buying agency you are considering will best fit your needs.

What is the total dollar amount for all media placed last year?

Find out just how much media your outside resource placed last year and then compare those numbers with those published in *Media Week* or another media-focused publication. You should know where your outside resource ranks in comparison to other media-buying agencies so that you can better understand how much negotiating power it will have to work with on your behalf. In general, the more media placed, the more leverage the agency will have when placing your media dollars. The exception to that rule is with local media buys where a smaller agency can often work with the individual media companies (broadcast stations or local editions of publications, for example) in which you are interested.

What is the average size client (in terms of media dollars) for whom you place media?

This question will help you determine where *your* media buy will fall in terms of priority. If your media buy is relatively small, a small to mid-size media-buying agency may be a better fit as your dollars will mean more to them as an agency. Whereas a smaller media buy will have less priority with a large media-buying group, a small to mid-size agency would welcome your business and likely provide more individual attention.

Is your agency promotions focused? If not, what is your media-buying specialty?

Some media-buying agencies are focused on promotional media. When you're buying media to support your online promotion, it's helpful to have a media resource that understands promotional needs and can go beyond a traditional media buy to integrate your promotion into the media itself. With radio, this can usually be a tie-in with the radio stations themselves. Online, your promotion may be mentioned elsewhere within the Web site content itself. In each medium, there are ways to get a little extra bang for your media bucks and a promotions-focused media buying agency will know just what to ask for and what you can expect to get above and beyond the traditional media buy.

What types of "promotional extras" can we expect to get for our media dollars?

If the media agency is promotions focused, it can usually tell you up front what kinds of extras you can expect to get with the dollar volume of media you're buying. Of course this is all subject to actual negotiations and availability, but the right agency partner can help identify what it's planning on going after and give you some realistic expectations of what will be achieved. There are a lot of factors that play into how many of the promotional extras will be granted, but it's a good idea to know up front what you can expect.

Do you have an example of a past media plan?

Find out what the media plan will look like—especially if you're new to media buying. How are the media findings and examples of media schedules presented? Check out the likely format of your media plan and ask questions before you start the process of negotiating your own media buy. The more you know up front about the media buy, the better off you will be when it comes time to place your media.

What is your fee structure? Do you charge flat fees or a percentage commission on the media buy?

It used to be a standard 15 percent commission on all media buys, but this is not always the case. Some media-buying agencies will charge a flat rate for planning, which could be more or less than the standard 15 percent commission. Find out what you will be expected to pay for the media-buying agency's services before you engage it and have it start working on your media plan. It should also be noted that the larger your media buy, the more room you'll have for negotiation of rates and fee structures with your media-buying agency.

Partnerships

Identifying good outside agencies to use for partnership negotiations is probably one of the more challenging areas associated with outsourcing your online promotions. Sometimes the best partnerships happen by pure chance. While these past partnerships look fabulous to you as an outsider looking in, it's difficult to ask the right questions to find out how much of the partnership was due simply to dumb luck versus shrewd negotiating skills. Below are some questions that will help you evaluate an outside resource for partnership negotiations, but of the different categories listed here, it's been my experience that partnership negotiations are the least consistent. Sometimes they work out great, and sometimes even the best negotiators strike out. These questions should at least help you identify the agency that will give you your best chance of an ideal partnership.

What do you consider to be a successful partnership program?

While this question is certainly open-ended, it will help you discover what your outside agency considers to be a *successful partnership* before any negotiations are completed on your behalf. While you are looking for a shrewd negotiator, it's best to have someone who is reasonable and realistic so that both partners feel that they are benefiting from the program. This will help breed long-term partnerships versus short-term gains.

Do you consider your past partnerships to be a "win-win" for all parties?

This question is less open-ended and gets right to the heart of the matter. If your outside partnership resource is only interested in your needs, then even when a partnership program is established, it will usually be for a single program and not lead to any long-term opportunities. When partnership programs are truly a "win-win" for all parties involved, they have a much longer-term viability than a single online promotion. You should seek an outside resource that is interested in helping you not just with this single program, but with establishing a relationship that lasts.

What was the biggest deal you put together? What were the gives and gets?

Find out the caliber of the outside resource you are considering. What was the best deal it put together and why is it considered the best? Find out what both partners gave to each other and what they received in return. Was it a fair exchange or was the deal lopsided? Do you recognize the program or the players involved? Would you be happy if you worked with either of the companies that were involved with the deal?

Can you give some examples of past partnerships?

Besides the best, what about the rest? Was the biggest success story a one-time deal or were there other partnership programs you'd be interested in? Check out the different partners and find out how the deals were put together. In most cases, the outside resource has one partner as a client—who was the client that initiated the deal? Is that company still a client? Could you partner with them if you wanted to?

Who are some of your current clients? Can I tap into any of these clients?

Find out whom the partnership resource has as clients and if there are any clients that you might be interested in up front. If so, this should make the negotiations much simpler as the resource you're using is working for both sides and can easily work with both you and your desired partner to create a partnership program that works for both of you.

Customer Support

As stated previously, I firmly believe that customer support should be handled in house whenever possible. But, since there are times when this simply is not an option, it's a good idea to make sure your outside partner has what you need to provide quality customer support to your lifeline. If customer support is not handled correctly, then you will lose sales and future revenue opportunities. This is why I recommend keeping this component in house, but if you must outsource, then make sure you have a quality partner on whom you can depend.

Who are some of your satisfied customers? Can you provide contact names and phone numbers?

Who is currently being serviced by your outside resource? Find out the kinds of clients that it currently has and then ask to speak with them directly. If the customer support group is doing a good job, then its clients will have no reservations about singing its praises. If, on the other hand, it is not performing as promised, current clients will say so and identify the areas in which they are not satisfied. If you think you will have similar problems, you can ask the current client who else it is considering and help you narrow down your own search.

What is your total number of phone/email/IM staff?

Not just how many people are on staff, but who is dedicated to what. In some cases there will be some overlap between phone, email, and instant messenger (IM) support. When a trained staff member is not doing one, he or she can certainly be doing another. The key is who's dedicated to what. There should be enough dedicated staff resources to handle your needs. Make sure you clearly identify what you are looking for so that your outside customer support group can be clear about what it can and cannot handle.

What are your guaranteed response times?

How long must a caller stay on hold? Will email be answered in a matter of minutes, hours, or days? Are instant messages really instant? Knowing what your customers will experience will help you determine if the outside resource is a good fit.

What are your peak call volumes?

When does the customer service group get the most volume of calls/emails/instant messages? Do your customer service needs fall into the same time frames? Will this be a problem? How are peak volumes handled? Find out what it does about peak hours and how it handles the additional load.

How is the staff trained?

Find out what normal procedures are for training new hires and existing employees who will be working on your business. Determine what you need to provide to the customer support center in order to train its staff to suit your customer service requirements. When questions are asked and the answer is unknown, who will it contact and how will the new information be disseminated to the rest of the team working on your customer service requirements?

Administration

Remember that a chief success criterion for online promotions is attention to details. Outsourcing the administration components will save you significant amounts of time as long as you have chosen the right partner. The key to identifying the right partner is determining the amount of experience the company has with handling the administrative aspects of the online promotion. You want someone who can handle every last detail and has the right staff in place to make sure all the details are handled correctly. Here are some questions to ask to find out if the administration agency you're considering has what it takes to handle the administration details.

Can you provide a listing of all the promotional details that your agency handles and/or an example of a promotional checklist?

Let the agency tell you what it covers in its administrative duties. There are several components associated with the back end of online promotions. A good agency partner can easily list all of those components for you and may even have an internal checklist that it uses to ensure that every last detail is taken care of. Review the checklist or promotional details and make sure you're satisfied with what it will cover on your behalf. Even if you've never completed an online promotion before, the number of items on the list itself will show you if the agency you are considering can meet your expectations.

How many promotions does your company handle administratively?

Make sure you're not the first client who has asked the agency to handle the administrative duties associated with online promotions. Administrative duties are tricky and should not be given to an agency that lacks experience in this area. The more promotions an agency has handled administratively, the more likely it is to have the right amount of experience you need for successful online promotions.

How many promotional administrators do you have?

In other words, how many dedicated resources are associated with the administrative aspects of online promotions? The number is relative to the previous question of how many promotions the company handles administratively. In general, a good promotional administrator can handle between 10 to 20 online promotions in a month (depending on their complexity). It's also a good idea to find out the average number of promotional administrators to account executives, or how many account executives does one administrator support?

What kinds of insurance do you carry?

Nobody is perfect and mistakes do happen. The key is, when mistakes happen with your online promotions, are you responsible for those mistakes or is your promotions agency? By finding out what kinds of insurance the agency carries, you'll know what it is already covered for in the event that mistakes are made with one of your online promotions.

Do you indemnify your clients? If so, up to what dollar amount?

A good online promotions agency will provide some form of indemnification against mistakes and potential liability. This question directly corresponds to the previous question about insurance. If the agency has the right insurance policies, then indemnification will not be a problem. If not, then you might not be covered if any problems arise. Indemnification can provide you and the rest of your company with peace of mind so that if problems do arise, the promotions agency will handle it.

Fulfillment

Unfortunately, fulfillment is rather hit or miss these days. You can ask all the right questions and still get the wrong fulfillment company or the right fulfillment company with a bunch of problems and mistakes. Most fulfillment companies do not offer guarantees of service or guarantees against their mistakes. In short, good fulfillment resources are hard to find. The following questions will help minimize your risk of working with a less than adequate fulfillment company and should help you ask the right questions when searching for a fulfillment company to service your needs.

How do you handle mistakes?

Be blunt. Mistakes are bound to happen when it comes to fulfillment, and you need to know what your resource will do when those mistakes are made. Provide examples of common mistakes. What would your resource do, for example, if a prize is incorrectly delivered? How would it handle a consumer's inquiry that the prize/product promised was never received? What would it do if the list of winners is mislabeled or the congratulatory letter was not included with the prize? Try to identify what will happen *before* the inevitable mistakes are made.

Do you have a rate card for services?

While most fulfillment companies prefer to quote on a particular job, ask if they will provide you with a generic list of services. In most cases, there are usually monthly minimums associated with jobs, warehouse fees for items stored long-term, and standard costs associated with fulfillment of prizes and premium items. While fulfillment companies are reluctant to provide these rate cards, you can usually get something as a starting point if you are persistent enough.

What is your ideal fulfillment job?

Every fulfillment center has its specialty. Find out what the fulfillment center you are interviewing does best. While fulfillment centers like to think that they can satisfy just about any request, they usually have a particular kind of job in which they excel. It's okay if the job they tell you about is not what you are looking for.

By knowing what they are the best at, you can usually get a pretty good idea whether what you're asking them to do is much of a stretch from their ideal job.

What is the average volume of jobs handled?

How many jobs does the fulfillment center take on at any given time? What is the volume of one of those jobs? Here you are trying to find out where your job will rank in accordance with the fulfillment center's normal job load. In many cases, the bigger your job(s), the more attention you will receive.

Can you provide examples of tracking and reporting?

What will your tracking and reporting look like? Look at a past client's report and see if you like the way the information was reported. If the reports are easy to read and make sense, you should have no problem identifying potential problems or integrating these reports into the rest of the reporting for your online promotion.

Do you offer data entry of mail-ins?

Most fulfillment companies have the ability to keypunch write-in data so that you can include it as part of your database. This is not always necessary, but you should find out if it's an option with the fulfillment center you are considering and the appropriate cost of completing this request. This is especially important with rebates and mail-in offers, but can come into play with premium offers, sweepstakes, and contest entries as well.

How much online integration do you offer within your back-end fulfillment process?

Can your preferred fulfillment resource receive email attachments, utilize your FTP site, and/or open your database files? Find out what its limitations are with respect to your current process. You need to know how much information conversion and other integration issues you will need to complete before the fulfillment center can do what you're asking it to do.

Research/Analysis

When it comes to research and analysis, the key questions you want to ask up front will pertain to the types of research and specific specialties that the research group can perform on your behalf. Each research organization has its own ways of conducting research, along with specific areas of ongoing focused research. When interviewing a potential research and analysis resource, you're trying to find out if its areas of expertise match your specific needs. Here are some questions to help identify if the group you are interested in will provide you with the information you need to support your online promotions.

Is your research firm primarily focused on quantitative or qualitative research?

Most companies will respond that they provide both quantitative and qualitative research services, but the majority of research firms have a concentration in one or the other. Large research firms may have separate divisions or related companies, each providing a different kind of research. With quantitative research, you have a better chance of integrating the simple multiple-choice questions into your Web site to determine the feedback provided by your target audience. Even though qualitative research firms will help you set up a focus group of participants (either online or offline), that approach will provide more comprehensive information *but* with fewer respondents.

What is your unique selling proposition?

In other words, what makes you different from your competition? Most research firms have some version of a proprietary research methodology or vast number of respondents from which they can ensure that you receive the highest quality research. Find out what makes the research organization you're interested in different from their competition.

What are your online research capabilities?

Nearly every research firm has formulated some answer to this question. It might be that it has developed a core group of respondents from which you can easily get the information you seek. Others have developed research applications, which can help you quickly deploy surveys on your own Web site. Still others have online focus group technology that they believe is second to none. Find out what your outside resource has to offer and see if it's what you need as part of your online integration into your online promotions.

Can you provide a current client listing?

Find out what other companies are using this research and analysis research firm. Pay attention to any companies that are in a similar industry to yours. If there are some, this will tell you that the research group you're considering is not new to your industry. If it is new to your industry, you may need to spend more time up front explaining the background information about your company, your competitors, the information you're interested in, and what you plan to do with the research and analysis. You should also call a few current clients to determine their satisfaction level with the research organization.

Do you have examples of research projects and/or a sample executive summary?

The sample research project and/or executive summary will help you better understand the way that the research organization reports its findings and information. It's a good idea to review its methodologies for previous work to make sure that its findings are statistically relevant and that the research has no significant bias. Equally important is the presentation of the findings themselves and the transformation from statistical data to analytical information. This is what you will be paying for and you should make sure you're happy with previous work before you engage the group for your own projects.

When and How to Fire Your Promotions Agency

If the time comes when you are no longer happy with the level of service you are receiving from your promotions agency, then it's best for all parties that you be up front and honest. There is a correct way to fire your promotions agency and an incorrect way. Even if you are extremely unhappy with your agency, it will behoove you both in the long run to talk about what went wrong and why you are no longer interested in its services. In most cases, the agency will already know (or at least be aware) that you're unhappy with its performance. Taking the time to terminate the relationship will help you confirm what requirements the agency has not met. This will help you with your search for a new promotions agency, as you can be up front about your requirements as a client and what it needs to do to satisfy you.

This section will address the best way to fire your promotions agency and how to avoid the need to fire the next promotions agency that you hire.

When to Fire Your Promotions Agency

You shouldn't fire your promotions agency at the first problem in an otherwise smooth relationship. The best long-term relationships develop an understanding and trust between client and agency. At the end of the day, promotions are a people business, and people make mistakes. It's when these mistakes become common and begin to repeat themselves that it's time to let go of your current agency and find a new outlet to satisfy your online promotional needs.

If customer service is at the heart of the issue, then perhaps you need a new account executive (or supervisor) who will manage your business more effectively. If you don't think you're getting the attention you deserve, then escalate your frustrations beyond your primary contact at the agency to someone who truly cares about keeping you as a client. As you go up the ladder in the agency, you'll find that there are a number of people whose sole job is to keep clients happy. If you're not happy, it's time you discussed your frustrations with someone who can make changes in the agency that will result in your ongoing contentment.

The key to firing your promotions agency is to *be fair*. If you have already established your requirements for a successful relationship, then it should be an easy review of what was promised and not delivered on. In the best-case scenario, you will already have warned the agency that it is "on probation." If it still fails to deliver on your expectations, then it is unlikely that it will argue with your decision.

Before you fire your promotions agency, consider the reasons you wish to do so. Has it underperformed or not met your expectations? Have you had at least one conversation with your agency about not having your expectations met? Is its attention to your business inadequate? If you feel that you have discussed the problems with your agency and have not had any resolution to your satisfaction, then it is time to terminate any agreements currently in place and begin searching for a new agency.

How to Fire Your Promotions Agency

Once you've decided to fire your promotions agency, it should be as easy as a phone call or a brief meeting. Assuming that you've already had previous discussions about its lack of performance or attention to detail, this should be more of an exit interview than an angry yelling match. If you've already discussed your dissatisfaction, then confirming that little to no improvement has been made should not come as a shock to the agency being let go.

If you have given your promotions agency a chance to correct its problems, then it will usually be the first to admit that it has not met your expectations. While it may offer some additional suggestions for improvement, it will probably agree with your decision if it has not fixed previously identified problems.

If your expectations are unrealistic, however, the agency may tell you so when the time comes to part ways. Try not to dismiss this as retaliation for being fired. Try to keep an open mind *even during the act of firing your agency*. If you continue to be reasonable, you might find out that what you want is unlikely to be achieved. Of course, you will be the ultimate judge of this when you interview your replacement promotions agencies. But if the same problems occur with your next agency, then perhaps there is truth in what the first agency told you.

The point is that we're all here to learn. As the client, you can learn a lot from your agency even if you're unhappy with its performance. Make sure that you're being a reasonable client and that you're not firing your agency as a knee-jerk reaction to a single problem or an unrealistic expectation. If you are a reasonable client, then the next agency you hire should have no problems succeeding where your previous agency failed.

How to Start an In-house Promotions Group

If you're finding that online promotions are a big part of your company, then perhaps it's time to start your own in-house promotions group. In order for your in-house promotions group to be a success, you must evaluate the cost-to-benefit ratio associated with starting an in-house group. If you're spending a significant amount of money on your promotions and you are projecting that this trend will continue, then starting an in-house group may be the best way to go. This section will not cover how to evaluate this cost-to-benefit ratio because each company's situation will be different. Simply speak with your finance person about the costs associated with the people and other resources needed (versus the potential cost savings), and he or she will help you determine if starting an in-house promotions group makes sense. Instead, this section will cover what you need to begin your in-house promotions group.

If you have read the bulk of this chapter, then you probably already know (or at least have a good feel for) which parts of online promotions make the most sense to bring in-house first. If you want to "test the waters" of having an in-house promotions group, you need not invest in every aspect of online promotions. Instead, you can pick and choose the areas you feel will be most cost-effective for your company now and in the future.

Starting with the Right In-house Resources

When starting an in-house promotions group, it's best to build a solid foundation with the three core elements of strategy, legal, and administration. Each of these core elements will provide the right platform on which the rest of the in-house promotions group can be built. Without these three elements, the other seven elements (creative, technical, media, partnerships, customer support, fulfillment, and research/analysis) will not be very helpful. Of the three, the legal and administration elements are the most challenging and will limit some of the strategy because of logistics and/or legal aspects that affect the promotion.

If you had to start with a single in-house resource, I would recommend that you begin with an administrative expert who has handled the back end of several online promotions. Good promotional administrators understand all the details that are required to launch successful online promotions and usually have experience with the legal aspects as well. If you don't have any knowledge or experience with online promotions, the administrator will help guide you through the back-end process where all the details make or break the online promotion.

Promotional legal counsel will help you identify where your biggest liabilities are and what you need to do to protect yourself. A legal expert together with a promotional administrator will ensure that you have covered all the legal and administrative requirements that will keep your online promotions aboveboard. Of course the third element of strategy will be necessary to actually get to where you want to go from a marketing perspective. To use a metaphor, if the administrator is the shell of the car and the legal expert is the engine, your strategic resource is the driver. You can be the driver in the short term, but ultimately you'll want an expert to help drive your promotions group.

Some would argue that you should begin with the strategic expert. In this way, you select the right driver who can help you pick out the administrative shell of your new car and the appropriate legal engine. In the best-case scenario, you should hire all three elements to create an ideal in-house team of experts. With these three resources in place, the group will have enough forward momentum to grow, as the work requires. As more online promotions are created, additional elements such as creative and technology will be brought into the fold until the team is completely independent of outside resources—*if* this is your ultimate goal.

Evaluating Your Ongoing Needs

Customer support is a natural extension to your internal promotions group. You probably have some form of customer support already in place, and training your internal group to support your online promotions is a no-brainer. After a few meetings with the strategic, legal, and/or administrative resource, your customer support group will have the answers to your customers' most frequently asked questions.

As you continue developing your internal team over time, you may find specific areas that never quite make sense to bring in house. Fulfillment, for example, may never make sense to bring in house because of the costs associated with warehouses and labor. Likewise, promotional media may not be something that internal dedicated resources will ever be able to do better than the outside experts. The key to building a good internal team is to bring in only the resources that will ultimately benefit the company. Even the administrative duties may be more than you wish to bring in house (at least in the short term). To start out, you may prefer to buy the intellectual property of a strategic and legal resource and see what else makes sense after you've tested the waters for a while.

Once you have started an internal team of online promotions experts, continue to evaluate their effectiveness immediately, in 3 months, and again in 6 months. Are you more satisfied with these internal resources or were you able to accomplish more with your outside promotions agency? You may find that the biggest benefits are not so much financial, but speed to market and the constant availability of an internal team focused on *your* business. If you're unhappy with the internal team, determine what you liked better about outsourcing and address your concerns with the team. You may find that you can support their efforts with a smaller financial commitment to an outside agency that puts your company ahead of all the competition.

Refer back to the section When to Call a Promotional Marketing Agency to help you evaluate which elements you'd like to bring in house. If you're not sure you will need the dedicated resources for the long term, consider hiring out on a freelance basis to see what adding the different components does for the rest of your existing online promotions team. After the initial launch of your internal group, you can experiment with the other promotional elements (creative, technical, media, partnerships, fulfillment, and research/analysis) to see what makes the most sense for your in-house promotions group.

Conclusion

There will be times when outsourcing entire projects will be the best solution, other times when outsourcing only part of the project is ideal, and still other times when the best thing to do is to keep the project completely in house. Through understanding the advantages and disadvantages of both outsourcing and keeping projects in house, the best solution is to seek the right approach for *each* online promotion that you are planning. Strategy corresponds directly with the phase of the company life cycle you are currently in (*start-up* = in house, *growth* = outsource, *mature* = in house, and *decline* = outsource). You should bring legal, technical, and customer support resources in house if you can afford it. Creative, media, administration, and fulfillment should be outsourced. For partnerships, if you have more money than time, you should use an outside resource. For research and analysis, a combination of internal and external resources should be used.

Once you've determined your outsourcing needs, the next big question is "How do I find the vendors I need?" If you plan on outsourcing more than one or two components for your online promotions, you may want to consider outsourcing all your needs to a promotions agency. The main magazine of the promotions industry, *PROMO Magazine*, has its own directory of promotions agencies, which include online and integrated promotions agencies. Likewise, there are specific resources available for each aspect of online promotions. The trick is knowing what questions to ask of your potential resource *before* you hire them. By knowing what to ask before the project begins, you are less likely to be disappointed when you actually put your outside resource to the test.

How to Create a
Multibrand Promotion

Even though online promotions are relatively inexpensive compared to traditional promotions, there are a number of reasons why you might want to consider having another company become part of your promotion. The most common reason companies look for a partner is to help with the media space or funds needed to help promote the promotion (which I will cover in Chapter 7, "Promoting the Promotion"). While the promotion itself may not break the bank, the right amount of media exposure can certainly lighten most companies' wallets.

Another reason you might consider having a partner is to increase your prize pool. There are many companies that leverage their excess inventory in order to secure media exposure through various promotional opportunities. While you may have a strong media budget, you may not have enough prizes in your promotion to make it compelling for your target audience.

Cross-marketing is yet another reason why many companies decide to partner with each other. When your product has obvious tie-in products, it makes sense to pool resources to increase effectiveness. If you're a salsa manufacturer, then it's not rocket science to want to partner with the maker of tortilla chips and/or beer to maximize promotional impact. If you're a hotel chain, then airlines, rental cars, and travel agents (real or virtual) make great cross-marketing partners.

There are, in fact, many reasons why a company might want to include another company as part of its online promotion. This chapter will show you how to avoid the potential pitfalls of partnering with additional companies as well as the best practices to ensure a successful multibrand promotion.

Starting with a Clear Objective

Sound familiar? I've already driven home the importance of starting with a clear objective in previous chapters. However, it's important to reinforce the fact that with one or more partners involved in the same promotion, starting with a clear objective is not just a good idea—it's critical to success. While you may get away with "flying by the seat of your pants" with your own online promotions, the first thing your potential partners will want to know is, "What are you trying to accomplish?" If you don't have a good answer, you're not likely to attract effective partners.

A clear objective is the first and most important step in creating successful multibrand promotions. If your objective isn't clear, then it will be impossible for you to explain to your desired partners what you want to do and why you think *they* should be involved. Conversely, a clear objective will make all the other steps flow effortlessly, because you can simply ask yourself, "Does this support the objective?" If so, taking that step will move you one step closer to your goal. If not, you should find an alternative that does.

This also applies to your potential partners. If your own objective is crystal clear and your potential partner's objectives are in direct opposition to yours, then no matter how much the potential partner is willing to contribute, it will not make sense for you to combine efforts. Once you identify your own objectives, you will begin to seek out potential partners that have the same or similar objectives. Only then will a multibrand promotion truly make sense.

Avoid Multiple Objectives

At the other end of the spectrum lies the challenge of having multiple (often conflicting) objectives. Here, the problem is *not* that you are lacking an objective, it is that you have too many objectives, all equally important and expected to be addressed with a single promotion—with one or more partners, no less.

Perhaps you have taken the time to identify all the key objectives you want to solve. Although this is a good practice, problems arise when you decide to use a single online promotion to satisfy them all at the same time. Having multiple objectives per se isn't bad, but use caution. More often than not, when a promotion has multiple objectives, it shows.

It's difficult to effectively increase sales, when you're also trying to drive traffic or reinforce brand identity at the same time. When you have multiple objectives, one objective usually takes precedence, and when it does, the others suffer. This is assuming that the promotion works at all. Often when there are multiple objectives, the promotion ends up being a muddled mess, contradicting itself, and ultimately it doesn't work.

When one objective doesn't take precedence over the others, the promotion has a serious identity crisis. This identity crisis usually leads to an unrealistic expectation that the target audience is willing to jump through all the necessary hoops to participate in your promotion—they won't.

When your promotional objectives are all over the map, potential partners will see this as a sign of disorganization and will think twice about a tie-in to their products, media, and other support to your shotgun approach to online promotions (if you're lucky). If you're not so lucky, you might wind up with an equally disorganized partner who has a similar shotgun approach to online promotions, and you'll both end up wasting a lot of time and money.

The bottom line is that for a multibrand promotion to work, it must be simple, clear, and to the point. If there's any confusion, your partners may get the wrong idea about what you're trying to accomplish. Or worse, targeted consumers will go about their business and ignore you and your partners' promotional offer altogether. With a single, clearly defined objective, you will ensure that your promotion stays on course and you'll be in a much better position to identify first-rate partners to support your objective.

Identifying Ideal Partners

With your objective clearly stated, the next step is to determine which partners could best help satisfy your objective while at the same time solve a complementary objective for their own company. Perhaps you want to drive traffic to your Web site and know of a complementary company that also needs traffic. Or perhaps you want to build a database of potential customers and know of a similar company that could benefit from a customer database.

While a partner's objective does not need to be identical to your own, it must not contradict what you are trying to accomplish. If your objective is to increase awareness of your product and your partner's objective is to increase sales, you are at different phases of the marketing cycle (awareness/interest/desire/action) and someone's objective will not be met. The promotion may build awareness (with the right advertising support), but fail to increase sales of the partner's products or vice versa. A successful multibrand promotion can only be accomplished when the objectives are similar enough that they don't conflict with each other.

At the industry trade show *PROMO Expo 2000*, I was fortunate enough to attend a partnership marketing session with Joel Ehrlich, Senior Vice President of Promotions for Warner Brothers Consumer Products. In this session, Mr. Ehrlich outlined his "10 Commandments of Partnerships" (Figure 6.1). As partnership promotions are a big part of Mr. Ehrlich's responsibility, I found these "commandments" were not only insightful but also accurate (from my own personal experience). You might want to keep Figure 6.1 close at hand the next time you are identifying ideal partners for your next promotion.

10 Commandments
of Partnerships

by Joel Ehrlich, Senior VP of Promotions
Warner Brothers Consumer Products

1. Be sensitive to partner goals
2. Plan to plan
3. Don't follow a formula
4. Leave ego at the door
5. Move quickly
6. Get to know your client's organization
7. Integrate and be flexible
8. Experience the consumers' experience
9. Communicate and be honest
10. Begin at the end

Figure 6.1   Ten commandments of partnership promotions.

The Gets: Satisfying Your Biggest Needs

Beyond complementary objectives with potential partners, you need to clearly identify what you want to get from your potential partners. You are looking for other companies that satisfy your biggest needs, be they additional advertising support, nontraditional exposure, prizes, reduced cost, or leveraging a brand.

Think big. If you could have anything, what would it be? Perhaps you want television exposure, but you simply can't afford it. Or maybe you need tickets to the Super Bowl for prizes, but have no idea how to get them. Identify your absolute best-case scenario and start there. You need to shoot for the stars even if you don't end up with your ideal add-on components.

Next, think about what else you would like to have, even if it's not as great as the ideal add-on components. Perhaps it's more Web server capacity. It's not as flashy as Super Bowl tickets, but it could increase the number of simultaneous users who participate in your promotion. These second-tier items are added bonuses that will make your online promotion more successful.

The next step is to correctly list your "gets" in the order of importance. Even if you are doing all the partner negotiations yourself, you will still need this list to refer back to as a reality check to make sure that you're getting what you truly need from your potential partner(s).

The Gives: What You're Willing to Offer

For a successful multibrand promotion, you need to be realistic about what you will give up in exchange for that nice list of "gets." In the same way you prioritized your list from "best-case scenario" to "nice to have," you need to do the same thing with your "gives." Not all of your "gives" have to be tangible. There have been cases where one partner included another partner simply for the "coolness" that they represented. You can't effectively put a price tag on "coolness," but if you have a cool or hip brand, you can use that for leverage to your partners.

If you're in business for the long haul, you should give some thought to what value you are offering. The best multibrand promotions are repeated year after year with minor changes. If you really create a win-win scenario for you and your partners, you'll all want to think about extending your relationships further.

The best way to compile your list of "gives" is to think about the kinds of things your company is in a position to offer that might be attractive to potential partners. Perhaps you have an abundance of product that you are willing to give away as part of the promotion. Or perhaps you have invested in events or sponsorships that can be leveraged in your upcoming promotions. This is especially helpful if you have relationships that are difficult to match or duplicate. Start with the big-ticket items you can provide and then work your way down to the smaller things that you can bring to the table.

When the final negotiations begin, much of what you're willing to put on the table will receive an estimated dollar amount that will be compared to what you are asking for in return. Not all negotiations come down to dollar for dollar, but as this is an easy measurement tool to estimate the exchange, it typically happens that way.

Complementary Partners List

Once you've compiled your list of "gives" and "gets," the next step is to identify complementary partners. Make a list of as many complementary partners as you can, so that you can begin to identify the ideal partners for your online promotion. If you're having difficulty getting started, I recommend using a company directory from a publication such as *Brand Week* or an online search engine. Company directories typically list by product and service offerings. Perhaps you are looking for a travel partner, but are not sure whom to include. Directories will provide you with a list of potential partners that you can then condense based on your own needs.

After you have created your complete list of potential partners, you then need to prioritize the ones that seem to be most important to your company and the promotion itself. This will become obvious from your prioritized list of "gets." That is, your list of "gets" will tell you what kinds of partners your promotion is in need of, and your list of complementary partners should make it easy to identify which partners make the most sense.

Identifying the *right* potential partners is usually the most challenging component of multibrand promotions because you need to widen your universe beyond the obvious choices. As you create your list, it's important to include as many potential choices as possible so that you can refine your choices to those that make the most sense. In this way, if your top choices don't work out, you have additional options to return to (rather than starting the process all over again).

Finding the right partnerships can take time, but is usually a worthwhile investment as the right partner can exponentially increase your chances for successful online promotions. When you combine complementary assets and skill sets, you have the potential to extend your reach, frequency, and marketing messages that will drive home the essence of your online promotion.

Put Yourself in Your Partner's Shoes

Determining what you want out of the promotion is easy—you want to satisfy your promotional objective and use your desired partners to help you do that. However, now you must place yourself in your partners' shoes and think about what you would want from your company if you were approached. Anticipating what your partners want from your company will help you negotiate the best deal for both parties.

Before you begin making phone calls and sending emails to solicit a partnership in your upcoming online promotion, be sure to ask yourself, "Why would I want to participate in this promotion? What will I get out of it? Would I be interested in what is being offered?" The best negotiations begin with the final end product in mind. If you can envision the kinds of responses that a potential partner will have to your request to combine marketing strengths, then you will be in a much better position to formulate your answers to questions ahead of time. The more you put yourself in your partners' shoes, the more likely you are to understand their requirements and potential concerns about your online promotion.

Contacting Potential Partners

At this time, it is important to consider how you would want to be contacted if the situation were reversed. Would you prefer to get a phone call, an email, a Microsoft Power Point presentation, or some information through the mail? Depending on the complexity of the online promotion and the kinds of things you're looking to get from your partner, you may need to do some additional up-front work before you begin contacting potential partners so that you have all your information in an easy-to-understand format.

The kind of solicitation will also depend on how well you know your potential partners. If you've never worked with them before, you will need to spend more time providing some background on your company and why they might want to consider working with you. If you've had previous contact with individuals within the company, then you may need less background information initially and can get to the point of why you think they should be interested in joining forces on your upcoming online promotion.

In general, it's a good idea to have your promotion clearly defined in some form of document or presentation. A Microsoft Power Point presentation or a few Web pages describing the online promotion is usually sufficient to provide basic information. The more information you can provide about the promotion and the more "buttoned up" your presentation materials appear to be, the more likely you are to interest a potential partner.

While some partnership negotiations can be completed without any supporting documentation, these partnerships usually have some other element, such as a previous working relationship or unique opportunity, that would justify the lack of documentation. Even if you begin contacting your potential partners via phone, they will usually ask you to send them an email that outlines your proposal. If you haven't prepared materials previously, this will slow you down during a critical time in the introductory process. The longer you take to get back to a request for additional information, the farther your initial contact will fade from their minds. If, on the other hand, you respond quickly to a request for follow-up information, you are more likely to close a partnership negotiation.

Keeping Track of Responses

The more potential partners you are contacting, the more you will need to keep records of your contacts. The easiest way to do this is to create a spreadsheet that tracks all your contacts, their needs, as well as follow-up action items associated with each potential partner. There are also software programs, such as *ACT*, which provide support with contact management.

The more responsive you can be, the more likely you are to interest a potential partner. In general, if a potential partner is seriously considering your offer to join forces, it wants to make sure that yours is the kind of company that it wants to be associated with. Beyond your brand and position in the marketplace, your potential partners need to know that your company is well organized and will not create more work for them than if they decided to create their own online promotions.

If you can demonstrate your efficiencies and effectiveness during the initial courting period, then you are in a much better position to attract your potential partner and encourage participation in your upcoming online promotion.

Selecting the Right Partner

The act of selecting the right partner is usually the easiest part of creating a multibrand promotion. If you've come this far, you should already have a good feel for your best potential partner. In some cases, you may not have many options, and the first potential partner that agrees to provide what you need may be the one you go with. However, there are times when there is more than one partner that is interested in participating. When this happens, you have a few different options.

Are all the partners offering the same things?

If you have more than one partner interested in your online promotion, you can sometimes prioritize based on what potential partners are willing to offer. If one partner is willing to provide a significant number of additional prizes, while another is offering extensive media coverage, then you can decide which is more important to the success of your promotion.

In other cases, the offerings are more like apples-to-oranges comparisons, making it difficult to prioritize one offering over the other. That is, if you need support in more than one area and different partners are offering different components, it may be difficult to simply choose one component. If this is the case, you will need to determine if more than one partner is a viable option. If not, you'll need to choose which additional component is most critical to the success of the promotion.

Does it make sense to include more than one partner?

If there is a potential for partnering with more than one partner on the same promotion, it will usually be based on the needs of the online promotion and the strengths that each partner provides. For example, if you are providing all the administrative, technical, and creative aspects of the promotion, you may need additional media coverage as well as a better prize package. If one partner can provide the media support and the other the prizes you need, then you might consider having two partners.

The trick is, if you were initially looking for a single partner and now are considering two, you need to introduce the idea to both potential partners. The more partners you have in an online promotion, the more complex it becomes. You will need to increase your own coordination and management efforts, but this will be worthwhile if you are able to accomplish your objectives. If all the potential partners are complementary and provide different (but equally important) aspects of the promotion, then it is unlikely they will object to having more than just the single partnership. By being up front with your potential partners about your desire to include additional partners, you will quickly determine if having more than one partner is a viable option.

What are the long-term benefits?

When selecting a potential partner, it's important to think beyond the initial promotion. While the promotion itself will take precedence, you should be thinking about a more long-term relationship that your partnership could provide. These benefits may be intangible items such as leveraging a trusted brand, introducing new vendor relationships, or providing additional PR value down the road. When you select a promotional partner, you're associating that company with your own. Make sure that the company you're considering has similar goals and can provide you with the right kind of "guilt by association." Your customers will associate you with your partner, and you want to make sure that association has positive long-term benefits.

By taking a long-term view to the relationship, you may be able to identify other unique opportunities that would interest your partner. As joint marketing efforts continue to grow, you can avoid going through the one-off partnership negotiating process each time if you think about your own future marketing efforts, how your new partner may fit into your long-term needs, and how you may be able to help your new partner.

Are there future opportunities?

The other consideration when selecting a potential partner is future opportunities. In some cases, you will find potential partners that would be ideal except for the fact that they can't participate in the current online promotion. Rather than going your separate ways, find out if there are any future opportunities for you both. If the potential partner is important enough, you will find ways to create future joint marketing efforts if none currently exist.

This holds true for the partners that you *do* select as well. Make sure you express your interest in future marketing opportunities if you are happy with the partnership. Your new partner may be involved in other venues where some additional support may be needed. While you may have initiated the current multibrand promotional opportunity, if it's a good relationship, further opportunities will arise.

Who Is in the Driver's Seat?

To use a football analogy, every online promotion needs a quarterback. While there are multiple players interested in the success of the online promotion, it's the job of the quarterback to drive the promotion, manage the key milestones and deliverables, and ensure its success. If there is no clear quarterback, then you run into the problem of having too many people in charge. When this happens, assumptions are made about who is responsible for what, and important aspects of the promotion can fall through the cracks.

If you have developed the online promotion, then you should assign the quarterback if you do not plan on playing that role. The quarterback will be the key individual who will be responsible for every aspect of the promotion. In essence, the quarterback is the producer of the online promotion. If changes need to be made, they need to be cleared with the designated quarterback. If there are problems with the promotion, it is the responsibility of the quarterback to address the problems and come up with the best solution.

In a client/agency relationship, there is usually a producer or account executive who plays the role of the quarterback. What's important in multibrand promotions is that one agency is deemed the lead agency that represents all the client interests. Multiple quarterbacks are just as bad as not having any quarterback.

Although each company usually has its own agency of record, everyone must agree on the single person who is the catalyst for the promotion. If everyone agrees on who the quarterback is, then it becomes much easier to establish roles and responsibilities for the rest of the players involved.

What to Do with a Weak Quarterback

The person playing the role of quarterback needs to take charge as soon as he or she is identified or else he or she will lose the necessary control over the promotion. If the lead producer of the promotion is weak, it will become obvious immediately. Meetings will be held without much benefit or movement toward the end goal. Disagreements will not be resolved quickly. If the direction of the promotion is not clear to everyone, then chaos will reign.

A quarterback maintains control over the promotion by creating a production schedule and assigning the key deliverables and their due dates to each of the team members. By providing a clearly defined game plan to everyone involved, the disagreements will be much more focused and have a better chance of being resolved quickly.

The best thing to do with a weak quarterback is to find a replacement as quickly as possible. When this isn't an option, you can sometimes provide the necessary coaching from the sidelines to empower the weak quarterback and help him or her get back in the zone. That is, identify the need for the game plan (including the production schedule and key deliverables) and perhaps even help create one. The key to good coaching is helping the quarterback identify the problems he or she is causing without assigning blame.

The Production Schedule

The production schedule is simply a list of deliverables with the names of the person (or company) responsible, deliverable dates, and any contingencies associated with the deliverable. If the production schedule is short, it can be created in a number of different programs (such as Microsoft Word or Excel), but if the production schedule is rather lengthy, it's a good idea to use scheduling software such as Microsoft Schedule. Production schedule programs will help with issues like contingency, where one deliverable is dependent on another, and help identify incomplete deliverables. If the project begins to fall off schedule, the program will help identify the impact of missed deadlines on future requirements.

Table 6.1 illustrates an example of a sample production schedule.

The production schedule is important to have when developing multibrand promotions because it helps identify who is responsible for what and when. The production schedule, when combined with flowcharts and other necessary documentation, is the "architect's blueprint" for an online promotion. If anyone is unsure about the progress of the promotion or what he or she is personally responsible for, the production schedule will help clear up the confusion. As dates are changed and priorities shifted, the production schedule should be updated and redistributed to everyone involved.

Table 6.1   A Sample Production Schedule

TASK DESCRIPTION	WHO IS RESPONSIBLE	DATE DUE	CONTINGENCY	STATUS
Signed contract	ABC Company	April 20, 2001	None	Complete
Media plan	Kelly, Scott & Madison	April 27, 2001	Final budget	Pending final budget
Write official rules	Seismicom	May 18, 2001	Need final prize descriptions	Pending prize list

NOTE   The current version of Microsoft Project has online collaboration utilities that allow for changes and updates to be made online, including the ability to send out email notifications to everyone involved.

Key Milestones

As part of the production schedule, milestones are identified as key dates when all parties come together to make important decisions on the development of the promotion. Key milestone dates should be identified up front so that timely reviews and approvals can be scheduled ahead of time by all parties. Key milestones are usually scheduled to review creative and technology work during the critical decision-making phases (rough comps, demo of the game, navigation treatments, and so on). Key milestones usually require client sign-off from each company involved in the online promotion so that no surprises occur at the last minute.

Key milestones are important to keep projects on track. They are checkpoints that help clients and agencies review work and make changes while there is still time left in the promotion. Without milestones, promotions can come to a grinding halt as final approvals are not received in time to make the required launch dates. Moreover, milestone dates give all parties involved a chance to provide feedback on the promotion and request changes prior to the launch.

Flowcharts and Other Documentation

The production schedule does not provide everything needed for a successful multibrand promotion. Flowcharts are often a necessary component of the preproduction phase of online promotions; they help everyone see a visual representation of how the promotion will work. The flowchart is usually a simple diagram but may include screenshots of the rough creative currently in development. In either case, the flowchart shows visually how the online promotion will flow from the main promotional page throughout the entire process.

Figure 6.2 illustrates a sample flowchart that provides a snapshot of the different content areas that might be included in an online promotion. While the specifics of the promotional flowchart will change, depending on the nature of the online promotion, most follow a similar construct.

In addition to the flowchart, other support documentation may be provided depending on the complexity of the online promotion. In some cases, a page-by-

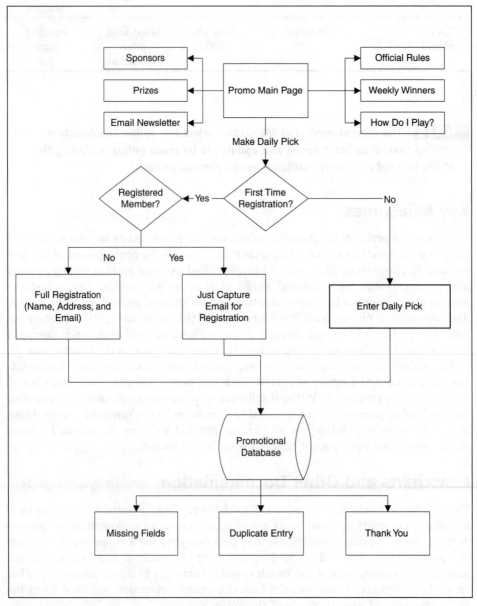

Figure 6.2 Sample flowchart.

page production "bible" is required so that team members can review the contents of each page before it is programmed. In other cases, sell-sheets are required to help solicit potential partners. These sell-sheets identify the objectives of the promotion and the various components that will be developed in support of the promotion.

In general, the more information you have at your disposal, the less confusion there will be about the promotion and what is in development. While you don't want to get bogged down in the documentation, as my grandfather used to tell me, "It's better to measure twice and cut once."

Contingency Plans

Nothing ever goes as smoothly as it is planned. Let's face it, problems do occur. The secret to successful multibrand promotions is having good contingency plans so that when things don't work out as planned, you have alternative options to consider. The best thing to do is to expect the unexpected. That is, take time to think about what could possibly go wrong with your online promotion ahead of time so that when it does, you're prepared, rather than caught off guard.

Contingency planning also means having first-rate outside resources that can help you when you're in trouble. Keeping good vendor relationships really comes in handy when things don't go as planned and you have very little time to fix what went wrong.

In the world of multibrand promotions, the success of the promotion depends on the designated quarterback. If the quarterback is constantly looking for alternatives and ways to keep the project moving forward, the obstacles on the field will not affect the outcome of the promotion. A good quarterback has a plan, but also knows when and how to effectively deviate from the plan to keep the project on schedule.

Create Partnership Agreements

Once all parties have given the promotion a green light, it's time to put it in writing. While this is true for all successful online promotions, partnership agreements are critical for multibrand promotions. A partnership agreement clearly spells out what each party will provide, along with the roles and responsibilities of all parties. Depending on where the promotion is when the partnership agreements are drafted, it's a good idea to include a completed production schedule outlining specific deliverables and their appropriate dates along with any applicable flowcharts and supporting documentation.

This is the time to bring lawyers into the development of the multibrand promotion. Agreements are designed to spell out exactly what was agreed on by all parties so that there is no confusion as to who is responsible for what when the time comes to deliver on the promises. At the signing of the partnership agreement, verbal commitments become real and the viability of the multibrand promotion becomes official.

While legal preferences differ, the creation of most partnership agreements is not a lengthy process. If the parties involved are all in agreement, then the official document simply represents on paper what each party has agreed to in the promotion. The fine print can sometimes cause some back and forth between each company's representative legal counsel, but if everyone agrees to agree, then the written agreement should be a simple matter.

Avoid Contract Templates

Beware of contract templates. It is not advisable to use another company's partnership agreement or to reuse a previous agreement for a new promotion. Legal verbiage changes with the introduction of new laws, the new interpretation of current laws through court findings, and general understandings between legal organizations. Partnership agreements are an important aspect of the multibrand promotion and should be prepared by a legal expert who is protecting your best interests.

While contract templates can provide a good starting point, they do not address the specific and unique requirements of the promotion itself. In most cases, broad or generic statements are difficult to enforce if the need ever arises. If you are developing the promotion, it's a worthwhile investment to engage a lawyer on your behalf to prepare an official partnership agreement for your specific promotion. If your partners have in-house legal counsel, they may offer to provide the first draft of the partnership agreement. While this may save you time and money, it would still behoove you to enlist the support of your own legal counsel so that your own interests are reviewed, interpreted, and protected.

Amendments to Partnership Agreements

Once the partnership agreement has been created, amendments can be made as long as the original parties all agree to the changes and do so in writing. The agreement was created for everyone's protection, but it's not intended to cripple the promotion if a change is required. In most cases, amendments will not be necessary if the promotion was well thought out prior to the drafting and signing of the agreement. However, unforeseeable issues have a way of coming up at the most inappropriate times and may require amendments to the original agreement to solve the potential problem. As long as everyone who signed the original agreement is okay with the required change, then amendments can be made.

Terminating the Agreements

In most cases, the agreement terminates at the conclusion of the multibrand promotion. However, there should be provisions in the agreement in which nonperformance of one party can provide an option to terminate the requirements of the other parties. While it is rare to terminate a partnership agreement prior to the launch of the promotion, not all partnerships work out as planned and early terminations do happen. The key to successful termination is avoiding potential lawsuits and nonperformance liability. These sections should be clearly outlined in the contract and, as long as they are followed, should allow for early termination of the agreement. This may be the only answer to a failing multibrand promotion with good intentions, but one that just doesn't seem to be going anywhere.

Manage the Ongoing Relationship

Once the contracts are signed, you have the official green light to start building the multibrand promotion that you've been cooking up. But while the production schedule may outline who's doing what and when, you still need to spend a good deal of time managing the ongoing relationship—especially if you've never worked with your partners before. Managing a relationship usually boils down to good communications skills between you and your partners. By keeping everyone informed about developments and changes in the original game plan, it is less likely that there will be major upsets, surprises, or unhappy partners.

The level of management of the partners will vary depending on what phase of the promotion you are currently in. Prelaunch, for example, requires much more ongoing communication to ensure the proper approvals and necessary feedback with enough time to incorporate changes before the launch of the promotion. At the launch, most of the development should already be in place, so it's more of a final checklist than detailed communications or updates. Once the promotion launches, partners will require updates on progress, reports detailing consumer participation, and a measurement of overall success. Even once the promotion has ended, there will be a need for a recap of the good, the bad, and the ugly associated with the promotion.

Managing the relationship has other longer-term benefits as well. If your partners come to rely on your expertise and knowledge of online promotions, they are likely to come back to you in the future for similar projects. If your partners like working with you, then the relationship has the potential to yield more benefits than future online promotions. In this section, we will focus on the specific requirements of managing the ongoing relationship during the different phases of the promotion.

Prelaunch

The most critical time for the management of the ongoing relationship between the newly established partnerships is the time between the contract signing to just before the promotion is launched. Whether you have one partner or several, your partner(s) will need constant updates on the development of the promotion as well as the ability to provide feedback and the appropriate approvals. Without question, the prelaunch period is the most difficult in terms of managing relationships.

In the prelaunch period, you will become aware of changes to the original game plan. Assumptions made during the precontract phase may prove false. What you thought would be the easiest components to provide may turn out to be the most difficult. The up-front work is time-consuming and the last thing you want to do is take the time to send out emails to your partners to provide updates regarding where the promotion stands, *but this is exactly what you need to do.* By updating your partners on your progress, you are keeping them informed of what's happening with their promotion. If dates slip, they need to plan accordingly—especially if you need their help to get back on schedule.

While the prelaunch period can be the most taxing phase of the multibrand promotion, it is also the most rewarding. If you pull it off, your partners will know it was because of all your hard work and constant communication with them. You will demonstrate your ability to cope with the pressures associated with a multibrand promotion and exhibit your value as a partner. The prelaunch period is the make-it-or-break-it period that either unites you and your partners, or destroys any chance of a future relationship.

At Launch

Just prior to the launch is the final checkpoint phase. While there is less need for management, it is the critical time to get everyone's final approval before the promotion goes live. Getting final approval can be a nightmare in itself—especially with multiple partners involved. The solution to the problem can be found back in the previous prelaunch phase. If you have done a good job keeping your partners updated on changes and developments, then they already know the importance of getting final approval and the act of getting it should be simple. If you have lagged in your responsibility to your partners prior to launch, it will become obvious when you need their final approval to go live.

During the Promotion

Once the promotion is live, you switch from update mode to reporting mode with a dash of crisis management. You should still be proactive with your partners, providing them with weekly updates and progress reports. But here your real strength will be tested when a disaster strikes. How do you handle a hosting failure and your targeted consumers can't reach the promotion? What if the database is compromised and a hacker replaces all your entrants with his or her own name? Problems will occur, and your ability to cope with them will again demonstrate your value as a partner. The faster and better you react when there's a problem, the more your partners will come to rely on your company and its abilities.

An important part of crisis management is how you interpret results. If something seems wrong with the promotion, your ability to examine the problem and come up with possible solutions will again demonstrate your value as a partner. This is also the time to listen to what your partners recommend. Perhaps you have identified the problem, but your partner has the best solution to address the problem. You need not have all the answers to be a good partner, and it helps to be a good listener.

Concluding the Promotion

Once the promotion has ended, you will still need to recap the success or failure associated with the promotion. What was the final outcome? Were all the goals met? If not, why not? It is important to create an open forum between you and your partners to discuss the results of the promotion. Were they happy with the success of the promotion? What would they have done differently? Would they consider partnering with you again in the future?

If you are interested in a future relationship with your partners, then the conclusion of the promotion should end with a recap of the good, the bad, and the ugly associated with the promotion. Be honest. If mistakes were made, revisit them as a learning experience and decide how you would handle the situation differently if you had another opportunity. Problematic multibrand promotions teach you far more about your partners and your own abilities than the unusual promotion that goes off without a hitch. Mistakes will be repeated if they are not learned from, so take the time to analyze what could be done better.

But try not to beat yourself up. Take time to recognize the impressive aspects of the promotion as well. Were you able to launch the promotion in a relatively short time frame? Did you keep the promotion under budget? Try to see the positive associated with the promotion as well as the negative. While the negative events will provide you with a list of things to improve in future multibrand promotions, the positive events will mark all the things you did right and help you keep a constructive outlook (which will encourage you to try again).

What Could Have Been Done Better?

No online promotion is ever perfect. While this was touched on in the previous section, it's important to go beyond partnership discussions and closing communications for the purpose of managing your relationships with your partners. Finding out what could have been done better means digging deep into the archived data and reports and taking a look at the drop-offs points and various reporting trends throughout the site.

In your search to find out what could be improved in future multibrand promotions, you can begin to create your own benchmark from which future multibrand promotions will be compared. By reviewing the log file information, you can discover additional information and trends about the participants in the promotion as well as where they came from prior to visiting your site. The on-demand reports created for the promotion will track your entry information and can usually separate the entry count into whatever time increments you're interested in. This can be helpful when comparing this information to your advertising schedule to see what was most effective.

For more in-depth analysis, you can grab the raw data from the promotion and create your own database queries. Clearly, the information you retrieve will depend on what information was gathered, but sometimes looking at the source information will help provide a different perspective from what you saw in your on-demand reports. Over time, you will be able to compare your results with those published by the research industry covering online promotions. Currently, this information is comparatively sparse, but as the online promotions industry continues to blossom, more in-depth research and information will become available.

Creating Your Own Benchmark

There are a number of reasons why creating your own benchmark is a good idea. Internally, creating a benchmark will provide you with comparative information for future online promotions efforts. The next time you create a multibrand promotion, you can compare your results to the previous promotion. The benchmark will provide your current partners with an additional perspective on the effectiveness of the promotion. The same information can be used when you are soliciting partners for a future multibrand promotion. The benchmark can also provide an easy segue into a case study of the online promotion.

To create your own benchmark, there are essential pieces of information that you will want to capture. Below is a list of questions that will help you formulate your own benchmark. Depending on the kind of multibrand promotion that you have completed (sweepstakes, sampling program, rebate offer, or premium giveaway, for example), you may have different kinds of information to document as your benchmark.

NOTE Promotional benchmarks are not necessarily compatible with different promotional types. That is, a sweepstakes may generate more unique customers, but a sampling program may generate more sales. Benchmarks work best when compared to the same promotional type (a previous sweepstakes compared to a current sweepstakes).

The following questions are applicable to all types of multibrand promotions and will help you create an initial benchmark.

GENERAL BENCHMARK QUESTIONS

- What was the objective of the promotion? Was the objective satisfied? Why or why not?

- What strategy was used to satisfy the objective of the promotion? Was the strategy on target?

- What promotional tactic was used to meet the strategy? Was this the best possible promotional tactic? If not, what might have worked better?

- What did each partner provide in this multibrand promotion?

- What was the total budget for the promotion?

- If outside vendors were used, which vendors were used and what services did they provide? Were they satisfactory?

- What media vehicles were used to advertise the promotion?

- What was the media budget?

- What was the biggest failure associated with the promotion? How can it be avoided in the future?

- What was the biggest success story associated with the promotion? How can that story be repeated in the future?

SWEEPSTAKES-SPECIFIC BENCHMARKS

- Why was a sweepstakes chosen as the promotional tactic? Would another promotional tactic have worked better?

- What was the total number of unique customers?

- What was the total number of sweepstakes entries?

- What was the average number of entries per customer?

- What prizes were offered? How many of each prize? Was the prize pool sufficient?

- Was there any consumer confusion about the sweepstakes? If so, what was it and how might it be made clearer in the future?

- What was the chief drop-off point in the desired promotional click-through path? Why did consumers leave that specific Web page?

SAMPLING-SPECIFIC BENCHMARKS

- Why was sampling chosen as the promotional tactic? Would another promotional tactic have worked better?

- How were samples distributed (online request, guerrilla marketing, or in store, for example)?

- How many samples were distributed?

- What was the total cost per sample distributed?

- What was the call to action? What percentage of consumers heeded that call?

- If coupons were distributed, how many coupons were redeemed?

REBATE-SPECIFIC BENCHMARKS

- Why was a rebate chosen as the promotional tactic? Would another promotional tactic have worked better?

- Which partner covered the cost of the rebates?

- Was overredemption insurance purchased?

- How many rebates were submitted?

- Were there any major customer service issues related to the rebate offer?

- Did the rebate offer incrementally increase sales volumes? Were the increases statistically significant?

PREMIUM-SPECIFIC BENCHMARKS

- Why was a premium offer chosen as the promotional tactic? Would another promotional tactic have worked better?

- Was the premium well received? Was there a high demand for the premium item?

- Did the premium offer incrementally increase sales volumes or membership acquisition goals? Were the increases statistically significant?

- Was there a specific action that was required in order to receive the premium offer? Was this requirement a significant barrier to participation?

- Were you satisfied with the results derived from the premium offer?

COUPON-SPECIFIC BENCHMARKS

- Why was a coupon offer chosen as the promotional tactic? Would another promotional tactic have worked better?

- How were coupons distributed [online, direct mail, newspaper Free Standing Insert (FSI), or magazine, for example]?

- What was the total number of coupons distributed?

- What percentage of the coupons distributed were specifically requested by the customer?

- How many coupons were redeemed?

- Did the coupon offer incrementally increase sales volumes or in-store visits? Were the increases statistically significant?

As online promotions evolve, so too will the key benchmark questions. These questions should be used as a jumping-off point whereby you formulate your own specific benchmark questions beyond these basic questions. Your questions should address the specific nature of the promotion and highlight key successes and failures so that you and your colleagues can learn from both over time.

Log Files

The log files of an online promotion can often provide the "hidden" information that will tell you more about the promotion's success or failure and perhaps some additional trends that may not be so obvious. Every time a Web page is requested, a record of that request is captured in the Web server's log files. Beyond the hits that measure each graphic and HTML file, additional information such as where your consumers came from and what browsers they are using, can be studied.

In their raw format, log files can be quite daunting. Fortunately, there are several software programs that, once installed, will take the raw log files and turn them into useful information that you are interested in. When it comes to multibrand promotions, the log files can help you understand where the drop-off points are in the promotion, that is, when a consumer decided that they had too much information or didn't know where to go next and decided to leave your Web site. Large drop-off points are usually associated with a promotion that requires several clicks to get to the actual entry form where consumers can participate. Short attention spans coupled with slow Internet access mean that your online promotions must be lean and to the point. Too much information will usually result in potentially interested participants going elsewhere.

While there are several software programs to help analyze a Web server's log files, I recommend WebTrends (www.webtrends.com). WebTrends is the easiest log analyzing program that I've come across and it seems to be the most commonly used in the programming community. While new software is constantly coming out with the latest and greatest features, WebTrends seem to provide the right amount of information without too many options, which can make this type of program overly complex.

If you take the time to review the log files, you may find that even your most successful program could have been even better if your links between pages were more obvious. Or you might find that a recent online promotion failure was due, in part, to massive drop-off prior to the entry form. Log files also capture where consumers came from prior to entering your promotion, so you can find out which partner provided the most traffic via the referring URL information. If most of your target customers use a Netscape Navigator browser, but your Web site was designed to meet the specifications of Microsoft's Internet Explorer browser, then you might think twice about which browser to design your creative and layouts around for your next promotion.

Custom On-Demand Reports

Beyond the log files, you should have some version of a custom report that you can use during the promotion to monitor its success. This can be as simple as providing entry count information or as complex as providing a statistical model that compares your target demographic profiles with that of the participants of the promotion. Of course, you can only create reports from the information that is provided, and some promotions collect only email addresses from participating consumers.

At a minimum, however, on-demand reporting should provide information about which of your partner's Web sites the consumers came from. This can be either from the referring URL information automatically provided in the log files or a number of other technology solutions. For example, each partner could have a separate Web page that they link to. The page can look identical to the target audience, but included in the entry form is a hidden field that passes partner information to the promotional database for tracking and reporting. The same information can be provided through Web server *Post* and *Get* commands created prior to the launch of the promotion.

Regardless of how the information is captured, your on-demand reports should tell you which partner provided the most Web traffic and subsequent entries to the multibrand promotion. Because these reports are dynamic, allowing you to find the information you need during the promotion, you can often make changes to the promotion before it's too late. If a partner isn't providing the kind of traffic and entries you had expected, you can talk with your partner and figure out what the problem is and how best to fix it. Perhaps its link to the promotion is not prominent on its site, or perhaps there are too many links before consumers get to the entry form page. The point is, you can't fix a problem you don't know about. By having access to this information during the duration of the promotion, you have a better chance of catching and fixing problems before it's too late.

Database Analysis

Database analysis goes beyond the log file and on-demand reports and helps you dig as deeply as you can. Once the promotion ends, you can take all the data collected from consumers and start cross-referencing it with other database information. Zip codes, for example, can be grouped to provide additional information regarding where the bulk of your consumers live who participated in the promotion. Opt-in information will help you understand what percentage of all participating consumers are interested in hearing from you again.

If you have previous promotional databases, you can cross-reference which consumers participated in previous promotions and either chose to be contacted in the future or not. Previous promotional databases can help you spot trends. Are the majority of promotional participants interested in future marketing efforts from your company? If not, why not? Are consumers coming from the same geographic regions or do they change from promotion to promotion? How do different partners influence the results of your online promotion?

With your database in hand, you have the maximum ability to extract information and analyze results. You may find that in future promotions, you wish to ask for more information about your consumers. Be careful. While information is power, it can also become a detriment to successful online promotions. The more information consumers must provide to enter your online promotion, the less likely they are to take the time to do so—even if you're offering a wonderful prize package. This becomes especially difficult when you add partners into the mix. Each partner has its own questions that it would like to ask consumers. If you're not careful, consumers will be required to complete a 10- to 20-question survey before they can participate. This will definitely decrease your response rates.

Protect Your Customer's Privacy

As long as you are analyzing information in the aggregate (that is, all the information as a whole and not individual consumers), then you are unlikely to violate privacy and protection policies. What you don't want to do is sell the valuable database you've just created from your online promotion. Allow consumers to opt in to your and your partners' future marketing efforts. By having consumers ask to receive additional information from you and your partners, you now have permission to segregate the database and weed out those consumers who wish to never be contacted again versus those who are interested in your company and/or your partners'.

A customer's information should be treated *like gold*. While this was discussed in previous chapters, it's important to bring up this issue again with respect to multiple partners. While you may appreciate the worth of your customers' information, you can't be sure that your partners hold the same respect for your customers' privacy. That is, if the database is shared with your partners and they resell the database to email marketing companies, then your multibrand promotion has violated your consumers' trust.

Be sure that your partners are equally responsible for the private information that consumers provide. If you're not sure about your partners, ask them for their company's privacy statement (if it's not clearly posted on their Web site). If you think they will not respect your privacy statement, you can include this demand in your partnership agreement.

Compare Your Results with Research Reports

Comparing your online promotion's results with research reports will be difficult. Even though online promotions have been popular since 1995, they have not been the priority of most research organizations. I do not believe this will be the case for very long. Forrester has already published a research report dedicated to online promotions, as has *PROMO Magazine*, and I believe that others will follow suit. As the new economy continues to equalize, online promotions will play a more important role in satisfying marketing objectives. As research on online promotions catches on, more information will be available for comparison. For now, you can use your own internal benchmarks and call upon Find/SVP to help gather secondary sources of information (that is, magazine and newspaper articles) that speak to online promotions results.

Conclusion

Multibrand promotions can provide numerous benefits if you know what you're getting into. Starting with a clear objective is the first step. If you have a clear idea of what you want to accomplish, then moving to the next step of identifying ideal partners becomes a snap. A clear objective will enable you to achieve the desired end result with your multibrand promotion and will help you identify the ideal partner(s) to help you get there.

Successful online multibrand promotions are created through effective communication among the partners. If the relationship among the partners is managed correctly, very few surprises will occur. Moreover, effective communication will likely result in well-managed expectations and future multibrand online promotions opportunities.

No promotion is ever perfect. The trick is to learn from your mistakes so you can avoid repeating them in the future and to discover the reasons for your successes so you *can* repeat them.

The most common reason companies join forces to create a multibrand promotion is to increase the overall advertising and exposure for all companies involved. In the next chapter, the focus will be turned to the best ways to maximize this effort. Knowing how best to promote the promotion can ultimately mean the difference between success or failure.

Promoting the Promotion

A promotion without the right amount of advertising support is like opening up a lemonade stand and hoping people will drive by. Simply put, it's foolish to have a promotion at all if you're not going to promote your promotion effectively. If the purpose of your promotion is to drive traffic to your Web site, but the only place you talk about the promotion *is on your Web site*, how will anyone know about your fabulous promotional idea? Or let's say you're trying to build a database. Unless you are interested only in existing customers who visit your Web site during the promotional period, you will want to promote your promotion with the help of your friendly neighborhood media groups.

The few exceptions to the promoting your promotion requirement include Web site surveys and sales offers (Buy One, Get One Free, for example) that are targeting consumers who happen to be at your Web site already. If you're not interested in growing your existing consumer base, then simple promotions with a banner or button on your home page will be sufficient.

Otherwise, if part of your marketing objective includes expanding your current customer base and/or motivating your existing customers to take action, you will want to promote your promotion as heavily as you can. This chapter is dedicated to the *who, what, when, where,* and *how* of promoting your online promotions (the *why* should be obvious).

Where and How to Advertise Your Online Promotion

Once you've built your online promotion (or are confident in the agency building it for you), it's time to turn your attention to where and how to advertise and promote. There are plenty of options. The question is, which media vehicles are right for your promotion? If you have a multibrand promotion, then chances are your partner(s) will have some say as to where and how the promotion is advertised. But if the primary decision is up to you, the question is, where do you begin?

For the sake of simplicity, I will divide today's media into two groups: online resources and offline resources. Online resources include Web site portals, search engines, banner ads, Web site links, and email marketing. Offline resources include television, radio, print, direct mail, outdoor, and guerrilla marketing tactics.

If you talk to the different online and offline media-buying services, all will argue that without question the media they're selling is the only media to buy. (When you're a hammer, everything looks like a nail.) Online media-buying services argue that the high targeting ability of online advertising is unparalleled in the traditional media world, while offline media-buying agencies will counter that you just can't match traditional media's reach and frequency with banner ads. The fact is, both arguments are correct. However, that doesn't mean you should buy some of each. In many cases, you only need the right media support from one group. The challenge is to determine which media group—online or offline—is the right choice for your online promotion.

The answer is that there is a media vehicle for every promotion. The best vehicle depends on what you are trying to achieve balanced with what you can afford. By highlighting the advantages of each medium, you should be able to quickly determine what kind of promotional media is required for your promotion. By talking to the right media experts, you will quickly learn what kind of budget is required to accomplish your marketing objectives. Together, these two criteria will help you determine where and how to advertise your online promotion.

Online Resources

There are numerous occasions when online media is the perfect vehicle to promote your online promotion. Soft launches (or prelaunch test marketing programs) are a great way to generate enough traffic to test the waters before introducing your promotion to the volume of consumers that can be reached from traditional media. Sales-driven promotions, where awareness and interest are already high, are perfect for the online medium where consumers can "buy now" with immediacy unparalleled in the traditional marketing world. Promotions that drive online research are another obvious choice for online media support where speed is important.

A wonderful advantage of online media is its flexibility. If you're unsure which creative campaign will be most effective, you can test several different approaches, remove the ineffective ones, and increase exposure of the more effective ones. This is much more difficult to accomplish with traditional media and could never be done within the same time frames as online media.

In this section, I will review various online media options and identify when each option works the best. If, after reading this section, you're still unsure about which online media vehicle is best for your upcoming promotion, you may want to run some tests with your promotions agency or online media-buying group to measure effectiveness. The beauty of online media is that you can afford to test various options with significantly less money than you would need to spend on traditional media.

Promotions Portals

A *portal* is a term used to describe a launching pad. When analysts began describing Web sites, they broke them down into several categories including commerce, destination, and portal sites. A *commerce* site is where consumers shop and use their credit cards to purchase products and services. A *destination* site is where consumers "end up" to review information, chat, email, conduct research, or play games. A *portal* site helps consumers find destination and commerce sites. In their purest form, search engine Web sites such as Yahoo!, Excite, Lycos, and AltaVista are all considered portal Web sites.

> **NOTE** Online services such as America Online, CompuServe, and MSN are in the unique position of having all three elements of commerce, destination, and portal. Of the three, America Online is (by far), the largest online service, representing over 25 million subscriber households and 50 million users. According to the September 2000 Media Metrix report, the AOL family of brands reaches 76 percent of the online audience.

A *promotions portal* is simply a site where consumers go to find out about online promotions. Webstakes (www.webstakes.com) is a perfect example of a promotions portal. Consumers go to Webstakes to find out about the latest online promotions. Another example is Sweepstakes Advantage (www.sweepsadvantage.com). Sweepstakes Advantage lists hundreds of online promotions by category so consumers can easily participate in the ones that interest them. These promotions portals can be quite effective at boosting the response rates to your online promotions. Webstakes has millions of active subscribers who have requested to receive an email newsletter describing different kinds of promotions. If your online promotion needs exposure, a promotions portal is a great way to get it in front of a mass audience that is specifically interested in online promotions. When consumers go to a promotions portal, they are in the frame of mind to enter sweepstakes, contests, instant win games, get a free product sample or reward for shopping online.

But there *is* one catch to consider. While many of the consumers may truly be interested in your products, there will be many more that have little to no interest in your products and are only participating because of the prize or discount being offered. In other words, your marketing dollars may fall prey to "gamers" who have no interest in doing anything other than entering the promotion for their chance to win. Companies like Webstakes address this problem with an opt-in check box that separates those interested in future marketing efforts from the "gamers" interested only in the promotion. Still, the percentage of people who opt-in can often be significantly low because of the frame of mind consumers are in when they are exposed to your promotion.

Sweepstakes Web Sites

Similar to promotions portals are Web sites dedicated to sweepstakes. Again, with a sweepstakes Web site, you are essentially "fishing where the fish are" by promoting your promotion to consumers interested in promotions. While these sites may not specifically point consumers to several different promotions, they drive their existing audience base back to their site on a daily basis to enter their (usually large) promotion.

Examples of sweepstakes Web sites include Iwon.com, FreeLotto.com, and LuckySurf.com. Each of these sweepstakes Web sites offers million-dollar prizes for consumer participation. While Iwon.com rewards consumers for using their search engine (and other features on their site), FreeLotto.com and LuckySurf.com are structured as a free version of a state lottery where consumers pick several numbers for their chance to win a million dollars or more.

Like promotions portals, sweepstakes Web sites have the similar problem that they attract consumers interested in the promotion and not the advertised products or services. The difference is that with ad banners on a sweepstakes site you can bring consumers into your site yourself (rather than depend on the sweepstakes entry form page) and expose them to your brand before shuttling them off to your online promotion. This is not to say that many of the consumers who participate won't be gamers—chances are, they will be. But, if you're looking for ways to boost your numbers, sweepstakes Web sites can certainly deliver.

Search Engines

True portal Web sites, such as the traditional search engines, can often help move you away from "gamers" and into a mass audience base. Interestingly enough, Yahoo! (one of the original search engines) quickly discovered the power of online promotions and created a mandate that all banners on its home page be some form of promotion. Check it out. The next time you visit Yahoo! take a look at the banner on its home page. The creative and company continually change, but unless Yahoo! is promoting itself, you'll find a promotional banner.

With search engines, you can tie your promotional advertising directly to key words that make sense for the promotion. For example, if you were promoting a new color printer, you could work with the search engine company to identify key words such as "printer," "color printer," "computers," and other commonly used words or phrases consumers would use to search for a color printer. That way, when the results of their search appear, so does your advertisement promoting your promotion.

Search engines can help add relevance to your promotional advertising needs without targeting gamers who are only interested in entering sweepstakes, contests, or games. By tying your advertising to relevant search results, you have a better chance of capturing consumers' attention and driving them to your promotion. Interestingly enough, Yahoo!, Excite, Lycos, AltaVista, MSN, and AOL all offer "beyond the banner" promotional advertising opportunities to help you capture their existing loyal users. Some of these applications include email newsletters, which their consumers have requested to receive on specific topics that may tie in quite nicely with your promotion. Each Web site has its own applications for features like free Internet access, free email, instant messaging, and other free software utilities that provide additional advertising opportunities that may be perfect for effectively promoting your promotion.

Related Web Sites

When it comes to advertising on destination Web sites (that is, Web sites with content rather than links to content), it's best to find sites that have a similar association with your own. One way to do this is to spend some time online reviewing Web sites that are complementary to yours. This is a good exercise, as you can see for yourself who else is out there that your existing customers may be currently visiting. While I highly recommend this exercise, many people involved in promotions find that they simply do not have the time to check out what's online. Fortunately, there is an alternative, but some time should definitely be set aside to do some focused surfing. The best way to find potential consumers for your Web site is to take the time to *be* one of those potential consumers and see what's out there.

Without spending time online yourself, you can turn to affiliate networks such as LinkShare (www.linkshare.com), which has developed an extensive network of Web sites and affiliates that provide traffic to each other. In the next section, I will talk about online media specialists such as DoubleClick and 24/7 Media, which have turned these networks into massive media placement agencies. The difference between media placement agencies and affiliate networks is how you purchase advertising. That is, with media placement agencies, you buy per *impression* (or exposure), whereas with affiliate networks, you buy on a *pay for performance* model, paying only for consumers who click on your banner advertising or URL links.

Currently, the lines between affiliate networks and online media specialists are extremely blurry, as affiliate networks often charge for impressions instead of the pay for performance model that they started with, and online media specialists offer the pay for performance model at a much higher cost than the impressions they sell. What hasn't changed is the effectiveness of related Web sites. If you can find a Web site (or network of Web sites) that currently captures your targeted customers, then there's a good chance you can attract those customers to your online promotion.

Online Media Specialists

If your eyes are starting to glaze over, don't worry. There is an abundance of online media choices out there, and I've only scratched the surface. Online media specialists like DoubleClick (`www.doubleclick.com`) and 24/7 Media (`www.247media.com`) have worked diligently to create partnership agreements with several of the top-rated Web sites and can make the right online media recommendations to fit your promotional advertising budget. If you identify the target audience you're interested in, the budget you have to work with, and any relevant demographic and psychographic information on your target audience, these online media specialists can make recommendations as to where to place your advertising dollars.

Groups like DoubleClick and 24/7 Media act as brokerage houses for their media partners. They often have excess inventory at a discounted rate as well as information on new online media vehicles that their partners are interested in promoting. Since they have their fingers on the pulse of online media, it is usually a good idea to speak with one of their online media specialists to get his or her recommendations before you decide to venture off on your own.

The downside is simply that they do *not* represent every major Web site and so their recommendations will not always include some of the sites in which you may be interested If, however, you cross-reference their media recommendations with online media reports published by Media Metrix, you can evaluate for yourself if their recommendations make the most sense. That is, Media Metrix will show which Web sites are the top-rated sites in a particular category, and you can then compare with the Web site properties that DoubleClick or 27/4 Media recommended.

As stated previously, one of the best applications of online media is the reporting element that allows you to understand how well your campaign is doing on a daily (and even hourly) basis. Another wonderful advantage of using an online media specialist to place your media is that he or she has built a proprietary system for reviewing the performance of the ads. This helps you clearly identify which of your creative campaigns works the best and allows you to increase the visibility of the most effective campaign.

Email Marketing

Email is still the most widely used application on the Internet. While people may not visit a particular Web site on a given day, they will most likely review their email. This is one of the reasons that email marketing has become so popular. If you take the time to ask for permission to market to your consumers in the future, those consumers who have granted you permission will be extremely receptive to your promotions. Sending an email to your existing customers who have opted-in on a previous promotion is an extremely effective marketing strategy.

But beware. A natural assumption can lead you down the wrong path. It goes like this, "Well, if my own customers are responsive to the emails I'm sending them, why don't I buy someone else's list and send emails to them?" Because they didn't ask for it, that's why. Forget quadruple opt-in lists that aren't your own. True opt-in means that consumers have given your company explicit permission to send them information, discounts, or future promotional offers. The notion that a consumer's permission can be bought or sold is false. The most effective email marketing campaigns will come from your very own homegrown efforts. Buying email lists as part of your marketing strategy is not as effective as developing your own. And, in some cases, this strategy will result in angry consumers who have no interest in your promotions.

When it comes to email marketing: Build it, don't buy it. Drive traffic to your online promotions from other traditional media (discussed in the next section) and online media vehicles such as search engines, promotions portals, and other Web sites previously discussed.

The one exception to this rule is a partner's or trusted media group's newsletter. If you are cross-promoting a multibrand promotion, your partners can effectively drive traffic to their own online promotion, which includes you. While it's not a good idea to send emails directly to your partners' email lists, they can certainly include your promotion as part of their normal communications to their subscribers. Likewise, a trusted email newsletter coming from a news organization such as *The Wall Street Journal*, *The Industry Standard*, CNN, NBC, or humor email can include a link to your promotion and will not offend the recipients of that newsletter. Recipients of the newsletter realize that they can get the information they want for free because of advertisers and may even check out the promotion if it has relevance.

HTML versus ASCII

A common question regarding email marketing is whether or not HTML-formatted emails should be used so that when consumers open an email from you, they see a slick colorful Web page rather than a black-and-white text-only email with a URL link. While plain text with URL links is still the most common form of email marketing, HTML-formatted emails have been shown to be much more effective *if consumers have HTML-compatible email viewers.* That is, if you know that your consumers can receive HTML-formatted emails, then there is no question that you should be sending them HTML-formatted emails. While the typical response rate for plain text emails with a URL link averages between 5 and 10 percent, HTML-formatted email response rates are closer to 20 or 30 percent, and we have seen response rates as high as 40 percent. The reason is that graphics are much more compelling.

Part of the drastic increase in response rates is due, in part, to the newness of the graphic emails. When you see a compelling picture, your attention is captured even before you read the information included in the email. If 95 percent of all your email received is plain text and suddenly you open a colorful Web page, you're more likely to pay attention and check out the promotion behind the beautiful email.

The downside of HTML-formatted email is that if consumers receive the HTML email in a noncompatible email viewer, then they see a bunch of ugly HTML tags and the email is wasted on them altogether. The biggest problem is that most consumers don't know if they have an HTML-compatible viewer. The trick is to ask them what program they use to read their emails so that you can determine if they're likely to be able to see an HTML-formatted email or not. Web browsers such as Netscape Navigator or Microsoft's Internet Explorer will handle HTML-formatted email without any problems. Customers who use Web browsers to read email (through Hotmail or search engines like Yahoo!, for example) will also be able to view an HTML-formatted email.

The latest versions of Microsoft Outlook and Qualcomm's Eudora also read HTML-formatted emails; however, earlier versions do not handle true HTML formatting. Version 6.0 of America Online (AOL) handles HTML emails quite well. Some earlier versions of AOL, however, do not read any HTML tags, while later versions of AOL (up to version 5.0) read *some* of the more common HTML tags (which makes it really fun to test HTML-formatted emails). If someone is using an old version of Outlook, Eudora, AOL, JUNO, or IBM's Lotus Notes, then it is likely that they will see a bunch of HTML tags that look something like this:

```html
<HTML>
<HEADER>
<TITLE>Win Instantly with ABC Company!</TITLE>
</HEADER>
<BODY>
<TABLE>
<TR><TD><A
HREF="http://www.abccompany.com/promotion/index.html"><IMG
SRC="http://www.abccompany.com/images/cool.gif" alt="Click to
play."></A>
</TD>
<TD>Welcome Bill Carmody. We thought you might be Interested In
playing our Instant win game. Simply click on the graphic to see If
you are an Instant winner.
</TD>
</TR>
</TABLE>
</BODY>
</HTML>
```

Try that on for a marketing message. While some programmers will know to copy the HTML tags and save the email to an .html file (that is, "email.html") so they can open the file from their Web browser, it's doubtful that they would even take the time to do so. In essence, you've lost a potential consumer because your email came through as code versus a plain text message that they could read.

To avoid this problem, ask your consumers what program they use to read their email and then segment your email lists so that consumers with the ability to read HTML-formatted emails will receive them, while those without the ability to read HTML-formatted emails will receive plain text. Or better yet, you can send out a "sniffer" email message that is primarily a text-only email but includes a single line of HTML code. As long as the consumer opens the email message, that line of code will automatically identify (and report back to you) if the targeted consumer has the ability to see HTML-formatted emails or not.

Offline Resources

When online promotions really got started in late 1995, the basic assumption was that the best way to promote an online promotion was via the Internet. But this assumption, for the most part, has been proven false. In the next section, I will discuss in more detail why targeted offline media can be more effective than online media. The short answer is greater reach. While traditional media is more difficult to track and less flexible for changes than online media, traditional media still delivers the optimum reach numbers.

In this section, I will review various traditional media options and their inherent advantages and disadvantages for promoting online promotions. With this information and the restrictions of your own marketing budget to promote the promotion, it should be evident which traditional media vehicles will provide the best results for your next online promotion.

Television

One Super Bowl does not an advertising campaign make. It was obvious enough that the dot coms who blew their entire marketing budgets on Super Bowl ads in January 2000 did not repeat that mistake in January 2001 (perhaps because they were no longer in business). But television can be an effective medium to promote your promotion *if you can afford to do it right,* and by that I mean, the ability to hit the right reach and frequency that are required for household penetration without breaking the bank.

Fragmentation of Television

Television has become extremely fragmented. What started out as the big three networks (ABC, NBC, and CBS) has now mushroomed into over 200 cable stations—not including DirectTV and other forms of satellite television. Television continues to fragment itself into special interest stations. From sports to cartoons, comedy to drama, history to weather, consumers have a ton of options. The good news for promotional marketers, however, is that this fragmentation has lowered the cost of buying television commercials, especially if spot cable buys are utilized. As more cable options become available, the different stations must find ways to compete for advertising dollars, thus driving costs down while increasing flexibility.

If you can afford the right amount of reach and frequency, you will find that television advertising will significantly increase participation in your online promotions. With the fragmentation of cable stations, you are able to do a better job of targeting your ideal consumers and waste less money on consumers who are outside your target. When you break this down even further into geographic regions within the United States, it is possible to isolate your media buys to specific cable shows in fairly precise geographic regions, thus further limiting the amount of potential waste on consumers who are not within your target.

It's also a good idea to get a better understanding of what's really going on in the world of television. There's a big difference between national buys versus spot buys and networks versus individual stations. Companies like PromoTV (www.promotv.com) have perfected the business of finding creative ways to get air time during off-peak hours and on a much more localized level, so that reach and frequency requirements are met for far fewer media dollars than would be required in a national or network buy. It truly depends on your specific needs, but it's often worth talking to promotional media specialists about your marketing objective and target audience, as they may be able to find a creative solution that will significantly increase the effectiveness of your online promotions.

While television is still one of the most expensive mediums available today, the fragmentation of the industry has allowed a more creative approach to buying media. This means that television advertising should not be immediately ruled out simply because of budget. Conversely, if your promotional media experts (your promotions agency and/or promotional media-buying group) agree that, based on the assigned budget, even the most creative media plan would not be effective by including television, then it should not be used.

Don't Forget about Their Web Site

Everybody has a Web site, and the television networks and local stations are no exception. Even though the purpose of using television is to promote your online promotion, don't forget to ask about all the extras that the network or local station has to offer. In many cases, the Web site was originally created to inform consumers about programming content on a specific channel, but has since developed into a very useful tool. On the CBS Web site (www.cbs.com), you can subscribe to various email lists, including David Letterman's Top Ten List from the previous night. When you're looking for creative ways to leverage your media buys, email newsletters and other online assets are an excellent way to tap into a large loyal audience and extend your television coverage. By including follow-up about your promotion on the station or network's Web site, you can reinforce what the consumer saw, may not have paid close attention to, or forgot to write down (such as your URL) to participate in your promotion.

Future Television

I'll close with an interesting anecdote about Microsoft's WebTV union with DirectTV. WebTV is a great product, but still has a number of limitations for high-end users. When Microsoft's WebTV joined forces with DirectTV, two things were accomplished: WebTV received an install base of over 1 million subscribers and DirectTV added value to its existing users and advertisers. Suddenly WebTV had a much larger audience to tap into, and DirectTV had the Internet functionality it was desperately lacking. Now more sports enthusiasts could order pizza from their television sets while watching the game.

It's clear that television devices are becoming more promotional in nature. The future of television (as has been promised for the past decade) is the ability to respond directly to TV commercials—not by calling an 800 number, or visiting a Web site, but by taking action *via the television set*. Television is by far one of the best media vehicles for promoting online promotions (read: generate awareness) and, as the lines between television and the Internet become more blurred, it will become one of the best media vehicles for *conducting* online promotions (read: get people to take action).

Radio

In my opinion, radio is still the best medium for advertising online promotions. The reason is that consumers can (and do) listen to the radio while they're online. Radio, as a medium, has the unique advantage of being engaging, but not overwhelming. People still listen to the radio while at their desks at work and at home while in front of their computers. URLs can be mentioned on-air and consumers can easily type them in as a welcomed distraction to their current endeavors. If the creative is compelling and the online promotion sounds interesting, radio can be an extremely effective way to drive traffic to a promotion. In this fast-paced, I-don't-have-time-for-anything mentality, people keep coming back to radio as background music and a source of information.

Taking Full Advantage of Personalities and Free Stuff

The radio and the Internet went hand-in-hand from the beginning, and today's radio stations realize the power of their medium. They are working with promotions agencies and promotional media groups to make the most of yet two additional advantages that radio can offer: their on-air personalities and their war chests of free stuff. A radio on-air personality, for the most part, is local (Howard Stern and other network personalities excluded). These personalities are wildly famous in their local circles and are there for the asking. Above and beyond all the 30- and 60-second spots, there are a host of "value ads" that these on-air personalities can provide. From in-store appearances to on-air giveaways, the best promotions integrate these on-air personalities into the program. While the stations rarely offer this directly, they are often extremely creative when it comes to a large buy. If you're spending a large chunk of your media budget in their geographic region, it only makes sense to find ways to include the on-air personalities.

And radio stations get a ton of free stuff, from music CDs to concert tickets to station-branded hats and T-shirts. If your prize pool could use some help, ask for free stuff from radio stations as part of the media negotiation. For the most part, they are looking for creative ways to get rid of all this stuff and if you can offer them a unique promotional idea that helps promote your promotion at the same time, well, so much the better.

Radio Station Web Sites

Radio is, and will continue to be, an ideal medium for promotions—online or off. And now, as every radio station attempts to increase its advertising revenue with links and banners on its radio Web site, there are even more opportunities to tie in with the radio station. Now radio stations send consumers to their Web sites to vote on popular music (the top nine at nine), to see what the on-air personalities look like, and to enter on-air sweepstakes and loyalty programs. As the radio station continues to drive traffic to its own site, the value of their Web site to your online promotion increases. Find out what online sponsorships are available that would help promote your online promotion.

Moreover, your online promotion can actually *help* the radio station achieve its objective of driving consumers to its site. Consider local radio stations as potential partners in your next online promotion. If one of your objectives is to increase traffic to your online promotion, radio stations can help by cross-promoting their own Web site in conjunction with your prize offerings. "Win $25,000 from [your company] and [local radio station]. Enter at [local radio station Web site]." Think about it. Most radio stations only have a few large promotions with which they can encourage consumers to listen more often or entice them to visit their Web site. If you work with the radio station manager responsible for promoting the radio station's Web site, you may find unique opportunities to increase the amount of exposure of your own promotion and help the radio station accomplish its own objectives (see Chapter 6, "How to Create a Multibrand Promotion").

Magazines and Newspapers

The best thing about print publications is that they are physical and you can take them with you. The high gloss factor of magazines makes them a pleasure to read. Newspapers and magazines have the distinct advantage of allowing their subscribers to take in the news and other content whenever it's convenient for them. In this information-rich age, the challenge for newspapers and magazines is to provide enough information without causing information overload. Because of their informative nature, magazine and newspaper advertising is often a continuation of the "what's out there" inquiry of consumers. For this reason, print publications can help drive awareness of an online promotion.

When it comes to magazines, I have a love/hate relationship. On the one hand, the right trade magazines can be an extremely effective way to reach your target audience. The *Industry Standard*, for example, is an excellent magazine for people who work in what they call the "New Economy." While the *Industry Standard* is chock-full of important information interesting to online marketers, it also has the largest amount of advertising I've seen in a weekly publication. So while this magazine may have the exact target audience you're interested in, you're forced to compete for the same consumer's attention with a hundred or more companies. Clever advertising can grab a consumer's attention, but placement of the ad becomes critical for success. Thus begins the love/hate relationship. Trade magazines typically have a loyal following, but their loyal following attracts substantial advertising dollars, making it difficult to break through the clutter.

Newspapers face a different problem: waste. Like television ads, newspapers are a great medium if you're trying to reach a mass audience—especially in a specific geographic region. With the media conglomerates, you can easily run national advertising or regional advertising, but either way, it's difficult to target a specific demographic. With newspapers, you have a fairly wide range of consumers. The specific sections of the newspaper will appeal to different psychographics, but the range of subscribers is large. So while your reach and frequency will be high, there is a large portion of consumers who will have no interest in your advertising efforts because they are simply outside your target demographic.

Having identified this problem of waste, Valassis Communications has come up with its own unique solutions to more highly target-specific (by zip code) demographic regions *within* newspaper circulations. In this way, Valassis Communications is able to utilize the massive reach of newspapers, but minimize the amount of waste typically associated with this medium.

Shrink Wrap and Belly Wraps

When it comes to exposure to reach your target audience, sometimes you need to use something besides the actual publication. Most magazine publishers have the ability to wrap your advertising message on the outside of the publication so that your ad is the very first thing that their subscribers see. The cost associated with this solution is a bit high, but the impact that it has is often worth the extra expense.

Of course, there are limitations on what you can print on plastic bags or small bands that go on the outside of a magazine. Oftentimes, the shrink-wrap solution is used for product sampling or CD-ROM distribution. If you're interested in the publication but need to break through the clutter, shrink-wrap and belly wraps are interesting alternatives to traditional ads.

Newsletters and Updates

Most publications have free email newsletter subscriptions that offer a unique way to leverage the loyal subscribers who have Web access and who want to keep current with news that is important to them. Typically, consumers subscribe to these services because they want the publication to automatically filter only the information in which they are specifically interested. This filtering effect further qualifies a publication's subscribers into specific interest groups that can be targeted.

Links from these email subscriptions can be an effective way to promote your online promotion without sending unsolicited emails to these consumers. In other words, consumers who sign up for these newsletters are likely to read the emails they receive. By advertising within select email lists, you have a much better chance at effectively promoting your promotion than if you bought a list of email addresses and sent out a bunch of junk emails. Again, this is the basic concept of opt-in and consent. With subscribers to an email publication, your advertising link as part of that subscription is only a minor intrusion on a service that has been specifically requested, whereas directly emailing a notification of your online promotion to consumers who have *not* asked for such an email is spam (unsolicited email).

Direct Mail

Many marketers still argue that the Internet is nothing more than the ultimate direct-mail medium. Perhaps they are right. What possibly makes the Internet the "ultimate" direct-mail medium is its ability to segment consumers, test campaigns, and measure response (or effectiveness) all in *real time*. What makes traditional direct mail an effective medium for promoting an online promotion is the *personal touch*. By sending a personalized invitation to participate in the promotion, you can engage consumers directly. Granted, direct mail works best with known lists. Ideally, direct mailing to subscribers of a magazine or newspaper or some other personally identifiable source is a good way to attract consumers to your online promotion.

What's great about integrating direct mail with an online promotion is the element of a printed game piece. Where traditional scratch-off game cards have a one-time use, a direct-mail piece with a unique code can be used multiple times. That is, each consumer receiving the direct mailing can be invited to participate in your online promotion and, at that time, receive a unique code to use to participate. What you do next with that code is up to the design of the online promotion. You could have consumers match their code with one posted to your Web site each day so that while their card never changes, your Web site does. This gives their static game card ongoing value during a 30- to 60-day promotional period. Or perhaps the code allows them to play a daily scratch-off game online and again can be used multiple times. The code can be used to earn special discounts and offers during key sales periods. And, in each example, the code links back to your database providing invaluable tracking information.

With direct mail, your advertising dollars are focused. Direct mail by its very nature is not meant to be a shotgun approach, but rather an effort to target a specific segment of your audience. With direct mail, you have the ability to track your advertising expenditures down to the individual consumer level and learn some very interesting things about the dollars you spend to promote your online promotion. While codes in broadcast media can sometimes be used to track effectiveness, direct mail has a much better chance of providing feedback and information about the effectiveness of the advertising dollars spent.

Outdoor

As consumers spend less time in front of the television and more time commuting to and from work, advertising on billboards, in bus shelters, telephone booths, subways, buses, taxicabs, and other forms of outdoor advertising continue to grow in popularity. For online promotions, however, it becomes difficult to inspire consumers to participate unless large prizes (either in amount or quantity) become the key message. "For a chance to win $1 Million, visit . . ." Outdoors, there's not much room to introduce a product, company, or idea. The key to outdoors is exposure. Outdoor advertising is great for sound bytes, but your promotional URL had better be easy to remember.

In general, I would recommend using outdoor media only *in conjunction with* other traditional forms of media unless the URL is short and easy to remember. It's difficult to create a compelling message that someone will remember in addition to the URL. What outdoor advertising can do effectively is help remind consumers to play again if you've spent enough money in another medium promoting the promotion. When used to give the promotion a boost, outdoor advertising can work well. On its own, it's much more difficult to be an effective medium for promoting online promotions.

Guerrilla Marketing

While it's still gaining in popularity, I believe guerrilla marketing tactics are underutilized by most companies. Getting face-to-face time with consumers is an excellent way to promote online promotions and spread word of mouth. Guerrilla marketing works best if you have a small premium item you can give consumers with your promotional URL branded on the premium. Consumers can then take away something fun that will remind them of your promotion later when they are online. Capital One recently proved this with their "Cyberize Your Credit Card" campaign where *the only advertising vehicle* behind the online promotion was 550,000 URL-branded choc keys—500,000 promotional "credit cards" and 50,000 picture frame mouse pads with the URL `http://www.cyberize.com` printed on them. During the 6-week promotional period, over 80,000 consumers participated in the promotion.

Feet on the street campaigns work wonders. Nobody knows this as well as Di-Ann Eisnor, CEO and founder of Eisnor Interactive, whose tag line is "Offline Promotions for Online Brands." Di-Ann Eisnor has made a solid promotions business out of helping online marketers figure out their "real world" strategies to drive traffic to their Web sites. The concept that online brands need real world exposure has taken off like wildfire as clients of Eisnor Interactive quickly see the effective results of guerrilla marketing.

With guerrilla marketing, the focus is on a limited geographic region that is densely populated so that street marketers can have maximum impact. The interesting thing about guerrilla marketing is the shock value that it can have and its relative effectiveness. With real people breaking social norms in the name of online marketing, consumers react—sometimes positively and sometimes negatively—but the reaction spreads the tremendously valuable word of mouth that cannot otherwise be bought. Guerrilla marketing is the spark that ignites the incredibly powerful buzz that all your marketing efforts attempt to achieve. Even the potentially negative buzz disrupts the status quo and breaks through the clutter—sometimes this is all that is needed for a successful promotion.

Perhaps the best part of guerrilla marketing is its cost-effectiveness. For relatively little money, you can now maximize impact and exposure of your online promotions and use word of mouth and other viral components to spread the buzz about your marketing objectives and promotion. In short, guerrilla marketing works, but you must be willing to take risks and try things that no one else is willing to try. If you're worried about your corporate image, then perhaps guerrilla marketing is not for you—or perhaps it's exactly what you need to break out of the norm.

Promotional Media Buys

Promotional media buys are different from traditional media buys in that they center around many of the "extras" that can be included—but only if they are specifically asked for. Radio, more than any other medium, has the best opportunities for promotional extras. While inventory can often be tight during the fourth quarter (preholiday season), a good promotional media specialist can help leverage a traditional media buy into something much larger and more engaging by involving radio personalities in an on-air promotion, getting additional mentions, increasing the existing prize pool with station-provided merchandise, leveraging existing email lists, and taking other actions that make sense to the specific promotion. The extras usually don't amount to a whole lot, but when added together they can make a big difference in the effectiveness of the buy.

For this reason, it's a good idea to make sure the person negotiating the media buy is familiar with available promotional extras. Otherwise, like every other part of the negotiating process, if they are not asked for, they will not be included. Promotional media should be purchased through experienced media buyers who understand what to ask for and can leverage the media budget to create maximum impact. The right media buyers will identify what is realistic to expect with a specified budget, and will make recommendations for how to maximize the exposure that is needed.

Promotional media experts include companies like Kelly, Scott & Madison, PromoTV, Initiative Media (formerly Western International Media), and Media America. While there is a plethora of choices when it comes to media-buying agencies, not all agencies understand the importance of a promotional media buy. If you haven't received promotional extras in the past, it's a good idea to consult with one of the above-mentioned groups or a promotions agency that can provide specific recommendations based on the needs of your promotion.

Targeted Offline Media

When the media experts discovered the Internet (around the end of 1995), you would have thought they had discovered the Holy Grail. Several mantras such as "Media buying will never be the same!" and "The Internet has (once again) changed everything" could be heard just about everywhere you went. In truth, online media has some very distinct advantages over traditional media: uppermost is its ability to track and target consumers and do real-time reporting. These two aspects alone were enough to make most media experts think they had discovered the Holy Grail of the media-buying business. Why? Because that's what companies want: targeting ability and accountability. And perhaps online media will someday be the Holy Grail that today's media experts still tout. But that's at least version 6.0 of online media and we're still at version 3.5.

The problem is that while the Internet audience continues to grow, it is more fragmented than the cable industry. I dare not say how many millions of Web sites currently exist today, for as soon as this book is published, at least another hundred thousand or so will pop up and the number will be inaccurate. Media Metrix publishes the top Web sites in terms of unique users and site traffic, but today's Internet simply cannot compete with traditional media *even when the reach numbers are similar*. The reason? There is very little urgency online. People don't sit down at exactly 8:00 P.M. and log on to a Web site to watch the top-rated sitcom. They might check their email, read a few articles, and look at their stock portfolio, but there are many Web sites where they can go to do this.

While the Internet has penetrated the home and workstation, it has yet to deliver on the same sense of urgency that traditional media offers. A few companies like America Online can counter that they have large chat rooms and famous guest speakers who draw large crowds at specific times of day. Others may counter that they have loyal customers who visit their sites on a daily basis and that the sense of urgency is not a requirement for successful online media. The bottom line is that while online media has by far the most sophisticated tracking and reporting tools, the reach and frequency numbers have yet to rival that of traditional media—but online media continues to grow on a daily basis. The one exception is America Online. According to the September 2000 Media Metrix report, the AOL family of brands reaches 76 percent of the online audience.

Why Targeted Offline Media Works

Targeted offline media works because you can catch your target customers outside of the Internet and in their normal daily lives when they're *not* thinking about the Internet, online marketing, or online promotions. With offline media, you can often break through the clutter of traditional advertising with a compelling online promotion and drive people back to the Internet specifically to participate in your online promotion. With compelling prizes, clever creative, and an attractive product or service, offline media can get consumers' attention and attract them directly into the promotion.

With the mass exposure that offline media can provide, online promotions get the attention and advertising support needed to effectively satisfy the promotional objective. Offline media complements online promotions with true integration between traditional and online marketing efforts and takes advantage of the strengths of both mediums.

The specific type of offline media (broadcast, print, direct, or guerrilla marketing) will depend on the specific nature of the online promotion, what the objective of the promotion is, who the target audience is, and how best to reach that target audience. In general, however, offline media can capture the attention of your prospective consumers when they are doing other things besides gathering information and shopping on the Internet and help drive them directly to your online promotion.

Why Offline Media Can Be More Effective

Traditional offline media is intrusive—more so than banner ads and most other kinds of online advertising. Let's face it, no one watches television for the commercials, but when consumers are engaged in a television program, they are interrupted by the commercials. That interruption is difficult to ignore. While consumers can certainly change channels, they will usually be interrupted by commercials on other channels. If the commercial is done correctly, the interruption can be an effective way to gain awareness and drive traffic. The same holds true for radio commercials, print ads, billboards, direct mail, and guerrilla marketing. All of these media vehicles are effective ways of interrupting people from what they are trying to do and get them to pay attention to the advertising message.

With radio, people are interested in the music, sporting event, or talk show. But the commercial gets their attention during the breaks in between. With print ads, they're thumbing through to the articles they're interested in and stop to check out something that catches their eye. Consumers don't intend to read billboards, but they get bored while driving, riding the subway, or waiting for a bus and they can't help but look. No one rushes home to read junk mail, but most people leaf through it and the catchy mail gets opened—even if it's over the trash can while it's being read. Guerrilla marketing is especially intrusive when people do strange things outside of accepted social norms—from wearing strange costumes or billboards around their necks or to passing out premium items in crowded locations.

Banners are much less intrusive. As multimedia becomes more accepted as part of the banners, this will change over time. Most banners today have some form of animation, but most do not include sound and streaming media (or even Macromedia's Flash). The banner real estate is small and, for the most part, consistent, which allows consumers to be trained to block out anything that appears to follow the dimensions of a banner ad. Less intrusion means that consumers care less about having the banners on the site, but also means that most of the banners go unnoticed—hence the decreasing click-through rates.

Offline media that supports online promotions builds true integration of both worlds. So while you get more exposure (that is, interruption time) with traditional offline media, you get the better tracking and reporting of online promotions. As the state of the banner evolves, so, too, will its effectiveness. With so many of today's Web sites surviving primarily from banner ad revenues, the death of the banner is a very scary concept and is unlikely to occur anytime soon. Instead, as companies demand more effective online advertising vehicles, banner ads are likely to morph into higher-impact forms of advertising—more intrusive and more effective. For now, however, targeted offline media can be more effective than online media when promoting online promotions.

Problems with Banners

One of the biggest challenges with the current state of online media is the banner itself. While banners can be quite appealing to the newest members of the Internet community, they are nearly invisible to consumers who no longer surf the Internet in search of the cool and new, but use it more for targeted shopping, research, and information gathering. Think about your own experience with the Internet. When you first started, you were in "explore" mode and would get lost in the endless sea of content that exists out there. But as the Internet became more a part of your daily life, you were less apt to wander aimlessly throughout the Web. Your first exposure to banners was probably a positive one as these billboards would take you to the new and different that you were specifically searching for. But after you felt comfortable with what the Internet had to offer you and your business, the banners became distracting and you began to tune them out.

Perhaps the best example I can give is a personal experience not too long ago. I was using MapQuest (www.mapquest.com) to get driving directions to a party, and at the top of my directions was a banner ad that *I didn't even see*. It was in plain sight, but I never really looked at it as my Internet-trained eye simply blocked it out. It was only after I had printed out the driving directions that I first *saw* the banner and recognized it as one created by the in-house advertising group for a recent promotion that I had been working on for over 2 months. For several weeks, I had been working with the creative that was used in the promotion and if I had even been generally aware of the banner ad, I would have recognized it immediately, but I didn't see it until after it had been printed out on the directions.

The point is, even the most easily recognizable and interesting creative can be ignored with the right training. It doesn't happen overnight, but as Internet users get more and more inundated with banner ads, they will begin to ignore the ads altogether and simply focus on getting done what they went online to accomplish. While banners are unlikely to disappear anytime soon, I recommend using them for testing and, in some cases, as support for other media vehicles. I do not recommend that the bulk of your advertising dollars be spent on banner ads to promote your online promotion.

The "Catch 22" of Email Marketing

Joseph Heller, author of the best-selling novel *Catch 22* could have a field day with email marketing. On the one hand, email is a wonderful way to promote an online promotion, but *only* if you have already built up a substantial internal email list. You can't buy a quadruple opt-in email list and expect it to perform in the same way as your internal email marketing list—it won't. If you buy an opt-in email list from a list broker, you are likely to get a maximum response rate of 5 percent— much better than direct mail's typical 2 percent response rate, but nowhere near the 15 to 20 percent response rate that an internal email list can generate. So sending out an email to your current opt-in subscriber base is an excellent way to promote your online promotions, but to get an opt-in email list, you need effective online promotions—hence the Catch 22.

As stated previously, leveraging a partner's email list is effective as long as the email is generated directly from the partner. If you send emails out to your partner's customers, it is the equivalent of sending out unsolicited email because you were never given permission to send emails to the individual customers. Instead, if your online promotion is included as a link in your partner's normal communications efforts to its consumers, then the emails are more likely to be read and help increase the impact of your online promotions.

The Long-Term Perspective

It should be noted that the goal of online promotions should ultimately be to move away from the traditional methodologies of advertising and promotions and move into the "relationship building" stage that most companies have not quite figured out how to accomplish. That is, each time that money is spent to meet specific promotional objectives, the objectives should be part of a master plan to build a relationship with customers and provide them with their specific needs. Customer relationships are incredibly important, and the identification of your best customers is even more so. In Chapter 8, "What to Do after the Promotion," I will further discuss best practices for relationship building and what to do with and for the customers who have opted-in to your future marketing efforts and wish to hear more from your company. The point here is that while offline media can provide you with the exposure needed for successful online promotions, the goal is to find better and more efficient ways to market to your best customers directly.

Integrating Communities and Portal Sites Effectively

By now, it should be obvious that I truly believe in the integration of online promotions, not just with offline media but also with the rest of your company's marketing efforts. Online promotions as stand-alone marketing efforts are much more challenging than if the online promotion is integrated into every other aspect of your company's marketing efforts (meaning each contact you have with your current and potential customers). Only with truly integrated promotions will you be able to become part of Internet communities and portal sites effectively. The reason is, if you are simply trying to use a well-established Internet community to create buzz for your promotion, you'll have a much more difficult time if the members of the community have never heard of the promotion. In fact, there is no such thing as the concept of "using" a community. It's simply not possible to "use" a community effectively. Instead, you can become *part* of a community and use a grassroots approach to spreading the word.

The integration of online promotions means using the online promotion as part of your "call to action" within the rest of your marketing efforts. While your online promotion is the place where consumers actually participate in your sweepstakes, contest, game, coupon, or premium offer, the availability of the online promotion should be promoted throughout the company as part of the rest of the marketing messages so that the online promotion becomes yet another benefit of your product or service. Assuming that you have done a good job of internalizing your online promotions with the rest of your marketing efforts, integrating communities and portal sites should be fairly easy.

What Defines an Internet Community?

After my first online marketing job in 1995, I struggled with the question of what made something interactive. After brainstorming with my then partners Gregg Alwine and Thelton McMillian, we came up with a formula for interactivity:

$$\text{Audience} + \text{Empowerment} + \text{Contribution} = \text{Interactivity}$$

This formula was the result of numerous evenings and weekends discussing why some Web sites suffered from "dead Web"—static Web pages that don't really do anything—while other Web sites were extremely active and engaging. I think what we were really talking about was defining an Internet community—not interactivity. A community by its very definition has the two elements of audience and contribution. The Internet adds the element of empowerment that allows communities to form all over the world. Most Internet communities are created because of a shared special interest. From a desire to find romance to financial investments to the discussion of automobiles to ski clubs, most Internet communities center around a general interest.

Online communities are similar to the fictional bar on the television show *Cheers* "Where everybody knows your name, and they're always glad you came." Perhaps the last part goes a bit far, but the first part is certainly true enough. Online communities are formed around special topics or areas of interest, but they're "of the people, by the people, and for the people." The debates can get heated as people are passionate about their areas of interest (hence their participation), but they are very real.

This is where most companies fail. Companies see a healthy online community that is centered on a topic related to their company, and they immediately think "advertising opportunity." And, if done correctly, an online community *can* be a worthwhile advertising opportunity. But most marketers rely on the interruption marketing techniques they learned in school and miss the whole point of the online community. Online communities are about peoples' passions. Nobody wants the intrusion of advertising, but especially not in a community built around discussions and an important exchange of information.

Be a Real Person, Not a Company

If you're truly interested in harnessing the power of online communities, you should read *The ClueTrain Manifesto* by Christopher Locke, Rick Levine, Doc Searls, and David Weinberger (Perseus Books, 2000). If it does nothing else for you, *The ClueTrain Manifesto* will teach you how to stop being a marketer for 10 minutes and just be a real person. Online communities recognize marketing propaganda a mile away. If you attempt to distribute your company's marketing propaganda via an online community, you will receive the exact opposite reaction that you want—negative word of mouth. Suddenly no communication is a wonderful alternative to all the hate mail and negative postings your company will receive as a direct result of incorrectly marketing your company.

If you want to get the word out about your upcoming online promotion, you first have to *listen* and become a part of the online community. Follow their discussions, take your marketing hat off, and listen as a consumer. What are they talking about? How could your promotion benefit these people? Throw away all your marketing collateral and speak from the heart about why you think people might be interested in your online promotion. If you seem like a person genuinely interested in helping the online community better itself from your input, then you will likely get at least some of the results you're looking for. At a bare minimum, your company should not receive angry hate mail and negative reactions to your contributions to the group. If it does, you can honestly respond as to why you thought people might be interested and avoid the corporate bashing.

Online communities are similar to real-life communities in that real people speak their minds—only without the fear of social repercussions that happen in real life. But if you act like a real person and not a company, you can respond appropriately and become part of the online community. And that's the real key to becoming part of an online community—acting like an individual who's speaking on behalf of a company rather than a company speaking corporate-speak through an individual.

Allow Your Employees to Do the Same

Fear doesn't get very far on the Internet. Companies that encourage their employees to spend time with their customers will reap the benefits. Many companies feel that the time their employees spend online is nonproductive, when this is usually not the case. Employees who use the Internet to support the requirements of their jobs often discover organizations filled with useful information and people resources that would otherwise be costly to hire out on an individual consultative basis. By contributing to online communities, employees make "deposits" into an online community's wealth of information, which will then allow them to make "withdrawals" when the time comes.

This is not just for the customer service department, but all levels of the company. The online communities that are related to your industry have different groups focused on different aspects of the business, and employees should be encouraged to become part of these online communities—not just when additional grassroots advertising support is needed, but as ongoing relationship marketing. Think of your employees as extensions of your integrated marketing efforts. Their time as part of the online communities will yield great dividends when you attempt to spread viral marketing. If they have taken an active role in their respective online communities, when the time comes to spread the word about online promotions and other online marketing efforts, the message will come from a respected member of the online community, and not from an outsider clearly looking to take advantage of the members of the group.

If you do ask your employees to help spread the word, make sure you let them do it in their own way. If you force them to post predetermined marketing messages, you will be asking them to stop being an integral and respected part of the online community and, instead, they will become the target of antiadvertising postings and emails. Instead, by letting them use their own voice to talk about what's going on in the company, their contributions will more likely be accepted and even acted upon.

Portal Sites

Traditional and promotional portal sites were discussed earlier in this chapter. The main difference between traditional and promotional portal sites is the audience they attract. While traditional portal sites attract a broad audience of consumers looking for information and commerce, promotional portals attract consumers interested in participating in sweepstakes, contests, games, and getting free stuff. This section will review both kinds of portal sites and provide information on how best to utilize them.

Traditional Portal Sites

There are many books available that provide strategies about how best to elevate your Web site to the top of a search results list. From metatags to key words, there are several tricks that can be utilized to help your Web page appear to be the perfect match to specific key words searches. If the promotion will last several months, then taking the time to add the proper metatags and key words may actually help consumers find the promotion. But all these tricks take time to go into effect and usually are not much help with an online promotion that lasts only 4 to 6 weeks—especially if you don't have much time prior to the launch.

The better strategy is to make sure your main Web site complies with all of the search engine requirements, and focus on other strategies for elevating your online promotion within the traditional portal sites. Buying key word banners, for example, can provide your online promotions with timely additional exposure. A key word banner ad buy is when you purchase specific key words that pull your banner into the results page (rather than purchasing a "run of site" advertising buy, where your banner ads appear randomly throughout the site).

Good key words are *not* broad topics like "sweepstakes," but specific words that are relevant to your promotional objective. If you are using the promotion to increase sales of a particular product, the key words should center on the specific product and words that consumers are likely to use to find your product.

In addition to key word banner buys, individual portal sites often have advertising specials that you can either buy into or incorporate as part of your online promotion. Seasonal events such as Valentine's Day, Mother's Day, Back to School, and Christmas typically have specific promotional packages that are developed internally by the portal sites. Each portal has its own advertising and promotions plans centered around these holidays and specific banner ad buys that can be purchased. In some cases, this is in the form of a sponsorship. In others, your online promotion can simply tie in to the existing promotion being developed by the portal site.

Beyond the Banner

It's equally important to think beyond the banner when effectively integrating your online promotions with traditional portal sites. Each portal offers specific services such as free email, free Internet Access, Instant Messaging, and personal preferences for its members. With each of these services, there are specialty advertising opportunities that go beyond the traditional banner ad. This can be as simple as a link in a personal preferences newsletter that is sent out each day or as a 30-second streaming television-like ad that appears when a consumer signs on for free Internet access.

If you're interested in integrating your online promotion into these portal sites, the best thing to do is ask for additional advertising opportunities that go beyond the traditional banner ad. Each portal site will offer different kinds of advertising opportunities that you can evaluate based on your company's needs.

Promotional Portal Sites

While traditional portal sites can provide a good avenue for driving traffic to your online promotion, the key factor to consider when deciding to use *promotional* portal sites is the kind of consumer you're interested in attracting to your online promotion. Whereas traditional portal sites do not typically attract gamers (consumers interested only in the promotion, not your product or services), promotional portal sites are designed specifically for consumers who are interested in participating in sweepstakes, contests, games, and getting free stuff. This is an important distinction that should be considered before promotional portal sites are integrated into the advertising strategy of promoting your online promotions. If you are not concerned about attracting gamers, then promotional portal sites can be an effective tool to boost the participation levels of your online promotions.

Similar to traditional portals, promotional portals act as a listing service but they are completely focused on online promotions. Because of this, you have different options for listing your online promotions. Most are listed by promotional category such as: Sweepstakes; Contests; Instant Win Games; Free Samples; Coupons; Buy One, Get One Free; Rebates; and Rewards programs. Adding a link to your promotion in some promotional portals is free while others will charge for the listing. As promotional portal sites continue to grow, the simple text link to your online promotion may not be sufficient. You may also want to consider buying banner ads for your key category to ensure the maximum exposure of your promotion.

Buying banner ads for your online promotion on a promotional portal site makes a lot of sense. Whereas traditional banner ads can be somewhat of a distraction to consumers searching on a traditional portal, the purpose of a promotional portal is to funnel traffic to online promotions. Since this is exactly what you are trying to accomplish, the banner ad becomes less of a distraction, and more of a helpful aid to get consumers to your promotions Web site.

Beyond the Banner

Similar to the traditional portals, promotions portals offer different promotions-focused services and additional advertising opportunities beyond the traditional banner ad. The most common of these is the promotional newsletter that identifies hot online promotions based on consumers' self-defined interest profiles. Other options include having the promotional portal tie in to the promotion directly by allowing users to pass their membership information directly to your database without having to retype everything. Another option is to access members who have identified themselves as being able to receive HTML-formatted emails and to send them a game piece directly, which they can use on your Web site to see if they are instant winners.

Some promotions portals offer multibrand promotions that your promotion can tie into for additional exposure and the ability to leverage a larger prize pool. If your promotion needs some extra exposure and prizes to increase its effectiveness, a tie-in to a promotions portal may be just what is needed for success.

Each promotions portal has its own advertising opportunities. Because the different opportunities are unique to the specific promotions portal, it's worth some investigation into all the available options to find out what makes the most sense for your online promotion.

Nontraditional and Experimental Advertising

There's something to be said for the tried and true, but when advertising noise becomes a serious hurdle to getting your messages across, consider nontraditional or experimental advertising. In many cases, newer advertising mediums are more cost-effective as the inventors are usually hungry for advertising dollars. Significant up-front costs usually accompany new mediums, with owners interested in recouping their investments. Because nontraditional and experimental advertising is "outside the box" of traditional advertising, it typically commands more attention. The first time you saw a normal consumer's car covered with an ad, I'm sure it caught you by surprise. It's not every day that you see the neon purple and yellow color of the Yahoo! ad stretched across a Jeep Cherokee. And that's the point. Nontraditional and experimental advertising breaks through an otherwise cluttered marketplace full of ads.

Over time, as nontraditional and experimental advertising becomes mainstream, the shock value of seeing an ad "where it doesn't belong" wears off. Also, as the new medium becomes another standard advertising vehicle, you'll again face the problem of "too much noise."

The risk in publishing a book is that what is nontraditional at the time of publication may already be mainstream by the time it is read—especially with the current speeds of the Internet and the overall booming advertising growth. But, if you understand the premise behind using nontraditional and experimental advertising, the examples in this section can simply serve as case studies for why even more nontraditional and experimental advertising mediums should be considered.

Online Media Vehicles

Everyone talks about "beyond the banner," but once you get past direct email and sponsorships, many companies are not sure where to go next. This catch phrase was originally created so that research and industry analysts could accurately forecast the potential growth of online advertising sales. But what it currently represents is ingenuity in the online world of advertising. From free Internet Service Providers (ISPs) to Shopping Agents, Instant Messaging to 800 number Web access, and software to enhance your Personal Data Assistants (PDAs) and Web Access Phones (WAPs) (see discussion that follows), there is a plethora of advertising vehicles that can help you get beyond the traditional banner ad—or, at the bare minimum, at least decrease the clutter and create some continuity among your audience.

Free ISPs

Free Internet access is one service for which consumers are happy to receive banner ads as an exchange. Unlike many advertising-based models, consumers receive a direct benefit with free Internet service saving approximately $20 to $35 per month. This is an interesting value proposition. While some Internet advertising models pay for consumers to click on ads and surf the Web, a Free ISP absorbs a real cost to consumers. As free broadband services become available [free digital subscriber lines (DSL), for example], consumers will be more and more willing to jump through small advertising hoops in exchange for free (high-speed) access to the Internet.

While there are a number of companies working the free ISP model, one company seems to be winning the battle in terms of having the right partners, distribution models, and amazing customer service. Spinway (www.spinway.com) developed the back-end free ISP model that is the essence of BlueLight.com (the joint venture between Yahoo! and K-Mart) as well as Costco's free ISP service and several others. In the original version of BlueLight.com, K-Mart served up traditional 30-second television-like ads for Tabasco, Martha Stewart, and K-Mart itself. This was truly engaging and incredibly smart, although I haven't seen these television-like ads in some time now.

The full-motion video appeared when consumers signed on to their free Internet access account. Rather than watching the connection between two modems, onlookers could view the single ad that was a smaller digital version of actual television commercials. Even if you left your computer to do something else, the music and audio portion of the ad would reinforce the brand message. By the sixth time I logged on, I could recite the commercial in full. The interesting part, however, was that the future video advertisements were slowly streamed into the background while consumers were online. If they signed off before the next commercial was finished, it would play the previous commercial the next time the consumer logged on and then resume streaming the new spot until it had been completely downloaded.

The video was by far the most engaging part of the service, but it appears that this component has been placed on the back burner. For the past few months, BlueLight.com has not launched any videos during the sign-in process—perhaps it was only a prebroadband test that focus group consumers rejected. As a marketer, I thought it was brilliant. The video commercials caught my attention every time, and I could not complain about watching them as it was a small price to pay for free Internet access.

Instead, the current model is to display traditional banner ads at the bottom of the screen. Once the free Internet connection is established, a banner-sized bar appears at the bottom of a consumer's Web browser and stays in the foreground for as long as the consumer is connected to the free Internet service. If other non-Internet applications are brought up to be worked on, the free ISP banner at the bottom of the screen remains prominent until the connection to the Internet is disconnected. If the banner is closed, the Internet connection is immediately terminated.

Like most banner ads, the ads on the advertising bar initially catch the attention of the consumer who is not used to seeing them there. But, over time, users of the free Internet service learn to block out the ads from their peripheral view and focus only on what they are looking for online. The major advantage of the free ISP advertising opportunity as it stands today is that it's new and it's tied directly to a consumer's Internet access. That is, consumers are exposed to the advertisements for as long as they are online—even if they switch over to a different (non-Internet) application.

I hope the streaming video commercial model resurfaces. I have a feeling that the banner ad model of the free ISPs will follow a similar trend of traditional banner ads unless alternative sources of advertising (such as the streaming video) increase their overall effectiveness.

Shopping Guides

Similar to the free ISP model, shopping guides such as the Dash bar (www.dash
.com) have appeared on the scene to help consumers find the best places to shop
online (not to mention the ability to track shopping behaviors). They follow the similar free ISP model that provides a banner-size navigational bar at the bottom of
the consumer's Web browser. The difference is that, unlike most bottom ad banners, consumers make these shopping guides relevant to their specific tastes and
interests and, in the best-case scenario, use the shopping guide to help them make
purchasing decisions.

In the traditional banner ad model, this means that relevant banner ads are
served up based on a consumer's self-selected profile (male, head of household,
earning at least $50,000, and likes hiking). But beyond the traditional banner ad
model, these shopping guides can help provide more relevant information at critical decision points. With these shopping guides, a sponsor, such as Barnes &
Noble, can offer a deep discount to a consumer who is just about to purchase a book
from Amazon.com. Because the shopping guide identifies its own sponsors and its
sponsors' competitors, it can provide relevant offers at the critical decision points
during the consumer's shopping experience.

The other advantage of the shopping guide is that, when used, consumers pay
attention to the guide. They use it as a portal to various shopping categories. In
some cases they use it to track their purchases and/or gain loyalty points for shopping at specific store locations. Shopping guides offer the simplicity of the banner
ad, but, when used properly by consumers, are also a powerful e-commerce tool.

WebCertificates (www.webcertificates.com) by eCount, was the first Web
site where you could send and receive gift certificates that can be used online anywhere that Visa or MasterCard is accepted. While a WebCertificate is not exactly
a shopping guide, by offering several choices and tracking spending limits set by
the giver, it acts as one when consumers attempt to redeem their WebCertificate.
The receivers can also increase the value of the WebCertificate by using their own
credit card in order to purchase an item that costs more than the value of their
original WebCertificate.

Shopping guides, such as the Dash bar and WebCertificates, can help consumers
find what they are looking for and reward them for their online purchasing behavior. As shopping guides advance in their artificial intelligence, they will be able to
make recommendations based on a consumer's previous shopping patterns. When
the traditional advertising models are combined with online shopping guides, the
result is the ability to provide tailored promotional offers to key consumers at their
critical decision points when shopping online. Over time, shopping guides will continue to be effective not because they are cool or unique, but because they are effective, and that is key to having lasting staying power among all e-commerce brands.

Instant Messaging

As if email, a fax machine, cellular phone, pager, and voice mail were not enough,
the explosive growth of instant messaging tells me that this relatively new communications medium is here to stay. Instant Messaging was an early tool built

within America Online and other proprietary dial-up service providers, but when it hit the rest of the Internet, it spread like wildfire. By selecting a screen name, users of the same instant messaging software can "instant message" you when you're online. When a friend wants to reach you, a message pops up on your screen. By responding to that message, you essentially engage in a one-on-one chat session.

For dial-up users with only a single phone line, this tool is a must-have. When friends try calling the home number and get a busy signal, they can use instant messaging to check to see if the person they're trying to reach is online or talking on the phone. This can be as simple as asking a question in the form of an instant message or simply alerting the person online to sign off and call his or her friends.

The problem with instant messaging as it stands today is that there are multiple protocols being used by the major players (AOL, Microsoft, and Yahoo!), and consumers can't instant message between the different providers. That is, if I have an account with AOL and you have an account with Microsoft, I need to download the Microsoft version of instant messaging software to reach you (or you need the AOL version to reach me). Over time, this will probably work itself out. As competitors are forced to work with each other (because of the demands of their consumers, if not governmental agencies), I'm confident that there will be cross-company communication abilities. For now, however, the market is fragmented.

Instant messaging allows you to get your advertising message across to consumers via the available ad buttons on the instant messaging tool itself. Granted, the instant messaging tool is only seen when it is used—the rest of the time it sits minimized on the consumer's task bar. Still, as the growth of instant messaging continues, companies are able to offer advertisers another "beyond the banner" application—even if it's still ultimately in the form of a banner. Instant messaging is a service that consumers use consistently and will be exposed to advertising messages when they go to talk with their friends and coworkers.

Free Email

When free email services, such as Yahoo! Mail, Hotmail, Mail.com, and others, arrived on the scene, I admit I was skeptical. Why would I purposely add another email account to my work and play email addresses? The answer was simple: because you can keep it forever.

People change jobs and `person@companyX.com` quickly becomes `person@companyY.com`. People switch Internet Service Providers and `person@ispX.com` quickly becomes `person@ispY.com`. With free email accounts, consumers can always be reached at one email address, as long as they check that account. This is important. If the free email account is inactive, then it doesn't do anybody much good. However, if the free email account is updated and checked often, then it becomes the most reliable email address a person can have.

From an advertising perspective, there are a few different options. The most common is to catch consumers when they log in to their free email account online and serve them the traditional ad banner. Because the free email account has value to consumers, banner ads can be less intrusive. More importantly, because consumers filled out a profile on themselves when they signed up, the banner ads that are served tend to be more relevant. With increased relevance comes increased attention, and the result is more effective banner ad results.

But banner ads are not the only option. Most free email services also provide consumers with an opt-in option to receive newsletters and relevant offers from partners—relevant offers based on the profiles consumers completed about themselves. While these opt-in email lists will not be nearly as effective as your own email list generated internally, they provide a good starting point for beginning email marketing efforts. This is especially true if you are sending a link as part of a sponsorship of a regularly scheduled email newsletter (which is much less intrusive than renting the list of emails and sending your own email blast).

There are also experimental advertising opportunities within the free email category itself. Birthday emails, for example, are one place where you can tie in with the free service's good will gesture and help provide a free gift (or special discount) within a happy birthday email being sent out to applicable recipients. Likewise, there are usually seasonal emails sent out about the holiday season, Mother's Day, Valentine's Day, and other relevant shopping events. With free email services, there are usually several options to capture the attention of an active, loyal audience.

Toll-Free Web Sites

With the telephone still holding the maximum household penetration in the United States (something to the tune of 98 percent of all households), toll-free Web sites have tremendous upside for bringing the Internet to consumers who do not have access to the Internet. Using the latest and greatest in voice recognition software, consumers can call Web sites like (800) 4BVocal or (800) 555-Tell and get updates on weather reports, traffic conditions, stock quotes, and other information. After establishing a membership with the service, consumers can get the information they need free of any long-distance charges.

Advertising your online promotions via a toll-free Web site may not make sense. It's too early to tell, but if it turns out that non-Internet users gravitate the most to these voice-activated Web sites, then telling consumers about an online promotion that they can't get to would not be money well spent. But, as the voice technology progresses, non-Internet users may want to participate in online promotions via this toll-free Web solution. In this way, consumers would have the option to enter for their chance to win or even order directly from your site when they call in to check the weather or traffic conditions in their local area.

Conversely, if it turns out that the wired population is the first to gravitate to toll-free Web sites, then this may even prove to be a good advertising vehicle for your online promotions. By combining current toll-free Web site information with the ability to send a reminder email to consumers requesting such a service, I can envision a program that alerts consumers to your online promotion and then allows them to provide their email address so you can send out a physical reminder. In this way, the next time they're online checking their email, they will receive your reminder with a link to the online promotion.

I see toll-free Web sites having tremendous upside, especially when you consider the overwhelming success of traditional 800 number promotions. By combining the ability to access virtually unlimited information via the Internet with a standard phone interface, the future of toll-free Web sites is very exciting.

Personal Data Assistants (PDAs) and Web Access Phones (WAPs)

Personal Data Assistants (PDAs) and Web Access Phones (WAPs) may become alternative distribution vehicles for newspapers and magazines, but it's still too early to tell. When the email subscription services to news organizations came out, many prophesied that email and screen saver news applications would replace traditional newspapers and magazine subscriptions, when, in fact, they only complemented them. The same may be true for PDAs and WAPs, but the reason they may have a better success story is due to their inherent portability. With emails and screen savers, you still need a computer to get the news and information in which you're interested. While even the best laptops are a pain to take with you wherever you go, PDAs and WAPs are different. They're small enough to keep in your pocket or purse and have the same attractive portability as traditional newspapers and magazines. When color PDAs and WAPs become the norm, then they will have a chance to become a primary source for news and information. What may ultimately prevent their success is their smaller screen size. Again, it's too soon to tell, but PDAs and WAPs make excellent experimental advertising vehicles.

At the time of writing, there is already legislation requiring the inclusion of Global Positioning Satellite (GPS) information in all mobile devices. This legislation is currently being fought on the basis of privacy concerns and who will have access to the GPS information. If the legislation stands, however, the inclusion of GPS in mobile devices may significantly change the way promotions are delivered to consumers.

Imagine driving within 5 miles of a Blockbuster store on your way home from work and receiving a "Rent one, get one free" coupon alert. The coupon is only transmitted when you are within a specified range of the physical store during key times of the day. The missing link is the store's ability to know when you're within that specified parameter, but with GPS, that problem is solved. Suddenly, you can receive offers and discounts at the time of consideration or while in route.

This will be a very interesting time for the promotions industry if GPS becomes standard in all wireless devices and marketers are allowed access to this information. As with successful email marketing campaigns, those companies who respect the privacy of consumers and get permission to market to them will win. If consumers agree to receive these special offers, they will be happy to get them. If no permission is requested or received, there is likely to be a huge consumer backlash in the same way consumers are still fighting unsolicited email.

The Next Biggest Thing Online

What's the next biggest thing on the Internet? I don't know, but I know where to find it. One good location is the industry trade show Internet World (by Penton Media). Each year Internet World brings together some of the brightest talent in a single forum so you can check out what's new. There's no guarantee that what you see at an Internet World show will actually make it, but you can usually tell what technology will quickly be absorbed industrywide and which technology barely made it to the show. Of course, this trade show only happens a few times a year. In between Internet World trade shows, you can review up-and-coming technologies in the magazine *The Industry Standard* or at various Internet-focused Web sites (including www.internet.com).

In Chapter 9 of this book, I will discuss some of the key emerging technologies that should also be considered as vehicles for nontraditional advertising and promotion. Among them are v-commerce, the next generation of DirectTV, the next generation of handheld devices, and the crossover of the gaming industry. The point is, there are several options for emerging technologies and the next big thing to happen in online promotions will likely be created by *you* when you connect all the dots as you look for new emerging technologies to promote and enhance *your* online promotions.

Offline Media Vehicles

Advertising is everywhere you look—or at least that's what the major offline media advertising conglomerates want. Clearly, some of the less traditional media vehicles work with mixed results and you have to decide what makes sense for your company and your promotions efforts. In this section, I will discuss a few of the current offline media trends that are catching on. As stated previously, the risk of writing this section is that what is emerging at the time of publication may already be mainstream as you read this book. If this is the case, please use this section to think about what today's equivalent emerging offline media vehicles are and how you might best take advantage of them to help promote your online promotions.

AutoWraps

The first time I saw a Jeep Cherokee that had been painted purple with the yellow Yahoo! logo, I about fell over. It was a lesson that there truly is no such thing as an original idea. In college, some 4 years earlier, I had dreamed up a simple concept that billion-dollar companies would someday subsidize the rising cost of automobiles and automotive insurance by printing their logos and advertising on the vehicles themselves. Sure enough, not one, but two companies launched with that very concept and, from what I gather, are doing well. On the AutoWraps Web site (www.autowraps.com) consumers submit the make and model of their car along with their daily commute to work, and consumers are matched with companies that are looking for additional exposure in that specific geographic region. Cars are then wrapped (or painted) with a billboard-type logo or message and consumers are occasionally followed to ensure that they are, in fact, driving their specified route to and from work at the specified time of day.

As long as the consumers keep the wrap or paint job on their cars and continue to drive the same commute, they receive checks for a couple hundred dollars each month for their "moving billboard." It's a three-way win as consumers get compensated for something they do every day anyway, clients get their advertising message on a virtually untapped medium, and the broker gets a piece of the action for matching consumer cars and driving routes with specific client needs.

I'm curious to see where this goes. Buses and taxies as moving billboards made a lot of sense as a simple additional revenue stream for the government or taxi company, but I'm curious to see how quickly consumer automobiles as billboards catch on. Will the car manufacturers get into the game and come out with a "Coca Cola Edition" Ford Explorer that costs less than a regular Ford Explorer? I believe it's too soon to tell. But as my economics teacher used to reiterate, "the market has a way of taking care of itself." That is, if consumers demand it, manufacturers and retailers will find a way to make it profitable.

As an advertising vehicle, AutoWraps also has the advantage of being extremely regional and targeted. At least at this stage of the game, it is a high-impact offline media "vehicle" that could seriously help "drive" awareness of your products, services, and online promotions. The one caveat is the timeliness aspect. If your online promotion is going up and coming down in a matter of weeks, advertising with AutoWraps may not be an effective advertising "vehicle" (no pun intended). However, online promotions can easily tie in to your corporate brand message and a URL that need not be so time oriented. In other words, the advertising draws traffic to your site and the site introduces the promotion.

Dry Cleaners, Lunch Bags, and Coffee Cups

At the 2000 PROMO Expo show, I met an exhibitor, Look WorldWide (www.lookworldwide.com), who was promoting his network of dry cleaners that adds magazine-style advertising to the plastic bags that protect consumers' clean clothes. Instead of the standard "Thank You. Come Again" message that is commonly printed on the poly bag, there was an ad you might see as a Free Standing Insert (FSI) in the Sunday newspaper. The technology to print on plastic has been around for quite some time and I've seen it done for magazines that include a special report, CD-ROM, or other attachment to the core periodical. The key difference was the network of dry cleaners that now allows marketers to target specific geographic locations (or run nationally) by using their traditional magazine or FSI ads at the dry cleaners.

Similarly, there has been a recent influx of advertising-supported lunch bags that are offered at the deli counter and other convenience stores. Starbucks has taken advantage of the rings around their coffee cups (to protect consumers from burning their hands) to sport various forms of advertising. It seems retail outlets are checking out their various cost centers (that is, supplies) and finding ways to turn them into profit centers through creating new advertising vehicles.

I believe that, with some ingenuity, it's not difficult to make the leap from these current trends to what's next in your particular industry. Perhaps you're interested in getting more exposure at gas stations. In addition to the straightforward ad banners hanging off the price-per-gallon signs, perhaps you can make a deal with the blue towel suppliers to superimpose your ad onto the gas station's towels to drive down the cost of your ad. Gas stations offer these disposable blue towels so customers can check their oil while at the pump. But because these blue towels cost the gas station money and are given to consumers for free, the blue towels are a cost center. By providing a way for gas stations to get these disposable towels for free, you have created a new advertising medium.

In-store displays in the supermarket were supplemented by ads on the carts and on the floor. With just about every inch of the supermarket covered with ads or price discounts, can the parking lot be far behind? What better way to remind you to buy frozen dinners than with a promotional ad on which you can park your car?

Clearly, lines must be drawn. Products like public toilet paper have yet to enter the ad space (nor are they likely to ever get there), but small entrepreneurial media groups have already started placing magazine-size ads in front of the men's urinals in restaurant and nightclub bathrooms. Let's face it, where there's a captive audience and some free space, some advertising-focused individual will find a way to turn a profit. The key for using these nontraditional advertising spaces for promoting online promotions comes down to timeliness. How quickly can ads be incorporated and distributed to their key locations? The faster the turnaround times, the more likely these new mediums will be used for experimentation.

Next-Generation Billboards

As traditional billboards spill out onto actual buildings, streets, and sidewalks, it appears as if they are taking over the major cities. No longer can tourists appreciate the historic buildings for their unique architecture. Now, they marvel at all the major brands that are fighting for their attention.

If Times Square in New York City is any indication of the future of outdoor marketing, we're in for an interesting ride. For one thing, Times Square is no longer full of static billboards. At the very minimum, static images surround entire buildings and are not contained within the traditional billboard shape and sizes. The next step up is a billboard with single-line tickers at the top that are posting approved emails from customers. Fake or not, they appear to be emails from actual consumers and often include real email addresses. I believe Joe Boxer was the first to do this, but they certainly will not be the last. From there you have larger tickers that are in full color and combine some smaller static images that rotate in conjunction with the text messages. But perhaps the most impressive are the massive movie-theater-size television screens that literally run television commercials and selected programming. Suddenly billboards and television programming have somehow merged.

As full-motion billboards replace the static images we see today, it will become more and more difficult to ignore the billboards or look away. If you're in the general vicinity of one of these billboards, you are compelled to see what's going on. The next step is for someone to connect these action-packed billboards with direct response. Perhaps you will one day be able to use your PDA to beam information to and from these billboards and place orders directly from them. Traditional billboards continue to evolve, and if full-motion billboards become the norm, they will provide an excellent medium to promote your online promotions.

Conclusion

No matter where or how you advertise your online promotions, the bottom line is that advertising is required for successful online promotions. As you can see from this chapter, there are a number of options you can use to promote your online promotions. I have found that traditional (targeted) offline media can be more effective at driving awareness of online promotions than the traditional online banner ads and purchased opt-in email lists. This doesn't mean that traditional offline media is right for everyone, but in many circumstances it can be more effective. Of course the ultimate goal is to move away from constant awareness and acquisition goals and into longer-term relationship management programs that target your existing customer base. Online promotions can help you get there, but they are only the first step. In the next chapter, I will review some of the things you should do once your online promotion has ended.

What to Do after the Promotion

After the promotion ends, the tendency is to take a deep breath and then jump into the next most urgent project. The Internet has increased the pace of business to the point where people expect tasks to be done in a matter of hours, when those very same requests used to take days. Even people whose job is dedicated to the field of online promotions have a difficult time taking a time-out once the promotion has ended. The value of analysis is downplayed and issues that are more urgent take precedence.

Regardless of the reason, most companies stop thinking about their promotions as soon as they've ended. When this happens, of course, companies are more likely to repeat the same mistakes and "roll the dice" with their next online promotion. Valuable learning that is packaged neatly in the form of a database of promotional entries and/or redemption data tends to get put aside in the things-to-deal-with-at-a-later-date pile. Opt-in customer segmentation is captured, but is not always used appropriately. When this happens, the list becomes stale, outdated, and decreases in value for the company.

In this chapter you will learn that to cross the finish line you must take the time necessary to measure the results of your promotion, manage and integrate your promotional database, and follow up with special discounts and offers targeting the very consumers who have given you permission to market to them in the

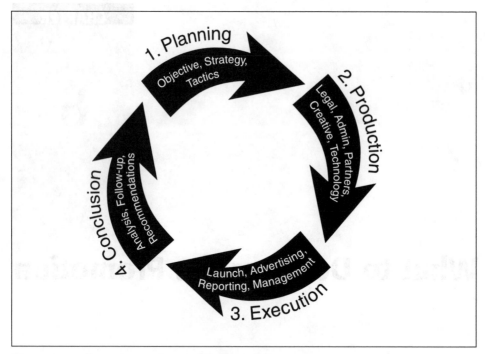

Figure 8.1 The circle of online promotions.

future. This chapter will also focus on how to better integrate your online and offline marketing efforts and how to apply what you've learned to your future promotional marketing efforts—online or traditional. When you have read this chapter, you will have completed the circle of online promotions, as shown in Figure 8.1.

Measuring the Results of Your Promotion

If your promotion began with a clearly defined objective, then measuring the results should be fairly straightforward. With online promotions, on-demand reporting capabilities are the norm. During the promotion itself, it should be easy to track the response to your promotionally driven advertising, follow the spikes in traffic (usually attributed to various advertising vehicles), see the abandon rates, and measure the ultimate goal of the promotion (that is, increased memberships, increased sales, retention, participation, etc.).

Sometimes, however, when you're in the middle of the promotion, it's difficult to see the forest for the trees. Individual problems are usually dealt with, but global problems are often difficult to detect on a day-by-day analysis. Only when you crunch all of the data gathered from the promotion can you spot other (forestlike) trends that can only be seen from the 10,000-mile-high vantage point. When measuring the results of your online promotion, it's important to stop looking at the trees long enough to see the forest.

In this section, we will examine both kinds of reporting—the specific "tree-focused" information as well as the 10,000-mile-high "forest-focused" information because both contain important information that you can use in future promotional marketing efforts.

On-Demand Reports

For the most part, on-demand reporting is more "tree-focused" by its very nature. On-demand reports provide the day-to-day information about your promotions. Because you're dealing with an online promotion, information is gathered in real time and, in most cases, can be reported in real time as well. The kinds of online reports will depend on the kind of promotion you're running.

With each online report there are areas of customization along with standard information. Log files, for example, are standard protocols that capture hits and page views across all online programs. The reports that access those log files, however, have different levels of customization and ways to display the information. When collecting information in a database, the same database can be queried in a number of different ways depending on the information that is needed (and how taxing the query is on the database server itself). The point is, there are some limitations to online reporting, but, as a general rule, if you know what kind of information you need *prior to the launch of the program*, you can usually get a report that suits your specific needs.

This section will review some of the kinds of online reports that are typical in the promotions industry and, more importantly, what to look for when reviewing these reports. While most reports will vary slightly depending on individual preferences and requests, there is general information that will help you analyze your success rates and immediate results both during and after the promotion.

Types of Online Reports

For simple sweepstakes, the most basic information will be the entry count. How many sweepstakes entries were received today? Different companies have different reporting styles, but this basic piece of information can usually be charted both on a daily basis as well as a running total. For example, perhaps you received only 2,500 entries today, but have received 20,000 since the launch of the promotion. By being able to track entry count on a daily (or even hourly) basis, it becomes easier to track advertising results (as was discussed in Chapter 7, "Promoting the Promotion").

Instant win games need to provide more information than entry count. With an instant win game, you have a set number of prizes to be given away instantly and, based on your odds of winning, a set number of game plays. Instant win reporting will display the total number of game plays to date, game plays remaining, the number of prizes in each category that have been awarded, prizes still remaining, and detailed information on the prize winners. On-demand reporting for instant win games is especially important as these reports can help you identify potential fraudulent game plays before all the allocated game plays have been used up. Once you've identified players who are playing fraudulently, you can take steps to prohibit them from future game plays and disqualify them as winners.

Online coupon and rebate programs can track the number of requests made and can help you prepare for potential spikes in sales and/or potential overredemption problems. By monitoring the number of rebate requests, you can see how close your projections are to reality, which helps with forecasting and communication efforts with the fulfillment house. Online coupon distribution can help you track the response to your offer—especially if your campaign is driving consumers to a physical retail store. While the offline component is slightly more difficult to track in real time (as storewide systems vary), online reporting can help prepare offline stores for potential spikes in traffic and sales.

General traffic reports are less specific to entry count or the number of downloads, but center around the traffic coming into the program. As stated earlier, most Web servers are configured to capture all the pertinent information in a log file. The problem, however, is that the log file is extremely ugly and can be overwhelming for large programs. Reports generated from log files typically break up the information and display it in a much more user-friendly way. WebTrends (www.webtrends.com), for example, is a popular reporting program that does a great job of making log files readable. Through WebTrends' reporting software, you can easily determine your most active pages, where that traffic is coming from, where consumers are leaving the program, and other useful information.

Advertising Results

With these different kinds of reports in place, we are able to move past the *information gathering* stage and into the more *critical analysis* stage. The first step is the ability to answer the question, "How are we doing?" In some cases, it doesn't matter which advertising vehicles are providing the best response to the program, as long as the overall numbers are high. But more often, people are interested in not only how the promotion is doing but also where the traffic to the promotion is coming from. If only one media vehicle is used (other than tell-a-friend viral marketing), all traffic can be attributed to the single advertising source. Usually, there is more than one advertising vehicle and the reports need to show which vehicle is doing the best for the promotion.

This is not a problem if the tracking for each media vehicle has been set up the right way, or if you allow consumers to self-select where they heard about the program. With print, direct-mail, email, and online advertising vehicles, it's easy enough to set up advertising-specific paths for the purpose of tracking responses. By establishing separate URLs for each media vehicle, you can track the separate entry points and attribute the traffic to that particular advertising vehicle.

Television and radio broadcasts, however, can be a bit trickier. The reason is that in the broadcast world, it becomes more important to get the shortest URL possible so that consumers remember where to go. In these cases, it's better to allow consumers to come directly to your home page and link to the program than to try to get them to remember a longer URL for purposes of tracking the advertising results. If the home page is the only place consumers are linking to the program (that is, other media vehicles have their own URL path), then the broadcast spike can still be measured, but not with as much accuracy as the other media vehicles. To help with the accuracy issue, you can also allow consumers to self-select (via a drop-down box) as to where they heard about the program. When you combine these answers along with the various advertising-based URLs, it provides you with a good idea of where the traffic is coming from.

If you see that a particular advertising vehicle is doing better than the others, what do you do? If you have additional media dollars, the answer is simple: Buy more advertising in the medium that is pulling the best results. If you don't have more advertising dollars, then it comes down to what was negotiated during the media buys. Are you getting your guaranteed impressions (or click-throughs)? Do you have alternative advertising creative that can replace what is currently being used? Often, it's the creative execution that compels consumers to participate. If the media vehicle isn't working very well, see if you can use an alternative creative that works better.

In some cases, there's not much you can do other than learn from the program and allocate the media dollars to the most effective medium in the next promotion. By tracking the various media vehicles and scrutinizing the results, you can learn from mistakes and improve your next promotion.

Abandon Rates and Pages

But what if advertising isn't the problem? Perhaps, through your traffic reports, you've discovered that the promotion received quite a heavy load of traffic coming into the main page, but huge drop-off rates prior to the sweepstakes, contest, game, or promotional offer. There may be different problems occurring that need further investigation—usually associated with technology or navigation difficulties.

On the navigation front, you may have too many choices that confuse potential participants. If consumers come to the main page and don't know where to go next, they go elsewhere. In general, you have about 3 seconds to show consumers where to go next. If they don't see what to do, they're not going to spend a lot of time trying to figure it out. If you see a large amount of traffic coming to the main page but then very few people going to the next phase, then the problem may be with the navigation. To fix this problem, see what links can be removed or minimized. Consider enlarging the graphic or highlighting the link that you want consumers to go to next. If you want to get consumers to complete an entry form, consider shortening the amount of questions or information you require for participation. Perhaps consumers are seeing the entry form and are scared off by the amount of information you are asking them to provide.

Online navigation and Web site usability are often overlooked, but can be critical to the success of online promotions. Ideal navigation is transparent. That is, consumers know exactly where to go and how to get there and don't have to stop and think about what to do next.

On the technology front, check out what Web browsers (and what versions of the browsers) people are using to participate in your promotion. Perhaps you have included components in your online promotion that require plug-ins or technology that is more advanced than your core consumers currently have. If consumers have to stop and download additional software just to participate in your promotion, you've created yet another barrier to entry. Even if the technology components make your promotion cooler than any other programs out there, if they stop people from participating, you're defeating your own purpose by including them. Instead, consider an alternative way to play the game without the technology requirement.

Even with Java games, I recommend a non-Java version that allows consumers participating from work (behind firewalls) to play. Even though the vast majority of Web browsers can read Java programming, for security purposes some companies block Java from unknown sources. If your promotion has its own unique URL, then it's probably not recognized by large corporations that do not allow Java into their company's network.

Entries, Instant Win, Memberships, and Sales

In the promotions world, true results come by satisfying the objective. The measurement of success will depend on the specific promotional objective and form of measurement available. If your objective is to convert anonymous browsers into permission-based customers, an opt-in sweepstakes is a great way to accomplish this objective. In this case, your interest is not just in the number of sweepstakes entries you received, but the number of entries that also opted-in to future marketing campaigns. This is the core of the online reporting that you're interested in for this type of promotion. It's wonderful to know how many consumers were exposed to the ads that drove them to the promotion. It's even better to know how many actually participated. And better yet to know how many have chosen to continue to participate with you in the future.

On the instant win side of the equation, your game play information will help you stop fraud before it gets out of control. If the database has been compromised, or consumers have figured out a way to play the game more often than they are allowed, then it's better to know immediately so you can terminate their ongoing fraudulent entries and take measures to void their previous fraudulent activities. Besides fraud, your instant win game reporting will help you send out your instant win prizes immediately and increase the effectiveness of the game. Consumers associate online promotions with the immediacy of the Internet. The faster you can send them their prizes, the better your chance to positively impact their entire promotional experience. More than that, you increase their word-of-mouth referrals to their friends. "Check out what I got from ABC Company. You can get your own by going to…"

If your promotional objective was to increase memberships, you can see how many consumers sign up each day during the promotional period. If you're not getting the response you expected, consider making changes to the sign-up process. Perhaps you're asking for a lot if information up front. See what information is actually required versus information that is nice to have (or that may be used "at some future date"). Or, if you can't change the membership form, consider adding a premium offer on top of the sweepstakes or instant win game. "Sign up today and receive [*insert premium item here*]. You'll also be entered to win [*insert sweep-*

stakes prize here].” Or perhaps you need to bump up the value proposition. Why should a consumer become a member? What are the benefits to membership? With the exception of the sweepstakes, contents, or the legal requirements of the offer, the beauty of online promotions is that you can change many of these aspects on the fly and test to see what works best.

The sales front is similar to memberships. If consumers are not responding to your promotional offer, there are many things you can do to change or modify the communications of that offer (and in some cases even the offer itself). By knowing your sales figures and promotional participation, you can increase the effectiveness by changing the creative, reducing the required information, and finding more compelling offers that encourage your consumers to buy more products.

En Masse Reports

Once the promotion has ended, you still have access to the online (on-demand) reports, but you can begin to move away from the tree-focused information and get the 10,000-mile-high forest-focused information. En masse reports look at the information as a whole rather than the individual components. Although you can get a sense of the forest when you’re staring at a tree, it’s much better to take a step back and look at all the information gathered from your promotion as a whole.

Database queries, for example, can be done in chunks while the promotion is under way. But some of the more telling information that is captured is easier to review once the promotion is complete. Similarly, offline information such as retail sales figures and coupon redemptions can be circled back into the promotion such that all the pieces of the promotional puzzle can come together.

Besides the quantitative number crunching, it’s equally important to get to the qualitative feedback of your internal team and external partners and customers. Did everybody like the promotion? What would they do differently? This is especially important if you plan to repeat this or a similar version of this promotion in the future. If you thought it was a disaster, it’s still important to identify the key things that went wrong so you can avoid similar problems in the future.

Once you’ve compiled everything, the final step is to create a summary of the program for future use. This can be as short as a single side of a single page, or as long as a 200-page report. It all depends on who needs the information that has been compiled and how much detail is needed.

Database Queries

Assuming that the information gathered from your online promotion was not already tied into your main marketing database, at the conclusion of the online promotion you are typically left with a promotional database (or tab-delimited text file to be imported into a database). This database includes all of the information captured about consumers who participated in your promotion—information that was provided by your consumers as well as information provided about your consumers (via log files). While your dynamic reporting provided the immediate information that was needed, the complete database can be utilized for additional information and data mining.

Good database queries follow the age-old "Garbage in, garbage out" principle. Meaning that if you have good information contained within the database, you will be able to extract that information in a very usable format. Conversely, the database can only provide answers with the information that was captured. If sufficient information is not available, even the best data miners cannot help you.

This can be a difficult situation. On the one hand, you want consumers to participate in your promotion. To boost the participation levels, you optimize the process so that you're only asking for pertinent information. On the other hand, if you don't collect enough information about your consumers, it becomes a daunting task to extract meaningful information about them for a report.

This is where third-party software can be extremely helpful. Let's say you want to identify which regions of the country where most consumers live. Your promotional database most likely includes demographic information, such as address, city, state, and zip code, for contacting winners. In a text format, you can sort by city or state, but it's difficult to truly analyze this information without a visual representation. This is where mapping software can be extremely helpful. By overlaying national or regional maps, you can develop clusters for your entrants to help you better understand where consumers are coming from geographically.

Or perhaps geography is less important than where consumers came from online to get to the promotion. Referring URLs are included in standard log file reports. Using WebTrends, you can identify the top referring URLs. But you can also dig deeper and review the less prominent, but perhaps equally important, referring URLs. This information may lead you to natural partnership selection in future promotions, or may help you identify or confirm the competition.

Another common query is an overlay of the consumers who participated in the promotion versus target demographic profiles (either online or offline) to see if they match or are different from what was expected. This can sometimes be accomplished via zip code analysis, but often requires more information such as gender, education, and income levels—difficult questions to ask when you're trying to increase the participation in the online promotion. If the information is important enough, you can identify which consumers gave permission for you to contact them in the future, and you can follow up on the promotion with an invitation to participate in a survey that captures this information. If you can afford them, premium offers are a great way to entice consumers to participate in these studies.

In the next section, I will review how to manage and integrate your promotional database. When it comes to measuring the results of your online promotions, the promotional database can actually provide you with the majority of the information that is available from a quantitative, statistics perspective (with the exception of the offline overlays).

Offline Overlays

The most successful online promotions are integrated with the rest of your offline marketing efforts. For purposes of measuring the results of your online promotions, it is often necessary to circle back to the more traditional offline components for the complete story. Typical offline components include things like retail sales information, coupon redemption statistics, in-store participation (entries filled out in-store), partnership marketing results, and fulfillment statistics.

In the best possible cases, this information is accessible via electronic files that can be imported into the same promotional database. Even if the data fields are completely different, the two data files can be cross-referenced to gather important findings. Coupon redemption, for example, will tie back to the number of coupons that were distributed online to provide you with the redemption percentage. Retail sales spikes can be analyzed to determine just how much of the sales increase can be attributed to the online promotion. In-store participation statistics for a sweepstakes will help you understand the balance between the online entrants versus the offline entrants, and how consumers prefer to participate in your programs.

Partners included in the promotion may have important information that, once included, will provide a different picture than you might have had otherwise with your information alone. At the Institute for International Research and Promotion Marketing Association conference called "Promotion Partners," Leanne Jonas, Director of Partnerships for *People* magazine, noted that in a recent partnership promotion with Kodak, the promotion yielded great results for Kodak, but did not achieve the subscription goals that *People* magazine had set. From Kodak's perspective, the program was a tremendous success. It reached its goals and would repeat the program again and again. Because Kodak was a dependable advertising client, it was less important that the promotion drive the subscription goals that *People* magazine had set, but without comparing the results of the program with its partner, Kodak might never have known that its extremely successful program yielded dismal results for its partner.

By adding the offline overlays to the online reports, you can generate a precise quantitative perspective of the promotion. In other words, you will have a wealth of statistics from which you can draw conclusions about the success or failure of the promotion.

Internal Review

Once you've compiled all the statistics you could ever want on the promotion, stick them in a file and put them aside for a moment. It's time to find out what the rest of your company thought about the promotion. Oftentimes what people say and what they do are very different things. Even promotions that failed miserably when it came to the numbers may have had an extremely positive impact on the company and/or your customers. In order to get a true sense of what happened, it's time to start talking to people.

Start with the people closest to the promotion. What do your colleagues think about the promotion? Did they like the concept? What about the execution? If they had to do it all over again, what do they think could be improved? It's important to document the internal perceptions of the promotion even before the final reports are released. If people thought the program was a tremendous success, find out why they think that—especially if you know otherwise. Sometimes the reverse is true. Perhaps the perception is that the promotion was a flop—even though the statistics prove otherwise. Either way, try to capture the internal opinion of the promotion.

Also, be sure to talk to any of the vendors who worked on the project. Your promotions agency, prize partners, hosting facility, and other players that were involved all have valuable input on the program. The goal is to capture that information as best you can. Perhaps the hosting never went down, but got dangerously close to overloading. Even though no problems were reported, the hosting facility may recommend that future programs be upgraded to better equipment. Perhaps the promotions agency only had a few weeks' notice before launch. While the program was a success, more notice could have yielded even better creative or technology solutions. As you talk to your internal colleagues and vendors, you should have an even better understanding of how the promotion went—above and beyond the statistics associated with the program.

External Review

The final step in the information gathering process is the external review. Some might argue that this would include the vendors used in the promotion, but I included them in the internal review since they were more part of the "behind the scenes" look at the program. For external review, I'm referring to your promotional partners (if any), the press (if they had any comments), and your customers.

As stated earlier, partners may have a very different perspective on the success or failure of the promotion. If your company's or your partner's goals were not met, it's important to find out why. The numbers don't always tell the whole story. Perhaps your partners have some insight as to what failed and why. Or perhaps neither of you knows what went wrong, but together you can recommend changes in an effort to try something different.

If there was any publicity for the program, what was it? Did the press like the program or did they pan it (and for what reasons)? If you have copies of articles, they should be included in the final report. Even if there was no coverage of the program, you might consider talking to a writer or an analyst to get his or her feedback on your promotion.

But the most important external review comes from your customers directly. If you have customer support via email or phone, speak with your customer support team. What kind of feedback (if any) did they get on the promotion? If emails were sent, make sure you have copies of these emails for your report. Did customer support managers have a good feeling about the program or did it confuse customers? Was the customer support team able to provide answers to promotions-related questions from customers? How were these inquiries handled? Can that process be improved in the future?

If you don't have a customer support group, or if they didn't get any significant feedback on the promotion, your next option is to get customer feedback via an online survey. Research facilities, such as Greenfield Online's QuickTake (www.quicktake.com) group, have online tools that allow you to tap into your existing customers or even the general Web audience as a whole. This research can provide you with valuable customer insight on your online promotion and how best to improve it in the future.

Spotting Trends

In Chapter 6, "How to Create a Multibrand Promotion," I referred to the need to create benchmarks for online promotions so that you can compare previous programs with current ones and better evaluate the overall success or failures. As you complete the last phase of measuring the results of your promotion, you are in effect creating a benchmark to compare against future promotional marketing efforts. With analysis of both the quantitative statistics and qualitative interview and feedback, you can draw some basic conclusions about the good, the bad, and the ugly associated with the promotion.

On an individual promotion level, you might begin to see some specific trends. Perhaps you notice that many of your consumers participate in your promotions late at night. Or perhaps there are peaks associated with specific advertising vehicles that show which medium works best for reaching your consumers. While spotting these trends is sometimes challenging on an individual basis, it becomes clearer over time with multiple reports from previous promotions. With each additional promotion that can be compared against the benchmark, possible trends become obvious.

As stated previously, if the promotion began with a clearly defined objective, then measuring the results of your online promotion should be fairly straightforward. This is also true with respect to spotting trends. If your promotional objectives are clearly defined and remain somewhat similar to previous promotions, it will be easier to spot specific trends.

Overall, the analysis of each individual promotion will help identify and archive the results on an individual basis. While some trends can be spotted on an individual basis, the more important trends will be captured after reviewing an archive of past promotion analysis. These trends will help provide you with the information you need to take advantage of these trends and increase your effectiveness.

Managing and Integrating Your Promotional Database

In addition to ignoring the results and analysis, another common mistake is not taking advantage of the newly developed promotional database and corresponding permission-based requests for future marketing efforts. In most online promotional campaigns, one of the biggest assets created is the promotional database itself. In the midst of putting out other fires and moving on to the next hottest thing, newly acquired customers are forgotten. The problem is that while consumers have granted permission to be marketed to in the future, this newly granted permission is for a limited time only. The longer the delay between granting permission and follow-up marketing efforts, the more likely that permission will be revoked when the time comes to actually complete the next marketing program.

It is difficult to measure lost revenue when you fail to take advantage of newly found hot prospects. It's clear, however, that lost revenue is the ultimate result. Ignoring the very customers who were sought out by the online promotion in the first place results in wasted time and money. There's no reason to seek out new customers or gather new opt-in email lists if there is no follow-up marketing to support these new acquisitions.

The biggest hurdle to managing the promotional database is the way in which it was created for purposes of the online promotion. Because of timing and integration issues often associated with online promotions, most promotional databases are not developed within the overall marketing database. Instead, they are created as a separate database, often by an outside vendor or promotions agency. The challenge then is to incorporate *this* promotional database into the core marketing database so that the newly acquired customers are not ignored because of internal technical difficulties.

This section will cover the importance of managing your promotional database and the best ways to integrate it into the rest of your marketing efforts.

Managing the Promotional Database

Most people realize that promotional databases are valuable—they simply do not understand just how truly valuable they are. The promotional database is like gold in the sense that newly established relationships with new customers have been identified and these hot prospects require attention. Especially with those customers who have opted-in to future marketing efforts, it becomes critical to quickly follow up and find out just how hot they truly are. Some consumers will barely respond to any offer you throw at them. Others will jump at the first discount or offer you provide them. The trick is to identify which consumers are truly your best customers and keep marketing to them to make them happy.

If you don't manage the promotional database, its value decreases over time. With each passing week that no communication is sent out following up with customers who have requested information, discounts, or offers, their interest in your company declines and eventually goes away. By managing the promotional database immediately, the risk of losing potential customers is minimized.

If there has been too long a gap between the online promotion and the follow-up marketing efforts, the result will be that few consumers (if any) will respond to your special discount or offer. In order to overcome this problem, the answer is to provide offers that consumers can't refuse, such that you regain the attention that was lost during the delays and regain the permission that was originally granted.

The Golden Promotional Database

After spending money on the online promotion and the advertising to promote the online promotion, it makes no sense to ignore the very customers who have been obtained, but this happens more often than it ever should. The promotional database is the very essence of what your online promotions have delivered—even if building the database was not your primary marketing objective. Consumers who have asked to be marketed to in the future need attention—*and fast*.

Anyone in sales can tell you that hot leads don't stay hot for very long. As soon as new potential customers have been identified, there must be a smooth transition straight into the next phase of follow-up marketing. In most cases, the opt-in customers identified in the newly developed promotional database are more relevant and important than customers found in a company's larger prospect database. The contact information is much more current, for example, for consumers who have recently participated in an online promotion. Because of their participation, their attention to your company and its products is higher than that of other consumers who may have been identified via other means. The opt-in customers from a promotional database result in a *demand pull* strategy where they are asking for information versus the typical *demand push* of other marketing efforts where consumers have not asked for the information provided.

Value Decreases over Time

The tragedy is that a promotional database is like fresh milk from the supermarket; it goes bad in a couple of weeks unless it is used. Marketers who jump into the follow-up marketing efforts (described later in this chapter) will reap the benefits of having developed a core group of valuable customers from the online promotion. Through testing and continued interaction, the complete lifetime value of these new customers will be identified and the initial acquisition goals can quickly be transformed into retention goals.

If action is not taken, however, the permission recently granted becomes stale and is eventually revoked. The longer the pause between a consumer opting-in and a follow-up offer, the more likely the offer will be ignored when it eventually makes its way into a consumer's email or physical mail box.

Immediately Follow Up with a Discount or Offer

The key to taking advantage of the newly granted permission from the online promotion is to immediately follow up with a discount or offer. The type of discount or offer will depend largely on your business and what makes sense based on sales needs and the overall cost per acquisition. The beauty of email marketing efforts is that you can send out a variety of different discounts or offers and keep track of which consumers respond to what offers. By starting off small and increasing the value proposition, you can begin to measure the effectiveness of your different offers along with the kinds of consumers you have recently added via your promotional database.

Consumers who respond to your smaller (less generous) offers are likely to be your better customers. Consumers who only respond to the deepest discounts or offers are less likely to be long-term loyal customers as they are responding only to the specific offer without having any real interest in your products or services. By establishing sufficient tracking, you can take your original promotional marketing database and begin to segment it further into categories such as "best customers" and "fair weather consumers." This will be discussed in greater detail later in this chapter.

The point is the need for immediate follow-up in order to keep the newly granted permission fresh and valuable. If no follow-up marketing is completed, or if it takes too long to generate the follow-up marketing efforts, you risk losing the most valuable asset gained in your online promotions—permission for future marketing efforts.

What to Do If You've Waited Too Long

Just because something is stale doesn't mean it's dead. If, for some reason, too much time has passed between your original online promotion and your follow-up marketing efforts, it's time to get down to guerrilla tactics and resuscitate otherwise dead prospects. This can be done via a wake-up marketing message that is essentially an offer they can't refuse. Again, the specifics of this offer will vary depending on the type of business and the specific products and services being marketed. In essence, it's your best possible offer. Short of giving your product away, this may even include taking a loss on the specific offer with the goal of regaining attention and bringing these previously hot prospects back into the consideration spectrum. The purpose of doing this is to regain the faith that was lost due to delays in the marketing efforts.

If this doesn't work, then the prospects are truly dead and it's time to move on to greener pastures. It's an unfortunate loss, but a good marketer knows when to stop wasting money on the wrong target. Rather than continuing to throw money at the problem, attention should be turned to the next project with the resolve that the same mistake will not be repeated in future marketing efforts. Perhaps the follow-up offer is agreed on even before the next online promotion. In that way, the offer can go out instantly—perhaps as a follow-up email confirming participation in the promotion.

Integrating the Promotional Database

The only reason I'm diving this deeply into database conversion is that it's an important step that must be considered when building an online promotion. Without consideration as to how the information will be later integrated, the usual result is that the information is not integrated (at least in a timely manner) and potential leads and hot prospects are lost in the shuffle.

No one plans to delay follow-up marketing efforts. It's usually the result of having several priorities to deal with while simultaneously trying to integrate a promotional database into a preestablished marketing database that causes the delay in the first place. To avoid these costly delays, steps can be taken prior to the launch of the online promotion to shorten the time frame from conclusion to integration. Likewise, if the established marketing database is rather complex, software conversion tools can be developed to support timely conversion and integration.

Speed is one of the most important aspects to reaping the benefits of integrating a promotional database into the established marketing database. The faster consumers receive an offer that they just granted permission to receive, the less likely they are to ignore it or become angry because they received it at all. Of course, with speed comes the caution of not making conversion mistakes that render the promotional database useless. Balance between speed and accuracy with the integration of a promotional database is the desired goal.

By recognizing the database requirements prior to the launch of the online promotion, many costly mistakes can be avoided and the integration becomes much less challenging. If a conversion tool has already been created, the tool should make the conversion process even simpler.

Making the Database Compatible

The most challenging marketing databases are usually not the more recently established databases, but rather legacy systems that are still being used to centralize internal marketing efforts. Older databases require more up-front work on the promotional information that was recently captured in order to accurately integrate the promotional data into the main marketing database. While this "scrubbing" of data is not that intuitive, there are usually standard procedures provided by the database administrator that, once followed, will allow for a smooth importing of the promotional data.

If the main marketing database is a recent version of any of the major database applications, such as Oracle, SQL, Informix, or Sybase, integration can be as simple as importing a tab-delimited text file with the same field records.

In either case, successful database compatibility comes down to the main database schemata. Even the same database applications can vary widely when it comes to the information architecture. In order to integrate separate promotional databases into the main marketing database, it should be clear how the information is formatted and where it resides in the main database. With clear database schemata (and any relevant instructions on legacy systems), conversion becomes a lot easier than it would seem at first.

Conversion Tools

Database conversion tools apply more to legacy database applications than more recent database applications, many of which have conversion tools built directly into the software itself. Conversion tools are simply a software application designed to make importing external data easier than manually manipulating the newly developed files so that they are compatible. In other words, conversion tools are programs that automatically scrub external files to make the integration process easier.

Some database conversion tools are actually scripts developed as a separate software program that will import data from one format into the existing database format. The raw data is converted into the required format of the database application. There are other tools that act as "import wizards," which are already built into database applications. When a file is imported, a series of questions is asked to determine file type and specific requirements that will enable the file to be imported into the existing database.

Conversion tools help identify the requirements of the legacy system and provide the step-by-step process required for converting tab-delimited text (or other character-delimited) files into the proper format that is readable to the legacy system. If these conversion tools exist, the database administrator of the legacy system can usually provide the software and some general guidelines to conversion. By having the necessary tools and software up front, the promotional database can be designed to support any specific requirements and less time will be required for conversion once the program is completed.

Speed Is Important

The faster you integrate, the faster consumers can be part of the rest of your marketing efforts. When conversion stumbling blocks occur, the consumers are the ones who miss out on the ongoing communications efforts. The longer the delay between the time when consumers opt-in and the time when they receive follow-up marketing, the less likely they are to respond to the offers being sent.

While speed is not the only factor when it comes to response rates, when it comes to Internet-related programs, speed is critical. The consumer expectation is that when they participate in online marketing programs, they are immediate in nature. This expectation has been created over the past 6 years through instant gratification. When the Submit button on a form is clicked, a "Thank You" page is immediately received. When an email request is made, the expectation is that it will be followed up with a response in a matter of hours (and the faster, the better). This is why speed has become so important. When consumers opt-in to an ongoing marketing program, they expect to reap immediate benefits or else they will choose to opt-out.

The next section describes how best to follow up with the initial permission that has been granted. It is important to remember that the recommended offers and discounts become less attractive over time. It would be like visiting a car dealership because you're in the market to buy a new car, and a salesperson tells you that he or she will be with you in about 6 to 8 weeks. The very fact that you went out of your way to visit the car dealership means you're hoping not to have to wait that long.

So think through the kinds of follow-up offers and discounts you're willing to make before you add the opt-in component to your online promotions. If you already have a plan or program in place, it will be much easier to add the list of recipients and take advantage of the newly established permission that they have granted you as a result of the online promotion.

Following Up with Special Discounts and Offers

From the beginning of the chapter, I've made the point that timing is important to follow-up marketing efforts. The longer the delay, the less likely consumers are to respond to your follow-up marketing efforts. As soon as permission is granted, it's best to begin following up as soon as possible. But with what? It's one thing to send out offers immediately and an entirely different challenge to send out offers that are appealing to your consumers and get them to respond.

Enter basic direct marketing, but with a twist: reduced cost and increased segmentation. For years, the direct marketing experts have driven home the point that testing several different offers using various creative strategies will tell you what offers work best. Then there's the 80–20 rule that states that 20 percent of your customers are responsible for 80 percent of your sales. What the Internet does is allow companies to test more cost-effectively and truly identify the online customers who are responsible for the most sales. True, the Internet population has yet to rival traditional household penetration, but each year the gap between these two markets gets smaller.

This section will review some of the basic principles of traditional direct marketing techniques and their applications to follow-up marketing once an online promotion has ended. From keeping tabs on your best customers to testing various offers, follow-up marketing efforts are important for ongoing success and online promotions can help. There comes a time, however, when even promotions are not enough to motivate targeted consumers and it's time to find out more about the root of the problem.

Loyalty programs can provide further leverage for your ongoing marketing efforts, but only if the basic offer is relevant and you're past the initial sales phase. While loyalty programs should not be leaned on to make up for basic marketing problems, they can serve as an excellent device to drive preference of your company's products and services over that of the competition's.

When direct marketing methods, research, and loyalty programs follow the conclusion of a successful online promotion, the online promotion becomes a bridge to the rest of a company's ongoing marketing efforts. It is this integration that separates the one-off promotions with the truly successful programs that engage consumers and keep them coming back for more.

Differential Marketing

My first internship out of college was for Ogilvy & Mather Direct and one of my first assignments was to provide support for Garth Hallberg's book, *All Consumers Are Not Created Equal* (John Wiley & Sons, Inc., 1995). After studying several chapters, I became convinced that the concept of differential marketing should be standard procedure for direct marketing. The oversimplified version of differential marketing is that only a small percentage of your customer base is truly responsible for the most profits. A much larger percentage of your customer base is much less profitable and can easily be swayed to purchase competitive products. Consumers who are motivated by price alone are not brand loyal and are not worthy of the bulk of your marketing dollars.

But it was only after my experience in the online promotions world that I found direct applications for and benefits to different kinds of marketing to different consumers, depending on what level of sales volume they represented. While traditional direct marketing could market by zip codes and, in some cases, by preferred mailing lists, online marketing databases could be developed in real time and be segmented much more accurately based on transaction history. That is, online marketing took the guesswork out of the equation and allowed for true differential marketing to occur at a fraction of the cost of traditional direct-mail efforts.

In other words, online marketing efforts didn't replace traditional direct marketing strategies and tactics; it took them to new levels never before possible, while keeping the costs down significantly. When you combine Garth Hallberg's book with that of Bob Stone's *Successful Direct Marketing Methods* (NTC Business

Books, 1994) and Less Wonderman's *Being Direct* (Random House, 1997), you cover the spectrum of direct marketing strategy, tactics, and case histories. Online promotions are about providing motivation and getting people to take action. Once this first step is achieved, it's back to traditional marketing (and direct marketing) basics when deciding how best to move the relationship forward.

Keeping Tabs on Your Best Customers

Think of online promotions as a corporate dating service. Eligible customers are matched up with companies and, through the online promotion itself, the initial contact is made. Relationships that are worth keeping are not made in a single contact. The first meeting is about getting to know each other. If your consumers enjoyed the initial contact, they might be inclined toward further meetings, which could eventually lead to the initial sale and, over time, long-term loyalty. However, there are some consumers who are not interested in long-term loyalty, but rather a bunch of one-off chance meetings. They might buy your products or visit your Web site, but they're not advocates of your products or services—they just use them from time to time.

Good database marketing separates your truly loyal customers from the fair-weather consumers who are only interested in your products when they are the least expensive or are tied to some amazing offer. Loyal customers buy your products or services because they *like* them. That is, the products provide real value for which your loyal consumers are willing to pay—not just once, but continuously over time.

If you can't distinguish your best customers from the rest, you're not likely to keep them. This is what good database marketing is all about—identifying your best customers so you can market to them differently from the rest and encourage their loyalty. By keeping tabs on your best customers, you can help increase your profit margins by offering unique opportunities without drastically cutting the price for your products and services. While you can still market to less loyal customers, you can begin to segment the most profitable consumers from the least profitable and spend your marketing dollars accordingly.

Keeping tabs on your best customers has another advantage—you know when they leave for your competition. When a loyal customer stops buying your products or services, you can immediately find out and contact them as to why. Truly loyal customers will even take the time to tell you why they've stopped buying and, in most cases, will be happy that you noticed and took the time to contact them. If your competitors have released a better product or have some amazing offer, your most loyal customers will usually tell you what attracted them elsewhere and what you can do to regain their loyalty.

If you listen to your best customers, they will tell you everything you need to know to keep them for life. If you have a good relationship with your best customers, they will let you know when things go wrong and when they expect you to fix obvious problems. With good database marketing, you can not only accomplish this task but also get this information in real time—not several weeks after the events have already taken place. That's the power of online marketing.

Tracking Is Essential

To have good database marketing, tracking is essential. Reporting will only display the quality of information that is captured. If your tracking is poor, then your resulting database and accompanying reports will be poor too. Having good tracking in place is critical to successful database marketing efforts and keeping track of your best customers. In fact, once you have studied your customers' behavior (through the available tracking and reporting), you can recognize patterns that can be slowly modified over time. Perhaps your best customers buy your product every week, but the next best customers are only buying once a month. By targeting these second-tier customers, you can create promotions that will encourage them to buy a second time in the same month and slowly increase the profitability from your second-tier customers.

Tracking is the key that unlocks all the hidden information about your customers and patterns that determines what kind of customers they are relative to your sales goals. Often, your best customers can help you identify other best customers with whom they associate themselves. Without violating your customers' trust, you may be able to create a referral program that encourages the introduction to new customers. With good tracking engines supporting these marketing efforts, you can reward your best customers for helping your business grow.

Tracking will also show you where your biggest weaknesses are. Good tracking and reporting will help you identify drop-off points, abandoned shopping attempts, and help pinpoint the major hurdles to sales growth. Good tracking and reporting will identify the good, the bad, and the ugly truth about what the company is doing right and what it is doing wrong that is resulting in a loss of market share.

Without the right information, your marketing efforts are essentially just shots in the dark. There is no excuse for poor tracking when it comes to the online world of marketing. All marketing efforts should be tied into an overall tracking and reporting engine that helps you identify the information you need to know about your customers and the successful programs that keep them coming back for more.

Keep Testing Different Offers

Testing different promotional offers will help you move from an opt-in email database derived from an online promotion to a more robust database that segments customers based on their value proposition. This gets down to traditional direct marketing basics and has a proven track record for successfully segmenting your customer base. Different consumers will respond differently to promotional offers—not just to the offer itself, but how the offer is presented and the creative approach that is used. While consumers may not respond at all to a "50% Off" promotional offer, they may be much more inclined to respond to an offer of "Buy One, Get One Free." Various premium offers will appeal to different consumers, depending on their demographic and psychographic profiles.

What's different about online marketing versus traditional direct marketing is that you can avoid the cost of printing the various offers and the weeks that pass between mailings and responses. With online campaigns, emails can be sent out and responses tracked in the same hour, day, and week. By the end of the first few days, you already have a handle on whether or not the offer is successful.

After various offers are tested among your consumers, you will begin to sense the kinds of consumers that are part of your newly established database. Over time, it will become easy to segment your customers into your best, worst, and in-between categories. Continued testing over time will help you hone in on your best offers, depending on what kind of customer you are targeting. As consumers respond differently, you will be able to identify them and better focus your own marketing efforts based on your goals for each customer segment.

When Promotions Are Not Enough

David Ogilvy once said, "Nothing kills a bad product like good advertising." There are times when the harsh reality of the market convinces you that no matter what your offer is, your product or service just isn't as appealing as you might have first thought. No one wants to face this cold, hard fact, but there comes a time when promotions and special offers simply are not enough. When that time comes, it's best to call in the experts to help figure out what might be the problem. I hope that you never have to deal with this unpleasant crossroad, but if you do, my advice is to do your best to keep an open mind and listen without prejudice.

If your customers are confused or simply don't see the value proposition, then it's time to reposition, reevaluate, or move on to the next best thing. Research organizations can help take the guesswork out of this difficult situation. Through focus groups, surveys, and one-on-one interviews, a research organization can help identify the problem and, in some cases, help make recommendations to fix the problem.

And don't forget about your promotions agency, direct marketing, or brand agency—all of which can help provide answers to tough questions. If you have a good relationship with your agency, it will tell you the truth rather than sugarcoat the problem. It's in everyone's best interest to figure out what went wrong and make recommendations to fix the problem or move on.

Loyalty Programs

Loyalty programs have been discussed earlier in this book, but it's important to bring them back into the discussion when talking about following up with special discounts and offers. When it comes to email marketing, it's all about relevance. While consumers may have asked to receive information about your products and services, if you don't engage them early on in the marketing cycle, they are likely to revoke the permission they previously granted and request that you stop send-ing them emails. After you've encouraged them to make that initial purchase, rel-evant loyalty programs can encourage them to keep buying from you.

One way to make your email marketing relevant is to customize the email so that the contents are specific to each individual customer. Beyond welcoming the customer by name, you can begin to show value in the email by alerting each cus-tomer right at the top of the email as to how many points he or she has accumulated. You can tie your loyalty program into a special offer that he or she will receive just for responding to the email and/or buying additional products for a limited time.

Loyalty is about finding ways to reward your best customers and to keep on doing it. In the long run, retention is more important than acquisition. What's the point of filling a bucket that is full of holes? If your retention efforts are poor, eventually every customer that you acquire will move on and all the money that was spent on acquisition will be wasted.

Integrate Reward Status into Emails

With loyalty programs, you can make your email marketing efforts much more relevant. Rather than getting the same old product offer, customers can get an email that informs them of how many points they have earned and how many more they need to get the things they desire. Promotional offers can be integrated into the loyalty program to help encourage customers to buy more.

But the email shouldn't stop there. The more relevant the email is, the more likely a consumer will be to take the time to respond. Perhaps the email includes a sample newsletter that provides news and information with a link to subscribe on a weekly or monthly basis. Perhaps there is new research or product information that was recently posted to the Web site that would be helpful to the customer's decision-making process. The more informative the email is, the more likely that consumers will take the time to review it and not delete it.

Retention versus Acquisition

In the early phase of dot-com marketing, it was better to acquire than retain. Companies boasted of their membership numbers and conveniently forgot to mention how many of those members were actually active. Unique visits were important, but repeat visitors were downplayed. The bottom line was less about the bottom line and more about growth—how fast can you capture the growing Internet population?

Then, in the summer of 2000, all those Wall Street analysts got the glory of the "I told you so" when profitability became more important than growth projections. Suddenly double-digit growth was out and making money was back in style. It seemed that online marketers pulled back on everything that wasn't vital and a contribution to the bottom line.

But just ask a company that's been around for over 100 years. S&H Greenpoints (formerly S&H Green Stamps) knows that the key to keeping loyal customers is not drastically reducing prices or creating unattainable loyalty programs that require years of point collection before the reward is ever achieved. No, the most successful loyalty programs get rewards into consumers' hands within a maximum of 90 days from the time they first sign up for the program. Successful loyalty programs reward a consumer's behavior over time (but not too much time), and any attempts to change a consumer's buying behavior are made carefully.

In the long run, not only is retention less expensive than the costs associated with acquisition, but it's more important. Keeping your best customers should be priority number one. Getting more sales from your best customers should be priority number two. Database marketing efforts will help you segment your customers, but loyalty programs will help you keep them.

Planning Your Next Promotion

Before building a house you need a blueprint. When a new house is to be constructed, the blueprint is drafted, studied, and reviewed by the experts. Changes are made on paper because, as my grandfather used to say, "It's easier to measure twice and cut once."

Successful online promotions are no different. You can either jump into the promotion feet first and see what happens or you can take the time to plan your marketing strategy and decide how promotions (online or traditional) will help you reach your objectives and meet your short- and long-term goals. Planning doesn't solve every problem, but it helps you identify potential problems and create contingencies when and if these problems arise. Good planning requires a combination of experience, research, and forward thinking. Of these three, I contend that experience is the most helpful. While research can provide statistics and information that are useful for planning, and forward thinking allows you to envision what's next (and what's possible), there is no substitute for the experience gained on previous promotions.

What I have attempted to do in this book is share my experiences in an effort to help you better understand the many aspects of online promotions and how they fit into the overall marketing mix. The following section consolidates much of what has already been presented in this book into a top 10 list of online promotional pointers. Think of this list as the summary version of this book, and refer to it when planning your next online promotion.

1. Begin with the Objective

This has been a consistent theme throughout this book and for good reason. Beginning with a clearly defined objective is perhaps the best thing you can do to control the success of your promotions—online or off. When you have a clearly defined objective, you know where you want to end up and the best strategies you need to use in order to get there. While everything else may not fall into place once you have identified your marketing objective, planning the rest of the promotion will be a lot easier if you have a clear idea of where you want to end up.

A clearly defined objective will also help you accurately measure your results and create on-demand reporting. By knowing where you want to end up, it becomes easier to identify the necessary information and reports you will require in order to measure your success. These reports will allow you to know if the promotion was successful or not.

On the multibrand promotional side of things, a clearly defined objective will help you identify potential partners who have similar marketing objectives. This will also help you when you negotiate the partnership agreements and determine what your promotion needs in order to be successful and what you're willing to give in order to have those needs met by your partner.

Without a clearly defined objective, failures are likely to be repeated and chaos will reign. Speed and effectiveness are not the same thing. In the world of online promotions, the speed of the technology often becomes a problem in itself just because it *is* possible to launch an online promotion in a matter of hours or days instead of several weeks or months. Before running full speed ahead, take 1 minute to ask yourself, "Why are we doing this promotion?"

Starting with a clear objective helps get you through the rest of the process. It helps you determine if your strategy is on target. If the strategy brings you closer to reaching your objective, then it makes sense. If not, then it doesn't. Before investing in the promotion, a clearly defined objective will allow you to conduct research ahead of time, and even turn failures into learning experiences. When you know what you were trying to achieve, it's much easier to see what went wrong and how to avoid making the same mistakes in the future.

2. Integrate Your Online Promotions

The second most important aspect to online promotions is to integrate them into the rest of your marketing efforts. Successful online promotions typically arise from high-quality integration with offline promotions and traditional media support. Stand-alone online promotions are not nearly as successful as an integrated campaign in which every aspect of your communications to your customers includes the call to action of the promotion itself. From your advertising down to the voice recording your consumers hear when they are on hold, the more integrated your online promotion is with the rest of your marketing efforts, the better chance it has for success.

This is especially true with offline integration and traditional media support. Without offline integration, an online promotion is not likely to get the proper attention that it deserves and, subsequently, is unlikely to achieve the desired results. If the only place that a consumer hears about your promotion is online, then it is unlikely that you will achieve the amount of reach and frequency numbers that are required for a successful online promotion. Creating traditional media campaigns, in-store signage, PR support, and other more traditional advertising support will help generate the necessary awareness of the promotion and drive traffic from the offline world into the online promotion.

Integration takes advantage of both worlds. The online world is replete with all the immediacy, tracking, reporting, cost efficiencies, and real-time information that could ever be desired. The traditional world has better opportunities for exposure, reach, frequency, and the mass audience that will help make any online program a success. By integrating the two, you take advantage of both and give yourself the best chance of creating highly successful promotions.

3. Keep Up with Technology

In October 2000, I attended the first PROMO Expo where it became clear to me that not only has the Internet penetrated the promotions industry but it has also affected just about every aspect of how promotions are currently conducted. From premium suppliers to promotional application service providers, technology is continually changing the way we do business—online and off. It's important to stay current. As new technology becomes available, so do the applications of that technology in the promotions industry.

In 1994, online promotions relied on ASCII text and simple PERL scripts to capture data. Today we have extremely robust databases that can handle much larger volumes of data. These database applications were not even available in an online environment—let alone for something as "trivial" as an online promotion. Now, with the addition of robust databases, instant win games are now possible. Collection and real-time reporting of information become much easier to handle during the promotion and even easier to manipulate at the conclusion of the promotion.

In 1994, flat graphics and magazine-styled content was the best you could hope for. Shortly thereafter when animating gifs came on the scene, very little animation could be accomplished. Now with streaming media, the Java programming language, Macromedia's Flash, and 3D environments, the only limitation is bandwidth—and this is becoming less and less of a true limitation every day. As access speed to the Internet continues to increase, and compression technology continues to reduce file size, rich media experiences will become the norm. But don't think of rich media as glorified television. With rich media over the Internet, consumers maintain control and challenge the traditional broadcast model. It's more like the old "Choose Your Own Adventure" books or multiplayer video games that have grown up into cooler online promotions.

In 1994, online promotions were only promoted online. Today, successful online promotions are truly integrated into the rest of the marketing mix (see Number 2 above). The original online-only advertising was restricted to text links and banner ads. Today there are a plethora of online media options that range from rich email campaigns, to free Internet access, to instant messaging software. Because of the "advertising-supported" nature of the Internet, there are several categories to choose from when buying online media.

But remember, technology is just the icing—not the cake itself. Do not fall into the trap of using technology just because it's *new* and *cool*. The most effective promotions find effective ways to integrate technology *without* losing sight of the promotion's objectives.

4. Listen and Learn

Your customers will tell you everything you need to know if you just take the time to listen and learn from what they tell you. Marketing has always been about consumers—finding out what they want, how much they're willing to pay for it, and where they'd like to find it. Promotions are no different. If you run an online promotion with dismal results, your customers are in the best position to tell you why. While you can make assumptions about what went wrong, your consumers can tell you what happened from their perspective. Perhaps they didn't even know about the promotion. Or perhaps they heard about it, but weren't compelled to take action. With these facts in hand, you can change your advertising strategy, increase prize values, or a host of other options that will improve the effectiveness of your online promotions.

Email is a great way to get feedback on your promotions, but is often overwhelming. Many companies have customer support centers that answer emails and phone calls from customers. Make sure you have the people resources in place to answer potentially large volumes of emails and phone calls. The better your customer service, the more likely you will hear your customers and respond to what they are saying.

5. Promote the Promotion

Building a cool promotion without the proper advertising support is like opening a lemonade stand and hoping that people will drive by. Successful promotions require advertising support to alert your customers about what you're doing and get them to participate. It doesn't matter how compelling your promotion is; if people don't know about it, they won't participate. *Promoting the promotion is critical to the success of online promotions.* With a host of advertising options—both online and traditional—there is no excuse for creating a promotion without the right amount of advertising support.

Here again, the integration of online and offline promotions is important. Often, the most successful online promotions have significant traditional media support driving traffic to the promotion. While advertising support for the promotion can be accomplished in an online-only environment, most online promotions require traditional media support to be truly successful.

Regardless of the medium, advertising support will make or break the promotion. If the promotion is integrated within the rest of your company's marketing efforts, promoting the promotion will not be a challenge. If the online promotion is treated as separate from the rest of the company's marketing initiatives, then it will be much more difficult to get the right amount of advertising support necessary.

6. Identify Reporting Needs *before* Launch

One of the biggest advantages of online promotions is the reporting capability. In the traditional world of promotions, it can take days, weeks, and even months to gather all the information necessary to track the success of the promotion. In the world of online promotions, reports can be generated on the fly giving you up-to-the-second measurement of performance and consumer participation.

But while online promotions have the capacity to track as much information as is asked for, once the promotion begins, it's extremely difficult (and sometimes dangerous) to change the database structure and information gathering. This gets back to the basic "garbage in, garbage out" principle of computers. You can only report on the information that is collected. If you don't ask for the information, or the tracking engine is not set up to track the specific results you're interested in, it becomes difficult (if not impossible) to gather the information that is needed.

By knowing what kind of information is required, it will make the data collection and reporting that much easier. Desired information can be built right into the entry form process or pulled from the appropriate log files. If too much information is being requested (and may become a barrier to entry), then the design of the entry form will clearly identify this problem before the promotion goes live. By taking the time to identify your reporting needs before the launch of the promotion, you're more likely to get the kinds of reports and information that you desire.

7. Opt-In: Ask for Permission

Learn from Seth Godin's book, *Permission Marketing* (Simon & Schuster, 1999). Permission is an extremely valuable asset and all you need to do is ask for it (and then respect it once it's granted). Do not assume that you have permission for anything other than what was expressly given to you. Through permission marketing, your customers have granted you—and only you—permission to market to them in the future. Never rent or sell your customer list. By doing so, you will violate your consumers' trust and permission will be denied.

If your partners wish to leverage your existing customer base, move with extreme caution. There are ways to introduce your partners without violating your customers' permission, but it's a delicate situation. If you have a newsletter, you can introduce your partners' programs with links to their promotion. Or you can introduce your partners in a separate email generated by you and explain that you have not given your partners your customers' names, but are making an introduction in the event that they might be interested. The key is to always maintain your customers' trust and never make them feel like the permission they granted you has been abused. Otherwise, they will choose to cut off their communications with you and take their business elsewhere. And that doesn't help you or your partners.

By the same token, you can't use someone else's permission—you must earn it on your own. Even if your partners are willing to give you their customer lists, don't expect that you can send out emails to your partners' customers and get the same kind of response that you get with your own customers. Your partners' customers have *not* granted you permission to market to them, and if your introduction is not directly through your partners, your email will be perceived as unsolicited junk mail.

Buying an opt-in email list may generate some awareness of your products and services, but don't confuse someone else's opt-in email list with permission marketing. Permission must be granted to you directly from your customers. Third-party list brokers can provide email addresses and names, but not permission.

Once you have been granted permission directly from your customers, you must use it or lose it. If you do not immediately follow up, the permission previously granted will become stale and void. If too much time passes between consumers' granting of permission and your follow-up marketing efforts, consumers will forget that they ever granted permission in the first place.

8. Begin a Relationship

Earlier in this chapter, I used the analogy of online promotions as a corporate dating service, and I believe this is the best way to reinforce the point that the most successful relationships are not the single contact. It's true that online promotions help match companies with eligible consumers. When a company creates a compelling promotion to introduce a product, generate awareness, or even encourage consumers to sample the product, the promotion brings new customers to that company.

But a relationship is not built on a single contact. In order for a relationship to succeed, it must be two-way. After consumers have given you permission to market to them in the future, the onus is on you to keep the lines of communication open and to encourage feedback and participation in future marketing efforts. Successful online promotions simply make the introduction. The actual relationship with consumers is not a quick fix, but rather a long-term dedication to making customers happy with the products and services offered by your company.

By listening to your customers, you can learn what interests them and what they need to keep your company in their minds. As with all relationships, the more you listen, the more you learn how to make the relationship better. With each contact from your customers, you begin to see things as they are (which is not necessarily the same as how you might perceive them to be). With the knowledge of what consumers want, it becomes easier to create ongoing marketing efforts to satisfy their needs and build successful relationships with them.

9. Build Your Database Marketing Efforts

In order to build your relationships with your consumers, you need to keep track of each contact with them and keep good records of their feedback and requests. Beyond good customer service, however, the goal should be to identify your best customers based on sales and profitability. The old 80–20 rule states that 20 percent of your customers are responsible for 80 percent of your sales. The trick is to identify those consumers who represent the top 20 percent so that you can market to them differently.

With database marketing, this becomes possible. When the database is then connected to online promotions and other online sales efforts, database marketing becomes essential. With each sale that is made and each promotion that is acknowledged, additional learning about your customers is taking place. By using this information, you can then begin to segment your customers so that you can market to your top-tier customers differently—make them feel special and reward them for their loyalty.

There is no excuse for not marketing smarter to your top-tier customers. With all the tracking capabilities of online marketing and promotions, you should clearly see which customers are responding to your different offers and which represent your best customers. Once in place, your database marketing efforts will pay for themselves, as your top-tier customers will become more loyal as you treat them differently. While all customers are important, your most loyal customers should feel that they are getting that little extra because their business is incredibly important to your company.

10. Ensure Legal Compliance

Perhaps the most important aspect of online promotions does not get enough attention. No one wants to think about the dark side of promotions. Legal disclaimers and the official rules of the promotion are often treated as less important and are usually something people think of when they are a week or so away from the actual launch. Online promotions means real-time changes and updates, so often the legal aspects of the promotion are overlooked. Make no mistake, legal matters can make or break the promotion. If the promotion is illegal, it can be shut down (not to mention the fines and negative publicity).

Rather than wait until the eleventh hour to find out what the legal ramifications are, the legal experts should be included in the concept phase of the promotion. Why spend time and energy on a promotion that is not legal? Rather than dancing around potential legal problems, it's much better to come up with promotional concepts that have clearance from the legal experts. If you don't know the law, then make sure your legal counsel or promotions agency does.

Conclusion

When crossing the finish line, the last thing you want to do is analyze how you did, but that's exactly what will help you improve your next online promotion. By taking the time necessary to review the success of the promotion, examine what could have been done better, and document the important learning experiences, you're on your way to building the most compelling and successful online promotions for your target audience. Measuring the results of your promotion will help you identify what you did right and what could have been done better. While you don't need to beat yourself up over the mistakes that were made, it is important to recognize them so that you are not doomed to repeat them in the future.

If you've taken the time to document your previous successes and failures, then planning your next promotion becomes that much simpler. The top 10 list of online promotional pointers summarizes much of what has been included in this book and should serve as a guideline when planning your next promotions. In the last chapter, "The Future of Online Promotions," I will examine some of the trends that should be taken into account when planning your next online promotion. While not all of these trends may apply to your specific business model, they may help spark some ideas for your next online promotion.

9

The Future of Online Promotions

Predicting the future is like predicting the stock market. You can spend weeks and months crunching numbers and compiling research, but studies have shown that throwing a dart at a listing of stocks to identify the best stock to buy can yield similar, if not better, results. Ultimately, it's an *educated* guess, but a guess all the same. Even as I sit here writing, I wonder how foolish some of my predictions will seem in a matter of a few years (maybe even sooner). Some of my educated guesses may prove to be wrong, but the basic ideas in this chapter will still be relevant.

While nobody truly knows what the future holds, there are a number of trends that point to rather obvious conclusions. While these conclusions can change, based on new information (not available at the time of writing), that doesn't mean that the predictions are irrelevant. It just means that new information became available that changed the direction of what otherwise would have been the logical conclusion.

Interestingly enough, many of today's online promotions will not need to change or evolve for quite some time. While the creative and technology will continue to evolve, the basic premise of a random draw sweepstakes will stay the same—as will instant win games, contests, coupons, rebate offers, and just about every form of online promotion that is available today. While better ways of doing things will offer lower costs or better results (or both), much of the core of today's online programs has been around since the beginning and is likely to remain even as newer and better ways become available.

This chapter should be read with the understanding that while this book provides information, there is undoubtedly new information out there that should also be explored. While I truly believe that many of the current trends will result in new advances in online promotions, I also believe that there are a number of up-and-coming trends that could be equally or more important in determining the future of online promotions.

That said, this last chapter will take a look forward to the road ahead (to borrow the title of a book by Bill Gates). There are a lot of exciting possibilities in the world of online promotions, and I for one am happy to be a part of these new possibilities. At the end of this chapter, you should have a good understanding of what the current trends are today and what will likely change the face of today's online promotions in the future.

Integrating Your Online and Offline Marketing Efforts

The future is *now* when it comes to integration. The future of online promotions is that people will stop calling them "online promotions" altogether and will simply call them "promotions," a term that will include the online medium as the primary or secondary data collection point (depending on the promotion and the overall marketing objectives). Online promotions are fun and can provide a unique user experience, but should not be isolated from traditional promotions and offline support.

The best online promotions are truly integrated into the rest of the marketing mix. From retail to the Internet and back to retail locations, online promotions provide a number of advantages over traditional promotional marketing tactics, but are much less effective when segregated from the rest of the overall marketing plan. Through integration, companies will stop thinking about their online promotions as separate from the rest of the company's marketing efforts and begin to look at online promotions as simply another avenue to help increase awareness, interest, desire, and action. A truly great example of this integration is discussed on pages 296–297 in the Kraft Game of LIFE promotion.

When Online Promotions "Grow Up"

I can't wait until the day when the majority of online promotions are no longer treated as "new and different." Soon, the vast majority of online promotions will be truly integrated into traditional promotional campaigns, and when that happens, online promotions will grow up and cease to be called "new media."

You can see it happening all around. There is a movement toward using print, radio, television, and direct mail to promote online sweepstakes, contests, and games. Banner ads are no longer the dominant media to drive traffic to online promotions. Web sites are being used more and more to check promotional codes on package goods products. URLs from print ads are being used to track effectiveness. And keypunching BRC cards, once an expensive part of the direct-mail world, is on the decline as more and more consumers do the keying themselves.

While technology continues to make the Internet faster, better, and easier to use, the truth is the Internet is simply another tool to accomplish your marketing objectives. Your *objectives* haven't changed. There are just more strategies and tactics you can now use to *accomplish* your objectives.

New and Different Phase

Historically, every medium—television, radio, magazines, direct mail, and so on— has gone through the "new and different" phase, until enough marketers understood how to use the medium effectively. Some of television's first programs were simply radio shows that had the visual element added to them. The first broadcast commercials were in the form of sponsorships until the program managers decided to change the format to distinguish content from commercials.

What the Internet has done is put fun back into the promotions industry by providing promotional marketers with new tools of the trade. Think about it: Companies are now demanding that promotions be completed faster and cheaper while simultaneously taking on objectives that, on the surface, seem insurmountable by traditional standards.

The Internet has presented what Andy Groves (former CEO of Intel) calls a *strategic inflection* point. That is, if you tracked the growth of the promotions industry, the point at which the Internet gains acceptance is the very point at which growth climbs an exponential peak. The reason is that there are all sorts of new ideas and new kinds of promotional tactics that were never before possible.

Truly integrated promotions, for example, allow mass marketers to communicate directly with their consumers—breaking down the corporate walls that have existed for many years. Integrated promotions allow measurements of campaigns in real time that, before the Internet, would have been impossible or extremely expensive. But most importantly, by combining your online efforts with your offline strategies, your integrated campaign gives you the ability to accomplish seemingly paradoxical objectives.

When you combine the power of the Internet with your traditional promotional marketing strategies, you can appeal to a mass market on an individual basis. You can segment your database with multiple offers and test your marketing strategies and still keep the costs way under your traditional direct-mail efforts. You can give out more game pieces than ever before, but with the highest degree of security. It's not the technology that gives you the ability to accomplish seemingly paradoxical objectives—it's a new way of thinking. The Internet essentially destroys the "box" that you've been asked to think outside of all along.

Everything Is Up for Debate

This is an exciting time because everything that promotional marketing experts thought they knew about the promotions industry is up for debate. This will be a

CASE STUDY: INTEGRATING THE KRAFT GAME OF LIFE

In August of 2000, Jeff Shirley, Manager of ePromotions for Kraft Foods, launched an extremely comprehensive and integrated promotion with the help of many Kraft employees as well as support from Ryan Partnership and Promotions.com. This promotion was unique for many reasons, but perhaps the most notable was the true integration between the online promotion and the in-store promotion that was found on 22 participating Kraft brands.

While the online and retail promotions each had their own separate rules and prize packages, this is where the segregation ends. Each game cross-promoted the other and consumers who chose to participate in both the retail and online promotions had a seamless user experience.

The key objectives for the retail (or "Land Based") promotion were to: (1) drive everyday volume, (2) build awareness and "connect" the Kraft portfolio, and (3) reinforce Kraft's image as contemporary. The key strategies to accomplish these objectives were to: (1) leverage packaging companywide to create a consumer "must-buy" factor, (2) motivate consumers to purchase across the Kraft portfolio, and (3) leverage an established game property that is consistent with Kraft's imagery and core values.

Hence, the "Kraft Game of LIFE" was born. Using the popular Hasbro game, "Game of LIFE," Kraft designed a game board that had both instant win and collect and win components. With 22 participating Kraft brands, this meant that there were 90 million game pieces delivered on 68 SKUs. Collect and win prizes for the retail promotion included: (1) a $1,000,000 family fortune, (2) $250,000 for a new home, (3) groceries for life, (4) a new kitchen, and (5) a Hawaiian vacation. Instant win prizes included: (1) $10,000 scholarship, (2) $500 pay day, (3) a Hasbro family game, (4) free Kraft coupon, and (5) free groceries.

The online promotion leveraged the retail exposure not only by having the URL of the online promotion on the retail game, but by leveraging the look and feel of the game and integrating the brand message throughout the promotional site. The objectives of the online promotion were to: (1) drive Kraft core consumers to the Kraft Foods Web site, (2) build a relationship with Kraft's core consumers (that is, get them to register),

difficult time for people who are set in their ways. In many cases, while the more traditional approach is accepted, it is not necessarily the best solution. Conversely, keeping an open mind and remembering what has worked in the past will help you come up with some exciting new promotional ideas that will cost less, be more profitable, and totally revolutionize the way people think about promotions. What's not exciting about that?

If you have an Internet department, online promotional segregation will be an issue in your company. Bring your tech people into your marketing meetings and see what happens. Once the fear and novelty fade, you'll find that your tech team wants nothing more than to help the company succeed—the same goal as your marketing team. Once they start putting their heads together early in the process, they will begin to bridge the gap between online *only* and offline *only* promotional campaigns. And when this happens, we'll no longer refer to "online promotions," but instead will simply talk about *the* promotional campaign, which has elements of print, radio, email, and Internet applications. And *that*, my friend, is when online promotions will have grown up to become an important part of the overall promotional campaign.

and (3) encourage repeat visits to the Kraft Foods Web site (that is, Kraft Interactive Kitchen). Online support for the retail promotion was provided by communicating the game rules and how to play, having a printable game board online, and providing details on prizes.

The online promotion itself was a spin and win game with instant win prizes that included: (1) Maytag appliances, (2) the "Game of LIFE" CD-ROM game, and (3) $10 worth of free groceries. There was also a sweepstakes overlay with a grand prize of $10,000 worth of free groceries. Consumers were entered into this grand prize drawing just for playing the spin and win game, sending recipes to friends, or for playing either the memory or word search games.

With each play of the online spin and win game, consumers received a different Kraft recipe from a database with over 90 recipes in rotation. Repeat game plays would generate different recipes and, of course, all recipes used participating Kraft brands as ingredients.

In addition to the integration and look and feel of the retail promotion, Kraft also utilized its "Interactive Kitchen" to help build relationships with their core consumers. While the online promotional elements were fun and engaging, Kraft knew that the best way to build a relationship with its core customers online would be through providing true added value.

Perhaps the most engaging online component was the "Family, Food & Fun Night" which truly tied together the Kraft Interactive Kitchen with the extensive retail promotion with a program that worked extremely well online. The concept was simple: "Plan a Family Game Night" and let Kraft Foods help make that night fun and delicious. The key components that were provided were: (1) the game night planner, (2) invitations — printable and electronic, and (3) recipe suggestions. With these tools in hand, it was simple for any family member to create a fun family night — sponsored, in part, by Kraft Foods and Hasbro. Even before the retail promotion had ended, the online promotion had exceeded expectations for unique visits and registrations for Kraft Interactive Kitchen. A key learning from this integrated promotion is that the most successful online promotions tend to have heavy traditional (offline) promotional support. Integrated promotions work better than stand-alone programs, and Kraft Foods is leading by example.

Offline Promotions for Online Brands

Interestingly enough, a close personal friend of mine, Di-Ann Eisnor, started her company, Eisnor Interactive, with the tag line, "Offline promotions for online brands." Her original vision was that online-only companies (otherwise referred to as "Pure Plays") would not succeed without offline marketing support. Her concept caught on like wildfire and soon she had several of the larger dot com companies coming to her for help with their offline strategies.

Around the end of the summer of 2000, however, Eisnor Interactive dropped the "Interactive" from its name to become Eisnor. In addition, it stopped promoting the very tag line for which it had become famous. Why? Because it's no longer about online versus offline marketing—it's finally just about the marketing. While Di-Ann is still the queen of viral marketing (at least from my perspective), her company has focused on the integration of online and offline marketing campaigns and the current client list is no longer made up of the online-only dot coms that helped launch the company. Today the company is much more balanced with traditional brands that seek out Eisnor's help with their "clicks-and-mortar" strategies.

This brings me full circle to the statement that was made at the beginning of this section: The future is *now* when it comes to integration. Online promotions are not likely to continue as stand-alone programs. They will be integrated into the rest of the marketing mix regardless of whether they are central to the promotion or another vehicle for participation. The movement toward integration of online promotions with more traditional promotions and marketing has already begun. The success of this integration will encourage more and more integration until the term *online promotion* is used to describe the medium—not the promotion itself.

Mobile Devices

Until recently, there was very little happening on the promotions front when it came to mobile devices. Sure, there were a number of traditional promotions that were used to encourage consumers to buy mobile devices, but not much was happening within the mobile devices themselves. A few companies ventured to use pagers to provide marketing messages and a chance to win prizes instantly, but, by and large, cellular phones were used primarily for phone calls, pagers for getting alerts and messages, and personal data assistants (PDAs) for contacts and calendars.

Then the separate worlds of the cell phone and the PDA began to merge. Next-generation cell phones had larger screens that allowed consumers to use limited functions of the Internet. This included checking email, instant messaging, and accessing Web sites specifically designed for handheld devices. At the same time, PDAs were connected to the Internet via cellular modems and their synch cradles. Using free software from AvantGo (www.avantgo.com), PDA owners could download information from the Web to their PDA and even their Web-enabled phone. For consumers with PDAs who wanted real-time access, there was also a subscription-based service from OmniSky (www.omnisky.com).

With a connection to the Internet, consumers can now begin to connect to online promotions from their mobile devices, but there are two problems: most Web sites were not designed for handheld devices and current handheld devices can't handle Java and rich media applications. Both of these problems, however, will be solved in the very near future. With the advent of XML, there are many companies that can now help Webmasters create an alternative version of their existing Web site that will function on handheld devices. Likewise, as companies like Intel design smaller and smaller hardware chips, handheld devices will eventually become as robust as desktop computers (and the rich media problem will solve itself).

Promotions on PDAs and WAPs

Current promotions on personal data assistants (PDAs) and Web Access Phones (WAPs) are reminiscent of early Web-based promotions in 1995. The promotions are by and large random draw sweepstakes. Consumers are either required to enter their email address only or complete their name, address, city, state, and zip and submit their entry via their PDA or WAP.

Because of the challenge of typing on a WAP, most handheld promotions limit the required entry information to an email address or telephone number. While this creates less of a barrier for entry, it makes it somewhat difficult to award prizes. If the only information collected is an email address, then in order to award the prize, you must contact the potential winner via email. Think about your own email "In" box. If you received an email from a company telling you that you had won a prize, would you respond to it or would you just think it was junk mail?

In most cases, with a random draw sweepstakes, the winners entered the promotion several weeks prior to winner notification. By the time they receive the notification email, they've forgotten that they even entered it at all. This makes awarding the prizes a difficult task as many potential winners must be disqualified because they delete their winner notification emails or simply do not respond to them.

When the technology embedded in PDAs and WAPs is far enough along to allow for Java and rich media promotions, instant win games will likely replace the current random draw sweepstakes promotions, and handheld devices will simply be another way to participate in the online promotion.

Global Positioning Satellite Technology

Earlier in this book, I noted the fact that there is current legislation mandating that all newly manufactured handheld devices come standard with Global Positioning Satellite (GPS) technology. GPS essentially pinpoints your location on the earth and helps you find where you're going or helps others find you. Sailors were the first consumers outside the government to use GPS to help them locate their position out at sea and make sure they were moving in the right direction.

The controversy about having GPS standard in all handheld devices is the potential privacy concerns of who has access to this information. While GPS is a great technology to help you find your way around a city, it can also serve as a violation of your privacy if there are no measures to protect you against unwanted companies or individuals pinpointing your location.

But let's fast forward past these privacy concerns for just a moment. For purposes of our discussion, let's assume that the U.S. government, in conjunction with privacy advocacy groups, comes up with a solution to the privacy issues. What an interesting time for promotions. Imagine that you're driving home from work, and your PDA alerts you that Blockbuster is having a "Rent One, Get One Free" promotion tonight. This alert goes off because you are within 5 miles of a Blockbuster and you are a Blockbuster Rewards member. Suddenly, promotions become situational and a whole lot smarter.

Let's assume for the moment that new legislation blocks your GPS signal, but it still comes standard on your PDA. Before you left the house for work, you entered your grocery shopping list. On your way home from work, you are reminded by your PDA to pick up your groceries, and, based on your personal shopping preferences and grocery list, your PDA automatically downloaded virtual coupons that save you an additional $20 on your bill.

GPS allows the handheld market to get extremely local—down to individual stores and shopping preferences. Promotions can now be beamed to participating consumers with handheld devices. The possibilities for the promotional marketing industry are endless.

Built-In Scanner Technology

And if GPS were not enough, several consumer-side scanning technologies are working their way back to consumer handheld devices. Presently, there are several companies running test programs to see if consumers are willing to use these hardware devices to essentially scan bar codes that appear in print magazines, outdoor advertising, and even on television commercials.

The consumer benefit is essentially an electronic coupon as well as a way to remind consumers to further investigate and (ideally) purchase products they were exposed to via advertising. The scanning units all have different ways of synching back to the Internet. Some plug into your computer directly while others don't even require a computer—just a phone line. The information can be sent via the mail or the product itself can be ordered through the unit to arrive at your doorstep. Scanning technology could lead to ultimate convenience, and may even lead to a more automated ordering process from the supermarket and other stores.

The corporate benefit is a new technology that allows better tracking and accountability for print, television, and outdoor advertising. By adding scan codes to various forms of visual media (including television), the bar codes will allow for better tracking of advertising performance. While this can be accomplished today via toll-free numbers, the phone solution doesn't allow for much consideration time. If consumers don't act immediately, they tend not to follow up at a later time. This scanner technology would allow consumers to scan advertising that interests them and to find out more information (via the Internet) before they make their final purchasing decision.

Who knows if this scanner technology will catch on the way analysts think it might. It seems like a win-win value proposition, but only the test markets will show just how willing consumers are to scan advertising and use bar codes as part of their decision-making process. If it does catch on, there may suddenly be some interesting online promotional opportunities just around the corner. Forget "Watch and Win" promotions, now you can "Scan and Win."

V-Commerce

To date, I have heard the term *v-commerce* used for two completely separate categories. The first was in reference to *Vehicle Commerce*. Sound crazy? Not really. Most of us spend more time in our cars than we would like. Please understand, I'm opposed to drivers who steer with their knees, with one hand on a cell phone and the other around a coffee mug, and whose eyes are on a laptop or a newspaper on the passenger seat. I think it's dangerous and should be illegal. But I'm less concerned when people use hands-free technology to talk on the phone. The first phase of hands-free phone technology came via speakerphones and earpieces. The second phase actually incorporated the phone into the stereo unit of the car.

V-commerce goes way beyond standard phone technology, however, and essentially turns your car stereo into a Web-enabled unit capable of checking your email, stock quotes, weather, driving directions, and a host of other features. Now instead of simply having a conversation with another person in your car, you can truly be conducting business, buying products, and staying connected. While I haven't seen or heard of any computer monitors available for passengers, I don't imagine that we're too far away from having monitors built into the luxury vehicles the same way that televisions and VCRs (soon to be DVDs) come as an available option. The next generation of family trips could be both a blessing and a curse. While you won't have as much fighting with each family member connected to his or her own virtual world, there's something to be said for the potential loss of communication within the car itself.

The second reference I've heard for v-commerce is *Voice Commerce*. This is the new craze of speech recognition software that many companies have integrated into their networks so that you can access your email, stock quotes, weather, driving directions, and make purchases using any phone by dialing a toll-free number. Speech recognition software has been around for some time now, but only recently has it been truly integrated into some of the top Web sites. Currently, these sites ask that you create preferences online to activate your account, but some newer voice-only companies do not require that you have Web access at all. This has some interesting implications for helping the Internet reach nearly 100 percent penetration of U.S. households. While not every home has a computer, just about every home has a phone, and everyone at least has access to a pay phone—even if they don't have their own personal phone for some reason or another.

Regardless of which version of v-commerce ends up sticking, both are equally exciting and have some wonderful applications to the promotional marketing world.

When "V" Is for Voice

Voice recognition has started to come into the limelight again. One of the reasons that previous voice recognition technology didn't really catch on was because the computer needed to learn an individual's voice. Accents and different kinds of pronunciation for the same words made it difficult for computers to achieve the accuracy levels necessary for voice recognition to gain acceptance. Another challenge was distinguishing synonyms, or "which witch is which." Words that sound the same but have different meanings are a real challenge for voice recognition software.

Some of the bugs are still being worked out of today's voice recognition software, but it's getting better all the time. While it's not likely that voice recognition software will ever be foolproof, it is safe to say that today's technology is ready for prime time. Some voice recognition applications have already been integrated into the Web and could be the key to creating 100 percent Internet penetration. While computers with Internet access have not reached every home in America, the opportunity exists to potentially bypass the computer requirement altogether and provide Web access via toll-free numbers to consumers.

Granted, there are limitations on how much of the Internet's resources can be duplicated without the visual elements associated with them. Applications, such as Macromedia's Flash, streaming video, and all the visual components that make the Web such an engaging medium, would be lost. But information without the sizzle would remain. Consumers without computers could get a taste of what everyone has been talking about for the past several years. Suddenly, the computer hardware requirement—the last barrier to accessing the Internet—may be history.

Or perhaps I'm making too much out of what could turn out to be a fad. That's the trouble with writing about the impact of future technologies. While the potential is certainly there, only time will tell if voice recognition will truly take off this time around and become the last piece in the Internet access puzzle. As a promotional marketer, it's certainly something worth exploring, specifically with some of the existing applications that are currently available.

A Few Examples

While there are several voice-to-Web portals currently out there, I'd like to touch on a few examples. I'm not focusing on industry-specific applications such as the financial industry, where consumers have been able to check their portfolios via the phone for years. I'm also not focusing on interactive voice-response systems that are now tied into back-end Web applications for additional content.

Instead, I'm looking at general Internet portals that now allow you to access information from the Internet via your phone. The purpose of reviewing a few examples is to give you an idea of what's currently available as well as spark some ideas as to what's likely to be available a few months to a few years from now.

AOL by Phone

In conjunction with the release of America Online (AOL) Version 6.0 in the fall of 2000, AOL by Phone was heavily promoted as another way to check email, weather reports, financial information, headline news, and other popular services to be added at a later date. AOL users who elect to pay an additional monthly fee of $4.95 per month, can simply call (800) AOL-1234, enter their PIN number, and access popular features of the online service. Simple voice commands allow consumers to navigate from the main menu to various choices. Checking email works well as long as you're willing to listen to a computer-sounding voice read back the contents. Even though there may be some errors, you certainly get the essence of the messages without much trouble.

When checking weather, the computer automatically assumes you're interested in the weather in your home area, but you have the option to check weather anywhere within the United States just by speaking the city and state. In the finance section, you can get a summary report for daily activities or a stock quote (delayed by approximately 15 minutes) even if you don't know the ticker symbol.

While all of AOL service is not available via the AOL by Phone, the email feature will come in quite handy for road warriors and people who want to keep in touch when they're away from their computers. At this time, you can only check email—not reply or create new emails via the phone. This may be due in part to the limitations of the software to take dictation. While preset voice navigation commands can be trained so that accents can be taken into account, open-ended voice dictation becomes a whole other ball game. This feature may be added in the future, but for now consumers are limited to hearing their messages read to them.

Yahoo! by Phone

Yahoo! by Phone, powered by Net2Phone, has many of the same features as AOL by Phone, and then some. As with every amazing product that Yahoo! has, the product is free to consumers with the help of advertising support. Consumers sign up online and create an account that includes a 10-digit number (home phone number), which becomes the account number plus a four-digit PIN number. With that, consumers call (800) My-Yahoo, enter their PIN, and access the free service.

From the moment you sign on to the service, you hear quick 5-second ads promoting various sponsors. Advertisers can choose to run their ads on the main menu or specific content channels such as email, finance, news, weather, or sports. What's different about Yahoo!'s content is that Yahoo! integrates radio-quality content into the phone-to-Web service. That is, when you want to listen to actual news, it's not a computer reading a Web page, it's a broadcaster talking to you as if you were listening to the radio. This is an interesting approach, as Yahoo! by Phone combines phone-to-Web technology with traditional broadcast to achieve an extremely positive user experience.

What's truly amazing about Yahoo! by Phone, however, is its ability to reply to emails. After listening to your email read by the computer voice, you can choose to reply to the email *by leaving a voice message*. The recipient of your reply receives an email from you. At first glance, it seems that you simply replied from your computer. But, on opening the email, the recipient is provided with a long URL string that links him or her to a Web page where your voice message is played.

So, rather than tackling the voice-type dictation challenge, Yahoo! by Phone simply emails a URL where a voice message can be heard. If the recipient of the email is on a high-speed Internet connection, then the voice message is no problem; your voice can be heard loud and clear. On a dial-up connection, it takes a while to load the message, but once it's loaded, you can play it as often as you wish. This is a great fix to a difficult problem. It would be incredibly difficult for the computer program to accurately dictate an email and allow the sender to review it before it's sent. Rather than do it, a digital voice mail message attached to an email works just fine.

Yahoo! by Phone also works in conjunction with your My Yahoo! Web page. If you have configured your My Yahoo! Web page, then Yahoo! by Phone can read back your current stock portfolio—rather than having to key in individual stock quotes one at a time. Yahoo! by Phone can also provide you with weather in the regions you've indicated. By keeping your My Yahoo! Web page current, you can get the information you're interested in without much talking.

BeVocal

I included the toll-free service (800) 4Be-Vocal because it's one example of a phone-to-Web portal that does not require Internet access to use. With BeVocal, you can access flight information, driving directions, and even find a business (restaurant, movie rentals, etc.). Through using BeVocal's business finder, you can have the service automatically connect you to the phone number it lists free of charge. You can also check stock quotes, weather, and traffic conditions.

BeVocal does have a Web site, but consumers do not have to sign up to use the BeVocal service. What the Web site does is allow consumers to save their home and work addresses so they do not have to speak them each time they use the BeVocal business finder service. The Web site also allows consumers to save up to 12 securities in a portfolio that can be read when they check their stock quotes. In essence, the BeVocal Web site for consumers is intended to make the phone experience that much more personal and pleasurable.

The main reason for the BeVocal Web site, however, is to up sell their phone-to-Web portal services to enterprise customers. BeVocal provides phone-to-Web portal solutions to businesses so that they can provide mobile Internet phone access to their employees and customers. Perhaps their Telecom overview page says it best:

> With more than 1.5 billion phones and over 450 million mobile phone users worldwide, the telephone has become the ultimate access device to the Internet. According to Nomura Research, there will be more mobile phones connected to the Internet than personal computers by 2002; and the Kelsey Group predicts that there will be more than 128 million voice portal users by the end of 2005, creating a $12.3 billion industry.

BeVocal has created a consumer phone-to-Web solution as a way to demonstrate its ability to do the same for its clients. I believe this is an interesting way to spread the word about the BeVocal technology and create demand pull in the marketplace.

"Tell Me," BeVocal's competitor, offers a similar service which can be accessed by dialing (800) 555-TELL. Like BeVocal, Tell Me is using a consumer phone-to-Web solution to attract corporate clients interested in creating their own phone-to-Web applications. Again, only time will tell if phone-to-Web applications will take off and traditional service-based companies will decide to use companies like BeVocal and Tell Me to create phone-to-Web access to their Intranets and Extranets.

Promotional Applications

It's clear that in each of the previous examples, advertising is or will be a key enabler to providing Web content via toll-free numbers. I see a whole new era of AOL Movie Phone. In the same way AOL Movie Phone runs through a trailer of a new movie release before allowing consumers to make their choices, these toll-free Web applications will likely have "a word from our sponsor" prior to allowing consumers into the content.

And this is where I see the promotional applications. Suddenly, your online promotions can have legs via toll-free numbers without creating a separate stand-alone interactive voice-response application. When consumers sign up for these programs, they have some version of a profile assigned to their account. Now with a few voice commands or numeric choices, consumers can participate in your online promotions via a toll-free number.

While toll-free promotions have always been an option, I have not seen the clear integration from the phone to the Internet. These phone-to-Web applications combine the power of the Web with simple voice commands that negate the computer requirement. Rather than transposing a traditional radio commercial to this phone-to-Web medium, there is a wonderful promotional opportunity that ties back into direct response. Whether it is a sweepstakes, contest, game, or special offer, you can now capture a consumer's undivided attention and allow him or her to participate in your online promotion by phone. Soon, as the voice commands for e-commerce become a reality, consumers will be able to shop online via the phone. When this component is added, these short interactive commercials will become invaluable to companies.

Voice-response promotions are nothing new. In fact, they predate Internet promotions. The challenge in the past, however, was that these voice promotions were stand-alone programs. If you wanted to participate in the toll-free promotion, that's all you did. You'd call a toll-free number, speak your contact information, participate in the promotion, and hang up. Now these voice promotions can be tied in to broader phone-to-Web content portals, thereby increasing their appeal to consumers.

In other words, if phone-to-Web applications take off, then we will have come full circle back to interactive voice-response promotions that are tied into online and traditional promotions. As Harry Truman said, "The only thing new under the sun is the history you haven't learned."

When "V" Is for Vehicle

Vehicle commerce, more than anything, reminds me of the old *Jetsons* cartoon show. With v-commerce, we can all be more productive during our commute to and from work. While you still can't pack today's car into a light briefcase, cars from General Motors and Ford already have the ability to connect to the Internet and allow you to conduct business right from your car. This is not some futuristic technology that is currently being tested—this is an option that is currently available and will soon be standard on all vehicles—foreign or domestic. Forget the fact that an emergency call is made on your behalf when your air bags inflate or that your car's exact location is reported to the proper authorities via GPS when it is stolen. These are cool features but are merely the tip of the iceberg.

On March 15, 2000, *Revolution Magazine* released an article entitled, "Ford and Sprint PCS Collaborate on In-car Services." It was this article that brought to my attention a whole new medium that would soon be everywhere. Suddenly there is another monitor-free medium with access to the Internet and core online services. While it's too early to tell if consumers will take a fancy to checking their email while driving, or using these in-car services to buy products, there is a huge potential for vehicle commerce to take off.

It's the same reason that in-flight magazines work so well: When you're traveling, you're a captive audience. What's the most popular and expensive time of day to buy radio advertising? Morning and evening drive time, of course. Now imagine if you could not only advertise your products during these peak hours, but could motivate consumers to act right then and there—in their cars. If the advertising is compelling enough, v-commerce could very well become the next hot direct marketing medium. With empowered consumers stuck in the morning and evening commute, it seems only logical that they will take advantage of their connectivity and either continue to conduct business or use this extra time to take care of errands.

I can't even begin to imagine all the different possibilities with which marketers will be able to experiment. Suddenly, prime time is not just for television any more. Imagine car manufacturers competing with each other, not on the physical features of the car itself but on the basis of their Internet capabilities and in-car service options.

Promotional Applications

In-vehicle promotions will be similar to voice promotions. In both instances, consumers are not able to use their eyes to participate in the promotion. In the car, consumers are not likely to use a keyboard or even a numeric touch pad. So any vehicle commerce promotions will rely heavily on the audio elements as well as voice recognition software.

Participating consumers are likely to have some form of Internet access, so they will probably be able to customize a personal home page that the in-car services will have access to in order to determine individual preferences. This will be helpful as consumers using a customized home page will not have to speak their contact information to advertisers of the in-car services to participate in promotional applications.

Assuming that there is more than one way around this hurdle, the in-car promotional applications will be high-end voice-response programs that directly or indirectly tie back to online promotions. That is, sweepstakes, contests, games, coupons, discounts, rebates, and loyalty programs can all be integrated into this new medium—as long as the visual elements are removed from the equation.

Interestingly enough, even the visual elements may be optional for the passengers in the car. While drivers will certainly not be able to look at a monitor and participate in a promotion, passengers with built-in monitors will be less restricted on the visual elements of the promotion. As most of today's cars do not offer this monitor feature, it may be some time before this aspect comes into play, but it's entirely possible that monitors and entertainment screens will allow for the visual components that will be missing for the driver of the vehicle.

It's also interesting to consider applications beyond the one-way advertised promotion in-car. For example, rather than hearing about a promotion from your in-car service, email, or radio station, v-commerce will allow consumers to see a billboard on the freeway and use their in-car service to participate in the promotion. As in-car promotions are tailored specifically to this new medium, they will still need to be promoted and outdoor advertising becomes a powerful way to break through the clutter once again.

Overall, the promotional applications for v-commerce are as broad as promotions built for radio stations, voice-response promotions, and online promotions that are modified to remove the visual element. With some creativity, there truly is no end to the possibilities for this new medium.

High-End Interactive Promotions

The promises of broadband sound a lot like the claims of interactive television almost a decade ago. It's true that when the world stops dialing in and everyone has high-speed Internet connections, there will be a lot more high-end content that we can begin to provide. Since day one, Internet connection speeds have prohibited the high-gloss content that television-prone consumers are used to seeing.

While fast Internet access continues to become more prevalent, true broadband applications are still not a reality for the majority of consumers. With DSL and cable modem options, household Internet speeds are increasing, but still haven't reached critical mass. So, while you may be interested in high-impact, television-like promotions, broadband applications are not yet the best answer.

There are alternatives, however, to flat HTML, magazine-looking promotions with Submit buttons. Earlier in this book, I touched on various Java applications. With Java, you can create instant win scratch-off games, collect and win games, and a host of other more interactive applications. And while Java programming continues to improve and have higher multimedia applications, there are some interesting alternatives to consider for your high-impact, televisionlike promotions.

One such application is Macromedia's Flash. With Flash, companies are beginning to provide high-impact multimedia applications in a near-television-quality environment that doesn't take more than a few seconds to load. Those who have high-speed connections never miss a beat. Your less fortunate consumers on dial-up connections, however, are not punished because of your desire to move beyond flat Web pages. While Flash is not the answer to every broadband wish, it's getting better every day and may turn out to be the best solution to broadband content desires—without having the broadband speed requirements.

I've also not given up on 3D environments. While they tend to come and go, 3D environments still have some niche applications that make a lot of sense. When they are combined with chat applications, there is a whole world of adventure that can be quite entertaining. While I don't believe that 3D environments will take over the Web, there are certainly nice promotional applications that still apply.

Multiuser gaming continues to flourish and attract the gamer market. From PC games to Internet subscription games to more traditional gaming hardware, the Internet connection has upped the ante on traditional single- or double-player games. If your demographics match this core gaming demographic, there are endless possibilities to consider promotionally.

And last, but not least, is the flourishing DVD content that will only continue to grow. From now on, most computers will come standard with DVD drives. Forget about everything you thought you knew about DVDs. While the DVD format is certainly great for playing movies in your home theater, the best DVD applications are not meant for your VCR. The best DVDs take advantage of computers and gaming hardware to provide all sorts of new and innovative programming and content that simply have not been previously available.

So while broadband applications are still a thing of the future, there's nothing stopping you from providing broadbandlike applications today—even without the broadband connectivity.

Macromedia's Flash

Macromedia's Flash is one application that continues to evolve and become more and more like the high-end broadband applications—without the broadband. Advertising and marketing agencies that are experimenting with Flash are beginning to see the televisionlike possibilities that were previously not possible because of slow Internet connection speeds.

While statistics vary depending on the source, roughly 90 percent of the current Web browser market is already Flash-enabled. But, with about an hour or so of additional programming time, you can easily set up a Flash "sniffer" that instantly checks a consumer's Flash capability so that non-Flash viewers receive an alternative version of the promotion without skipping a beat.

Even if consumers are required to have Flash to participate, the few consumers who do not already have Flash installed will note that downloading the Flash plug-in is perhaps the fastest download they've experienced. It's so fast that some companies are crossing the line in terms of Netiquette and are simply forcing the download while they tell consumers what they are doing. While I don't recommend this approach, the point is that of all the plug-in barriers to entry, Flash appears to be the least trouble.

What's truly compelling about Flash applications is not the prevalence among Web consumers—it's what you can do with the Flash files. Music, full-screen animation, televisionlike content, and commercials are now available online. Forget the "eye candy" of the past, this is true animation at its finest. While video conversion is not there yet, just about everything else appears to be available. That is, while you can't broadcast video with Flash, you can create animating graphics and illustrations with background sounds and music.

If you haven't been to Macromedia's Web site in a while, you should point your browser to www.macromedia.com or www.flash.com (also by Macromedia) and check it out. Macromedia has links to all kinds of examples of what you can do with their software.

Promotional Applications

So where do the online promotional elements come in? Just about everywhere. Is there a better way to launch into an online promotion than with a consumer's full attention? If your marketing objective is to generate awareness, a sweepstakes or instant win game might get a consumer to go online, but a Flash movie will get their attention. One application is to use Flash to introduce your products and services before launching into the online promotion itself.

But why stop there? You can also design the entire online promotion using Flash so that your entry forms and data collection points are integrated into the Flash movie. Or perhaps you're creating a collect and win game. Rather than flat image files, why not allow consumers to collect various Flash movies that highlight specific product features? With sound and animation, there are all kinds of gaming possibilities. Perhaps a game centered around your products and services will provide the interaction you're looking for with your customers.

The point is, while Flash provides the ability to create televisionlike animation and music, it's still a two-way medium. Rather than one-way television content being broadcast on the Web, there are numerous ways to integrate the high-end content into your marketing and sales objectives. Even "commercials" should be interactive and give control back to consumers.

3D Environments

Three-dimensional environments have been around for a long time. Since 1994, there have been various explorations into how 3D can be integrated with the Internet to create the "virtual worlds" that most of the early authors wrote about when they envisioned the Internet. Even before I had ever been online, the book *Snow Crash* by Neal Stephenson (Bantam Doubleday Dell, 1993) drew pictures in my mind about what the Internet would one day be all about. It was fantastic. People created virtual avatars that were the visual representation of how they wished to look and would interact with each other as they would in the real world, only from anywhere in the world.

When most people get online, however, they are exposed to flat catalog-looking pages, which is a much different experience than the virtual worlds that most fiction writers (and even Hollywood movies) like to describe. I'm not sure why 3D environments never really caught on. Perhaps the early limitation of just the visual sense (that is, lacking sound, smell, touch, and taste) coupled with slow connection speeds and Web server limitations made the virtual worlds feel like a cheap imitation of the real world. Or perhaps, the revenue models just didn't make for good business. Or maybe 3D environments are still ahead of their time. Whatever the reason, 3D worlds have yet to gain in popularity in the same way the rest of the catalog-looking Web pages have caught on.

I mention them here because I believe there are still times when a 3D world makes sense. As technology continues to grow and improve, some of the early limitations will take care of themselves. With advances in Internet telephone technologies, it's conceivable that future versions of 3D worlds will include the sense of sound—allowing consumers to talk and listen to each other rather than type their communications. There are even companies experimenting with smells over the Internet. You can now buy a printerlike device that combines various smells from data that is received online.

The point is, there's a good chance that 3D environments may flourish and become the next generation of Web sites. But even if that doesn't happen for some time, there are still online promotional applications that should be considered.

Promotional Applications

I consider 3D environments a means to connect special-interest groups together for the purpose of communication and interaction. In other words, I look at virtual worlds as a very different application for event marketing. From booths to theaters, 3D environments seem like the logical application for taking event marketing specialties online.

To me, it would seem that a virtual concert theater would be a very different way for music groups to promote their concerts and upcoming shows. Using the visual elements of a 3D environment, fans could see and hear music from their favorite artists while getting to know each other.

If specific 3D environments gain in popularity, you would have the advantage of using both traditional "at show" promotions as well as the integration of all the online promotional applications discussed in this book. By "at show," I'm talking about drawings that happen in real time the same way that they occur at a booth during a trade show in the real world. The drawing is among all eligible participants who are present at the time of the drawing. Even if this is not high on your priority list, it's something to consider when you're looking for that breakthrough idea to engage your consumers.

Multiuser Gaming

Multiuser gaming is taking the gaming industry by storm. Whether the game is played from your PC or gaming hardware, multiuser games continue to grow in popularity. I was amazed at how far they have come. In a few short years, the quality of the gaming experience has increased dramatically and the limitations on the number of simultaneous users playing the same game have virtually been eliminated. Rather than 10 people playing the same game at the same time, imagine several hundred thousand people all competing against each other. Now the 10 people you tried to defeat are now your allies so that you don't immediately get squashed by other bands of gamers.

It should also be noted that gaming technology has dramatically increased in the last few years. Now there are paging and email services that alert you when your team is under attack. Imagine minding your own business when your pager goes off to alert you that your virtual community is being trashed and you only have a few minutes in which to defend yourself. It might sound a bit crazy, but that's what's going on right now. Hard core gamers are constantly being challenged to go further and be part of a gaming community. It's no longer about you versus the computer, it's about you and your allies against your attackers (who have banded together from various parts of the world).

One company in particular, Mythic Games (mythicgames.com), has built its success around a subscription gaming model. Forget paying for software, just sign up for a monthly subscription to the game of your choice and join in the battle (whatever battle that may be) with your friends—or make new friends online. Mythic Games' parent company, Abandon Entertainment (www.abandonent .com), is taking the next step and working on promotional applications using Mythic Games' 3D gaming technology.

Promotional Applications

Multiuser games are compelling by the very nature that they are alive with a gaming community. Let's face it, games are cool—especially to younger demographics.

If your target is teenage boys, there are few online promotions that will get their attention like a multiuser game.

Product placement in these games is much like it is in the movies. Fees are paid to the creators of the content to place icons and products directly into the game. From billboards in driving games to branded foods used to increase power or health, there are many ways to work products and brands into multiuser games.

Alternatively, tournament games can be used to challenge gamers. By setting up the game so that players compete on score or battle it out among each other, the game itself can be used as the online promotion. Granted, there is a lot of legal gray area here, so lawyers and/or promotional agencies with a good legal background should be consulted. But with the right setup, tournament games can be a compelling way to drive the success of your promotional marketing objectives.

Digital Video Disks

I'd like to end this section on nonbroadband applications by mentioning the endless possibilities of digital video disks (DVDs). As stated earlier, DVDs are not just for the living room anymore. As most computers will come standard with DVD players, movies are just the beginning. First and foremost, DVDs are about compression. Depending on the format you use, there are several gigabytes of space available on a single DVD. To put this into perspective, one floppy disk holds about 1.5 megabytes. The average CD-ROM holds about 550 megabytes. DVD-5's hold 5,000 megabytes (or 5 gigabytes of information). There are also DVD-9 (9-gigabyte) and even DVD-18 (18-gigabyte) formats currently available.

This is important, because, like music CDs, movies only take up a fraction of the available space on a DVD. While this doesn't matter much for the DVDs that are meant to be played in your VCR, it's a whole other ball game when it comes to your PC. Imagine having a small CD that has the ability to contain more information than most computer hard drives.

Apple Computer saw the possibilities, and has decided to use encrypted DVDs to hold virtually all the major software titles that Apple would like to sell to its customers. In its fight to win shelf space, Apple has taken advantage of this massive amount of available space so that consumers can simply buy the DVD and then call an 800 number or visit a Web site to unlock the encrypted software. Forget downloading massive software files; now you can simply unlock them with the right codes when you buy the software license.

DVDs have the potential to change everything once again. Retail chains that sell movies and software would be wise to closely follow these trends. This new distribution channel has the potential to change the way that consumers buy their software products. While there are solutions to every problem, being unaware that there is a potential problem is the biggest problem of them all.

Choose Your Own Adventure

Do you remember the old "Choose your own adventure" books from the 1980s? With these books, you determined the outcome of the book based on decisions that you made at critical decision points. The simplest example is that you came to a fork in the road in the story, and you could go left or right. If you chose to go left, you turned to page 25. If you thought right was the better way to go, you turned to page 53.

In essence, these books were wonderful because you could read them several different times, each time with a completely different story and endings based on the choices that were made. Early on, some Web pioneers (myself included) attempted to replicate this experience with Web pages. Rather than turning to a different page, you would simply click on the appropriate link to choose your own adventure. While this was a different medium, it was still not much of an improvement from the books.

But with DVDs, this technology may come back in a hurry—only this time from Hollywood. One company already experimenting with this idea is Abandon Entertainment (www.abandonent.com). If you go to its Web site, you can watch movie clips with this technology already built in. But this is only the beginning. While the "choose your own adventure" style programming never made much sense in the movie theater, DVDs are all about the customized experience.

Some movies already provide various camera angles so that aspiring directors can create their own movie based on the raw footage. But what if you're not an aspiring director? To appeal to a much broader audience, I foresee the next big wave of movies that go directly to the DVD format will incorporate this "choose your own adventure" format so that the movie can be played over and over again with different outcomes and a plethora of story lines. This is what interactivity is all about, and I don't think it's too far of a stretch for Hollywood.

Promotional Applications

Forget traditional product placements in movies; now, choosing the wrong beverage can be an actual plot in the movie. If a Pepsi is ordered instead of a Coke, then a different path can be taken in the movie with an entirely different outcome. In the real world, consumers have choices. Now with the "choose your own adventure" styled movies, the same choice can imply good or bad decision making. It can be subtle or blatant; either way, there are new promotional opportunities just with product placements.

Then consider the fact that the majority of consumers with DVD players will also have access to the Internet. Why not include e-commerce right in the very contents of the movie? If consumers see something that they like, why not allow them to order it right then and there—just by clicking on it at the time they see it? This is not impossible, and savvy marketers will find ways to take advantage of this new medium in ways that have direct results. Now you can go beyond traditional exposure and branding. With DVD movies and an Internet connection on your PC, the possibilities are endless.

And what about all that extra space on the DVD? Those purist nonmarketers who demand to separate movie content from sponsors can have their way when actual interactive advertising becomes the norm. Forget the standard movie preview before the film starts—that's so one-sided. With all that available space on the DVD, why not create compelling interactive promotions and advertorials that actually increase the value of the DVD? It could be a game, an e-commerce storefront, or even encrypted software (discussed in the next section). Think of all that extra space on the DVD as what consumers might enjoy online if they had a broad-band connection and Internet speed was no longer an issue. Spark any other ideas?

Encryption

Encryption has been around since roughly the first government computer. To keep sensitive information from falling into the wrong hands, data has been encrypted so that only the intended viewer could decrypt the information. What's new is that this encryption technology keeps morphing itself into the marketing world and has taken on a whole new perspective when it comes to DVDs. It's no longer about intercepting secret information—it's about a new way to buy and sell digital assets—be they software, games, music, movies, or anything else electronic.

Promotional Applications

There are plenty of promotional applications wherever DVDs are being sold or freely distributed. Premium items are a perfect example. A game developer might decide to freely distribute one of its games in order to up sell higher-end games that are encrypted on the same DVD. The value to the consumer is the free game, but once the DVD is installed, it becomes a marketing tool to up sell to higher-end games in which consumers are most likely interested.

Music is another example. Perhaps several songs on the "B-Side" of a particular album are freely distributed (in whole or in part) such that interested consumers can decrypt the rest of the album through buying the appropriate unlocking code. But why stop at a single album? Perhaps a music club will distribute all its top-selling albums for a specific kind of music (rock, alternative, country, pop, or classical, for example) on a single DVD. A sample of all the albums is free, but each album is priced separately and can be bought online or via a toll-free number.

Movies are no different. If the space is available, why not include additional movie titles that a consumer might be interested in purchasing on the very DVD that was just purchased? Or perhaps an entire trilogy is included on a DVD created specifically for the first of the three movies. If the consumer wants all three, he or she simply unlocks the other two.

And then there are a host of applications that are outside any one specific category. Perhaps a movie, game, or software is used to reward new members for signing up for Internet access or for subscribing to a magazine or newspaper. Wherever an incentive is needed, encryption can provide a way of getting the message and the potential reward into the hands of targeted consumers. Once the desired action is taken, the premium item is easily unlocked and the consumer is rewarded immediately.

Beyond Television

First there was black-and-white television, then there was color, then there was cable, then there was satellite, and now there are several set-top boxes with several subscriptions and features to choose from. The interesting thing is, they are all beginning to converge. Cable television and cable Internet access are starting to be sold hand-in-hand across the United States. DirectTV is working in conjunction with WebTV for online and interactive content and with Tivo to allow consumers to intelligently capture television programming that is of interest.

Where's it all going? Will interactive television ever be a reality to the degree that it was once promised? Will television and your PC become so interchangeable that it will no longer matter which one is used for entertainment or productivity? And what will differentiate a future television with high-speed Internet access and a computer that is finally connected via broadband? While there are still a lot of questions that have yet to be answered, one thing is for sure: Today's television is not likely to be "the same old thing" in a few years.

At its core, television is primarily used for entertainment while computers are primarily used for productivity. But as the lines begin to blur between televisions and computers, what will remain is high-end content that is at least somewhat interactive. Many of today's televisions already come preprogrammed with interactive guides that make watching and recording programs much easier. As the various types of set-top boxes continue to converge, standards in television programming will emerge.

I don't believe it will be much of a leap to continue to integrate more and more interactive content that accesses a specific program's Web site, so that consumers can spend as much time as they wish with their favorite shows—even when they are not currently broadcasting. With services like Tivo, consumers can be less concerned about tuning in at the exact moment when a television program is airing, since intelligent set-top boxes will already know their interest in the show and will simply record it and archive it. Imagine combining an archive of every episode of your favorite television show with the ability to more closely interact with the television content through the show's Web site. This is where I see things headed. We're not there yet, but all the pieces of the puzzle currently exist.

Promotional Applications

WebTV already has some interesting promotional applications in place. From the ability to order pizza online when you see selected commercials to online extensions of game shows, WebTV continues to plug along with promotional applications tied into television content. But, as I see it, this is just the beginning. It's one thing to be able to play the "home game" version of a game show in real time and an entirely different thing to be able to click on the actual set of the show you're watching so that you can order the clothes, furniture, and anything else you see that has been incorporated into the programming. This is the catalogue of the future. Home shopping channels may have started the ball rolling, but an e-commerce overlay to a television show is the next level.

Watch and win games will likewise take on an entirely new spin as the game piece will be distributed electronically during the broadcast—not via magazine and television guides ahead of time. Sweepstakes, contests, and games can be conducted with the viewing audience and results are immediate. While I'm not sure if the "choose your own adventure" style of programming would work with shows that are episodic in nature, polls could certainly be taken in real time to determine how audiences would like to see the program evolve.

The basic premise is that wherever a one-way broadcast previously existed, now some form of two-way interactive content can join the mix. Promotional applications are no longer a broadcast scenario, but can be more involving of the viewing audience much like online promotions are today. Imagine consumers actually rating the television shows in real time. There are lots of ways this can go, and it will be interesting to see how the convergence of television and the Internet will evolve over time.

Conclusion

This concludes my version of the future of the online promotions industry. I have no doubt that some of these technologies will absolutely take off while others will surely die a slow and painful death. At this point, it's too soon to tell which technologies are which. In fact, only time will reveal the truth about which online promotional applications are truly breakthrough and will catch on and survive. The point of this chapter was not to predict the future. If any of us could do that we'd be wealthy beyond reason and would turn our attention to more important things than online promotions. The purpose of this chapter was to take a good hard look at the various pieces of the online promotions puzzle so that trends and new technologies can be dissected and better understood.

There are many trends that will affect the future of online promotions, and successful companies will keep their eyes open for opportunities that make sense. The most logical of all these is to move away from the term *online promotions* altogether and to view the Internet and online marketplace as one more medium in which to conduct promotions. If you start with a clearly defined objective, then promotional marketing goals will be met regardless of online or traditional promotional marketing tactics. While there are distinct advantages to the online medium, promotions are, at their very core, the same—online or off. Promotions that take advantage of both mediums and are truly integrated will outperform one-off promotions that are segregated from the rest of the marketing mix and are limited to one medium or the other.

With each new advancement in technology comes new promotional applications. Those with vision will take advantage of these opportunities and evolve their current (online) promotions. While the basic premise of the promotion will change only slightly over the years, the tactical executions will evolve and change with changing technologies.

Thank You

I want to take this opportunity to thank you, my reader, for taking the time to read this book. I hope that you have found it informative and helpful as you journey deep into what is currently dubbed the online promotions space. I have attempted to provide you with the tools and techniques of the online promotions industry and to give you the resources you need to create successful online promotions. I want you to know that I welcome your comments and feedback. If you have found this book helpful, or have any questions about the material covered in this book, I invite you to contact me via email: bill@seismicom.com or bcarmody@ yahoo.com. I can't promise that I will reply to every email that I receive, but I will try. Good luck with your next online promotion. I wish you all the success in the world.

Index

A

Abandon Entertainment, 310, 312
Abbreviated rules, 134–135
Acid Tested, 183
Active consumers, tracking, 93. *See also* Best customers
ActiveX, 9
ACT software, 213
Ad Age, 180, 182
Ad banners, 234, 248. *See also* Banner ads
Ad campaigns, generating ideas for, 37–38
Ad Club, 183
Added value, 25
Addresses, for differing functions, 131
Administration, 169
  in-house, 169–171
  outsourcing, 171–173
  questions concerning, 196–198
  of random draw sweepstakes, 4
Administration support, choosing, 185
Administrative experts, 203
Advertising
  nontraditional and experimental, 254–263
  offline resources for, 239–246
  online resources for, 232–238
  of promotions, 231–264, 289
Advertising results, analyzing, 268–269
Ad Week, 180, 182
Affidavits of eligibility, 128–129
Agency.com, 182, 183
Agency reel, questions concerning, 191
AllBusiness, 110
All Consumers Are Not Created Equal (Hallberg), 281
Alliance for Internet Security (AIS), 110
Alphanumeric codes, 35, 64, 71
Alphanumeric passwords, 114
Alta Vista, 233, 235
Alwine, Gregg, 250
Amazon.com, 173
America's Funniest Home Videos, 20
American Advertising Federation (AAF), 183
American Family Publishers, 43, 135–136
American Institute of Certified Public Accountants, 99
America Online (AOL), 212, 233, 246, 247, 258
Analysis, 176
  of advertising results, 268–269
  database, 228
  in-house, 176–178
  of online promotion results, 75–76
  outsourcing of, 178–180, 199–201
  postpromotion, 223–229
Analysis support, choosing, 185–186
Anderson Consulting, 182
Antivirus software, 112
AOL by Phone, 302–303
Apple Computer, 311
Application Service Providers (ASPs), 154, 155
Arizona, contest registration in, 120–121
Arrowhead Fulfillment, 185
Art contests, 15, 18
Attorneys, in-house, 150–152. *See also* Legal issues
Attribute reinforcement, 30–32
Audio components, adding, 66
Automated backups, 112–113
Automatic entry sweepstakes, 6–7
  as a sales driver, 32
AutoWraps Web site, 261–262
AvantGo, 298
Average retail value (ARV), 121
Awareness
  as a promotional objective, 83
  building, 30–32, 43

B

B2Bnow, 110

Backups, security and, 112–113

Banner ads, 258–259. *See also* Ad banners

Banners
key word, 253
problems with, 248–249

Barnes & Noble, 257

BBB*Online,* 99

Being Direct (Wonderman), 282

Benchmark questions
for coupons, 226
general, 224–225
for premiums, 226
for rebates, 225–226
for sampling, 225
for sweepstakes, 225

Benchmarks, creating, 223, 224–226

Best customers. *See also* Active consumers
identifying, 22, 276
tracking, 282, 283

Better Business Bureau, 99

BeVocal, 303–304

Billboards, full-motion, 263

Blockbuster Video, 23

BlueLight.com, 3, 256

Blue Marble, 182, 183

Blue Shield of California Web site, 8

Boxer, Joe, 263

Brand identity, reinforcing, 36–37

Brand loyalty. *See also* Online brands
building, 35–36
customer support and, 167

Brand Week, 180, 182, 211

Browsers. *See* Web browsers

Built-in scanner technology, 300

Bulk mailings, 21

Bulletin board systems (BBSs), 59

Buy.com, 23

BYC (Because You Can) rationale, 81

C

Cable Internet access, 313–314

Cable stations, 239

Cable television, 313–314

Call/email support center, 166, 167

Canada, sweepstakes in, 137–142

Canadian Institute of Chartered Accountants, 99

Cash back, 22

Cash prizes, 121, 122

Casino-style games, 63–64

CBS Web site, 240

CD-ROM, writeable, 112

Cell phones, 74

Chance promotions checklist, 125–133

Chaos, internal, 85

Chief technology officer (CTO), 157

Children's Online Privacy Protection Act (COPPA), 99–106
exceptions to, 105–106
FTC regulation of, 101–105
scope of, 100–101

Child safety, parental consent and, 106

Circle of online promotions, 80, 266

Client referrals, questions concerning, 191

ClueTrain Manifesto, The (Locke, Levine, Searls & Weinberger), 251

Coca Cola Company, 145

Code ownership, questions concerning, 190

Coffee cup advertising, 262

Collect-and-win games, 64–65

CommerceNet Consortium, 99

Commerce sites, 233

Companies, internal chaos in, 85

Complementary partners list, 211–212

"Compliance Assessment Questionnaire," 99

CompuServe, 233

Computers, as prizes, 121

Concept testing, 82

Confidential information, 96–99. *See also* Privacy

Consideration, 3, 116–119
in preselected sweepstakes, 10
problems with, 7

Consultants
finding, 180–186
strategy, 182

Consumer-driven email, 69

Consumers. *See also* Active consumers; Best customers
disqualification of, 130
good, 87–88
relationship with, 291
understanding, 16

Consumer trust, abuse of, 96–97

Contest registration, 120–121

Contests, 12–20
additional types of, 19–20
brand identity and, 37
essay, 15–18
games as, 18–19
objectives of, 15
photography and art, 18
programming, 19
reasons for choosing, 14–15

Contingency plans, for multibrand promotions, 219

Contract templates, 220

Control, in online promotions, 54

CoolSavings.com, 23

Corporate life cycle, stage of, 205

Corporate strategy, 182

Costs
of guerilla marketing, 245
of loyalty programs, 26
of online promotions, 56
of outsourcing, 175
of research, 177

Coupon redemptions, 273

Coupons
benchmark questions for, 226
electronic, 21–23
as prizes, 119
smart, 33

CPA WebTrust, 99

Cracker Jacks, 33

Creative briefs/case histories, 191

Creative needs, outsourcing of, 158–159

Creative resources, 157
choosing, 183–184

Creative strategy, questions concerning, 192

Creative teams
in-house, 157–158
questions concerning, 191–192

Creativity, 184

Creativity awards, questions concerning, 192
Crisis management, 222
Cross-marketing, 207
Cultural blunders, avoiding, 143
"Current list," 10–11
Customer acquisition strategies, 85–86
Customer database, 177
Customer participation, 58
Customer privacy, protecting, 96–99, 228–229
Customer problems, 166
Customer profiles, 54–55
Customers
feedback from, 87, 274
importance of, 84
knowing, 176–177
listening to, 288–289
new ideas from, 37
segmenting, 284
Customer support, 165–166, 204
in-house, 166–167
outsourcing of, 167–169
questions concerning, 195–196
Customer support center, 166
Customer support services, choosing, 184–185
Custom on-demand reports, 227–228
Custom programming, 14

D

Daily instant win games, 35–36
Daily prize awards, 34
Dash bar, 257
Data. *See also* Databases
collecting, 90, 92
managing, 93–94
Database administrator (DBA), 92, 105
Database analysis, 228
Database applications, 279, 288
Database conversion, 278
Database conversion tools, 279–280
Database management, 275–280
Database marketing efforts, building, 291–292
Database plan, 91

Database queries, 223, 271–272
Databases
building, 90–94
compatibility of, 279
designing, 91–92
effective use of, 92–93
planning for, 91
Data collection, in online promotions, 55
Data encryption, 113
Deadlines, for receipt of entries, 131–132
"Dead Web," 250
Deception, avoiding, 135–136
Decision making. *See* Key milestones
Demographic information, 91, 96
collecting, 38–41
Demographic profiles, 227
Design
of databases, 91–92
of emails, 72–73
of random draw sweepstakes, 5
Destination sites, 233
Differential marketing, 281–284
Digital signatures, 102
Digital subscriber lines (DSL), 255
Digital video disks (DVDs), 307, 311–313
Direct-mail advertising, 243–244
Direct-mail sweepstakes companies, 108
Direct marketing, 20, 281
Direct marketing firms, 47
DirectTV, 240, 314
Disclaimer of sponsor's liability, 132
Disclaimers, developing, 133–135
Disclosure, tell-a-friend emails and, 108
Discounts
as prizes, 119
as promotion follow-ups, 277, 280–286
Dispute of email address, 133
Disqualification, of consumers, 130
Documentation, in multibrand promotions, 217–219

DoubleClick, 183, 235, 236
Download.com, 113
Downloadable demos, 44
Drivers
sales, 32–33
traffic, 33–35
Duplicate entries, checking for, 17

E

ebooks, 53
eCount, 257
E-coupons, 53
eCoupons.com, 23
Ehrlich, Joel, 209
80/20 rule, 22, 67, 280–281, 291
Eisnor, Di-Ann, 245, 297
Eisnor Interactive, 245, 297
Electronic coupons, 21–23
overredemption of, 23
Electronic equipment, as prizes, 121
Electronic Frontier Foundation, 99
Eligibility, affidavits of, 128–129
"Eligibility requirements" disclaimer, 133
Email. *See also* Opt-in email lists
adding links to, 71
creative design for, 72–73
feedback via, 289
forwarding, 73
free, 258–259
HTML-formatted, 72–73
importance of, 77
integrating reward status into, 285
online promotions and, 57
permission to send, 69–70
personalizing, 70–71
preselected sweepstakes and, 10, 34–35
via mobile devices, 73–74
viral marketing impact of, 73
Email address, dispute of, 133
Email hierarchy, 69
Email marketing, 68–74, 236–238, 277
problems with, 249
relevance of, 284–285
Email newsletter subscriptions, 243

Email referrals, additional
  entries for, 118
Emails
  promotional, 35
  tell-a-friend, 107–109
Email viewers, HTML-
  compatible, 237–238
Employees, customer contact
  with, 252
Encrypted File Transfer
  Protocol (FTP) access,
  105
Encryption, 113
  digital video disks and, 313
En masse reports, 271–274
Entertainment Software
  Rating Board (ESRB),
  99
Entries
  additional, 118
  automatic checking of, 17
  deadline for receipt of,
    131–132
  free, 12, 130
  judging of, 127
  number of, 126–127
Entry forms, online, 5
Entry methods
  equitable, 136–137
  "free," 6–7, 117
Entry rules, 134
Environmentalism, online
  promotions and, 53–54
"Errors and Omissions"
  insurance, 170, 171, 172
Essay contests, 15–18, 37
  idea generation and, 38
  online advantages of,
    16–18
Ethical hacking, 110, 144
ethicalhacking.com, 110
European Union (EU) data
  protection directive,
  106–107
"Everyday low prices" policy,
  22
EVINCI company, 110
Evolution, of online promo-
  tions, 58–59
Excel, 216
Excite, 233, 235
Executive summaries, 201
Experience, role in strategy,
  147
Experimental advertising,
  254–263
External reviews, 274

F
Facsimile entries, 126–127
Fast Internet access, 307
Federal Trade Commission
  (FTC) regulation
  limitation of enticements
    and, 104
  notification and, 102
  online privacy and, 98–99
  parental consent and,
    102–103
  parental disclosure and,
    103–104
  security and, 104–105
Feedback
  customer, 271, 274
  email, 289
  from product offerings, 93
  on promotions, 51, 74–75
  real-time, 75
  from trivia games, 66
  from vendors, 273–274
Field Fisher Waterhouse, 183
Find/SVP, 185, 229
Firewall protection, 105, 113
555-Tell, 259
Flash "sniffer," 308
Flash technology, 9. *See also*
  Macromedia Flash
Florida
  consideration ruling by, 3
  sweepstakes registration in,
    119–120
Florin, Ken, 96, 98
Flowcharts, in multibrand
  promotions, 217–219
Follow-up marketing, 57,
  265–292
Foreign laws, 137–143
  country-specific chart of,
    138–141
Forrester, 185, 229
4BVocal, 259
Fraud, stopping, 270
Free, use of the word, 136
Free email, 258–259
Free entries, 6–7, 12, 130
FreeInternet.com, 3
Free ISPs, 255–256
"Free" lottery games, 63
FreeLotto, 34, 89
FreeLotto.com, 63, 234
FreeSamples Web site, 21
FreeShop Web site, 21, 85
Free-standing inserts (FSIs),
  53, 262
FreeStuff Web site, 21

Frequent flyer programs, 24,
  25
Frequently asked questions
  (FAQ) document, 166
Fritsch, Bill, 85
Fulfillment
  in-house, 173–175
  outsourcing of, 175–176,
    198–199
Fulfillment centers, 198
Fulfillment companies,
  choosing, 185
Fulfillment resources, 173
Fun, in online promotions,
  55–56
Future marketing, getting
  permission for, 38–41
Future promotions, planning,
  286–292

G
Gains, short-term, 84–85
Gambling, 2
"Gamers," 234
Games
  casino-style, 63–64
  collect-and-win, 64–65
  as contests, 18–19
  downloadable, 19
  "free" lottery, 63
  instant win, 60–68
  match and win, 64
  prediction, 68
  scrambled image, 62–63
  scratch-off, 61–62
  sports tournament, 67–68
  stock market, 66–67
  trivia, 31, 66
Gaming, 61
"Garbage in, garbage out"
  principle, 272, 289
Gates, Bill, 58
Geographic coverage
  statement, 127
Get command, 228
"Gives" list, in partnerships,
  211
Global Positioning Satellite
  (GPS) information, 260
Global Positioning Satellite
  (GPS) technology,
  299–300
Godin, Seth, 6, 38, 290
Goldstein, Linda, 142
GotSavings.com, 23
Grass roots marketing, 52–53
Greenfield Online, 185

Groves, Andy, 295
Guaranteed response times, questions concerning, 196
Guerilla marketing, 244–245, 248, 278
Guinness "Win a Pub" contest, 14–15, 16

H

Hacking
  ethical, 110
  of online promotions, 132
Hallberg, Garth, 281
Hall Dickler Kent Friedman & Wood, 142, 183
Halpert, James, 99
Handheld devices, 73
High-end interactive promotions, 307–315
Hot Jobs, 183
Hotmail, 53, 258
HTML entry forms, 64
HTML-formatted emails, 68, 72–73, 237–238
HTML links, 53, 71
HTML pages, for random draw sweepstakes, 5–6
Hyperlinks, 68

I

IBM "Quest for Java" promotion, 15
Idea generation, for ad campaigns, 37–38
Illegal lotteries, 116–119, 126
iMarketing News, 180
Immediacy, of online promotions, 52
"Import wizards," 279
Incentive Magazine, 180, 185
Industry-specific contests, 12
Industry Standard magazine, 180, 183, 242, 261
Information. *See also* Data
  collecting, 55
  confidential, 96–99
  single-use requests for, 105
Informix, 279
In-house administration, 169–171
In-house analysis, 176–178
In-house creative teams, 157–158
In-house customer support, 166–167
In-house fulfillment, 173–175

In-house media buys, 160–161
In-house partnership negotiation, 163–164
In-house programming capabilities, 190
In-house promotions group, starting, 202–204
In-house research, 176–178
In-house resources, 203–204. *See also* Promotional marketing agency
  versus outsourcing, 145–146
In-house strategy, 148–149
In-house technology staff, 154–155
Initiative Media, 184, 245
Instant messaging (IM), 257–258
Instant messenger (IM) support, 196
Instant win games, 60–68, 77
  collecting demographic information via, 40
  daily, 35–36
  reporting for, 270
Instant win sweepstakes, 8–10
  launching, 28
  with second chance drawings, 34
Insurance, 170, 171, 172
  promotional agency, 197–198
Integration, of online promotions, 58
Interactive Digital Software Association (IDSA), 99
Interactive promotions, 66–68
  high-end, 307–315
Interactive Week, 180
Interactivity formula, 250
Internal reviews, 273–274
Internal team, developing, 204
International Computer Security Association (ICSA), 110
  Web site of, 114
International legislation, 106–107
International promotions, 137–143
Internet
  advantages of, 48–50
  effect on promotions industry, 295

experimenting with, 94
  taking advantage of, 86–87
Internet access, as consideration, 117
Internet communities, 250–254
Internet Explorer, 227, 238
Internet law, 188
"Internet Legislation in the 105th Congress," 99
Internet security specialists, 111
Internet Service Providers (ISPs), 105, 155
  free, 255–256
Internet Service Providers Security Consortium, 114
Internet strategy, 182
Internet World trade show, 260–261
Intrusion detection systems, 114
Inventory, 174
IPSec, 114
IQ.com, 183
IWON, 89, 234
IXL, 183

J

Java applications, 9, 18, 307
Java games, 14, 270
Java programming language, 62, 66, 288
JavaScript, 67
Jiffy Lube, 23
Jonas, Leanne, 273
Judging
  internal, 170
  remote access, 17
  streamlining the process of, 17–18
Junk mail, 21, 68, 70
Jupiter, 185

K

Kelly, Scott & Madison, 184, 246
Key milestones, in multi-brand promotions, 217
Key word banners, 253
K-Mart, 256
Knowledge, role in strategy, 147
Kodak, 273
"Kraft Game of Life," 296–297

L

Laws, changes in, 95–96. *See also* Legal issues
Leader board, 52
Legal compliance, 135–137
  ensuring, 292
Legal expertise, 150–151
  choosing, 182–183
  in-house, 151–152
  outside, 152–153
  promotional, 203
Legal issues, 95–144. *See also* Foreign laws
  in creating partnership agreements, 219–220
  overview of, 115–124
  privacy and security and, 96–115
  questions concerning, 188–189
  understanding, 170
Legal precedents, 4
Levine, Rick, 251
Liability, disclaimer of, 132
Limitation of enticement, FTC regulation concerning, 104
Links, adding to email, 71
LinkShare, 235
Live Person, 185
Locke, Christopher, 251
Loeb & Loeb, 96, 98, 103, 183
Log files, 226–227, 267
Look WorldWide, 262
Lotteries
  defined, 2
  "free," 63
  illegal, 116–119, 126
Lottery laws, 2, 188
  breaking, 137
Lotus Notes, 238
Loyalty programs, 24–27, 281, 284–286
  in building brand loyalty, 35
  considerations for, 26
  increasing memberships via, 42
  online, 27
  as retention programs, 40–41
  as sales drivers, 33
LuckySurf, 34, 89
LuckySurf.com, 63, 234
Lunch bag advertising, 262
Lycos, 233, 235

M

Macromedia Flash, 62, 66, 248, 288, 302, 307, 308–309
Macromedia Shockwave, 9, 66
Macromedia Web site, 308
Magazine advertising, 242–243
Mail.com, 258
Management
  of crises, 222
  database, 275–280
  fulfillment, 174
  of partners, 221
  of privacy, 97
Management Information Systems (MIS) managers, 110
MapQuest, 23, 248
Marden-Kane company, 62
Marketing. *See also* Future marketing; Permission marketing; Promotional marketing; Viral marketing
  differential, 281–284
  email, 236–238
  guerilla, 244–245
  integrating online promotions into, 287, 294–298
  smart, 85
Marketing messages, changing, 54
Marlboro Miles program, 25–26
Match and win games, 64
McDonald's Monopoly game, 64
McMillian, Thelton, 250
Media America, 245
Media-buying services, 232
Media buys, 159–160
  fee structures for, 194
  in-house, 160–161
  outsourcing, 161–162
  questions concerning, 192–194
Media Metrix, 185, 236, 246, 247
Media placement, 74
Media placement agencies, 235
Media plans, questions concerning, 193
Media specialists, online, 236

Media support, choosing, 184
Media vehicles
  offline, 261–263
  online, 255–261
Media Week, 184, 192
Membership forms, 117
Memberships, increasing, 41–43
Micromanagement, of the fulfillment process, 174
Microsoft Gaming Zone, 19
Microsoft Outlook, 238
Microsoft Project, 217
Microsoft Schedule, 216
Microsoft virtual golf tournament, 15
Microsoft Word, 216
Minors, as winners, 129–130
Mistakes
  handling, 198
  quick response to, 174
Mobile devices
  email via, 73–74
  promotions using, 298–300
Mobility, of online promotions, 59
Modem Media, 67, 182, 183
MonsterBoard, 183
MSN, 233, 235
Multibrand promotions
  concluding, 223
  creating, 207–230
  ideal partners for, 209–212
  improving, 223–229
  objectives for, 208–209
  partner relations in, 221–223
  partner selection for, 212–215
  partnership agreements for, 219–221
  production schedule for, 216
  responsibility for, 215–219
Multiple-choice questions, 13
Multiuser gaming, 307, 310–311
mylifepath.com, 8
MyPoints.com, 27
Mythic Games, 310
My Yahoo! Web page, 303

N

Needs satisfactions, in partnerships, 210
Net2Phone, 303
Netcentives.com, 27

"Netiquette," 107
Netscape Navigator, 227, 238
Netscape Netcenter, 18
Network administrators,
    114–115
Network Associates, 112
NetZero.com, 3
"New Economy," 242
Newsletters, 237, 243
    promotional, 254
Newspaper advertising,
    242–243
New York
    state lottery in, 2
    sweepstakes registration in,
    119–120
Nielson, 185
Nondisclosure agreements
    (NDAs), 187
Nontraditional advertising,
    254–263
"No purchase necessary"
    disclaimer, 3, 126, 133
Norton AntiVirus, 112
Notification, FTC regulation
    concerning, 102
"Number of entries"
    statement, 126

O

Objectives
    conflicting, 82–84
    for future promotions,
    286–287
    for multibrand promotions,
    208–209
    for online promotions,
    80–84
Odds of winning, 127–128
    changing, 9–10
    rules for, 134
Offers
    as promotion followups,
    277, 280–286
    testing, 283–284
Official rules, 127
    importance of, 124–125
    making changes to, 74, 125
    preparing, 124–135
Official rules requests,
    separate address for, 131
Official winners
    investigation of, 137
    list of, 122–123, 134
Offline advertising resources,
    239–246
Offline marketing efforts,

integrating, 294–298
Offline media, targeted,
    246–249
Offline media vehicles,
    261–263
Offline promotions
    advantages of, 49
    for online brands, 297–298
Ogilvy, David, 35, 160, 284
OmniSky, 298
On-demand reports, 267–271
    custom, 227–228
One-time emails, 107–108
Ongoing needs, evaluating,
    204
Online advertising resources,
    232–238
Online brands, offline
    promotions for, 297–298
Online loyalty programs, 27
Online marketing efforts,
    integrating, 294–298
Online media specialists,
    236
Online media vehicles,
    255–261
Online navigation, 269
Online privacy, 98–99
Online promotion agencies,
    180–182
Online promotions. *See also*
    Promotional marketing
    advantages of, 48–60
    effective versus ineffective,
    89–90
    email components of, 68–74
    ending, 123–124
    experiencing, 89–90
    feedback and response to,
    74–77
    future of, 293–316
    goal of, 249
    ideal nature of, 59–60
    integrating, 250, 287
    legal aspects of, 95–144,
    115–124
    legal expertise in, 188
    locating, 88–89
    novelty of, 58
    objectives for, 80–84
    ongoing nature of, 59
    planning, 79–94
    repeating, 51
    successful, 47–77, 88
    tampering with, 132
Online reports, 267–268
Opt-in customers, 276–277

Opt-in direct-mail programs,
    53
Opt-in email industry, 6
Opt-in email lists, 237, 290
Opt in/out concepts, 39
Oracle, 279
Order fulfillment, 173
Outdoor advertising, 244
"Out-of-the-box" solutions, 28
Outside resources, questions
    concerning, 186–201
Outsourcing. *See also*
    Promotional marketing
    agencies
    of administration, 171–173
    of analysis, 178–180
    of creative needs, 158–159
    of customer support,
    167–169
    of fulfillment, 175–176
    of media buys, 161–162
    of partnership negotiations,
    164–165
    of research, 178–180
    of strategy, 149–150
    of technology requirements,
    155–156
    versus in-house resources,
    145–146
Outsourcing partners, 175
Oven Digital, 182, 183

P

Pagers, 74
Palm Pilots, 59, 73
Parental consent, FTC
    regulation concerning,
    102–103
Parental disclosure, FTC
    regulation concerning,
    103–104
Parents, contacting, 105–106
Participation rates, in online
    promotions, 57
Partners. *See also* Partner-
    ships; Potential partners
    long-term relations with,
    214–215, 223
    for multibrand promotions,
    209–212, 214
    selecting for multibrand
    promotions, 212–215
Partnership agreements
    amendments to, 220
    for multibrand promotions,
    219–221
    terminating, 220–221

Partnership marketing, 162–163

Partnership negotiation, 184
  in-house, 163–164
  outsourcing, 164–165

Partnership programs, successful, 194

Partnerships. *See also* Partners
  questions concerning, 194–195
  ten commandments of, 210

Partners list, complementary, 211–212

Passwords, 114

Penton Media, 260

People Support, 185

Permission marketing, 38–39, 54–55, 290

Permission Marketing (Godin), 6, 38, 290

Personal data assistants (PDAs), 59, 260
  promotions on, 298–299

PGPfreeware, 113

Photo contests, 18, 37

Pinging services, 189–190

Piper & Marbury, 99

Pizza Hut, 212

Placement agencies, 183

Planning
  database, 91
  long-term benefits of, 86
  of marketing strategy, 286
  for multibrand promotions, 219
  of online promotions, 79–94
  taking time for, 84–86

Plastic bag advertising, 262

Plesser, Ronald, 99

Portal sites, 232, 233
  integrating with Internet communities, 250–254
  promotional, 253–254
  traditional, 252–253

Post command, 228

Potential partners
  contacting, 212–213
  tracking responses from, 213

Power Point presentations, 212, 213

Prediction games, 68

Preferred tactics, for promotional objectives, 29

Prelaunch issues, 221–222

Prelaunch test marketing programs, 232

Premium Incentive Show, 40

Premium offers, 272
  collecting demographic information via, 40
  increasing memberships via, 42–43
  as sales drivers, 33

Premiums, benchmark questions for, 226

Preselected sweepstakes, 10–11
  as a traffic driver, 34–35

Primary research, 82

Priority escalation process, 189

Privacy, 96–115. *See also* Children's Online Privacy Protection Act (COPPA); Security
  customer, 228–229
  Federal Trade Commission (FTC) and, 98–99
  global positioning satellite technology and, 299

Privacy management, 97

Privacy policy, individual, 108

Privacy White Paper, 103

Private information, selling, 97–98

Prize pool, increasing, 207

Prizes
  awarding, 123
  descriptions of, 134
  as incentives, 2–3
  obscure, 122
  quantity and description of, 128

Problems, responding to, 174, 176

Product awareness, 32

Production "bible," 219

Production schedule
  for multibrand promotions, 216, 221
  sample, 217

Product loyalty, 22

Product preference, 35–36
  building, 35–36

Products
  creating interest in, 43–45
  launching, 28

Product sampling, 20–21

Product trials, initiating, 43–45

Professional help, obtaining, 135

Programming contests, 19, 37

PROMO Expo 2000 trade show, 209, 262, 287

PROMO Magazine, 142, 180, 185, 205, 229

Promotion administration. *See* Administration

Promotion agencies, online, 180–182

Promotional administrators, 203

Promotional banners, 234

Promotional checklists, 197

Promotional components chart, 181

Promotional databases
  integrating, 278–280
  managing, 276–278

Promotional emails, 35

"Promotional extras," 193

Promotional law, 188

Promotional marketing, 1–45. *See also* Online promotions
  choosing the type of, 27–45
  contests, 12–20
  electronic coupons and smart rebates, 21–23
  loyalty programs, 24–27
  product sampling, 20–21
  sweepstakes, 1–12

Promotional marketing agencies, 204
  when to use, 147–180

Promotional Marketing Association (PMA), 170, 188–189

Promotional Marketing Association (PMA) Law Conference, 99, 182

Promotional Media, 193

Promotional media buys, 245–246

Promotional objectives
  preferred tactics for, 29
  satisfying, 270–271

Promotional portal sites, 253–254

Promotional quizzes, 31

Promotion follow-ups, 277
  special discounts and offers for, 280–286

Promotion industry, 81

"Promotion Partners" conference, 273

Promotion portals, 233–234
Promotion results, comparing
   with research
   reports, 229
Promotions. *See also* Chance
   promotions checklist;
   Future promotions;
   International promo-
   tions; Multibrand
   promotions
   action orientation of, 77
   advertising, 231–264, 289
   beyond, 284
   digital video disks and,
      312–313
   external reviews of, 274
   feedback and, 51
   follow-up for, 265–292
   high-end interactive,
      307–315
   how to advertise, 232–246
   internal review of, 273–274
   in-vehicle, 306–307
   measuring results of,
      266–275
   multiuser gaming and,
      310–311
   preparing official rules
      for, 124–135
   start/end dates for, 126,
      133–134
   translating into multiple
      languages, 142–143
   using 3D environments,
      309–310
   using Macromedia Flash,
      308–309
   using mobile devices,
      298–299
   voice response, 304–305
   WebTV and, 314–315
Promotions.com, 182, 183
Promotions agencies, 162,
      164, 165
   firing, 201–202
Promotions group, in-house,
      202–204
PromoTV, 184, 239–240, 245
Publicity rights, reservation
   of, 131
Public key infrastructure, 114
Publishers Clearing House,
      43, 135–136
Purchases, added value to, 25

Q

Qualcomm Eudora, 238

Qualified entry sweepstakes,
      7–8, 30–31
   idea generation and, 38
Qualitative research, 200
Quantitative research, 200
Quebec, promotions in, 142
"Quest for Java" promotion,
      15
QuickTake, 51, 89, 185, 274
Quizzes, promotional, 31

R

Radio advertising, 241–242
Radio personalities, 241
Radio promotion, 184
Radio station Web sites,
      241–242
Random drawings, 127
Random draw prizes, 34
Random draw sweepstakes,
      4–6
   collecting demographic
      information via, 39
   daily entry/prizes in, 36
   design of, 5
   launching, 28
Rate cards, 198
RazorFish, 182, 183
RealTime Media, 182
Real-time reporting, 75, 77
Real-time responses, 76–77
Rebates
   benchmark questions for,
      225–226
   as a sales driver, 32–33
   smart, 21–23, 44
Recruitment agencies, 183
Red Alert, 189
Referrals, tell-a-friend emails
   and, 108–109
Relationships
   with customers, 176–177,
      282, 288–289, 291
   with promotions agencies,
      201–202
   strategic, 163
   with vendors, 219
Remote access judging, 17
Reporting needs, identifying,
      289–290
Reports
   custom on-demand,
      227–228
   en masse, 271–274
   offline overlays to, 272–273
   on-demand, 267–271
   online, 267–268

Research, 176
   analysis of, 177
   in-house, 176–178
   for online promotions, 51
   outsourcing of, 178–180,
      199–201
Research companies, 89
   questions concerning, 187
Research database, 177, 178,
      179
Research deployment, 177
Research project samples, 201
Research support, choosing,
      185–186
Reservation of publicity
   rights, 131
Resources
   finding, 180–186
   monitoring, 189–190
Response rates, speed of, 280
Responsibility, for multibrand
   promotions, 215–219
Results, analyzing, 75–76.
   See also Analysis
Retention programs, 41
Revolution Magazine, 305
Rewards, increasing
   memberships via, 42–43
Reward status, integrating
   into emails, 285
Rhode Island, sweepstakes
   registration in, 120
Rich media, 288
"Right customer at the right
   price" strategy, 85–86
Rules
   abbreviated, 134–135
   preparing, 124–135

S

Sales, driving, 32–33
Sales-driven promotions, 232
Sales figures, knowing, 271
Sales offers, 231
Sampling, benchmark ques-
   tions for, 225
Sampling programs, 30,
      43–44, 53
Saturn Networks, 182
Scanner technology, 300
Scrambled image games,
      62–63
Scratch-off games, 8–9, 40,
      61–62
Search engines, 89, 234–235,
      235
Searls, Doc, 251

Second chance drawings,
11–12
with instant win sweep-
stakes, 34
Security, 96–115. *See also*
Privacy
creating, 109–115
FTC regulation concerning,
104–105
technology solutions for,
110–115
Security policies, 143–144
"Seeding" winners, 5
Seismicom Company,
180–182, 183
Selling proposition, 200
Sell-sheets, 219
Server access, 114
Server crashes, 75
Services, launching, 28
Shareware, 113
S&H Greenpoints, 23, 27,
285
S&H Green Stamps, 24
Shirley, Jeff, 296
Shockwave, 61, 62
Shopping guides, 257
Short-term gains, avoiding,
84–85
Silicon Alley Reporter, 183
Single-use requests for
information, 105
Skill, defined, 13
Skill-based judging criteria,
19
Skill games. *See* Contests
Slippage, 22, 32
Smart coupons, as a sales
driver, 33
Smart marketing, 85, 93, 94
Smart rebates, 21–23, 44
Snapple "Win Nothing"
sweepstakes, 2
Snow Crash (Stephenson),
309
Soft launches, 232
Software
antivirus, 112
database, 156
downloadable demos of, 44
encryption, 113, 113
production schedule, 216
response-tracking, 213
third-party, 272
Spam, 53, 57, 107
Special offers, follow-up
with, 280–286

Speed, of online promotions,
50–51
Spinway, 256
Sponsor's liability, disclaimer
of, 132
Sponsorships, tie-in, 44–45
Sports tournament games,
66, 67–68
SQL, 279
Staff training, questions
concerning, 196
Starbucks, 262
Start/end dates, for
promotions, 126,
133–134
Stephenson, Neal, 309
Stock market games, 66–67
Stone, Bob, 281
Strategic experts, 203–204
Strategic inflection point, 295
Strategic plans, 187
Strategic recommendations,
187
Strategic relationships, 163
Strategic services, 186–187
questions concerning,
186–187
Strategy
as a core focus, 186
importance of, 147–148
in-house, 148–149
outsourcing of, 149–150
questions concerning,
186–187
Strategy consultants, 182
Streaming audio contests, 37
Streaming content, 65
Streaming media, 288
Street marketers, 245
"Subject to official rules"
disclaimer, 134
Success, of online promotions,
56–57
*Successful Direct Marketing
Methods* (Stone), 281
Support documentation, 218
Surety bonds, 119–120
Surveys, 117
Sweepstakes, 1–12
automatic entry, 6–7, 32,
118–119
benchmark questions for,
225
exclusive, 118
increasing memberships
via, 43
instant win, 8–10, 28

preselected, 10–11, 34–35
product preference and, 36
qualified entry, 7–8, 30–31,
38
random draw, 4–6, 28
second-chance sweepstakes
drawing, 11–12
tell-a-friend, 41–42
as traffic drivers, 34
Sweepstakes Advantage, 233
Sweepstakes entrants,
addresses of, 129
Sweepstakes entry forms, 87
Sweepstakes Online, 89
Sweepstakes-only entry form,
117
Sweepstakes registration,
119–120
Sweepstakes Web sites, 234
Sybase, 279
Symantec, 112

T

Tactics. *See* Preferred
tactics
Target audience
educating, 7
marketing to, 91
Targeted consumers, 21
Targeted electronic coupons,
22–23
Targeted offline media,
246–249
Taxes, 121–122
Tax liability, of winners, 131
TechieGold.com, 183
Technical support, choosing,
183
Technical training programs,
190
Technology
global positioning satellite,
299–300
keeping up with, 86–87,
287–288
online promotions and,
51–52
promotional applications
of, 315
scanner, 300
Technology requirements,
outsourcing of, 155–156
Technology solutions, 154
components of, 111
questions concerning,
189–190
security and, 110–115

Technology staff, in-house, 154–155
Television advertising, 239–240
Television network Web sites, 240
Television promotion, 184
Tell-a-friend emails, 107–109
Tell-a-friend programs, 53
Tell-a-friend sweepstakes, 41–42
Tell Me, 304
Ten Commandments of Partnerships, 209, 210
1099 filings, 121–122
Testing
  of concepts, 82
  of offers, 283–284
3D environments, 307, 309–310
Tie-in sponsorships, 44–45
Time, role in skill-based contests, 14
Tivo, 314
Toll-free numbers, 305
Toll-free Web sites, 259–260
"Total prize value" disclaimer, 134
Tournament games, 36–37, 311
Tracking, 283
Tracking and reporting, 199
Tradition, going beyond, 65–66
Traffic, driving, 33–35
Traffic reports, 268, 269
Travel prizes, 127, 128
Travel releases, 129
Treasure hunts, 7–8, 31–32
Trend spotting, 274–275
Trivia games, 31, 66
Trivia questions, 13, 50
Trust accounts, 119–120
TRUSTe, 99
"Try-before-you-buy" approach, 30
Turnkey technology, 183
Tutorials, downloadable, 44
24/7 Media, 235, 236

U
Unique Selling Proposition (USP), 36
United Marketing Services, 185
Universal resource locators (URLs)
  referring, 272
  for separate media vehicles, 268

V
Valassis Communications, 242–243
Value proposition, 271, 284
V-commerce, 300–307
Vehicle commerce, 305–307
Vendors
  feedback from, 273–274
  finding, 180–186, 205
  relationships with, 219
Video contests, 37
Viral marketing, 52–53, 56, 73, 297
Viral programs, 21
Viruses, 112
VirusScan, 112
Visual contests, 18
Voice recognition, 301–305
Voice recognition software, 259
Voice-response promotions, 304–305
"Void where prohibited" disclaimer, 132, 133

W
Wal-Mart, 21–22
"Watch & Win" games, 10, 314
Web access phones (WAPs), 260
  promotions on, 298–299
Web browsers, 62, 269
WebCertificates, 257
WebDecoder, 62
Web-enabled phones, 59
WebJones, 183
Web servers, security of, 109
Web site portals, 232. *See also* Portal sites

Web sites
  associated, 235
  launching, 28
  toll-free, 259–260
Webstakes, 34, 89, 233
Web traffic, 75, 228
WebTrends, 227, 268, 272
WebTV, 240, 313–315
Weinberger, David, 251
WHOIS searches, 109
Winners
  investigation of, 137
  method for determining, 127
  minors as, 129–130
  notification of, 123–124, 129
  in random draw sweepstakes, 5
  randomly selected, 13
  selection/notification of, 134
  tax liability of, 131
Winners lists, 52, 134
  official, 122–123
Winners' list requests, separate address for, 131
Wireless marketplace, 74
WIT, 183
Wonderman, Less, 282
Wood, Douglas, 142
Word of mouth
  encouraging, 52–53
  negative, 251
Work portfolios, questions concerning, 191
Worst case scenarios, thinking about, 116
Write-in entries, separate address for, 131

X
XML, 298

Y
Yahoo!, 38, 233, 234, 235
Yahoo! by Phone, 303
Yahoo! Mail, 53, 258

Z
Zip code analysis, 27